Education and Development

Education and Development

Measuring the Social Benefits

WALTER W. McMAHON

OXFORD

UNIVERSITY PRESS

OXFORD
UNIVERSITY PRESS

Great Clarendon Street, Oxford OX2 6DP

Oxford University Press is a department of the University of Oxford.
It furthers the University's objective of excellence in research, scholarship,
and education by publishing worldwide in

Oxford New York

Athens Auckland Bangkok Bogotá Buenos Aires Cape Town
Chennai Dar es Salaam Delhi Florence Hong Kong Istanbul Karachi
Kolkata Kuala Lumpur Madrid Melbourne Mexico City Mumbai Nairobi
Paris São Paulo Shanghai Singapore Taipei Tokyo Toronto Warsaw

and associated companies in Berlin Ibadan

Oxford is a registered trade mark of Oxford University Press
in the UK and in certain other countries

Published in the United States
by Oxford University Press Inc., New York

© Walter W. McMahon 1999

The moral rights of the author have been asserted

Database right Oxford University Press (maker)

Reprinted 2001

ISBN 0–19–829231–7

Printed in Great Britain
on acid-free paper by
Bookcraft (Bath) Short Run Books
Midsomer Norton

To Carolyn, my wife,
with love, for her counsel
and moral support

Preface

The field of economic growth has reawakened with a new emphasis on the combination of theory with empirical work. Education has emerged with the key role in the dissemination of new knowledge and of capacities to adapt as central to the growth process. This is of increasing strategic importance in the new environment of knowledge-based and globalizing economies.

But true economic development does not occur unless this pure economic growth is accompanied by other dimensions important to the quality of life, such as good health, reductions in poverty and inequality, improvements in participatory democracy, political stability, a sustainable environment of forests, wildlife, air, and water, less violent crime, and basic human rights. Yet these are also some of the aspects of human welfare to which education simultaneously contributes.

Unfortunately these other contributions are often not fully recognized. This is partly because they are hard to measure. There are measures, but usually they are only for some sectors, and many are very particularistic and piecemeal at the micro level, if they exist at all. Furthermore, a structural approach that systematically measures and traces indirect impacts has not yet been employed.

This book grew out of my concern for the need for more comprehensive and systematic measurement of the returns to education as well as concern for more effective economic development by cost-effective means in the poor countries. The subject touches the welfare of children and families throughout South and East Asia, Africa, and Latin America and the Caribbean but also those in the US, UK, and other OECD member countries. My work in the economics of education in the US and also in developing countries has been accompanied by an acute awareness that education systems have large underutilized potential for increasing their efficiency and equity as a means of contributing to growth and human welfare. There has also been increasing awareness in the US and UK of the significance of getting more comprehensive measures of the outcomes of education and research.

In part the interest in outcomes is the result of the pressures for accountability and greater use of programme budgeting, but it is also the result of uneasiness with the limited nature of outcome measures confined to instructional units and test scores. Faculty, education administrators, students, and their families generally are interested in knowing what the monetary and non-monetary outcomes of education over the life cycle really are likely to be, and not just the costs. But there is also a lack of awareness of the measures of the outcomes that currently exist, since the research in this field is relatively inaccessible. Some of it hypothesizes technically and abstractly on largely statistical grounds about the reasons why usable measurements of the returns to education need to be questioned. Much of it is very narrow and particularistic, which has some merits, but also means it cannot be the sole basis for education policies. There are some quality in-depth measurements, but they often neglect structural effects and other externalities as well as intergenerational and distributional effects. Perhaps most of all, the situation is characterized by benign neglect in spite of the importance of the subject.

A complementary step to what follows has been to draw recent relevant microeconomic contributions to this research together. This was done in a special issue of the *International Journal of Educational Research* devoted to 'Recent Advances in Measuring the Social and Individual Benefits of Education', for which I was the guest editor (vol. 27, no. 7, December 1997). Other steps are a more comprehensive survey of the microanalytic research as part of a 'Conceptual Framework for the Analysis of the Social Benefits of Lifelong Learning' in *Education Economics* (McMahon 1998b) and an article on 'Education and Growth in East Asia' published in the *Economics of Education Review* (McMahon 1998a). The journal has kindly given permission for the main thrust of this latter paper to appear in Chapter 3 of this book. The book has also benefited from other recent work on the social benefits of education in Behrman and Stacey (1997) that will be cited where relevant.

The book is intended for a general but well-informed audience who are interested in the outcomes of education and sources of economic growth and development but also for a professional audience of economists, educators, and advanced students. The fields to which it is relevant include economics (the economics of education, economic development, labor economics, and economic growth), education (educational policy studies, educational finance and administration), and also faculty, researchers, and students in the social sciences and other fields. I hope that economic policy-makers, and certainly persons in economic development agencies, may also have a special interest, albeit from a different point of view.

For the general reader the book should be understandable throughout. It may take patience in a few spots, such as thinking through the implications of the results of regressions, although most of the graphs and tables are very straightforward. For professional economists patience of another kind will be required since it is necessary to explain the use of concepts that are familiar to them in order to reach a broader audience.

I would like to thank several persons who have had a significant role in this effort. Most especially there is Dr Norman Rifkin and others at USAID. He made some key suggestions, and USAID provided the grant of support at the University of Illinois that enabled me to do much of the basic empirical work. Luis Crouch and Rob Feldman at the Research Triangle Institute made key contributions at the inception of this project to the programming of the initial model and especially to the health and labour force sectors, which draw in part on Luis Crouch's prior work for the Bridges project.

For research assistance on the other seven sectors I am indebted to Stephanie Leaphart (democratization), Remy Nauman (economic growth in LAC), Gamini

Premartine (growth in East Asia and growth in LAC), Ali Arifa (population growth in Africa), Beloo Mehra (crime and policy reforms), David Gerard (the environment), Song Gau (additional data collection to expand the model beyond LAC to cover most East Asia, Africa, and OECD economies), and Qui Mei Yang (for additional econometric estimation). As countries for additional regions were added and the model fine-tuned, Gamini Premartine and Sergey Makarevich were particularly helpful with the econometrics and with the simulations, and also contributed to the substance. Ye Zhang from computer science was extremely helpful in programming the re-estimated equations in Borland C++, as was Sergey Markevich. Gamini Premartine was especially helpful with the simulations and preparation of graphs for the publisher. I am deeply grateful to each of these people, without whom the project would not have been possible.

Chris Colclough, Martin Godfrey, and Adrian Wood were most encouraging and helpful during work on the manuscript while I was a Visiting Fellow at the Institute of Development Studies, University of Sussex. They and members of the ESRC Study Group on the Economics of Education made comments on the substance of the research and the simulations, as did persons at the World Bank during seminars delivered there. At the University of Illinois, Chancellor Michael Aiken and Vice-President for Academic Affairs Sylvia Manning supported me in a closely related project involving measurement of the outcomes of higher education which contributed insights to this book. Vernon Burton's invitation to present my interactive macrodynamic model on 'Simulating Investment in Education and US Productivity Growth' at a Beckman Conference and its refinement for Burton, Finnegan, and Herr (forthcoming) added perspectives to the simulation techniques. Ali Arifa was helpful with the analyses relevant to African countries and as co-author of that chapter. Economist discussants at professional meetings where I have delivered some of the chapters as papers and especially Moshe Justman of Ben-Gurion University in Israel have contributed useful comments. I am most of all indebted to the anonymous referees at Oxford University Press who went over the entire manuscript very thoughtfully and made excellent comments that have resulted in considerable econometric re-estimation, a completely restructured Part IV, and other changes that have improved the end result.

I also wish to thank the Academy for Educational Development, and particularly Beverly Jones and Francy Hays there, who were the channel for the initial grant from USAID. Neither AED, USAID, nor any of the persons mentioned above, however, are in any way responsible for any errors in the collection or analysis of data or for any conclusions drawn. I alone remain solely responsible for the final result.

Carol Halliday and her staff at the Word Processing Center at the University of Illinois have provided excellent and indispensable assistance as this manuscript has gone through various drafts.

Finally, I am deeply grateful to my wife, Carolyn. She frequently acted as a sounding board, helped edit major parts of the manuscript, and offered sustained moral support both as the research was done and as the writing of the manuscript progressed.

W. W. M.
Urbana-Champaign, Illinois, 1999

Contents

PART III.   MEASURING THE NON-MONETARY BENEFITS

PART IV. THE COMPLETE MODEL: EDUCATION AND ECONOMIC DEVELOPMENT

PART I
Introduction

1 Measuring the Returns to Education

Extensive reconstructions of economics are generally the result not of a frontal assault on traditional theory but of the systematic elaboration of a single basic idea which previously had been ignored or given only passing recognition.

(Anonymous)

The relation of education to a young person's economic well-being and satisfactions later in life has long been recognized by most families. After considerable neglect, education has also come into its own among economists as crucial to the dissemination of knowledge with the reawakening of the field of economic growth, due largely to the combination of theory with empirical tests, and to a spreading recognition that the results deal with the questions that really matter. Knowledge for development has also become a central theme for many economic development agencies (e.g. World Bank, 1998).

Overview

In the new endogenous growth and augmented Solow models economists now give education and knowledge the central role in the growth process. This has begun a reconstruction of economic theory with extensive implications that extend not only to the poorest countries like India or Sub-Saharan Africa, where hundreds of millions of people live in absolute poverty on less than US$1 a day, but also to the advanced OECD member countries. 'The consequences for human welfare involved in questions like these are simply staggering: once one starts to think about them it is hard to think about anything else' (Lucas, 1988: 3).

This book develops a single basic idea, the systematic measurement of the net returns to education, tracing these impacts on economic growth and development. The conceptual framework focuses on more comprehensive measurement and valuation of both monetary and non-market returns. This enables certain of the key Solow constants such as population growth, the saving rate, and even political stability to be treated as endogenous within the complete model and within about a 40-year medium-term context. In this sense this book seeks to reorient economic theory and analysis to encompass the central role of knowledge and its dissemination within the broader process not just of economic growth but also of a theory of economic development.

Some of the potential implications of the analysis, not all of which are developed in this book, include implications for measurement of the outcomes of household production in the newer system of 'total' social accounts, better measurement of the externalities of education, and the more comprehensive appraisal of outcomes of educational institutions to include more of the outcomes from the liberal arts and sciences apart from earnings, and apart from patenting, which is traditional for engineering and some other fields. Chapter 14 will explicitly consider insights on finding more cost-effective means of achieving faster growth and development in the poorest countries.

Recent Advances in Measuring Education Outcomes

There have been recent advances in measuring and valuing the market and non-market returns to education at the micro-level of the individual, the family, and the firm. A number of these are developed in surveys by others in a special issue of the *International Journal of Education Research* (see McMahon, 1997), in *Education Economics* (McMahon, 1998*b*), and in *The Handbook of Labour Economics* by David Card (1998). Recent advances surveyed include those in measuring the causal effects of education on earnings while controlling for innate ability and family factors using large samples of identical twins, together with a more precise offsetting correction for measurement error. The latter leads normally to understatement of the returns due to the omission of the quality of education and due to biases from the self-reporting of education levels. In the opinion of most specialists, this largely offsets the omitted variable (ability) bias. A second recent development involves the measurement and inclusion of dynamic trends in earnings within each age cohort and in education costs in computing pure internal rates of return. These trends have been dramatically upward for college graduates since about 1980 in the US and some other OECD countries. A third major development is in the methods for measuring non-monetary returns at the microeconomic level. Other recent developments in microanalytic research will be considered further as they relate to each topic in the chapters that follow.

There are other major recent advances in the field of economic growth at both the theoretical level and in empirical research. At their heart is a flurry of activity that develops the central role of human capital and of knowledge externalities in endogenous growth and augmented Solow models.

Together the microanalytic and economywide-growth theoretical insights and empirical tests can now be extended to include tests of the net non-market returns to knowledge and its dissemination and hence to become a key part of the explanation for broader economic development. As will be shown, the non-market returns to education are often correlated with pure economic growth returns but in different directions and by different amounts depending on the type of non-monetary return considered. Most studies of non-market returns are now beginning to control for money income or earnings in order to measure the non-monetary returns without double counting. But there are literally hundreds—perhaps thousands—of these studies, some of which do not control for monetary returns and hence do not fit into the theoretical framework very well. Most deal with narrow particularized aspects, which has its merits for certain purposes, but such studies are so specialized that it takes a serious effort to make broader policy-relevant sense out of them. Almost none of these microeconomic studies seek either a more comprehensive measure of the non-market returns or a valuation of these returns.

Two notable exceptions are the pioneering studies by Haveman and Wolfe (1984) and Wolfe and Zuvekas (1997) advancing the conceptual framework for valuing the non-market returns to education. The author has sought to set out and extend this more comprehensive conceptual framework at the microeconomic level to include its two aspects (measurement and valuation) and comparisons of cost-based valuation to other approaches (McMahon, 1997a, 1998b). These all rest on earlier basic contributions by Becker (1964) involving household production and the value of time, as well as other research on non-market returns to education surveyed in the sources cited.

This book now seeks to take the next step in pursuing the theme of the measurement of the returns to increasing the value of human time by disseminating knowledge through education at the economy-wide level. It is at this level that many relevant comprehensive measures must be made.

Endogenous Development Defined

The systematic measurement of education outcomes leads to a logical extension of the concept of endogenous growth, a concept which is well known, in the form of a closely related but different concept of *endogenous development*, which is new. Endogenous development still implies endogenous decisions by individual families, firms, and governmental units without exogenous interventions in the form of 'manna from heaven', but it can now be applied to the broader economic development process. Since education and knowledge are central to growth in the endogenous growth models, the decisions with which we are concerned relate primarily to decisions regarding the allocation of time to human capital formation through education. Parents refrain from consumption (i.e. save) and invest in their children's continuation in school. These decisions are sometimes influenced by subsidies decided on by governmental units responding to citizens (e.g., building schools and hiring teachers in rural areas). These are also decisions concerned with the allocation of time by parents and students to education.

Endogenous development has a second meaning within the context of simulations of the complete model in Chapter 12 and 13. The Solow constants such as population growth that will have been determined endogenously from an econometric point of view in Chapter 6 will also be determined endogenously within each time period in the process of generating simulations of the time paths in comparative dynamics 40 years into the future. The term 'endogenous' is used in the same way as in endogenous growth models in these respects, but it is not used here to apply to long-run steady-state solutions. Instead, the focus in this book is on the interactive solutions within each time period generating dynamic time paths for each of the 22 endogenous variables over the medium term. The main reason for the shorter time horizon is the commitment to empirical tests, empirical relevance, and policy relevance. The very-long-term fortunes shift. Even in a growth context, policy horizons, perhaps unfortunately, are often less than 40 years.

The contributions of education to the welfare of individual students and their families and to economic development include the direct contributions of education to economic productivity plus indirect contributions through community structural effects. These latter, to the extent they are due to education, also aid productivity growth within firms and households. In this context two levels of externality benefits can be distinguished. One level is within the firm or household. Some work environments, for example, contain many well-educated people, collegiality, and stimuli to new learning, facilitating an interchange whereby each individual's productivity benefits from knowledge gained from colleagues; the same is true within some households. A second level of shared externality benefits is from the environment in the community within which the firm or the household lives, which can also contribute to firm or household productivity. These community characteristics can include low crime rates, good public health, democratic processes, political stability, and other characteristics to which the level of education in the community contributes, and not just knowledge in the environment that is shared. Some of these advantages can even come from prior generations and their earlier knowledge, clearly an externality. This process is at the core of the new endogenous growth models. The result is an offset to the diminishing returns to physical capital that would otherwise occur. Within the context of these models, this means increasing returns, which allows per capita growth potentially to continue without bounds!

But also as part of endogenous development, the contributions of education to other important aspects of development lead to additional non-market satisfactions largely during leisure-time hours that are part of true development and also important to human welfare. These are over and above their contributions to pure economic growth; that is, non-market direct satisfactions from the community levels of human rights, poverty reduction, lower violent crime rates, environmental quality, and so forth, to all of which education has made some indirect marginal contributions.

The indirect structural effects of education are less commonly measured and understood. For example, the direct effects of education create a skilled labour force that raises productivity. But the indirect effects encourage higher rates of investment in physical capital and stronger export competitiveness with feedback effects on growth, as well as other indirect effects such as those on the environment (via poverty reduction, etc.) or on greater political stability (via democratization), all after long delays. Altogether these indirect externality-type effects of education will be shown to constitute about 38 to 40 per cent of the total effects of education on economic growth (higher in some types of countries and lower in others), with additional indirect effects on non-market returns that are higher in the case of certain non-market returns and lower for others.

Tracing direct and indirect measures of education outcomes has the further potential for finding more cost-effective means of achieving economic development in the poor countries and similar goals in the higher-income OECD member countries.

Education and Development: Other Recent Work

It is important to emphasize that this book is *not* attempting to *test* whether the human resource view of development is more or less correct than other views of development. This would imply an entirely different approach to the empirical analysis. Rather, the book is based on the proposition, consistent with the recent micro-level studies of identical twins and empirical tests of endogenous growth and augmented Solow models, that education contributes to economic productivity, has a central role in diffusing knowledge which is vital to the growth process, and is an important force for broader economic development. This proposition is widely held by specialists, but not by everyone. Yet this does not mean that education is the only such force, which it is not, or that it is both a necessary and sufficient condition, neither of which is suggested or tested here. The research in this book instead seeks to extend our knowledge of the range of outcomes, their magnitude, and the timing of the marginal effects of education.

Other views of development are not mutually exclusive, however, and education overlaps significantly with many of them. First, for example, innovation and new designs in the Schumpeterian paradigm that emphasizes innovation and new technologies are not inconsistent with education as an explanation of a key source of the capacities to create these innovations and perhaps even more important the diffusion of these innovations and new process and product designs. Second, and similarly, the emphasis on export orientation as in Ito and Krueger (1995) is another perspective. But looking at who has had success in increasing manufacturing and service exports, it is clear that such success is heavily dependent on a skilled labour force created by education plus learning on the job, which is highly correlated with prior education (Wood, 1994). Third, macroeconomic stabilization, structural reform, and reduced civil strife also deal with important sources of differences in economic development among countries. But I will show that widespread education, after considerable lags, is conducive to democratization and political stability. Therefore these sources of economic growth or the lack thereof are complementary to education over longer periods of time and not inconsistent with what follows. Fourth, *total* saving rates stressed by neo-classical growth models include saving that is immediately invested by parents and governments in human capital, as well as saving that comes from abroad in the form of money capital transfers when political stability is adequate. I do include investment in physical capital in all of the growth equations in this book. So tracing education's net impacts is not inconsistent with the analysis of the saving and investment process that dominates traditional growth theory. In sum, this book seeks to trace the net role of education as a catalyst in the development process, not to test whether it is more or less correct than other emphases, some of which overlap.

At the microeconomic level Behrman (1997) hypothesizes about which controls are needed for omitted-variable bias. Apart from the offset of ability bias by measurement error, on which I rely, some of the indirect structural effects that I seek to measure can be excluded by inappropriately imposed controls. In some cases, for example, there may be no direct effects from education whatsoever; there are only indirect marginal effects from education coming through its contribution to some 'community effect' which, if excluded, would be missed. Some of these involve long dynamic time lags.

Second, there are thousands of possibilities for omitted-variable biases. Through aggregation many offset one another and wind up in the disturbances uncorrelated with the explanatory variables. Many others are not empirically significant. Assuming reasonable precautions are taken not to omit factors that are known to have a logical basis and to be significant (such as investment in the growth equations, or per capita income when measuring non-market returns), the burden of proof must begin to shift to those advancing the hypothesis about an omitted effect: they must demonstrate that it is empirically significant in a comparable context.

Third, it is necessary to distinguish my primary objective of tracing the impact of human capital formation through education—much of which is done by households (e.g. Ben Porath, 1967), some via external benefits from other schools, and some by prior generations—from the measurement of the net value added by one particular school. Much of the literature is concerned only with the latter, which is a quite legitimate objective, but it is not the objective here. The basic theoretical framework for this book is concerned with human capital production by households to which current and prior schooling both contribute, as do certain community effects.

Fourth, in surveying recent research, and in empirical tests later, there are some controls that are vital to the conceptual framework that must be imposed. These include a control for per capita income when measuring non-market returns to education to avoid double counting and for investment in physical capital when measuring the market returns as mentioned, but also for cultural differences, political instability, and other disturbances when they are empirically significant (see also McMahon, 1997a).

With respect to interactive economy-wide models recent research has sought to trace some of the non-market impacts of education on development. The Education Impacts Model (EIM) by Crouch, Spratt, and Cubeddu (1992) comes closest, in that it deals with interactions among the health, population, and growth sectors. But it does not include interaction with other sectors such as crime, democratization, poverty reduction, and so forth. It also does not seek to separate direct from indirect externality-type impacts. And it does not do simulations so that patterns can be observed over time or across different types of economies. The model in this book was built initially around the EIM health and population sectors in particular, and the author is deeply indebted to Luis Crouch and Rob Feldman for their collaboration in the early programming of the entire model as indicated in the Preface.

Other international economy-wide models include those by Chenery *et al.* (1986), Wheeler (1984*b*), and the International Labour Office (Moreland, 1982). The Chenery *et al.* model contains reduced-form growth equations that initially contained human capital, but eventually omitted it because of the inclusion of other factors with which it is correlated (e.g. the shift of labour out of agriculture, the growth of exports, a measure of the level of development). It builds toward a computable general equilibrium model that simulates a market economy into which price incentive policies are introduced (Chenery *et al.*, 1986: 311). But although it explores several development strategies, it is not designed to measure the market impacts of education, and it does not explore any of the non-market outcomes or aspects of comprehensive development. An earlier well-known study of *Redistribution with Growth* by Chenery *et al.* (1974) does trace the impacts of primary and secondary school enrolments on inequality (ibid.: 28) and includes a model (with Ahluwalia; ibid.: 215) that has interactions among growth, distribution, and population growth. But it contains none of the other sectors and does not distinguish between direct and indirect effects.

The Wheeler model is a long-run socioeconomic model that does focus on education and the interaction between education and fertility, population, and income per capita in a simultaneous equation context. But although consistent with my results, it also does not contain the other sectors. The same could be said of the ILO model. There are other models that have mostly been of the input–output type, with linear production functions focused on disaggregated industry-level outputs and inter-industry interactions.

In this book simulations of endogenous development and of policy change options are possible for each of 78 countries in East Asia, Sub-Saharan Africa, and Latin America, and among the OECD industrialized countries. The newly independent nations of Eastern Europe and Asia are not covered since there is great difficulty in acquiring comparable data on key variables over the time periods required. Conditions in command economies raise somewhat different issues that would require separate treatment.

The Conceptual Framework

The economic growth process and the growth sector of the development model are discussed in the growth chapters below; they are heavily influenced by the *endogenous growth* models of Lucas (1988), Barro (1991, 1997), and others and the empirical evidence related to them. The purely market-related aspects are expanded in succeeding chapters to include important non-market aspects of economic development along the lines mentioned above. When so expanded, the development process is referred to as *endogenous development*.

The starting point is at the microeconomic level with individual firms, households, and governmental units. For firms, education's contributions to market-measured output arises from the human capital that is in the firm's production function as specified by Lucas (1988). His and the other production functions that appear as a central element in endogenous growth models contain externalities generated by the general level of human capital and knowledge within the firm and in the community. These externality benefits raise productivity within the firm and hence measured output.

In the case of non-market returns to education, there is *household* production of final satisfactions largely during non-labour market leisure-time hours. The household production function yields *private* non-market benefits, and yet this household production is also affected by externalities. Examples of *private* non-market outcomes include the contribution of education within the family after controlling for per capita income to better health in the family as measured by increased longevity or reduced infant mortality.

In addition to these *private* market and non-market returns, the public *social* benefits of education include the benefits that are shared by all in the society whether these benefits (or costs) be monetary or non-monetary. It does not matter whether or not they are fully anticipated. The key point, as noted by Lucas (1988), is that the externality-type benefits generally available as free goods in the society will not affect any single individual's decision to invest in education because the individual knows that they will be generally available to all and will be unaffected by any single individual's decision on whether or not he or she invests.

Finally there are distributional impacts of education. These include effects on poverty reduction and the net impacts on reduced inequality in income distribution. Poverty reduction constitutes an increase in social welfare if the rates of return to that education which reduces poverty are high. But there is also a distributional dimension to it, as there is to redistribution, which raises normative questions. To place a value on poverty reduction and the reduction of inequality it is usually necessary to accept the value placed by society on these items in the public budgets of democratic societies. Only by this means can they be included as part of the *social benefits* of education.

The Framework for Endogenous Development

The endogenous development model contains 8 sectors. Each sector consists of 2 to 4 subsector benefits or effects, each of which is represented by a behavioural equation estimated from the data. This comes to 30 endogenous variables, to which must be added 11 identities, some of which determine the sectoral benefit totals, which then makes them also endogenous. The sectors and respective subsectors are:

- Economic Growth
    Per Capita Growth
    Investment in Physical Capital
- Population and Health
    Net Population Growth
    Fertility
    Longevity
    Infant Mortality
- Democratization and Human Rights
    Democratization
    Human Rights
    Political Stability
- Reduction of Poverty and Inequality
    Urban Poverty
    Rural Poverty
    Income Inequality
- The Environment
    Forest and Wildlife Preservation
    Air Pollution
    Water Pollution
- Crime and Drug Use
    Homicide Rate
    Property Crime
    Drug Use
- Labour Force Participation
    Female Labour Force Participation
    Percent of Labour Force in Agriculture
    Total Labour Force Participation Rate
- Education Enrolment Rates (Totals)
    Male and Female Enrolment Rates in Primary, Secondary, and
        Higher Education (6)
    Investment in Education as a Percent of GDP (3)

The Data

All data are annual data, specific to a particular year, and for 78 countries in the world, the largest number for which consistent data are available on all of the essential variables. The economic growth sector is estimated separately for data specific to each region and over the time period 1965–95 within each country. This period includes the lags, given that education and initial GDP per capita are normally for 1965. The POOL method of estimation was used, correcting for heteroscedasticity in the cross-section dimension and for autocorrelation in the residuals in the time series dimension.

The Time Period

The time period with which I am concerned is the medium term, viewed as about 35 or 40 years with simulation projections from the present to the year 2035 A D . The *medium period* is defined as a period during which total capital deepening is continuing to occur. *Capital deepening* is defined as more physical capital per capita, and also more education per capita. In the case of some Sub-Saharan African countries, with rapid population growth and slow capital accumulation, there has sometimes been less physical and human capital per capita or *capital dilution* over time. This is still the medium term but in this case the whole growth process is reversed.

Solution Values for the Endogenous Variables for 2000–2035

The solutions, therefore, are in the form of dynamic time paths generated by solutions within each year for each endogenous variable. No long-term steady-state growth solutions are considered. This is because, apart from the reasons already mentioned over the periods covered here, there has been and continues to be continuous capital deepening (or capital dilution) which is characteristic of the medium term. The level of total physical and human capital per worker even in East Asia remains far below the levels attained in the more industrialized countries. There are numerous lags, so all lagged values are fed by the reduced-form solutions for the preceding period as dynamic time paths are generated.

Lags

The lags are decreed by the logic of each situation. This is supplemented by empirical exploration of the length of the lags to see if additional insight is offered by the data. These lags are sometimes as long as 10 to 25 years. Although the impacts of education policy changes begin to show up immediately, it can take many years before the cumulative impacts from changes in enrolment rates are large enough to affect the much larger stock of human capital in the society, which in turn affects GDP.

Because of these lags most parts of the structure of the model are recursive. This justifies estimation of at least those portions separately by ordinary least squares. This also facilitates making appropriate corrections for heteroscedasticity and autocorrelation. Simultaneous equation estimation is used, however, for the joint relation between economic growth and the rate of investment in physical capital within the economic growth sector. Where simultaneous bias is not found to be serious, the ordinary least squares estimates with the heteroscedasticity corrections are used and the simultaneous estimates appear only as a cross-check.

Feedback Effects

The lags indicate that the direction of the flow of causation is from the earlier event to the later event: for example, from investment in education early in the life cycle to earnings increments later or from secondary enrolments 15 years earlier to measurable net increments to economic growth later. The inference of causation must be from the logic and the underlying theory of the process, not from the empirical correlation alone, which can be spurious. However, in this case the cause-and-effect relation does not just run from investment in education to economic growth later; there are also feedback effects as higher per capita income contributes to further investment in education by households and by governments. This social demand for education means that governments generally respond to voters' wishes, so that the endogenous income elasticity of demand for basic education is about 1.0 (McMahon, 1971, 1992*b*), a fact that is incorporated in the endogenous development growth path in Chapter 11.

There is nothing wrong with this two-way flow of causation. There are many instances of it in economics. It does not diminish in any way the causal connection between investment in education and economic growth (with which I am primarily concerned) or the causal connection between rising per capita income and increased investment in education. The logic of the theory at the micro-level includes education's contribution to the skill levels of workers and through this to increased productivity in firms, as well as growth in the aggregate that finances further improvements in education levels. Although each of these relations is basically recursive, the possibility of simultaneity in aggregate data that distorts the net impacts of education on income growth in statistical measurements must continually be considered and tested for. This has been done, for example, in simultaneous equation estimates for Africa (McMahon, 1987), for the US (McMahon, forthcoming), for East Asia (Chapter 3 below), and earlier by Wheeler (1984) and others, with the result that with proper lags simultaneous bias was not found to destroy the relationship of education to income growth. Higher-income families invest more in the education of their children but in principle, investment that comes later cannot affect investments that have been made in the past.

Long-Run Equilibrium Relationships

The behavioural equations of the model make use of the concept of adjustment from one long-run equilibrium toward another as the underlying forces influencing households, firms, or governmental units change in each case. Economists make wide use of the concept of equilibrium. It is used for analysis of non-market behaviour by households (e.g. Becker, 1976, 1981, 1988) and for analysis of the decisions of firms and governmental units (e.g. Downs, 1959; Diamond, 1993).

Parameters estimated from cross-section data normally are interpreted as parameters relating to longer-run adjustments between old and new long-run equilibria after time has been sufficient to react to changes in factors impinging on them and to reach the new levels. There are many excellent examples in the consumer behaviour literature, for example, of longer-run parameters estimated from both cross-section and longer-run time series data that are then related to shorter-run disequilibria in both (e.g. Friedman, 1959). The normal view is that households, firms, or governmental units viewed in the sweep of cross-section data have found their microeconomic long-run equilibria, although there are recent arrivals at each level which have not fully adjusted (and which produce noise that is collected in the disturbances). There must of course be controls for differences in other relevant conditions, such as political stability, where they are relevant, which constitutes enforcement of the ceteris paribus conditions. But this is a matter of research design to isolate the effects of the key variables of interest with specifications that control for the preconditions, cultural differences, or external shocks that are significant, not a matter of whether cross-section or time series data is used.

Cross-section data is widely used as a basis for making predictions in all of the social and life sciences based largely on this concept. For example, democratization as measured by the Freedom House Index (Freedom House, 1998) has been interpreted by political scientists in the cross-section as reflecting movements in response to changes in the underlying conditions toward new longer-run levels of democratization. If underlying forces change it is reasonable to conclude that this same process will continue as development occurs. This is especially pertinent in Latin America, where the underlying per capita income, education, and industrialization levels have changed, with the result that many countries have moved generally but erratically toward democracy in the last 25 years. Yet these democracies are still fragile since most are in the 'zone of transition', as will be discussed in Chapter 7. The parameters predict progress in this direction as development occurs, but they do not predict what will happen 'next year'. They instead relate to a longer-run process. This will be considered in relation to China and other countries throughout the text. From a statistical point of view the outcomes are probabilistic, with the usual standard errors of the estimate, and also reflect the dynamic lags in tracing impacts within this context of longer-run processes. For these reasons the estimates should not be misinterpreted as speaking to what is going to happen in specific cases with certainty next year.

Uses for the Conceptual Framework and the Results

There are several potential uses of the conceptual framework, both micro and macro, for measuring the returns to education more comprehensively. One is certainly as a stimulus to the interest of those concerned with measuring education outcomes better. There is a need to move toward a more comprehensive measurement and valuation of the outcomes and perhaps in principle at least the equation structure suggested here could be used in additional ways, such as for estimates at state or local levels.

A second use is in tracing the impacts of human resource development through education on economic development with a view to finding more cost-effective development strategies. This is not only in appraising the impacts of changes in education enrolment and investment policies at the different levels, as well as other reforms, through simulations, but also in costing out these education policies, and considering the costs of alternative means of achieving these same outcomes.

A third use is in measuring social rates of return and non-market outcomes in countries where such measures do not now exist for use in policy dialogue with policy makers, many of whom may not be fully aware of these impacts. Most are interested in cost-effective policies and most are also interested in achieving the kinds of development goals discussed.

A fourth use is in suggesting hypotheses for further testing at the microeconomic level using data for individual households, firms, or governmental units. It is impossible of course to have every single explanatory variable, including the marginal ones, completely and fully delineated. So this should not be expected; also, I have only tried to seek out the main effects. A macro-to-micro research strategy of this type is common in physics, physiology, and other disciplines. The themes might encourage graduate students in economic growth, economic development, education, and human capital fields to explore the implications more fully.

PART II
Economic Growth

2 Human Capital, Endogenous Growth Models, and Economic Development

In the new endogenous growth models, as well as in the Solow models augmented with human capital, human resource development through education is central to the growth process in ways that will be considered more explicitly in this chapter.

Households make decisions about allocating their time to the formation of human capital through education with a view to future income and future satisfaction rather than allocating their time to the labour market to support current consumption. Firms directly use the human capital skills thereby created in production, but they also benefit from the average level of knowledge due to human capital in the community available to all as an externality and, in Romer's (1990) terms, 'non-rivalrous'. They are therefore able to produce under conditions of increasing returns. The result is that this knowledge embodied in human capital inside and outside of firms offsets the diminishing returns to investment in physical capital which would otherwise occur. There is no steady-state level of per capita income, and per capita growth becomes possible virtually without bounds.

Further development of this theoretical framework, including analysis of the dynamics of the growth process relevant to shorter periods of time (e.g. 35-or 40-year periods), will lay the foundations for the empirical analyses of education and economic growth in East Asia, Latin America and the Caribbean, Sub-Saharan Africa, and the OECD member nations in the chapters that follow. The development of the theoretical framework here involves five modifications to the formal long-term growth models found in the literature. The *first*, which is implicit in our focus on shorter-term dynamics, is that the regressions are not valid only if countries are in their steady states (as in Mankiw, Romer, and Weil, 1992: tables I and II), but instead will be comparable to their Solow model augmented with human capital, which is not subject to this restriction and does produce their best worldwide results (ibid.: table IV). *Second*, this chapter will introduce the influence of government decisions that encourage households to save and invest in education, an effect that will be included in the regressions later. *Third*, the contribution of education at primary, secondary, and higher levels is analysed separately, as well as the distinction between enrolments and investment expenditure at each of these levels. *Fourth*, the indirect effects on economic growth, as rates of investment in physical capital and population growth rates become endogenous as they are affected by education and by economic growth, is considered, effects that will be tested later in Chapters 3 to 6. *Finally*, although the theoretical framework focuses on the sources of pure economic growth, it also can be adapted to accommodate the non-market returns to education. They will be analysed explicitly in Chapters 7 to 10 and will become an integral part of the complete model of endogenous development in Chapters 11 to 14.

Human Capital in Economic Growth Models

There has been a flurry of recent theoretical and empirical research since about 1988 which constitutes a reawakening of the field of economic growth. This has been partly due to the theoretical insights offered by the new endogenous growth models and by the Solow models augmented with human capital, but it also has clearly been due to the wave of research that gives these models empirical relevance. Together these developments have identified the significance of human capital created through education, and the dissemination of new knowledge through education, to achieving sustained per capita economic growth. Furthermore, it is now strongly suggested that a set of government policies including the encouragement of higher rates of human resource development through education is critically important to achieving higher sustainable growth rates. It is no longer accepted that *nations are poor because they are poor*. Instead, it is now the more widely accepted view that *nations are poor because of poor policies*.

The per capita growth record differs widely among regions since 1985, a fast 6.9 per cent per year in East Asia, a slower 0.6 per cent in Latin America and the Caribbean, and a −1.2 per cent in Sub-Saharan Africa (World Bank, 1996a: Indicators, table 1). It also differs sharply among countries within each region. The framework set out in this chapter seeks to discuss the theoretical background for addressing empirically in the chapters that follow the source of these differences among regions and among countries within each region. These sources include differences in saving and investment rates, in population growth, and in political stability. Taken together with the chapters that follow this can be viewed as a step toward explaining the key constants or exogenous variables in the Solow model and to make them endogenous.

Medium-term dynamics was defined in Chapter 1 as a period within which total capital deepening continues to occur. That is, education levels per worker and physical capital levels per worker are changing and *are not fixed as they are in steady-state and steady-state growth solutions*. These total capital stocks per capita have in fact been rising, especially in East Asia, but also in Latin America. They have not been constant in Africa either, but have been rising in some countries and falling, with capital dilution occurring, as education and physical capital are spread more thinly in many others. But in all three regions the amount of human and physical capital per capita remains very low in relation to the much higher total capital per capita ratios in the more advanced OECD nations. This focus on short-and medium-term dynamics seems justified in that the Solow model augmented with human capital implies that economies reach only *halfway* to their steady state in 35 years as estimated by Mankiw, Romer, and Weil (1992: 29). In the endogenous growth models of Lucas (1988) and Romer (1990), with constant returns to total capital or increasing returns with externalities, no steady-state level of income is ever achieved, but instead steady-state growth. For this a constant level of total capital per capita is again assumed to be achieved. Capital deepening and capital dilution (with rapid population growth), however, appear to be more consistent with the data. This capital deepening is characteristic of the time paths generated by reduced-form solutions via simulation within each time period for all of the endogenous variables and is also typical of short-and medium-term dynamics.

Endogenous Growth and Related Research

A starting point is the Lucas (1988) production function, which features human capital in a central role, and whose levels in turn are endogenously determined by household time allocation decisions. In Lucas's model human capital is used by firms, which precludes its use by others; this is therefore the major 'rivalrous' component of knowledge (Romer, 1990: 579). But human capital is also available as an externality in the form of an average level of education in society, created by families and by educational institutions. The latter also raises productivity within firms.

A closely related starting point is the Solow model augmented with human capital, as exemplified by Mankiw, Romer, and Weil (1992: part II). In contrast to Lucas and Romer they assume constant returns to scale when human capital is explicitly included. So there are diminishing returns to human and physical capital. But countries with higher rates of investment in human capital nevertheless grow significantly faster in their regressions. Therefore Solow's model is consistent with the international evidence if the importance of human capital is acknowledged.

A third, also related, starting point is the empirical tests by Kim and Lau (1996) in their research on growth in East Asia. They conclude that high rates of investment in physical capital and in human capital explain essentially all of the rapid per capita growth on the Pacific Rim. That is, 'technical progress' (i.e., total factor productivity), after the accumulation of human and physical capital is taken into account, explains little or nothing. This makes it important to look more closely at the specific roles of human capital in the growth process in the developing countries of Latin America and Sub-Saharan Africa as well. Domestic investment in R&D as a source of new knowledge is likely to be more relevant to sustainable growth processes in the advanced industrialized OECD economies, but even there it is complementary to higher education, on which it depends for dissemination. R&D will be tested empirically in East Asia, Latin America, and Africa, but it generally remains more in the background in these regions.

Western technologies of course were imported and adapted in East Asia (and in principle could be in Latin America and Sub-Saharan Africa as well). But education facilitated this process. Education was also basic to the success of export-oriented growth strategies in East Asia, a point documented in depth recently by Adrian Wood (1994). Romer's (1990) term, 'endogenous technical change', perhaps has the advanced economies most in mind, but he also clearly has human capital in a central role. His 'non- rivalrous' inputs could be interpreted (as Lucas does) as a human capital externality enabling the dissemination of knowledge inputs and facilitating the adaptation of new designs.

Consistent Micro-level Evidence

Consistent with the endogenous growth and augmented Solow growth models, there is supportive new evidence at the micro-level concerning the significance of education to increments in earnings productivity. It includes that by Ashenfelter and Rouse (1996, 1998) based on large samples of identical twins. They impose very stringent controls removing the influence of innate ability, prior education, and family factors, and interview the other twin as a basis for estimating the offset due to measurement error. These and other related microeconomic studies are the basis for 'The Causal Effect of Education on Earnings' as inferred by Card (1998). There is also evidence of positive trends over time based on microeconomic data which shows that when trends in earnings at different levels of education are taken into account these 'growth factors' have been raising rates of return even above those rates estimated by standard methods from cross-section data (Arias and McMahon, 1998).

Relation to Other Growth Processes

Schumpeterian models based on innovation or R&D alone rather than education might logically explain this endogenous growth process, except for the fact that they do not explain where the capacities to innovate come from. Also, empirically they normally do not include human capital in the regressions. When they do, the results are very different. Export-oriented growth strategies such as those studied by Ito and Krueger (1995) also are not inconsistent with the empirical findings of these growth models. Exports undoubtedly help but the focus on exports alone does not take into account the extent to which they depend on prior education. Wood (1994) shows skill development through education to be almost a precondition for comparative advantage and good manufacturing export performance.

The Production Function

In the original Solow (1956) growth model the neo-classical production function contains only physical capital and raw labour. With constant returns to scale assumed, it displays diminishing returns to increased physical capital per worker. This can be offset by technical change. But human capital in the original Solow textbook model is not linked to the dissemination of technical change as it is in the more recent work by Lucas (1988), Romer (1986, 1990), Eliasson *et al.* (1990), Kim and Lau (1996), and Barro (1991, 1995: 198–200, 1997). It is strictly exogenously determined, and drops from the sky.

In contrast to the increasing returns in endogenous growth theory, Mankiw, Romer, and Weil (1992: part II) go back to the assumption of constant returns to scale as in the Solow model but introduce human capital as an explicit separate input in the production function. This does not generate growth without bounds in the very long run, but it does generate a very high rate of economic growth per capita in the medium term in response to larger rates of investment in human capital associated primarily with higher rates of enrolment in secondary education.

The empirical models to be estimated for each of the three regions are similar to both of these, but I will show only the Lucas (1988) production function below. I choose to do this partly because he treats the technology level, A, as a constant. This is consistent with the empirical work for East Asia by Kim and Lau (1996: 9–13), who find empirically that technical change adds nothing to total factor productivity if human capital investments are taken into account. So the technology level appears as a constant, essentially disappears when derivatives are taken with respect to time, and will only be brought back into the discussion when growth in the OECD nations is being considered. I also choose to show the Lucas production function because of the presence of externalities in it that are related to the average level of education or skill levels in the economy. This is consistent with the indirect structural effects this term contains that I identify and will investigate extensively later in this book.

In the Lucas production function in Equation (2.1) below the stock of human capital skills employed on the job is μH. This includes not just the vocational skills of the labour force but also technical and managerial knowledge, some of which may have been acquired in college and most of which is not patented. This is distinguished from raw unimproved labour measured by the number of workers, N. Lucas (1988: 17–19) discusses the aggregation procedures further. But these workers are in possession of sufficient human capital capacities that they can adapt to career changes and can adapt spillover knowledge that is available in the society as externalities. This latter average level of education available in the economy at large, which also raises productivity within the firm, is shown by the term H^α.

The Lucas production function, therefore, is:

$$Y_t = A(K_t, \mu H_t, N_t)H^\alpha, \tag{2.1}$$

where Y = output, K = physical capital, μ = the proportion of time each worker devotes to production in the firm, μH = human capital engaged within the firm, created by past investment in education and on-the-job training, N = the number of persons, and H^α = the average level of human capital in the community that reflects the external effects of human capital in the society on productivity within firms. A is the technology level, presumed as mentioned above to be constant, assuming that in order to be disseminated and effective, knowledge must be embodied in human capital.

The fraction of time that this Lucas production function implies to be allocated to the production of human capital is $1 - \mu$. It is taken here to be the result of decisions by households influenced by the decisions of governments to build schools, train teachers, buy books, and invest in education. These government decisions act as encouragement to households to keep their children in school. It can also include paying teachers, declaring basic education to be compulsory, and subsidizing higher education via means tests so that it does not drive out private investment in higher education. The effects on enrolments of lowering the effective price of education to families is demonstrated empirically for Indonesia by Prescott *et al.* (1993), and for the US by McMahon (1984c). As children remain in school longer, this involves forgone earnings for the parents, causing them to refrain from consumption (i.e. save) and simultaneously invest these savings in room, board, and tuition to provide for more years of schooling.

These government and private decisions are both part of endogenous growth in the sense that they are partially dependent on increasing per capita income as the economy grows. They are not the exogenous unexplained 'manna from heaven' in Solow or Schumpeterian models but instead are the result of deliberate decisions by governments and households to allocate time to human capital formation. This offsets diminishing returns to human capital and also creates a potential for increasing returns in Equation (2.1) as the exponents add to more than 1.

Turning to non-monetary final satisfactions, workers carry this human capital home with them where it is used in household production during leisure-time hours (Becker, 1965), yielding non-market returns to education. These non-monetary returns, both private and social, generate additional externalities that affect measured GDP but also the non-monetary quality of life.

To illustrate this growth process in Figures 2.1 and 2.2 the production functions that apply to consumption goods, physical capital, human capital, and household production of final satisfactions will assumed to be similar to Equation (2.1). That is, one unit of consumption can be transformed costlessly into either one unit of human capital, one unit of physical capital, or one unit of non-monetary Becker commodities. All workers in the economy will be treated as having the same skill level and choosing time allocation μ, so that total production can then be expressed in per capita terms as shown in Equation (2.2). This production function is expressed in implicit terms, since that will facilitate treating it either as part of an endogenous growth model with increasing returns to scale or a Solow model augmented with human capital:

$$Y/N = A(K/N, H/N, u), \tag{2.2}$$

where variables are as defined above, except that $H =$ human capital, and $u =$ disturbances.

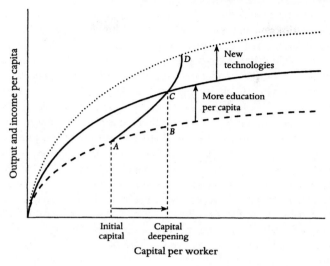

Figure 2.1 The economic growth process in the medium-term

This production function 25 illustrated in Figure 2.1 expresses output per capita Y/N on the vertical axis as a function of physical capital per capita K/N measured on the horizontal axis. As the stock of physical capital, K, increases faster than the number of persons, N, physical capital deepening occurs, increasing K/N along the horizontal axis. But if there are not sufficient increases in the education and skills of the workforce, this physical capital deepening in isolation encounters diminishing returns, as shown from *A* to *B* in Figure 2.1. This causes growth in output to slow down and eventually to reach a steady state in the Solow model.

With increased investment in human resources $\Delta H/N$, the production function expressed only as a function of physical capital on the horizontal axis shifts upward, as illustrated in Figure 2.1. In endogenous growth models with increasing returns to scale the shorter-or medium-term dynamic time path is from *A* to *C* as this total capital deepening occurs. It slopes upward, so output per capita, Y/N, grows, and could grow with increasing returns without bounds even in the very long run. In the Solow model augmented with human capital, per capita growth could also occur as human capital deepening continues, but it depends on continuing education inputs and would eventually slow down as diminishing returns to all inputs eventually take over, resulting in no further growth in Y/N.

All the later chapters will focus on the medium-term dynamics, where there is continuing human capital deepening as illustrated here. After suitable controls are imposed for other factors that vary among countries, the role of this human capital deepening will be tested in East Asia, Latin America, Sub-Saharan Africa, and the OECD nations.

Technical change in the OECD member nations has not reached the rural areas of Sub-Saharan Africa and the poorest nations in Latin America and the Caribbean, where most of the people live. This lack of information, stressed by Stiglitz (1998), can be interpreted within this endogeneous growth theory context as a failure of dissemination due to human capital deficiencies. In the OECD nations, however, in addition to the human capital investments, new knowledge of processes, products, and organizational techniques are generated through investment in research and development by governments and firms. This results in a second upward shift in the production function and potentially further growth in output per capita from C to D as shown in Figure 2.1. This can further offset diminishing returns to both physical capital and human capital, as evidenced, for example, by the rising rates of return since 1980 to higher education in the US (see Arias and McMahon, 1998). But leading-edge research and the financial capacity to support it, since there are major costs for all of the failed experiments and less productive research, is most feasible in the higher-income OECD member countries. It runs a severe risk of being relatively high-cost and having a low net return in the poorest countries, especially considering the high opportunity costs. New technologies created elsewhere can be imported and adapted, and an export-oriented growth strategy implemented, as has been done in East Asia.

But these things can be done successfully only if there has been sufficient prior investment in human capital. The capacity to adapt production technologies and product designs effectively and to manufacture and export goods depends heavily on a labour force with considerable secondary education and capacities to learn on the job (again, see Wood, 1994: 5–15, 22).

Investment and Saving Rates

To raise the level of stocks of human and physical capital in the production function shown above requires deliberate decisions to save and invest. The investment must be financed in the neo-classical model by high domestic saving rates. If the macroeconomic policies are not right, and investment is not financed by saving in periods when the economy is near capacity, then this can only be followed by inflation. This in turn leads to high interest rates dictated by the central bank or by lenders such as the IMF forcing reduction of deficits. The result is a recession to get rid of the inflationary expectations, as in Indonesia in 1998 for example, all of which slows long-run growth temporarily. So in the following sections of this chapter and in the rest of this book, higher rates of investment in human capital are thought of as financed in part with *total* saving (i.e. forgone earnings and taxes) so that this investment does not merely cause inflation and thereby slow growth.

Determinants of Investment Rates

Total investment is equal to saving in both endogenous growth and augmented Solow models. (See the investment = saving function in the bottom half of Figure

2.2.) Investment in human capital, however, which is a part of this *total* investment, is mostly done by families financing it by forgoing the real earnings of their children while they are in school, and paying room, board, and tuition. The institutional costs of public education are largely financed with taxes, which in a sense are a form of forced saving. Total investment in physical capital plus human capital per capita in Equation (2.3) is equal to total saving per capita, which includes personal saving but also forgone (parental) consumption as children are sustained in school and taxes are paid:

$$(I_K + I_H)/N = S/N. \tag{2.3}$$

Here I_K and I_H = investment in physical and human capital respectively, and S = total saving, composed of S_P = personal saving + S_T = taxes + S_F = forgone earnings.

In Figure 2.2, medium-term physical capital deepening occurs from $(K/N)_{65}$ to $(K/N)_t$. When this is augmented with human capital as a separate input (and in the case of the OECD member countries, with I_A = investment in new technologies via R&D), total investment in physical capita per capita, as shown by the line that passes through G, is higher since only physical capital is measured on the horizontal axis. *Total* investment and *total* saving per capita as measured on the vertical axis in US dollars is not at H but instead is at G. That is, if physical capital is augmented in Figure 2.2 with new investment in human capital via education and new investment in knowledge capital via R&D which are both greater than zero, *total* capital deepening would be shown by the line that passes through G rather than by the line that passes through H. A policy decision to invest suddenly in human and knowledge capital (say increase I_H above zero, which is exogenous here but is made

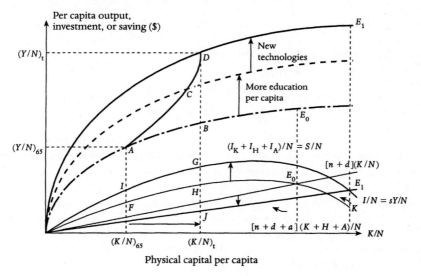

Figure 2.2 Medium-term and long-run growth

endogenous soon below) would shift total investment per capita from F to I and increase total saving and the stock of human capital. Output and income in the medium term would grow not from A to B but from A to D.

The question about what happens in the long run steady-state solution in the augmented Solow model or in the endogenous growth models is not addressed here but it is useful to look at it graphically for purposes of comparison. The preceding might be thought of as before and after a shift in policy, or as comparing an economy that does not invest in human capital to one that does. The sloping straight line at the bottom is a reference line that defines the amount of investment per capita required to maintain the constant per capita total capital stock that characterizes the long-run steady-state solution. It shows that some investment will be required to replace depreciation determined by the depreciation rate, δ, and some will be required to keep up with the rate of population growth, n. With actual investment occurring at G and less required at J to maintain a constant per capita capital stock, total capital deepening will continue to occur until the long-run solution is achieved at point E_1. This involves a much higher steady-state output per capita, read from the production function at the top of the graph, than at E_0, without human and knowledge capital, where it would otherwise be. Investment and saving per capita is also at E_0 before including human and knowledge capital and at E_1 after their inclusion.

These rates of investment feed into the production function (Equation (2.2) and the top of Figure 2.2) through standard stock accumulation equations:

$$K = K_{-1} + I_K - \delta_K K_{-1} \tag{2.4}$$

$$H = H_{-1} + I_H - \delta_H H_{-1}, \tag{2.5}$$

again treating A as constant for applications later to East Asian, Latin American, and Sub-Sahara African countries. Here δ_K and δ_H are the rates of depreciation and obsolescence for physical and human capital respectively. These investment rates in turn are endogenously determined:

$$I_K/N = I_K(Y/N, I_H/Y, (Y/N)_{65}, PS, \alpha_6, u_6) \tag{2.6}$$

$$I_H/N = I_H(Y/N, \alpha_7, u_7). \tag{2.7}$$

Variables are as defined above for Equations (2.1)–(2.3) except that PS = Political Stability, and u = disturbances. PS is the composite political, financial, and economic risk rating for each economy from the *International Country Risk Guide* (Coplin *et al.*, 1997), which measures positive stability and not negative risk. Other data sources are given in Chapters 3 to 5, where these hypotheses are tested. α is a constant treated as a parameter which sets the starting point in the investment function for simulations in each country that also allows the rate of *endogenous* investment in human capital (endogenous since $I_H = f(Y/N)$), to be changed by deliberate policy decisions.

Rates of investment in physical capital in Equation (2.6) are expected to be a function of income and output per capita, Y/N, which is a standard endogenous accelerator-related effect from investment theory and also in this case related to the dependence of saving on per capita income. Interest rates have opposite effects on investment and saving in the medium term, and also opposite effects on domestic investment and international capital flows. So since they were also tried in preliminary tests and found on balance not to be very significant they remain with the disturbances, u_6. Although shown as disturbances here this term also represents controls which will be sorted out in the chapters that follow for shorter-term fluctuations by introducing a term for the unemployment rate, oil shocks, or oil-exporter status. Although these are largely 'noise' here from the point of view of our focus on the medium and longer term, they are particularly important in the Latin American countries. Political stability is exogenous here, but only temporarily, since it becomes endogenous in Chapter 7 and also an important part of the complete endogenous development model in Chapters 11 to 14. Gross Domestic Product per capita in the initial year, $(Y/N)_{65}$, is a test for convergence in investment rates.

Rates of investment in physical capital are hypothesized to be dependent on investment in human capital after a lag because of the key role of an increasingly skilled labour force in offsetting diminishing returns to physical capital. This education and skills furthermore support manufacturing exports (Wood, 1994), which helps to earn foreign exchange and also to attract money capital from abroad.

Investment in education in turn becomes endogenous in Chapter 11, where impacts on the functioning of the education sector are investigated. In particular, private investment in education is dependent on average per capita income and hence on economic growth. These household decisions are assumed also to respond to the government's decisions to invest in human capital, which lower the effective price of education and which in turn also respond to the growth of per capita income among taxpayers and voters over time. The basis for this latter endogeneity of public decisions to invest in education is in the public-choice literature, which includes income effects that are reflected through voter preferences, sometimes collected into partially countervailing special interest groups (McMahon, 1992b). The degree of democratization which becomes endogenous in a later chapter may also lead to greater support for rural education. The endogeneity of private and public investment in education with no extra policy changes generates a rate of economic development that is fully endogenous, slower in some countries than in others.

The capacity to *change* this internally determined rate of endogenous development by *changing* the rate of growth of investment in education, and hence enrolment rates which depend on this, is retained, however, in the parameter α. The effects of extraordinary policy interventions of this kind can then be compared to the endogenous development path by means of simulations.

The long-run steady-state permanence of these policy effects has been explored by Kockerlakota and Yi (1995). They conclude that although taxes do reduce consumption, which forces saving (by definition), and which alone would have negative incentive effects if carried too far, government investment financed with these taxes can then raise total investment demand, raising productivity. The resulting growth will eventually induce additional saving, especially in the case of investment in education, which encourages additional forgone earnings as discussed below. They further conclude that there is evidence in time series data for the long-term permanence of policy effects on economic growth. This is in spite of the fact that their model does not have endogenous population growth effects, which is one important effect of a change in education policy that might reasonably be expected to be very permanent.

Total Saving in Open Economies

But will public investment in education merely cause excess demand and inflation followed by high interest rates, recession, and slower growth?

The answer is 'no'. First, assuming that the investment is financed with taxes, this reduces private consumption expenditures. The resources committed to meet consumption demands are released and can be transferred to meeting the new investment demand. Second, total saving and total investment are increased, not decreased, by investment in education. 'Free' public education induces additional saving and investment in the form of forgone earnings as parents sacrifice their own consumption to support their children and may even work harder to support them. Therefore there is no net inflationary increase in aggregate demand and there may be a higher level of total saving induced in the society as a result of this policy. There is some evidence that this is one important thing that happened in East Asia (see McMahon, 1994b). So current consumption has been diverted to investment in the future as children stay in school longer, with no significant increase or decrease in aggregate demand. To the extent that some taxes reduce not just consumption but also private investment or private saving, if the rate of return to investment in human capital is higher than the average rate of return that otherwise would have been obtained in alternative private investments, as it usually is, then resources have been redirected to more highly productive human capital investments with a net gain in economic growth. This ignores the additional non-market returns to individuals and to society. It has been shown by Arias and McMahon (1998) that rates of return on education in the US compare favourably to rates of return on other assets in the US and by Wolfe and Zuvekas (1997) that the non-market private and social returns to education are about equal to the market returns.

Third, since in most poor countries rural unemployment and underemployment are very high, additional time spent in school involves a significant investment in the future but at relatively low opportunity cost. Even though their parents forgo some of their children's help in agriculture or at home, the productivity of children in these employments is very low, and if they would have been unemployed otherwise, it is practically zero. Also, rural housewives are often employed as teachers and underemployed males as custodians or in school construction. This use of underutilized resources is not inflationary, a point that is of great concern to the IMF.

Fourth, in contrast to the neo-classical one-country model, internationally money capital is now very mobile and the rate of investment is not fully constrained by the domestic saving rate. There is a correlation; where domestic saving rates are larger, investment (and hence growth) is also higher. But investment is not totally limited by domestic factors in the medium term; countries can borrow from the World Bank or other international lenders, invest wisely, grow, and repay later out of higher per capita incomes and export earnings. The old divisive growth models, which argued that with higher inequality the rich would save more and invest for faster growth, are false; the rich in some of the poorest countries have put their resources in Swiss banks and skipped out (e.g. Haiti, the Philippines, Zaïre, Nigeria, and many others); the limits of domestic saving rates can be circumvented with international money capital flows given the right policies; and most important, investments in human capital formation tend both to utilize underutilized resources even more than other types of investments and to induce higher rates of total saving by parents. Fifth, although the contributions of these investments in education to political stability (after a lag) will be considered in Chapter 7, they are also germane here.

The overall basic point with respect to saving is that there are more degrees of freedom in the determination of total investment than is sometimes supposed. Put more forcefully, the older models, depending on inequality for higher saving, pay attention to saving rates but do not include public investment in education, where taxes force additional saving; do not include induced forgone earnings in their definition of saving; do not recognize that education in poor countries absorbs underutilized resources in the rural areas and hence leads to little crowding out; generally ignore both rapacious dictators and their supporting elites as well as international sources of money capital; and finally ignore net contributions of education investment to longer-run political stability and lower population growth. For all five of these reasons they are irrelevant and cannot be used as guides to meaningful policy.

Population Growth Rates

The neo-classical Solow growth model, the augmented Solow model, and endogenous growth models all predict a negative relation of high population growth rates to lower per capita output in the long run, and vice versa.

How this works for the long-run steady-state solution in the case of slower population growth as in East Asia can be seen in Figure 2.2 above. Interpreting Figure 2.2 first as the original Solow model in steady state at E_0, a slower population growth rate requires a lower rate of investment to maintain a constant per capita capital stock. This shifts the investment *requirements* function, which defines the amount of investment required to maintain a constant per capita capital stock, downward to point J (population growth is an exogenous parameter in the augmented Solow model). At the old steady-state solution (E_0) using the investment function that passes through F and H, the incentive to invest is increased since the vertical gap between the investment requirements function and this investment $=$ saving function is now positive below point E_0. The new solution for the steady-state level of income per capita is at a larger K/N along the new investment requirements function to the right of E_0. The steady-state solution for per capita output on the production function to the right of E_0 read off the vertical axis is larger.

Similarly, reinterpreting Figure 2.2 as an augmented Solow or endogenous growth model, the investment $=$ saving function passes through points I and G since it now contains total investment, including education, and total saving, including forgone earnings. A lower population growth rate again shifts the total investment requirements function downward to J, increasing the new steady-state solution to E_1 and output per capita to E_1 at the very top of the graph. This solution for Y/N in the augmented Solow model is given by Mankiw, Romer, and Weil (1992: 13), where the negative relation to population growth, n, can easily be seen on the right:

$$
\begin{aligned}
lnY/N =lnA + at - (\alpha + \beta)/(1 - \alpha - \beta)ln(n + a + \delta) \\
+ \alpha/(1 - \alpha - \beta)lnI_K/Y + \beta/(1 - \alpha - \beta)lnI_K/Y.
\end{aligned}
\tag{2.8}
$$

Here $a =$ technical change, which drops out in both places it appears if this is assumed to be zero for Asia, Latin America, and Sub-Saharan Africa (but not for the OECD nations), and α and $\beta =$ exponents from their constant returns to scale production function.

Income per capita in many countries in Sub-Saharan Africa, where population growth rates are higher, would be lower in the steady state than if this were not occurring. Per capita growth in 37 out of the 54 or so nations in Sub-Saharan Africa was positive in 1998, but was negative in the rest. So in the latter nations this whole process would be reversed, with the investment requirements function shifting upward rapidly, and the steady-state solution per capita output falling.

In the medium term where capital deepening (or capital dilution) has not ceased, the movements in Figure 2.2 are instead from A to C to D (with capital deepening) or D to C to A (with capital dilution). But except for the starting point, the rest of the graphical analysis of the growth process and the conclusions about the effects of slower population growth on *achieving* higher *per capita* income growth are the same.

These net population growth rates becomes endogenous in Chapter 6. They are heavily dependent on female education, as demonstrated there. More specifically, since more primary education improves health before it lowers the fertility rate sufficiently, and large numbers of Sub-Saharan African and Indian/Pakistani/Nepalese females are at these levels, population growth rates remain high and can be expected to rise in these places for some years into the future. Only after most females have some secondary education do population growth rates begin to slow down as they have in East Asia so that the process of capital dilution described above is reversed.

Summarizing this endogeneity in a reduced form:

$$n = n(Y/N, I_H/N, u_9).$$ (2.9)

The variables are as previously defined. This leaves out the details, but the expected positive relation of per capita income to population growth (the Malthusian effect) and the negative relation of investment in female secondary education to net population growth rates is apparent.

Endogenous Growth and Endogenous Development

This chapter has discussed the main features of the recent endogenous growth and augmented Solow models with a view both to setting the framework for the empirical analysis of the economic growth process in East Asia, Latin America, Africa, and the OECD nations in Chapters 2 to 5 and to setting out much of the endogenous development framework developed later in this book. Investment in physical capital is determined in the economic growth chapters, but there have been allusions to the determinants of political stability, investment in education (and total saving), population growth, and the treatment of technical progress so that the later chapters appear as part of an integrated whole.

From the point of view of non-linear comparative dynamics, the medium-term dynamic time paths for each of the variables are first generated by simulation methods to obtain the path of endogenous development. Then, since governments representing their citizens may not like what they see, the capacity has been retained to intervene in the model and change the otherwise endogenously determined education policies. This new time path is no longer fully endogenous, of course. But it permits a measure of the impacts of a change in education inputs on education outcomes, or on economic development, depending on which is the reader's primary interest.

When the substantial variation from country to country of these constants in the original Solow model, augmented Solow model, and endogenous growth models is explained econometrically and its feedback effects on per capita growth is taken into account, this should contribute to a more general theory and empirical explanation of the economic growth process. As this is extended in later chapters to include the main non-market returns to education, this should begin to extend the capacity to measure more comprehensively the net contribution of education to human welfare.

3   Education and Growth in East Asia

Although there has been a major slowdown recently due largely to financial crises, the sources of medium-and longer-run per capita economic growth in East Asia with which this chapter is concerned are based on relatively strong longer-run fundamentals there. These sources are particularly interesting because of the very high per capita growth sustained from before 1960 to 1997, essentially 40 years, in the Far East and because of fundamentals which are likely to re-emerge. Apart from the needed reforms now under way in the banking systems, there are additional lessons, that can be learned from the dramatic increase in per capita incomes and poverty reduction since the end of World War II that might be transferrable to other regions.

Per capita growth in real terms had been 5.2 per cent per year from 1965 to 1988 in the East Asia region, and 6.9 per cent per year more recently from 1985 through 1995. This compares to 1.9 per cent in the OECD member nations in the more recent period, 0.6 per cent in the Latin American region, and − 1.1 per cent in Sub-Saharan Africa. The recession in Japan and financial crises elsewhere in the Far East aside, this basic longer-term pattern is likely to remain much the same.

A starting point is the new endogenous growth model and Solow model augmented with human capital and the related empirical work as discussed in the preceding chapter (e.g., Lucas, 1988; Romer, 1990: 579, Mankiw, Romer, and Weil, 1992, Barro, 1991, 1995, and McMahon, 1984a, 1987), all of which give education a central role. A second, more empirically based, starting point with data specific to East Asia is Kim and Lau (1996), which concludes that high rates of investment in physical capital and in human capital essentially explain all of the rapid per capita growth there. That is, 'technical progress' (i.e. total factor productivity), after the accumulation of physical and human capital is taken into account, explains little or nothing. Other recent empirical work on East Asia such as *The East Asian Miracle* (World Bank 1993a) and Tallman and Wang (1993) tends to reinforce this. Work that emphasizes an export-oriented growth strategy whose success in turn depends heavily on prior education and capacity to learn in the labour force and on physical capital investment would also not seem to be inconsistent with this same starting point (e.g. Ito and Krueger, 1995).

In this chapter, however, I propose to look more closely at the different specific roles of primary, secondary, and higher education enrolments, and at the rates of investment in each which support these enrolments but also reflect the quality of education, albeit imperfectly. I will also consider effects of these investments in education on rates of investment in physical capital, with feedback effects on economic growth. Later chapters will consider extensively the indirect effects of education through its effects in slowing population growth, on democratization and longer-run political stability, and on poverty reduction, including the relevance of all of these in the Far East.

The nations included in this empirical analysis are South Korea, Thailand, Malaysia, Japan, Indonesia, the Philippines, India, Sri Lanka, Nepal, and Singapore. Background studies focusing on secondary education in the growth process were conducted as part of a larger study done for the World Bank for the first five of these countries respectively by Jang (1994), Tunsiri (1994), Rashid (1994), Kiso (1993), and McMahon (1994a, 1994b). A closely related supplemental study was done by Jayatunge (1993) for India, Sri Lanka, and Nepal.

The lags in the production function following either education enrolment or education investment decisions are long, given the many years most persons are in the labour force. Therefore, because of the slow impact of additions of new graduates on the overall education level of the labour force, the basic system is recursive in this respect and can be estimated by OLS. This will be done, but with corrections for heteroscedasticity and autocorrelation. Simultaneous equation estimates involving joint dependence between physical capital investment and economic growth will then be presented and discussed.

The Reduced-Form Production Function

I do not propose to estimate precisely the generalized Lucas production function presented as Equation (2.1) in the preceding chapter, but, as mentioned earlier, it provides a good starting point. Since the stock of human capital, H, must be used either in production of goods in the economy, μ, or household production of more human capital, $1 - \mu$, these fractional uses of human capital sum to 1 and in the aggregate, μ drops out. If the resulting reduced-form production function is written in implicit rather than explicit terms, totally differentiated with respect to time, and divided through by real output, Y, the result is:

$$\frac{\partial Y}{\partial t}\frac{1}{Y} = \frac{\partial Y}{\partial K}\frac{\partial K}{\partial t}\frac{1}{Y} + \frac{\partial Y}{\partial N}\frac{\partial N}{\partial t}\frac{1}{Y} + \frac{\partial Y}{\partial H}\frac{\partial H}{\partial t}\frac{1}{Y}. \tag{3.1}$$

Variables are as previously defined under Equation (2.1). The partial derivatives of output with respect to each input are the marginal products (e.g., $\partial Y/\partial K = MPP_K$, etc.). Lower-case letters can now be used in Equation (3.2) below to represent per cent rates of change with respect to time (e.g., $y = \partial Y/\partial t\ 1/Y$, etc.). Investment represents the change in each capital stock with respect to time (e.g., $I_H = \partial H/\partial t$, etc.).

$$y = MPP_K\frac{I_K}{Y} + MPP_N(n)\frac{N}{Y} + MPP_{H_1}\frac{I_H}{Y}. \tag{3.2}$$

Strictly speaking, each type of investment in Equation (3.2) is *net* investment. However, since replacement investment also embodies the more recent technologies in the new human and physical capital stocks, and is a major way new technologies are disseminated as part of the endogenous growth process, the investment terms in the production function are more appropriately interpreted as *gross* investment, which is also easier to measure without the need for nebulous depreciation and obsolescence estimates. Since these new additions to the human and physical capital stocks are of the most recent vintage, embodying the more recent technologies in both net new and replacement investment, this fact should be expected to reduce the explanatory power of the term for investment in R&D in the regression.

Investment and Enrolment by Levels: Definitions and Data Sources

To separate the effects of the various levels of education on per capita growth, I_H can be separated into investment in primary, I_P, secondary, I_S, and higher education, I_{HE}. n can also be subtracted from both sides so that per capita growth rates, $y - n$, are given by Equation (3.3). The variables are defined, and data sources are given, below each equation.

$$y - n = \alpha_1 \frac{I_K}{Y} + \alpha_2 \frac{I_P}{Y} + \alpha_3 \frac{I_S}{Y} + \alpha_4 \frac{I_{HE}}{Y} + \alpha_5 \left(\frac{Y}{N}\right)_{65} + \alpha_6 PRE + \alpha_7 n + \mu_4.$$

$$(3.3)$$

$y - n$ Average annual per capita GDP growth rate, in 5-year periods from 1965 to 1990, from World Bank, *World Tables* (1996).

I_K/Y Gross Private Domestic Investment in physical capital as a per cent of GDP, for the same 5-year periods, from IMF (1996).

I_P/Y Average annual gross public investment rate (per cent of GDP) in primary education, 1965, from UNESCO (1968: 297–346).

I_{HS}/Y Average annual gross public investment rate in secondary education, 1965 (ibid.).

I_{HE}/Y Average annual gross public investment rate in higher education, 1965 (ibid.).

    These education investment levels are expressed in local currencies, so GDP must also be expressed in local currencies from the UN National Income Accounts, cross-checked with the ratios and allocations by level in UNESCO (1968: tables 2.18 and 2.19). Using a formulation that calls for all investment components as ratios of GDP eliminates the need for using exchange rates.

$(Y/N)_{65}$ Initial GDP per capita in each country, 1965, in US dollars, from World Bank, *World Tables* (1996) and World Bank, *World Development Report* (1996).

PRE   Preconditions controlling for corruption and civil wars. It is measured here as a dummy variable for which the Philippines $= 1$ and other nations $= 0$. This roughly reflects the 'International Country Risk Guide' (Coplin *et al.*, 1980–97). (Particularly since 1990, some other nations probably should $= 1$.)

n Population growth rate; from ILO (1996).

l Rate of growth of employment, which will later be substituted for n in some of the regressions; also from ILO (1996). If $l > n$, then the hypothesis is that the per capita growth will be faster since there are higher labour absorption rates.

μ_4 Disturbances.

The initial GDP per capita fixes the intercept for each country. Empirically it is entered into the growth equation so that its coefficient represents the rate of conditional convergence. Its sign is hypothesized to be negative, reflecting conditional convergence within the region, an exogenous effect not explained here but very likely due to the high degree of communication, observation and introduction of similar policies, and (if there are diminishing returns as predicted by the Solow, 1956 model) the high degree of money capital mobility within the region.

With respect to preconditions, *PRE*, it is obvious from casual observation worldwide and from Barro (1995: 435) that the influence of physical and human capital accumulation cannot normally be observed under conditions where there are civil wars (consider Cambodia or Bosnia) or substantial government corruption (consider Zaïre). The one nation in my data set where conditions have been somewhat unstable due to some of both, and where growth rates uniquely plunged in 1980–90, is the Philippines, although things have dramatically improved there recently. Political stability, *PS*, is measured in a different way in the investment function and tested further below.

Enrolment Version

An alternative way to measure investment in human capital is to use gross enrolment rates. Enrolment rates and attainment measure quantitative additions in the form of years of schooling to the stock of human capital without regard to their quality, the way this has usually been measured, e.g. in Barro (1995: 422–31), World Bank (1993: table 1.8). Sometimes test scores increase without increases in expenditures, as has been noted in the *Economist* (1997*a*). On the other hand, investment expenditure, although by no means a perfect measure of quality, nevertheless is critically important to educational quality in poorer nations in providing textbooks, libraries, more adequate teacher training, and other inputs that are known to contribute to educational effectiveness (e.g., World Bank, 1995: 51). The problem is that enrolment rates and investment rates at each level are so highly collinear that it is not meaningful to put them into the same equation.

This leads to the substitution of *GER1*, *GER2*, and *GER3* for the rates of investment in human capital in Equation (3.3) above, yielding Equation (3.4).

The estimates for Equation (3.4) will be shown in Table 3.1, with those for investment rates in Equation (3.3) shown in Table 3.2.

$$y - n = \beta_1 \frac{I_K}{Y} + \beta_2 GER1 + \beta_3 GER2 + \beta_4 GER3 + \beta_5 \left(\frac{Y}{N}\right)_{65}$$

$$+ \beta_6 PRE + \beta_7 n + \mu_5.$$ (3.4)

$GER1_{65}$ Gross primary enrolment rate, 1965, from UNESCO (1968).
$GER2_{65}$ Gross secondary enrolment rate, 1965 (ibid.).
$GER3_{65}$ Gross higher education enrolment rate in 1965 (ibid.).
μ_5 Disturbances.
Other variables, with sources, as above.

Empirical Results: Econometric Properties

Empirical results that systematically explore the key sources of endogenous growth in East Asia are presented in Tables 3.1–3.4 and 3.6. Before discussing their

Table 3.1 Human Resource Development and Endogenous Growth (dependent variable: per capita growth rates, $y - n$, 1965–1990, 5 time periods; t-statistics in parentheses)

	Model 1	Model 2	Model 3	Model 4	Model 5	Model 6	Model 7	Model 8
I_K/Y	0.0221	0.1365	0.1651	0.0042	0.1227	0.1588	0.0580	0.0049
	(0.8595)	(6.024)	(7.764)	(0.2262)	(5.540)	(7.703)	(2.877)	(0.2717)
$GER1_{60-65}$	0.054			0.0621			0.0263	
	(5.738)			(9.603)			(2.294)	
$GER2_{60-65}$		0.1426			0.1898		0.2918	
		(2.985)			(4.147)		(3.213)	
$GER3_{60-65}$			−0.1361			0.6502	−0.6703	
			(−1.761)			(3.339)	(−4.962)	
GER_{60-85}								0.0561
								(9.955)
I_A/Y							−0.0421	
							(−3.353)	
PRE_1				−0.0484	−0.0568	−0.1117		−0.0621
				(−4.148)	(−4.666)	(-4.418)		(−5.959)
$(Y/N)_{65}$	−0.0121	−0.094	0.018	−0.0162	−0.120	−0.05971	−0.0630	−0.0537
	(−0.6794)	(−2.667)	(0.9504)	(−0.7598)	(−3.591)	(−2.419)	(−1.535)	(−3.680)
R^2	0.6784	0.4138	0.2175	0.9194	0.5423	0.4656	0.9639	0.9187
LH	4.22	2.127	0.81	0.59	0.06	0.02	0.38	0.40
rho	Before 0.383	0.245	0.114	−0.015	0.059	0.014	0.072	−0.075
	After 0.001	0.051						
BP (Q1)	0.41	3.60	2.43	0.409	2.30	1.79	0.894	0.399
BP (Q2)	0.18		0.18	0.412	0.045	0.038	0.0321	0.165
n	35	35	35	35	35	35	35	35

Note: All of these models were estimated with corrections for heteroscedasticity and, if needed, for autocorrelation in the residuals.

Table 3.2 Human Resource Development and Endogenous Growth (dependent variable: per capita growth rates $(y - n)$, 1965–1990, 5 time periods; t-statistics in parentheses)

	Model 9	Model 10	Model 11	Model 12	Model 13	Model 14	Model 15	Model 16
I_K/Y	0.0078	0.0074	0.1034	0.0099	0.0055	0.0117	0.0051	0.0568
	(0.4228)	(0.4018)	(4.579)	(0.5148)	(0.2934)	(0.6203)	(0.2701)	(2.80)
$GER1_{60-65}$	0.05702	0.0624		0.04733	0.1585		0.1415	0.0266
	(6.331)	(9.403)		(4.676)	(4.652)		(3.253)	(1.89)
$GER2_{60-65}$	0.0364		0.3141	0.1604		0.0565	0.0216	0.3094
	(0.6430)		(4.940)	(2.075)		(1.973)	(0.580)	(3.43)
$GER3_{60-65}$		−0.2988	−0.5530	−0.4550	−0.5075	−0.2451	−0.5200	−0.7253
		(−3.658)	(−4.643)	(−3.715)	(−4.222)	(−2.480)	(−4.235)	(−5.37)
$(Y/N)_{65}$	−0.0350	0.0196	−0.1602	−0.0734				−0.0496
	(−0.9472)	(1.153)	(−4.280)	(−1.715)				(−1.27)
I_A/Y								−0.0509
								(−3.79)
ℓ								0.1478
								(1.67)
CONST					−0.0663	0.0387	−0.0560	
					(−2.833)	(7.777)	(−1.961)	
R^2	0.9237	0.9239	0.6221	0.9205	0.9244	0.9200	0.9249	0.9606
LM	4.31	2.62	0.64	2.30	1.65	2.89	1.80	1.49
rho	Before 0.402	0.160	0.131	0.068	0.124	0.235	0.127	n.a.
	After 0.031							
BP(Q1)	0.905	0.587	1.43	1.21	0.037	0.021	n.a.	n.a.
n	35	35	35	35	35	35	35	35

n.a. = not available.

substance it is necessary briefly to comment on the steps taken to address the econometric problems of autocorrelation in the residuals, heteroscedasticity, and multicollinearity.

Autocorrelation

Since there are 5-year average growth rates over 5 time periods (1965–90) for each of the 7 countries it is necessary to ensure that the coefficients in Tables 3.1–3.4 and 3.6 are not biased due to autocorrelation among the residuals. To test for autocorrelation in the time series dimension only, the Baltagi and Li (1991) test was used, a modification of the Durbin–Watson test for panel data of this type. These statistics were computed based on the OLS residuals prior to corrections for heteroscedasticity, since autocorrelation among the residuals after such a correction is not meaningful in that they have been adjusted. On the basis of the Baltagi and Li statistic, a Lagrange multiplier test that follows the chi-squared distribution was then computed for all models, and is shown as *LM* (replacing the Durbin–Watson test) for each model in Tables 3.1–3.4. Where this *LM* statistic is greater than 3.84 the null hypothesis must be rejected. So models for which this is true, i.e., Models 1

Table 3.3 Human resource development investment and endogenous growth (dependent variable: per capita growth rates ($y - n$), 1965–1990, 5 time periods; t-statistics in parentheses)

	Model 1'	Model 2'	Model 3'	Model 4'	Model 5'	Model 6'	Model 7'	Model 8'
I_K/Y	0.1567	0.0361	0.0130	0.1534	0.0312	0.017	0.0570	0.0681
	(4.849)	(1.751)	(0.7152)	(4.724)	(1.320)	(0.7998)	(3.441)	(2.091)
$I_P/Y_{(60-65)}$	0.0835			0.2521			−1.232	
	(0.2008)			(0.5730)			(−1.602)	
$I_S/Y_{(60-65)}$		4.092			4.2407		5.466	
		(7.405)			(6.6542)		(9.752)	
$I_{HE}/Y_{(60-65)}$			20.633			20.087	2.126	
			(9.258)			(7.6919)	(0.5237)	
$I_H/Y_{(60-65)}$								1.124
								3.460)
I_A/Y							−0.0431	
							(−5.199)	
PRE_1				−0.026	0.0063	−0.002		−0.0237
				(−2.531)	(0.5082)	(−0.200)		(−2.429)
$(Y/N)_{65}$	0.0045	0.0083	−0.0749	0.003	0.0070	−0.0708	0.0903	0.0020
	(0.2552)	(0.5777)	(−4.599)	(0.1985)	(0.4795)	(−3.9959)	(4.637)	(0.1246)
R^2	0.2031	0.8406	0.9196	0.2750	0.8292	0.8950	0.9342	0.6285
LM	1.02	1.25	2.71	0.12	0.01	0.89	0.47	0.66
rho	0.225	0.171	0.145	0.115	0.161	0.177	0.087	0.237
BP(Q1)	2.11	0.348	0.908	0.908	0.484	0.725	0.357	0.959
BP(Q2)	0.029	0.018	0.326	0.480	0.121	0.090	0.0005	0.026
n	35	35	35	35	35	35	35	35

and 9 and 16–20, have been re-estimated making a correction for autocorrelation using the POOL method (Kmenta, 1986). The rho coefficients shown after the correction or for the model estimated can be seen to be small for all models in Tables 3.1–3.6. Therefore all of the coefficients shown in these tables can be said to be free of bias due to significant autocorrelation.

Heteroscedasticity

All models in Tables 3.1–3.4 and 3.6 have been corrected for heteroscedasticity, also using the POOL method. This method first distinguishes from among the 35 observations those that apply to the same time period across countries, and then applies the same correction for heteroscedasticity within each of the 5 separate time periods. To ensure that there is no reasonably detectable heteroscedasticity after the correction, a relatively powerful Breusch–Pagan (1979) Lagrange multiplier test is computed on the residuals after the POOL correction. This test is shown as $BP(Q1)$ and $BP(Q2)$ for each model in Tables 3.1–3.4, with the former applied to a model that contains only I_K/Y and $(Y/N)_{65}$, and the latter for a regression that contains only the other variables in each model to see if either causes any heteroscedasticity. Since these measures also follow the chi-squared

Table 3.4 Human resource development investment and per capita growth (dependent variable: per capita growth rates, 1965–1990; *t*-statistics in parentheses)

	Model 9'	Model 10'	Model 11'	Model 12'	Model 13'	Model 14'	Model 15'	Model 16'
I_K/Y	0.4232	0.0203	0.0236	0.0243	0.0087	0.0167	0.0122	0.064
	(1.733)	(1.009)	(1.083)	(1.105)	(0.478)	(0.7369)	(0.5825)	(3.11)
$I_P/Y_{(60-65)}$	−0.1110	−0.9511		−0.0802	−1.398		−1.049	0.015
	(−0.3605)	(−2.669)		(−1.795)	(−3.599)		(−2.241)	(0.886)
$I_S/Y_{(60-65)}$	4.1003		2.803	0.9932		2.9275	1.225	3.205
	(6.849)		(2.195)	(0.6929)		(3.178)	(1.068)	(3.27)
$I_{HE}/Y_{(60-65)}$		26.06	7.277	20.347	14.504	2.387	10.388	−6.94
		(8.086)	(1.141)	(2.372)	(3.650)	(0.7431)	(2.225)	(−5.01)
$(Y/N)_{65}$	0.0086	−0.0806	−0.0204	−0.0590				−0.069
	(0.5448)	(−4.685)	(−0.6952)	(−1.812)				(−1.62)
I_A/Y								
$n(POP)$								−0.045
								(−3.53)
CONST					0.0306	0.0103	0.0233	0.2102
					(4.098)	(1.044)	(2.058)	(0.813)
R^2	0.8124	0.8978	0.8703	0.8749	0.9207	0.8773	0.8954	0.976
LM	1.1639	1.3326	1.2016	1.3259	1.3784	1.2032	1.3653	1.52
rho	0.172	0.132	0.140	0.116	0.105	0.132	0.100	n.a.
BP(Q1)	0.397	1.35	0.578	1.38	0.037	0.004	0.00001	n.a.
BP(Q2)	0.028	0.394	0.270	1.08	1.43	0.291	0.00001	n.a.
n	35	35	35	35	35	35	35	35

n.a. = not available.

distribution, and none exceed 3.84, at the 0.05 level in Tables 3.1–3.4 the null hypothesis can be accepted, and under the conditions of this test all models shown are free of bias due to heteroscedasticity. Since none was found here, and all models in Table 3.6 have been similarly corrected, it is reasonable to assume that all models in Table 3.6 are free of heteroscedasticity as well.

Multicollinearity

Multicollinearity is a serious problem that must be addressed, particularly since I am trying to sort out as much as possible the separate contributions of the expansion of and investment in primary, secondary, and higher education. The correlation of the explanatory variables with the error term can bias the coefficients when there are unobserved or deleted variables, as indicated by Levine and Renelt (1992), and thereby cause the findings to be sensitive to the specification of the models.

To cope with the problem of multicollinearity, first a set of countries has been chosen in East Asia where most of the conditions that could exert major disturbances are similar in the 1965–90 period apart from the minor deviations in preconditions indicated above for which controls have been imposed. For this reason, countries like Vietnam, Cambodia, and China have been excluded. The major remaining difference has been a wide divergence in the policies followed with respect to secondary education. That is, most of the countries had nearly universal primary education by the beginning of the period. The difference is that first Japan, and then the other East Asian nations except for Indonesia, the Philippines, and Thailand, began with 25–73 per cent gross enrolment rates in secondary education during 1960–5 and have continued to invest in rapid improvement and expansion at that level since that time. However, the Philippines, Thailand, and South Korea have invested more heavily in the expansion of higher education, so there is some variation in this respect as well.

Second, a systematic approach has been used in what follows to try to distinguish the different effects where explanatory variables are collinear. Models 1–16 in Tables 3.1 and 3.2, for example, are identical to Models 1′–16′ in Tables 3.3 and 3.4, the only exception being that the human capital formation rates in Tables 3.1 and 3.2 are measured by enrolment rates in 1960–5 reflecting quantity of schooling ($GER1$, $GER2$, $GER3$, and their simple sum GER), and in Tables 3.3 and 3.4 by the respective education investment rates reflecting quality (I_P/Y, I_S/Y, I_{HE}/Y, and their sum I_H/Y).

Third, the systematic approach within Models 1–16 and 1′–16′ involves introducing each type of human or knowledge capital investment one at a time, and then in concert. There are, however, always controls for investment in physical capital (I_K/Y) and for a country-specific intercept $(Y/N)_{65}$ testing for convergence, both of which economists regard as essential.

Fourth, any remaining multicollinearity is shown in the zero-order correlation matrix, Table 3.5, and will be discussed further at a later point. Finally, the recursive lag structure and tests for simultaneity will also be discussed later.

Table 3.5 Zero-Order Correlation Matrix (variables in Tables 3.1–3.4)

	I_K/Y	$GER1$	$GER2$	$GER3$	I_P/Y	I_S/Y	I_{HE}/Y	$I-A/Y$	PRE_1	$(Y/N)_{65}$
I_K/Y	1.00									
$GER1_{(60–65)}$	0.35	1.00								
$GER2_{(60–65)}$	0.31	0.74	1.00							
$GER3_{(60–65)}$	0.10	0.75	0.61	1.00						
$I_P/Y_{(60–65)}$	−0.03	—	—	—	1.00					
$I_S/Y_{(60–65)}$	0.03	—	—	—	−0.42	1.00				
$I_{HE}/Y_{(60–65)}$	0.27	—	—	—	−0.02	0.60	1.00			
$I_A/Y_{(60–65)}$	0.20	0.25	0.83	0.19	−0.20	0.44	0.88	1.00		
PRE_1	N.A.	0.31	0.04	0.76	0.12	−0.76	−0.57	−0.25	1.00	
$(Y/N)_{65}$	0.41	0.55	0.92	0.37	0.01	0.15	0.83	0.82	−0.20	1.00

Impacts of Education on Growth

Overall, as hypothesized, human resource development through education is shown in Tables 3.1–3.4 to be a key determinant of economic growth, together with investment in physical capital. In East Asia secondary education can be regarded as a foundation for the successful export-oriented growth strategy common to these nations, a result that taken alone is not particularly novel. But it is also shown to be important to the rate of investment in physical capital, as will be shown in Table 3.6. Since this is particularly important in the follower countries such as Malaysia, Thailand, and Indonesia as they seek to attract money capital from Japan and world capital markets, it is plausible that human capital, and not necessarily diminishing returns, is one key factor helping to explain conditional convergence *within this group*.

This conditional convergence is revealed by the negative sign of the initial GDP per capita $(Y/N)_{65}$ in all of the regressions in Tables 3.1–3.4 and 3.6 in which it is significant.

Differential Impacts of Human Capital Formation

Primary and secondary enrolments taken separately or together (Models 1, 2, 4, 5, 7, and 9–16) *always* have a positive and *almost always* have a highly significant relationship to growth. This is true for *investment* in secondary education as well (see Models $2', 5', 7', 9'$, and $11'–16'$). However, the amount of public funds invested in *primary* education is always less significant than is investment at the secondary level, and sometimes even negative (Models $1', 4', 7', 9', 10', 12', 13'$, and $15'$).

This positive and more highly significant effect from public investment in secondary education is less surprising when it is realized that virtually all of these countries had universal primary education by 1965, the beginning of the period studied, and then Singapore, South Korea, Japan, Hong Kong, and Thailand raised test scores without significantly increasing public expenditure per pupil (OECD, 1997). But some were rapidly expanding access to and quality of secondary education, while others were moving more slowly.

Another tentative conclusion can be drawn from this comparison. It is that a higher rate of public investment in secondary education early on has paid off. This expenditure would have been necessary for building schools, hiring teachers before enrolments could expand, and inducing greater saving and investment in human capital formation by families as children stay on in school. But it also would have been necessary for improvement in quality through the provision of textbooks and the support of better training for teachers. Putting larger resources into primary education (once universal primary education at an adequate level of quality was achieved) does not appear to have paid off as well.

The pattern with respect to higher education is quite different. Taken alone, large enrolments in higher education have a negative relation to growth (Models 3, 7, and 10–16). This is not so when both *GER1* and *GER2* are excluded and the Philippines is removed by means of a dummy variable (*PRE* in Model 6), but in this model the R^2 is also relatively low. It is also not true in Tables 3.3 and 3.4 for *investment* improving the quality of higher education in East Asian countries, where I_{HE}/Y is positive and significant in Models $3', 6', 10', 11', 12', 13', 15'$, and $16'$).

This also is not particularly surprising. Barro (1991, 1995: 425–8) found this same negative result for initial levels of female higher education enrolments based on worldwide data, with insignificant coefficients for males, that we now find for total higher education enrolments in East Asian countries. World Bank (1993: 48) does not report any higher education enrolment or investment results in their worldwide regressions. Mankiw, Romer, and Weil (1992: 34–8) also do not test higher education enrolments, and also find strong positive relationships of secondary education enrolments to growth in their worldwide regressions. On the basis of observations from work in these countries, when higher education enrolments are allowed to expand greatly, especially at the early stages, the quality of higher education seriously deteriorates. With too many graduates, and too few jobs, higher education graduates are more mobile and sometimes emigrate. Higher education enrolments are highest in South Korea, but there are large private contributions by families so the quality there, relatively speaking, is sustained.

When no attempt is made to distinguish the separate roles of primary, secondary, and higher education, total enrolment at all three levels (*GER* in Model 8) and total investment at all three levels (I_H/Y in Model 8′) are both very highly significant. In these cases human capital investment even overwhelms the importance of increasing further the already high rates of investment in physical capital.

Models 8 and 8′ confirm the findings by others who have used measures of the total human capital stock, such as Kim and Lau (1995: 5–6) for East Asia, and Tallman and Wang (1993: 19–23) for Taiwan. Campos and Nugent (1996: tables 5 and 7) report a similar result for Latin America. But they all use educational attainment as a measure of the overall total human capital stock which is based on enrolments. This begins to sort out the negative effects of excess higher education *enrolments* (consistent with Barro), but suggests that this is tempered if a major effort (enrolment plus public investment) is made at the secondary level. The result in Model 8′ for total public investment in all of education as a per cent of GDP is fully consistent with Barro's (1995: 426, 433) result using essentially this same variable with worldwide data. He concludes that a 1.5 percentage point increase in government expenditure on education 'raises the growth rate by .3 percentage points per year' (ibid.: 433). He also interprets this as modifying the effects from years of schooling to include a rough proxy for the quality of schooling.

The results suggest that secondary education enrolments and investments in secondary education in particular were very important in offsetting diminishing returns to investment in physical capital in East Asia. Investment rates in physical capital certainly have remained very high. It also indicates that education investments have been a key source of relative convergence, as can be seen in Models 14 and 14′ when the initial level of GDP per capita is removed.

Determinants of Investment Rates: Feedback Effects

The rate of investment in physical capital is also a very highly significant determinant of growth in East Asia in essentially all models. The only exceptions are regressions in which primary enrolments in the initial period are included, in which case they are usually more significant than physical capital (Models 1, 4, 9, 10, 12, 13, and 15), or usually where higher education is included (3', 6', and 10'–15'). Barro (1995: 433–4) also finds physical capital investment rates to play a less important role than the central one attributed to them by others in his worldwide regressions when a wider range of human capital variables (and life expectancy) is included, even though he does not include primary enrolments. Investment in succeeding periods can be seen to be more highly correlated with starting primary enrolments than with anything else except GDP per capita in Table 3.5, however, as well as positively dependent on secondary enrolments rates and indirectly dependent on primary enrolment rates in the initial period in Table 3.6.

Turning therefore more directly to the influences on these rates of investment in physical capital shown in Table 3.6, investment rates are hypothesized to be determined by the following factors:

$$I_K/Y = \gamma_1 \left(\frac{Y}{N}\right)_{65} + \gamma_2 \frac{Y}{N} + \gamma_3(y - n) + \gamma_4 GER_1 + \gamma_5 PS + \gamma_6 UT + \mu_6. \quad (3.5)$$

Variables and data sources are as defined previously except:

Y/N GDP per capita in constant US dollars (World Bank, *World Tables*, 1996).

$y - n$ Per capita growth rates, accelerator-related effects from standard investment theory.

PS Political stability, an index of composite political, financial, and economic risk from Coplin *et al.* (1997 and earlier issues).

UT Utilization rates, measured as 1 minus the unemployment rate from ILO (1996 and earlier issues). This is to control for cyclical fluctuations to the extent that averaging I_K/Y over 5-year time periods, *PRE*, and *l* have not already done so.

μ_6 Disturbances.

Interest rates have opposite effects on investment and saving in the medium term, and on investment and international capital flows throughout any interval of time, so although they were tried in preliminary tests, they remain with the disturbances, μ_6. Rates of investment in education are hypothesized to be positively related after a lag to rates of physical capital investment because of the role of a skilled labour force in offsetting diminishing returns to physical capital, supporting manufacturing exports, and attracting money capital from abroad.

GDP, which logically is a determinant of Gross Private Domestic Investment, is not significant as a determinant of the rate of investment as a per cent of GDP, as seen in Models 17 and 18, so it is dropped. Political stability (*PS*) is not significant in Model 17, but is more significant than the precondition isolating the Philippines in Model 18, so *PRE*$_1$ is dropped from this investment function. With controls for the initial GDP per capita in 1965 and for utilization rates, the distributed lag on enrolments shows secondary education human capital stocks to be consistently significant in Models 17–19. Primary and higher education are also positive and

Table 3.6 Investment Functions and Feedback Effects, 1965–1990 (t-statistics in parentheses)

Dependent Variable	Model 17 I_K/Y	Model 18 I_K/Y	Model 19 I_K/Y	Model 20 I_K/Y	Model 21 I_K/Y	Model 22 (3SLS) I_K/Y	$y-n$	$GER2_{65}$
Y/N	0.0000003 (0.059)	−0.0000004 (−0.071)						
y − n						1965–90: 0.076 (0.159)		1960–5: 1.40 (2.97)
I_K/Y							0.054 (2.00)	
$GER1_{65}$				0.122 (1.01)			0.017 (1.63)	
$GER2_{65}$	0.205 (2.20)	0.228 (2.50)	0.207 (2.24)			0.080 (1.19)	0.297 (6.12)	0.158 (8.76)
$GER3_{65}$				0.675 (1.84)			−0.609 (−8.47)	
GER_{65}					0.126 (2.90)			
PRE_1		0.0020 (0.098)						
PS	0.0086 (0.742)	0.0009 (0.744)	0.0009 (0.744)	0.0038 (2.43)	0.0018 (1.57)	0.0045 (8.97)		
$(Y/N)_{65}$	−0.132 (−1.844)	−0.177 (−1.620)	−0.130 (−1.91)	−0.162 (−2.56)	−0.140 (−1.76)	−0.071 (−1.53)	−0.068 (−3.42)	0.330 (−3.54)
UT	2.57 (6.60)	2.57 (6.31)	2.59 (6.75)	2.81 (7.11)	2.46 (6.64)			
I_A/Y							−0.045 (−6.05)	
Constant	−2.28 (−6.13)	−2.24 (−5.66)	−2.30 (−6.29)	−2.76 (−6.81)	−2.32 (−6.11)			
R^2	0.92	0.90	0.93	0.85	0.89	0.65	0.74	0.91
rho	−0.059	0.131	−0.077	0.005	0.026	0.933	0.607	0.801

Note: Models 17–21 are corrected for heteroscedasticity and Models 17–22 for autocorrelation.

marginally significant in offsetting diminishing returns and/or attracting additional investment in Model 20, and the three levels taken together, *GER* in Model 21 reflecting total human capital, is the most significant and chosen for simulations.

Feedback Effects and Simultaneity

There are lags built into Models 1–21, with investment in education and/or expansion of enrolments preceding the impacts on the per capita growth rates by 5 years in 1965 with cumulative impacts over the next 25 years. So from this point of view the models are basically recursive, justifying the OLS methods with corrections for heteroscedasticity and serial correlation that have been used. But this is not true for the rates of physical capital investment. There is also great interest in feedback effects over longer periods. In the latter case, the growth in income finances further growth in enrolments and human capital formation.

These effects are captured in Model 22, where all three equations are estimated jointly by three-stage least squares. It can be seen in the last column of Model 2 that the initial level of secondary education enrolments, $GER2_{65}$, depends significantly on primary education enrolments ($t = 8.76$) as well as on per capita income in this initial period ($t = 3.54$) and the rate at which per capita income is growing at that time, i.e., $(y - n)_{60-5}$ ($t = 2.97$). This makes secondary education enrolment rates largely endogenous, although primary enrolment rates remain policy-determined. This *degree* of endogeneity of public decisions regarding education is analysed further in McMahon (1992b), but in a broader context than just East Asia.

Another feedback or joint effect comes through democratization, which I did not find to be significant, except through political stability. Political stability (*PS*) in turn is significant as a determinant of investment in physical capital (I_K/Y in Models 20 and 22) and hence of growth rates ($y - n$ in Model 22). Political stability tends to follow democratization in the very long run; after all, every OECD nation is a democracy and politically stable, whereas very few of the poor authoritarian nations in the world are stable. Some in East Asia such as Singapore, Indonesia, and South Korea are reasonably stable, although not yet full democracies by Freedom House (1997) measures. Endogeneity of this aspect of the model is developed further in Chapter 7. But for present purposes, the significant point is the major role of political stability in providing a stable environment for investment in physical capital ($t = 8.87$ in Model 22).

It is interesting how this compares to the results reported by Barro (1995). He also finds that democratization is not systematically related to economic growth and that 'the channel of effects has to operate indirectly from democracy to some of the independent variables such as educational attainment' (ibid.: 439). He also finds political stability, measured as revolutions per year, to be significant in his worldwide data (Barro, 1991, 1995: 435), while in my simultaneous system here we find it to be even more significant ($t = 8.97$), operating through its effects on the rates of investment.

In the growth equation of Model 22, bias due to simultaneity can be said to be removed from the coefficient of I_K/Y as the result of simultaneous estimation. But this coefficient is about the same as before in the comparable OLS equation (see Model 7 in Table 3.1). It is the inclusion of primary education, not bias due to simultaneity, that reduces the fraction of economic growth attributable to investment in physical capital. In the investment equation of Model 22, economic growth could feed back and contribute to higher investment in physical capital as well, but this effect is not significant. It is noteworthy that in the simultaneous equation estimates the size and significance of secondary education affects growth even more than before ($t = 6.12$).

Other Factors, Including Controls

Several other factors specified in the hypotheses or as controls, appear in the regressions in Tables 3.1–3.6, and require brief comment.

Investment in R&D

Public investment in R&D is introduced in Models 7, 7', 16, and 22 to check that this factor and its potential relation to technical progress is not being overlooked. The East Asian governments have played an important role in the promotion and transfer of technology, as noted by Stiglitz (1997: 14) for example.

The results in Tables 3.1–3.3, 3.5, and 3.6, with the 5-year averages of gross investment in R&D by firms and government lagged 5 years expressed as per cent of GDP (from IMF, 1994) are consistent with the findings of Kim and Lau (1996) for East Asia that technical progress did not help explain growth there. The signs of I_A/Y in Models 7, 7', 16, and 22, in fact, are all negative. One likely reason is that the lags after investment in R&D before product and process innovation can affect productivity are very long, probably longer than the 5-year lag, which is the longest lag possible here. A second probable reason is that the East Asian governments placed emphasis on the transfer of technology, which is more closely related to travel for businessmen, study abroad, and other types of expenditure than to investment in R&D and the costly failed experiments that are involved in achieving technological leadership.

Unimproved Labour and Employment Growth

Population growth (n), which reflects the growth of unimproved labour, is not a significant determinant of per capita growth, as shown in Model 16'. This was as expected; it would only be if there were higher labour absorption rates, i.e. $l > n$. But the rate of employment growth, l in Model 16, although positive, is not quite significant. So both n and l were dropped from the other models in Tables 3.1–3.4.

Labour force utilization rates, *UT*, enter the investment functions, Models 17–21, where they are significant and act as controls for cyclical instability when seeking to identify the other longer term influences in the investment function. In the 3SLS estimates, when utilization rates are introduced in Model 23 (not shown) and R&D, I_A/Y, is dropped, the results are much the same as those shown in Model 22; in the growth equation, *UT* was not significant $(t = -1.58)$. (Y/N) and $GER2_{65}$ are somewhat less significant in the growth equation in Model 23 but larger and more significant in the investment function $(t = 2.67)$, as in Models 17–20. The other coefficients are not greatly affected, so not much new is learned from this apart from what can be seen in Model 22 which will be used later.

Conclusions

Human capital formation is central to the growth process in the wave of new work on endogenous growth and related empirical tests, most of which have featured human capital aggregates. This chapter has sought to explore which levels of enrolments and types of public investment contribute the most, as well as how some of the feedback effects from endogenous development operate in the fastest-growing countries.

The major overall conclusion is that heavy initial investment in human capital by households and governments, as well as high investment in physical capital, and probably not 'technical progress', is largely responsible for the high per capita growth in East Asia. This is under certain preconditions, such as political stability, and confirms recent overall conclusions by Kim and Lau (1996) for East Asia, as well as being consistent with conclusions by Barro (1991, 1995: 425–51) and Mankiw, Romer, and Weil (1992). Krugman (1996) has suggested that long-run diminishing returns to physical capital may have set in recently in East Asia. But the model in this paper is not concerned with long-run steady-state solutions that may be more appropriate to Japan (or with shorter-term fluctuations which many believe characterize the situation in Japan), but instead with the medium term, a period during which capital deepening in the form of more physical and human capital persists. In East Asia (and in most of the developing economies) the amount of physical capital per worker is considerably lower than in the industrial economies. The amount of human capital per worker is also much lower: the average worker has received only 4 years of education in Indonesia and Thailand, and 9 years in South Korea, compared to 10 years or more in the OECD countries. From this point of view, and in spite of the sustained total capital deepening since the 1960s, East Asia is and continues to be in a medium-term period within which sustained human and physical capital deepening can still occur.

Turning to specific levels of investment in human capital and feedback effects, the conclusion is that initial secondary enrolments, government investment at the secondary level, and feedback effects, as secondary enrolments and political stability provide a good climate for higher rates of investment in physical capital, have been strategically very important. This holds also after taking into account the significant effects of higher initial per capita income and income growth on secondary enrolments in a 3SLS context. This is a widely recognized joint dependence (see, e.g., Wheeler, 1984b; McMahon, 1992b: 139–42 and appendices A and B; and Barro and Sala-I-Martin 1995: 432), although the key aspects of this relationship are recursive. Others have not dealt with these effects in this context, although on the basis of worldwide data, and not including primary education or rates of public investment at the secondary level, this is consistent with the significance of secondary-level educational attainment found by Barro (1991), Barro and Sala-I-Martin (1995), and Mankiw, Romer, and Weil (1992).

This conclusion concerning secondary education should not be regarded as inconsistent with that of Ito and Krueger (1995), who also consider growth in East Asia but with a strong focus on export-oriented strategies. A skilled labour force at the secondary level can be regarded as fundamental to the successful production and export of manufactured goods, which is an initial assumption in this chapter based on the work by Wood (1994), but also based on the education and training policies described by Kim et al. and tested by Pyo for South Korea (both in Ito and Krueger, 1995: 181–200, 229–45). Pyo concludes that human capital plays a significant role, and that those countries that continue to accumulate it can converge while those that do not may diverge (ibid.: 240). The latter conclusion is based on his study of South Korea only (as he admits), but it is consistent with my results here for East Asia.

This chapter also concludes that primary enrolments in the initial period are highly significant. But in a context where universal primary education has largely been attained, as in East Asia, additional public investment in primary education as a per cent of GDP does not provide a very good payoff. The finding concerning primary enrolments confirms the same result in the World Bank's (*World Development Report*, 1993: 48, 64) major study, although their data are worldwide, and there is no separate analysis of education investment rates as a per cent of GDP. One possibility is that East Asian governments have been able to continue increasing effectiveness at this level as measured by maths and science test scores without increasing expenditures as fast (see OECD, 1997; *Economist*, 1997a: 21). Another is that it is well known that reduction of class size beyond a certain point is expensive and not very cost-effective at increasing learning at the primary level (World Bank, 1995: 51).

Another conclusion, although somewhat more tentative, is that early increases in higher education enrolments are not effective as a strategic means of increasing growth. This is based on the fact that whenever they are included with other levels of education, their coefficient is negative and significant. Barro (1995: 431) finds a similar result, based on worldwide data for female higher education attainments, which he suggests may signify more backwardness (and hence more potential for growth through the convergence mechanism). An additional source could be that these nations which expanded higher education enrolments with very low tuition at an early stage also have overcrowded campuses, low quality, poor employability, and emigration among these groups, none of which is conducive to growth. Consistent with this, the regression results find that higher investment in higher education as a per cent of GDP, which hopefully improves quality and is targeted so that it does not drive out private investment, is usually positively and significantly related to growth later.

Other factors were considered, but were found not to contribute. The evidence on conditional convergence is more persuasive, in that the sign of GDP per capita in 1965 is almost always negative and significant. These nations tend not only to import technologies, but also to make peer group comparisons among one another in their education policies.

Finally, the feedback effects from human capital related to the endogenous development process warrants continuing attention. I have found here that not only educational attainment, but also political stability, is related to high rates of investment in physical capital, which in turn is significant to growth in a simultaneous equation context. But political stability and democratization in turn are related to human capital formation in increments above the direct effects of per capita growth, as are longevity and net population growth rates, in complex ways (see Chapter 6). I interpret the evidence in this chapter, however, in which some of these feedback effects are endogenous and others are exogenous, as providing a starting point for tracing the broader role of education in endogenous development. Capital accumulation has always been at the core of neo-classical growth theory. But endogenous growth based on the deliberate decisions by households to allocate time to education, and as suggested here also by decisions by governments to invest in education in particular ways, deserves to be at the core of endogenous development.

4 Education and Growth in Latin America

Economic growth in Latin America and the Caribbean has not been as steady or robust over the last several decades as it has been in East Asia. It has also varied widely among the countries in the region.

Nevertheless, after controlling for shorter run shocks such as the one in 1999 and for differences among countries, there is still an important element that can be detected. It is that prior investment in education that supports the dissemination of knowledge and the capacity to learn new skills is a consistently important source of sustained per capita economic growth there as well. Both direct and indirect effects of education must be taken into account, especially the indirect effects on rates of investment in physical capital, on political stability, and on democratization (after lags), all with feedback effects, plus effects in slowing population growth. Education is by no means the only source of growth, but it is a source that can be changed by deliberate policies and at relatively low cost.

More specifically, economic growth in Latin America was 5.7 per cent in the 1970s. It fell to 1.0 per cent in the 1980s and has risen to 2.5 per cent in the 1990s. When population growth rates are subtracted from that, per capita growth has been lower. It averaged − 1 per cent in the 1980s. It has risen to only 0.3 per cent in the period from 1985 to 1995, compared, for example, to per capita growth of 7.2 per cent per year in East Asia during this same period (World Bank, *World Development Report*, 1997: 215), though lower with the slowdown that began in 1997–8. The empirical evidence suggests that growth over time in Latin America would have been slower than it was, and population growth rates higher, if investment in human resources in the 60s and 70s had been lower.

I will not attempt to test here (or in other chapters) whether these impacts of human resource development have been more or less important than other factors contributing to per capita growth, such as trade liberalization, financial reforms, and privatization, all of which have also been occurring recently (see Inter-American Development Bank, 1994: 1–8). The objective instead is to trace the net direct and indirect impacts of education, taking into account the lags in its effects. In the 18 Latin American and Caribbean countries in this study, for example, after controlling for other key differences, the slow-growing countries tend to be those that made the least effort in the prior decade to improve their human resource base through education.

The countries covered by this analysis are Argentina, Bolivia, Brazil, Chile, Colombia, Costa Rica, Dominican Republic, Ecuador, El Salvador, Guyana, Haiti, Honduras, Jamaica, Mexico, Nicaragua, Panama, Peru, and Venezuela. These are all of the larger Latin American and Caribbean nations; only some of the smaller Caribbean islands and Cuba had to be omitted since comprehensive data are not available. Within this group, several have persistent large-scale political instability; all have been moving since 1960 toward higher, albeit fragile, degrees of democracy, to which education has also contributed (see Chapter 7). Economic instability characterized by large debt and inflation followed by recession-induced cutbacks in physical and human capital accumulation, often required by the IMF, have troubled many. In this environment it is more difficult to sort out the longer-run sustained influences of human and physical capital accumulation on per capita economic growth. But with the appropriate controls (or, in later chapters, explanations) for these factors that are constants in the Solow model (1956) as well as in the augmented Solow model (e.g., Mankiw, Romer, and Weil, 1992), and new endogenous growth models (e.g., Lucas, 1988; Barro, 1991, 1995), these underlying factors more clearly emerge.

This chapter builds on the logic of the conceptual framework for the economic growth process set out in Chapter 2. It will not repeat that framework here, beyond providing the reduced-form production function (or growth equation) and physical capital investment functions for reference and for explanation of how the controls are handled. It does seek to extend earlier research related to endogenous growth and augmented Solow models by tracing more specifically the influence not only of prior enrolments at primary, secondary, and higher education levels but also of rates of investment in education at these levels. The feedback effects on growth through impacts of education on rates of investment in physical capital are considered in the second section. Net population growth rates and their relation to labour force growth, political stability, and democratization that also have feedback effects on growth are treated as parameters, or controls, in this chapter, but become endogenous in the complete model in the chapters that follow. The final section summarizes the conclusions.

The Reduced-Form Production Function

The production function of the new endogenous growth models containing externalities and increasing returns (as in Lucas, 1988) that was shown as Equation (2.1), or the related Solow model augmented with human capital as in Mankiw, Romer, and Weil (1992), is again the starting point. The focus is also still on the medium term, not on long-run steady-state growth or long-run constant per capita income steady-state solutions.

By expressing the production function in implicit rather than explicit functional form and totally differentiating it with respect to time, it then can be divided through by real GDP. This latter step has the distinct advantage of converting investment and other variables into ratios to GDP that are largely independent of the wide fluctuations in exchange rates and inflation rates that have been experienced by a number of the Latin American economies since 1960. This can be simplified by using lower-case letters (as before) to represent percentage rates of change with respect to time in GDP and in the number of persons, i.e.:

$$y = \frac{\partial Y}{\partial t}\frac{1}{Y}, \quad n = \frac{\partial N}{\partial t}\frac{1}{N}.$$

n can then be subtracted from both sides, and investment in physical capital disaggregated to show investment at primary, secondary, and higher education levels to obtain per capita growth rates. Controls for initial GDP per capita, oil shocks, political stability, and unemployment rates normally thought of as part of the disturbances in the preceding purely theoretical frameworks are important in Latin America, so they are sorted out and shown explicitly in the following equation, and will be used as controls in the regressions.

$$y - n = \alpha_1 \frac{I_K}{Y} + \alpha_2 \frac{I_P}{Y_{60}} + \alpha_3 \frac{I_S}{Y_{60}}$$
$$+ \alpha_4 \frac{I_{HE}}{Y_{60}} + \alpha_5 \frac{Y}{N_{70}} + \alpha_6 OIL + \alpha_7 UT + \alpha_8 PS + \alpha_9 n + \mu \qquad (4.1)$$

The definition of each variable, and data sources for measurement, are:

$y - n$ Growth of real GDP per capita, measured as 5-year average annual rates of growth over the 1970–92 period, from World Bank, *World Tables* (1996).

I_K/Y Gross Private Domestic Investment as a per cent of GDP, also 5-year averages, 1970–92, from World Bank, *World Tables* (1996).

I_P/Y_{60} Investment in primary education as a per cent of GDP, 1960, from UNESCO (1968). (For all investment rates, a subscript of -10 $=$ lagged 10 years).

I_S/Y_{60} Investment in secondary education as a per cent of GDP, 1960, from UNESCO (1968).

I_{HE}/Y_{60} Investment in higher education as a per cent of GDP, 1960, from UNESCO (1968).

$(Y/N)_{70}$ Initial GDP per capita, in US dollas, 1970, from World Bank, *World Tables* (1996).

OIL Control separating oil exporter nations ($OIL = 1$) from oil importer nations ($= 0$).

UT Unemployment rate, a control for short-term fluctuations, from ILO (1996).

PS Political stability, from 'International Country Risk Guide' (Coplin *et al.*, 1997 and earlier issues).

n Percentage rate of growth of population (N = population), from ILO (1996).

μ Disturbances.

Political stability (*PS*) will also appear later in the investment function for physical capital, and is a function of democratization in later chapters. Also, enrolment rates with equivalent dates and lags will be substituted for the rates of investment in education shown above in alternative specifications that are the same in all other respects. The latter alternative tests for the quantity of human capital formation without the element of quality that expenditure levels reflect, especially in the poorer countries. Specifically:

$GER1_{60}$ Gross enrolment rate in primary education, 1960, from UNESCO (1995). (For all enrolment rates, a $- 10$ subscript $= 10$-year lag.)

$GER2_{60}$ Gross enrolment rate in secondary education, 1960, from UNESCO (1995).

$GER3_{60}$ Gross enrolment rate in higher education, 1960, from UNESCO (1995).

Equation (4.1) indicates that after controlling for the starting intercept in each country using $(Y/N)_{70}$ and other identifiable sources of disturbances, per capita growth is higher with higher rates of investment in physical and human capital. Investment in human capital and gross enrolment rates must be introduced with sufficiently long lags that the overall skill level of the labour force constituting the nation's larger existing stock of human capital is raised significantly.

Where $n =$ population growth is compared to labour force growth, shown as l in one later table, and l is larger than n, then labour absorption rates are higher than population growth rates. This growth of raw unimproved labour could be expected to contribute positively to growth of per capita output, although probably not very much. However, if $n > l$, the new population is not entering the labour force, and the coefficient of n could be expected to be negative. If $n = l$, the effects of the population growth rate and labour absorption rate offset one another, in which case either n or l, if entered into the equation, could be expected to be insignificant. Although n and/or l are shown in a number of the tables that follow, both are often not significant in the growth equation—note, however, that growth is defined and measured in per capita terms.

Properties of the Growth Estimates for LAC

Estimates for this equation are presented in Table 4.1 for the period from 1980 to 1990 using the rates of investment in primary, secondary, and higher education lagged 10 years. Directly comparable estimates using the gross enrolment rates, also lagged 10 years with other elements in the model, are then presented in Table 4.2. Both investment and enrolment rates represent gross *additions* to the human capital stock of the population. These occur slowly, relative to the much larger size of the total human capital stock in each nation, so it takes time to raise the overall level of the stock and a lag is appropriate. Both investment and enrolment are expressed as a per cent of the GDP or relevant population base respectively, so they are very close to measuring the change in human capital per capita, and hence human capital deepening or capital dilution characteristic of the medium term

Table 4.1 Investment in Primary, Secondary, and Higher Education and Growth, 1980–1990 (dependent variable: growth of real GDP per capita, $y - n$, 5-year periods; t-statistics in parentheses)

	Model 1	Model 2	Model 3	Model 4	Model 5	Model 6
I_K/Y	0.259	0.256	0.098	0.987	0.136	0.207
	(2.93)	(3.02)	(1.01)	(0.93)	(1.37)	(1.93)
I_P/Y_{-10}		0.080		0.304	−0.313	
		(0.479)		(2.82)	(−1.39)	
I_S/Y_{-10}	1.439	1.280	0.648	0.338	4.13	2.54
	(3.30)	(2.43)	(2.41)	(1.09)	(3.01)	(2.50)
I_{HE}/Y_{-10}					−3.47	−1.67
					(−2.16)	(−1.21)
$\ln Y/N_{70}$	−0.035	−0.034	−0.016	−0.016	−0.029	−0.033
	(−4.89)	(−4.97)	(−4.58)	(−5.11)	(−3.78)	(−4.01)
OIL	0.110	0.108	0.072	0.078	0.106	0.108
	(6.38)	(6.44)	(6.19)	(6.71)	(5.66)	(5.86)
UT	0.340	0.326				0.336
	(5.02)	(4.91)				(4.65)
Adjusted R^2	0.56	0.57	0.56	0.61	0.43	0.44
rho	0.11	0.12	0.11	0.09	0.12	0.17
R2	1.37	1.16	2.64	1.03	0.408	0.911
HT	5.64	8.02		9.03		7.16

Note: Sample size is 36. All models corrected for heteroscedasticity and autocorrelation.

discussed in Chapter 2. Investment in education is often necessary to expand enrolments (e.g., to build secondary schools in rural areas or to expand university access and hire teachers), but it also supports a better quality of education that gross enrolment rates do not capture, a factor that is very significant in Latin America, where school and college completion rates are low.

Brief comments are necessary on econometric aspects of the properties of the estimates before turning to the substance of the results.

Heteroscedasticity

To ensure that the estimates are not biased due to the variation in disturbances across observations remaining in the residuals, all models are corrected for heteroscedasticity. This was done using the POOL method of Kmenta (1986). It distinguishes the observations that apply across the 18 countries from those that apply to the two time periods within each country (a total of 36 observations) and applies the same correction for heteroscedasticity within each of the two time periods. To check that there is no heteroscedasticity after the correction, the residuals were saved, and a check made using R2 to see whether the disturbance variance across observations is constant. R2 (the number of observations times R^2) shown in Tables 4.1 and 4.2 follows the chi-squared distribution, and since it never reaches 3.84, the

Table 4.2 Enrolment in Primary and Secondary Education and Economic Growth, 1980–1990 (dependent variable: growth of real GDP per capita, $y - n$, 5-year periods; t-statistics in parentheses)

	Model 1'	Model 2'	Model 3'	Model 4'
I_K / Y	0.196	0.170	0.153	0.020
	(3.60)	(2.28)	(1.29)	(0.168)
$GER1_{-10}$		0.00007		−0.0004
		(−0.108)		(−0.453)
$GER2_{-10}$	0.0018	0.0016	0.0013	0.0016
	(4.08)	(2.25)	(1.92)	(1.73)
$\ell n\ Y/N_{70}$	−0.043	−0.037	−0.024	−0.013
	(−12.20)	(−4.64)	(−5.44)	(−1.23)
OIL	0.114	0.017	0.071	0.071
	(8.58)	(4.35)	(3.82)	(2.70)
UT	0.391	0.353		
	(9.33)	(5.67)		
R^2	0.88	0.64	0.71	0.41
rho	0.105	0.124	0.125	0.065
JB	2.02	1.31	3.38	2.29
R2	1.10	1.03		
BPG before	5.76	6.56	3.40	4.85
HT	3.18	4.87	6.18	

Note: Sample size is 36. All models corrected for heteroscedasticity and autocorrelation.

0.05 significance level, for any model, we can be confident there is no significant heteroscedasticity, and that the coefficients are therefore free of bias from this source.

Autocorrelation

All models have also been corrected for autocorrelation in the residuals in the time series dimension only, given that the POOL method distinguishes observations over time within each country from those across countries. The rho coefficients after the correction if any are shown in Tables 4.1 and 4.2 and are relatively small. We can therefore be confident that the coefficients are free of bias due to first-order autocorrelation.

Hausman Specification Test

The Hausman and Taylor (1981) statistic tests whether GDP per capita in 1970, a constant for each country, controls for the differences in the intercept among countries so that the estimated equation can be used for predictions within countries. However, I have introduced other variables as well to assist in controlling for differences among countries in the intercept (*UT*, *OIL*, and *PS* in the investment equation later).

The 'between and within' country estimates have been computed, and the Hausman test, *HT*, which ascertains the significance of the difference between them, is shown in Tables 4.1 and 4.2. Its level must be below 3.84 to indicate that shifts in the intercept have been controlled, which it is for Model 1' and Model 3', which omits UT and is the one actually used in the simulations in Chapter 12. It is higher in the other models, but as noted, *UT*, *OIL*, and *PS* also help to control for shifts in the intercept and this is not fully taken into account in *HT*.

Multicollinearity

A systematic approach has been used in Tables 4.1 and 4.2 to address the problem of multicollinearity. It arises almost exclusively among primary, secondary, and higher education levels of investment and the corresponding enrolment rates. The logical connection between them (e.g., secondary investment largely determining expansion of secondary enrolment rates as mentioned above) is the reason that they are not placed in the same models together, even though the former reflects an element of quality not captured by the latter that is especially important in poor countries. So first with investment in education, and then with enrolments, one level at a time is introduced, and then combinations in concert, while always including investment in physical capital as a per cent of GDP, I_K/Y, initial GDP per capita, $(Y/N)_{70}$, and other controls.

Empirical Determinants of Growth in Latin America

In general, the results shown in Tables 4.1 and 4.2 are consistent with the logic of the hypotheses as they relate to the medium term that were discussed in Chapter 2 and illustrated there in Figures 2.1 and 2.2.

Total Capital Accumulation

That is:

- Physical capital deepening, I_K/Y, contributes positively and significantly to growth in output per worker in Latin America, except when the control for the unemployment rate is omitted.
- Investment in primary education, I_P/Y_{-10}, and both investment and enrolment in secondary education, I_S/Y, in Models 1–3, 5 and 6, and $GER2$ contribute significantly to per capita economic growth in this period.
- Convergence *does* occur within this Latin American group of 18 nations. The group does not include the smaller and often very poor Caribbean Islands, however. The coefficients of Y/N_{70} are all negative, and significant. This

suggests that those nations with lower per capita GDP at the outset are growing at higher percentage rates.

Oil Exporters

The two oil exporter nations, Colombia and Venezuela, were able to shelter themselves from the high-interest-rate/debt shocks that came in the 80s. The coefficient for *OIL* is positive and highly significant in all models. This helps to stabilize the intercept among countries and allow the effects of human and physical capital accumulation on per capita growth be detected.

Unemployment Rates

Many of the increases in GDP per capita during the 80s were not sustainable long-run growth but instead shorter-term recovery from recessions brought on by the shocks from high interest rates and debt ratios mentioned earlier. Unemployment rates varied widely among countries (see Table 4.3), and their positive relation to GDP increases in those nations that had the farthest to recover is probably related to this. Unemployment rates are a useful control for extraneous factors and have the effect of increasing the significance of physical capital and secondary education when they are used. But the use of this control has little or no effect on the role of the other variables.

Growth over the Longer 1970–1993 Period

In Tables 4.5 and 4.6, the longer 1970–93 period is chosen, with growth rates for 1970–9, 1980–9, and 1990–3, and the same periods for investment in physical capital as before. The sample size is therefore 3 time periods within 18 countries or 54 time periods in all. Rates of investment in education are used in Table 4.5 and enrolment rates in Table 4.6 as before except that they are the initial rates in 1960 (i.e., lagged ten years). Since these are constant for each country, they can also be interpreted as a proxy for the level of human capital stock in use throughout the period in that country.

Now investment in physical capital continues to have a positive and significant relation to per capita growth in almost every model in Tables 4.5 and 4.6. Investment in primary education is not significant (Table 4.5) but enrolment in primary education usually is (Table 4.6). This is reminiscent of the same pattern found in East Asia.

Investment in secondary education, somewhat surprisingly, is not significant (Table 4.5) and even negative (Table 4.6). But it will be seen shortly that initial secondary enrolment rates are extremely significant as determinants of the rates of investment in physical capital in Latin America (Table 4.7), so they would therefore have an important relation to growth rates through this channel.

Enrolment in higher education is not significant as a determinant of growth rates (Table 4.5). This is the same as the pattern found in East Asia, and also with the findings by Barro (1995: 425–7) based on his worldwide data. Higher education enrolments also have an insignificant and tentatively negative relation to rates of

Table 4.3 Means and Standard Deviations

	Mean	σ	Minimum	Maximum
I_K/Y	0.22	0.07	0.11	0.47
I_P/Y	0.034	0.05	0.02	0.25
I_S/Y	0.029	0.07	0.02	0.32
I_{HE}/Y	0.015	0.02	0.01	0.06
OIL	0.17	0.37	0	1
Y/N_{70}	526	302	90	1,260
UT	0.20	0.11	0.017	0.40
n	0.07	0.15	−0.15	0.72

Table 4.4 Zero-Order Correlation Matrix, Latin America (36 observations)

	I_K/Y	I_P/Y_{-10}	I_S/Y_{-10}	I_{HE}/Y_{-10}	OIL	$(Y/N)_{70}$	UT	n
I_K/Y	1.00							
I_P/Y_{-10}	−0.19	1.00						
I_S/Y_{-10}	−0.11	0.94	1.00					
I_{HE}/Y_{-10}	−0.06	0.83	0.80	1.00				
OIL	0.11	−0.21	−0.15	−0.15	1.00			
$(Y/N)_{70}$	−0.08	−0.13	−0.18	0.10	0.42	1.00		
UT	−0.24	0.03	0.09	−0.01	−0.12	0.19	1.00	
n	−0.21	−0.02	−0.10	0.06	−0.17	−0.11	−0.15	1.00

investment in physical capital (Table 4.7). This perhaps is not so surprising when one takes into account the problems with the quality of higher education in much of Latin America. The World Bank (1993b) cites high dropout and repetition rates, little effective research output (ibid.: pp. vi, 6), low levels of cost recovery, and the expansion of admissions beyond economic capacities (ibid.: 20). Initial investment rates in 1960 in higher education have positive and significant effects over the period as a whole (Table 4.5, Models 3, 5, and 6), reflecting both the need to attend to quality and the long lags before higher education and R&D investments are effective. Investment in higher education more recently, lagged only 10 years, does not appear to be effective, at least as yet (Table 4.1, Models 5 and 6). It is true that some military dictatorships, as in Brazil, spent considerable amounts in this period on higher education that favoured the elite with low tuition, while failing to provide adequate basic education in most rural areas.

Political stability always has a positive relation as a determinant of growth rates, and over 66 per cent of the time is clearly significant (Tables 4.5 and 4.6). But as a determinant of the rate of investment in physical capital in Table 4.7 it really comes into its own, with high t-statistics ranging up to 5.9 and 13.7. Secondary education plays a complex role in this, related in part to the emerging democratization in many Latin American countries, which in turn contributes to political stability in the long run. So this is an indirect effect of education, but it will only become endogenous later, in Chapter 7.

Table 4.5 Education Investment and Economic Growth (dependent variable: per capita growth rates ($y - n$), for 3 time periods: 1970–9, 1980–9, 1990–3; t- statistics in parentheses)

	Model 1	Model 2	Model 3	Model 4	Model 5	Model 6	Model 7	Model 8
I_K/Y	0.052	0.052	0.091	0.094	0.075	0.089	0.089	0.089
	(1.86)	(1.83)	(4.30)	(4.16)	(2.79)	(4.08)	(4.03)	(3.48)
$(I_P/Y)_{60}$	0.004			0.004		0.006		
	(0.84)			(0.75)		(0.96)		
$(I_S/Y)_{60}$		0.001		−0.013	0.006	−0.004		
		(0.08)		(−0.91)	(0.45)	(−0.26)		
$(I_{HE}/Y)_{60}$			0.055		0.048	0.058		
			(4.10)		(2.97)	(4.10)		
$(I_H/Y)_{60}$							0.00359	0.00327
							(0.9764)	(0.869)
PS	0.0005	0.0005			0.0002			
	(2.77)	(2.52)			(0.76)			
OIL	0.009	0.007	0.013	0.0087	0.012	0.015	0.007	0.007
	(1.78)	(1.52)	(2.74)	(1.39)	(2.51)	(2.88)	(1.17)	(1.22)
$(Y/N)_{70}$	−0.00002	−0.00002	−0.000007	−0.000005	−0.00001	−0.00001	−0.000005	−0.000005
	(−2.09)	(−1.22)	(−1.13)	(−0.48)	(−1.14)	(−0.96)	(−0.54)	(−0.56)
UT	−0.086	−0.084	−0.074	−0.088	−0.075	0.072	−0.091	−0.092
	(−4.07)	(−3.98)	(−3.51)	(−4.14)	(−3.49)	(−3.45)	(−4.36)	(−4.22)
ℓ	−0.0010	−0.0037	−0.006	−0.0008	−0.005	−0.006	−0.001	−0.0009
	(−1.76)	(−1.47)	(−2.28)	(0.36)	(−2.12)	(−2.36)	(−0.47)	(−0.27)
Constant								0.00005
								(0.004)
Adjusted R^2	0.338	0.321	0.412	0.260	0.406	0.417	0.258	0.260

Note: All models were corrected for heteroscedasticity and autocorrelation. Sample size is 54 (3 ×18 countries).

Other controls behave in a fashion similar to that reported before, except that the unemployment rate is consistently negative and highly significant in relation to growth over this longer 1970–92 period (Tables 4.5 and 4.6). Oil exporters (*OIL*) do consistently better and the initial per capita income, $(Y/N)_{70}$, always has a negative sign whenever it is significant, indicating some degree of convergence within the region. The percentage rate of increase in the labour force, l, is negatively related to the growth rate whenever it is significant (Tables 4.5 and 4.6), but positively related to the rate of investment in physical capital (Table 4.7). This suggests that in the growth equation, increases in raw labour inputs alone, after controlling for improvements in the quality of labour through education and for unemployment rates, do not contribute to per capita growth. Increases in raw labour inputs also act as a proxy for population growth rates, which were never independently significant. In the investment function, the most likely possibility is that conditions that are conducive to higher rates of investment are also conducive to higher labour absorption, although since there is no lag, there could also be two-way joint dependence between I_K/Y and l.

Table 4.6 Education Enrolments and Economic Growth (dependent variable: per capita growth rates, $y - n$, for 3 time periods: 1970–9, 1980–9, 1990–3; t- statistics are in parentheses)

	Model 1'	Model 2'	Model 3'	Model 4'	Model 5'	Model 6'	Model 7'	Model 8'
I_K /Y	0.045	0.067	0.045	0.060	0.057	0.056	0.050	0.058
	(1.57)	(2.41)	(1.57)	(2.28)	(1.92)	(2.02)	(1.73)	(1.98)
$GER1_{60}$	0.0002			0.0003		0.0003		
	(1.41)			(2.11)		(1.97)		
$GER2_{60}$		−0.0004		−0.0005	−0.0004	−0.0005		
		(−1.60)		(−2.23)	(−1.61)	(−2.06)		
$GER3_{60}$			0.001		0.0004	0.0003		
			(0.74)		(0.73)	(0.24)		
GER_{60}							0.00006	0.0002
							(0.46)	(1.46)
PS	0.0003	0.0005	0.0005	0.0003	0.0006	0.0003	0.0004	0.0005
	(1.27)	(2.87)	(2.63)	(1.24)	(3.00)	(1.34)	(1.90)	(2.34)
OIL	0.011	0.006	0.009	0.011	0.008	0.011	0.009	0.008
	(2.078)	(1.21)	(1.82)	(1.89)	(1.47)	(1.97)	(1.67)	(1.630)
$(Y/N)_{70}$	−0.00002	−0.00001	−0.00002	−0.00001	−0.00001	−0.00002	−0.00002	−0.00003
	(−2.34)	(−0.90)	(−2.20)	(−1.37)	(−1.41)	(−1.54)	(−1.93)	(−2.57)
UT	−0.083	−0.078	−0.081	−0.072	−0.073	−0.0007	−0.084	−0.078
	(−3.99)	(−3.69)	(−3.83)	(−3.47)	(−3.41)	(−3.37)	(−3.98)	(−3.77)
ℓ	−0.005	−0.050	−0.003	−0.008	−0.005	−0.008	−0.004	−0.001
	(−1.97)	(−2.02)	(−1.51)	(−2.90)	(−2.02)	(−2.82)	(−1.63)	(−0.37)
Constant								−0.03022
								(−1.826)
Adjusted R^2	0.359	0.309	0.352	0.342	0.325	0.352	0.343	0.358

Note: All of these models were estimated with corrections for heteroscedasticity and, if needed, for autocorrelation in the residuals. Sample size is 54 (3 ×18 countries).

Investment in Physical Capital and Total Saving

The determinants of rates of investment in Latin American economies in Table 4.7 and the background for these estimates, need to be explained, although aspects of Table 4.7 have been cited above.

To focus here on rates of investment, first in physical and then in human capital, it must be explained briefly how these investment decisions are not totally dependent on personal and corporate saving rates, especially in the medium term. First, higher growth rates support higher investment in Table 4.7, but they also generate higher saving. Second, some investment can be attracted from abroad, particularly as education contributes to a skilled labour force that aids exports and earns foreign exchange, a factor that is particularly important in labour surplus economies.

Third, and most important in relation to the financing of government and private investment in education that underlies GER1, GER2, and GER3 in Table 4.7, which is part of *total* investment, such investment induces additional saving, which is then part of *total* saving. This occurs not just because taxes used to finance

Table 4.7 Determinants of Physical Capital Investment Rates (dependent variable: I_K/Y, 3 time periods: 1970–9, 1980–9, 1990–3 (Models 1–4) and 2 time periods: 1970–5, 1975–80 (Model 5); t-statistics are in parentheses)

	Model 1	Model 2	Model 3	Model 4	Model 5
$y - n$	0.365	0.607	0.339	0.339	
	(1.90)	(2.89)	(1.72)	(1.77)	
$GER1_{60}$	0.0017			0.0017	
	(4.67)			(4.68)	
$GER2_{60}$	0.0031	0.0047	0.0040	0.0028	0.0019
	(3.14)	(4.50)	(3.82)	(3.17)	(3.42)
$GER3_{60}$	−0.0039		−0.0045		
	(−1.03)		(−1.13)		
$GER2_{-10}$		−0.0003		0.0019	
		(−0.64)		(3.42)	
PS	0.0015	0.0024	0.0037	0.0015	0.0055
	(2.73)	(5.94)	(13.70)	(2.94)	(5.29)
$(Y/N)_{70}$	−0.00001	−0.00009	−0.00007	−0.00009	−0.0005
	(−1.72)	(−2.65)	(−1.82)	(−2.61)	(−2.99)
ℓ		0.023			
		(4.34)			
$(Y/N)_{70}^2$					0.0000003
					(2.51)
Constant	0.779	0.603	0.722	0.774	0.051
					(0.971)
rho					0.064
R^2	0.779	0.603	0.722	0.774	0.954

public investment in education reduce private consumption, which therefore is saving normally defined as refraining from consumption. To the extent they reduce private saving or investment, if the social rate of return to investing in education is higher than the average return that otherwise could have been earned, there is still a net growth payoff (and vice versa). Still more important is the impact on private investment of forgone earnings by parents when government subsidies induce parents to leave their children in school longer. These forgone earnings are simultaneously saving done largely by the parents as they refrain from consumption and finance their children in school. The decisions by governments to invest in education therefore operate to direct resources from consumption toward saving and investment that has a return to future economic growth and development.

This point can be linked to the new endogenous growth models discussed in Chapter 2. The decisions by government take the externalities into account that households take as givens, and that therefore do not affect private decisions. This fact, together with compensation for the imperfect capital markets for financing human capital, thereby counterbalances the underinvestment in human capital formation by private households and firms that would otherwise occur on pure efficiency grounds. It also helps to explain the source of the externalities in the new endogenous growth models, since externalities and hence government decisions play a crucial role as part of increasing returns to scale and hence sustained growth and development.

The Investment Function

Private investment in physical capital is shown in Equation (4.2) below as influenced by the public and private investment in human capital discussed above that supports increases in the gross enrolment rates, GER1 and GER2. The hypotheses are also that it is positively influenced by higher per capita growth rates, GN, and by political stability, PS:

$$I_K/Y = \beta_1(y - n) + \beta_2 GER1_{60} + \beta_3 GER2_{60} + \beta_4 PS + \beta_5 (Y/N)_{70} + \mu. \quad (4.2)$$

All variables have been defined and sources given previously under Equation (4.1). The rationale for the potential impacts of primary and secondary education, GER1 and GER2, is that a skilled and trainable labour force attracts investment. Perhaps this is a precondition for sustaining high rates of investment without facing diminishing returns.

Similarly political stability, and democratization to which it is related as discussed in Chapter 7, is conducive to private investment. PS becomes endogenous in the complete model (Chapter 12) but is a parameter here whose value is given by the data. PS is measured using the Political Risk Rating index in Tables 4.1 and 4.2 and in Models 1–4 in Table 4.7, but by the Composite Risk Rating in Model 5 in Table 4.7. Political Risk is an index reflecting weighted ratings of government pronouncements vs. reality, political leadership, corruption, the military in politics, rule of law, political terrorism, civil war, political party development, and quality of the bureaucracy. The Composite Risk Rating includes economic risk, which is highly correlated with political risk. Economic risk includes expropriation of private investment, repudiation of contracts, losses from exchange controls, loan default, inflation, and success with exports. They are referred to here as political stability because a higher index number indicates higher stability, not greater risk.

Empirical Determinants of Investment Rates

Physical capital investment as a per cent of GDP is shown in Table 4.7 to be very significantly related to initial levels of investment in primary and secondary education throughout the 1970–93 period, and to the expansion of secondary education but only in the later 1980–90 period (Model 5). This is consistent with the hypothesis that skill levels in the labour force encourage higher rates of investment.

Political stability is now much more significant as a determinant of the rate of investment in physical capital in Table 4.5 than it was as a determinant of growth rates directly in Tables 4.5 and 4.6. There has been a debate about this in the literature, with Barro and Sala-I-Martin (1995) finding that the more significant effects are through investment (ibid.: 451) rather than on growth directly (ibid.: 439), whereas Campos and Nugent (1996: table 7) find significant effects from a variable more akin to democratization on growth directly. My conclusion here is somewhat in between, but closer to that of Barro and Sala-I-Martin. I did not find democratization to be significant in the growth equation (and hence did not show it), although political stability marginally is. However, political stability is dramatically significant as a determinant of rates of investment in physical capital (Table 4.7) and so I conclude that its main influence, and indirectly that of democratization as developed later, comes through that channel.

The growth in real GDP per capita, $y - n$, is not a robust determinant in Table 4.7 of higher rates of investment in physical capital in Latin America, somewhat like the insignificance of log GDP in Barro's worldwide regressions (Barro and Sala-I-Martin, 1995: 451). The initial GDP per capita, $(Y/N)_{70}$, is in fact negative and usually significant, indicating falling rates of investment in physical capital *after controlling for investment in education* as growth proceeds, a phenomenon predicted by the original Solow model, although this is offset in the highest-income countries by the non-linearity in this term, as suggested by Model 5. The two countries with the highest GDP per capita, Chile and Mexico, also have the highest investment rates. Other aspects of the results in Table 4.5 have been discussed earlier, but it is notable that the R^2, ranging from 0.60 to 0.95, are good, and as good or better than those obtained by Barro and Sala-I-Martin (1995: 451) based on worldwide data.

International Trade Impacts

Finally, human resource development has been shown by Adrian Wood (1994) to have a very significant relationship to reducing the heavy dependence of many poor countries on extractive primary exports, and moving toward more human and physical capital-intensive manufacturing exports. Although I have not done original research on this point and integrated it as yet into the interactive simulation model, it is appropriate to summarize very briefly the results of Adrian Wood's work here. It is significant to the earning of foreign exchange, as mentioned above, which helps to pay debt service on foreign loans from international donors and investors, and thereby helps to support my emphasis here on investment in physical capital and in human resources.

Manufacturing exports, XM, relative to primary exports, XP, depend on human resources, controlling for the country's land area relative to its population in Wood's key regression:

$$XM/XP = 0.59 \; \ell n HR - 0.71 \; \ell n NR + 1.01.$$
$$(3.47) \qquad (-7.10) \qquad (1.94) \qquad\qquad (4.3)$$

Here: HR = number of years of schooling of adults over the age of 25 divided by the population, from Barro and Lee (1993).

   NR = the country's total land area divided by its population, from World Bank (1993).

This suggests that human resource development is important not only to earning foreign exchange but also to the success of an export-oriented growth strategy. It also has great significance for reducing the strain from extractive primary exports on the environment in developing countries. It therefore also relates to the important indirect effects discussed in Chapter 9 of human resource development on achieving a sustainable environment.

Conclusion: Tracing the Impacts of Education on Growth in Latin America

In simulations of endogenous development using the interactive model in Chapter 12, the data specific to each country in Latin America and the economic growth sector discussed here are used to estimate the potential impact of changes as they relate to that country, especially in primary and secondary education policies.

   If one has a homogeneous set of countries, then the Solow model with the same production function works quite well. But these conditions hardly hold across the nations in Latin America. Some have experienced military *coups d'état*, wild inflation, and other instabilities during the period studied. Latin America was not doing badly in the 40s, 50s, and 60s. But in the 70s and 80s, the region as a whole really looks bad *vis-à-vis* East Asia.

   It is therefore necessary to control for many of the preconditions for stable growth in Latin America before the underlying forces of physical capital accumulation and human capital accumulation, as in the augmented Solow growth model of Mankiw, Romer, and Weil (1992), clearly emerge. The preconditions I find most significant are political stability in both the investment function for physical capital and the growth equation, the initial GDP per capita, and the utilization rate. Given that political stability is related to democratization (both become endogenous in Chapters 7 and 12), the wave of democratization that has left no nation in Latin America untouched can be reasonably expected to have a continuing positive effect on economic growth there.

   When these controls are imposed, however, significant separate direct effects of physical and human capital accumulation on economic growth clearly emerge. For education, some of the most significant effects are of both primary and secondary education enrolments on rates of investment in physical capital and on trade, which helps to finance this through exports, and through these on per capita growth. However, there are also significant direct effects on growth. An interesting illustration in gross terms (without these other controls) is in Costa Rica and Ecuador, which invested much more as a per cent of GDP in primary and secondary education than did Venezuela and Bolivia. Costa Rica invested a high 2.2 per cent in primary and 1.5 per cent in secondary education, and Ecuador an even higher 5 per cent in primary and 1.4 per cent in secondary education. This is to be compared to a low 1 per cent and 0.9 per cent in Venezuela and 0.2 per cent and 0.4 per cent for each level in Bolivia. The per capita growth rate for the 1970–93 period was 3.8 per cent in Costa Rica and 5 per cent in Ecuador, compared to a much lower rate of less than 2 per cent in Venezuela and Bolivia. All four countries invested in physical capital at about equal rates.

This chapter finds, however, that there are different impacts at different times. Initial 1960 primary enrolment rates were directly significant to growth, but even more than this, initial primary and secondary enrolments were very significant determinants of the rates of investment in physical capital, and hence influenced growth rates in important but indirect ways. Rates of investment in higher education were positive only with longer lags going back to the initial period. But rates of investment expenditure on secondary education were very important to growth in the latest period, 1980–93, essentially after universal primary education had been achieved in most countries.

Although these are all aspects of economic growth in Latin America, they do not isolate the externalities per se from the economic returns to education realized privately. To the extent that the social product is larger, the external direct effects would be captured partially by the marginal products that are reflected in the coefficients for the human capital inputs in the production functions. All social benefit externalities also would not be captured by rates of return estimated from microeconomic data based on private earnings. Specifically endogenous development in Chapter 12 takes both the non-monetary returns and the indirect effects from interactions among sectors into account to relate the costs to the *total* impacts. From this point of view, microeconomic social rates of return, although positive and substantial, could be expected to underestimate the true contribution of education both to economic growth and to endogenous development.

5 Africa's Population Growth and Dilution of Human Capital

WITH ALI ARIFA[1]

Africa offers dramatic contrasts both now and into the future between economies enjoying rapid per capita growth, such as Botswana, Tunisia, and Uganda, and others facing per capita economic decline, great inequality, turmoil, higher infant mortality, shorter longevity, and starvation, particularly in the rural areas.

Faster overall average growth rates in Africa in 1996 of 5% reflect recovery from the depressed levels of the 1980s and early 90s, but fell to 3.7% in 1997, barely above the population growth rate. These Africa-wide averages do not reflect the wide differences between Africa's fastest-growing countries and those where per capita real growth is zero or negative. The longer-term per capita real growth in Sub-Saharan Africa from 1985 to 1996 is − 1.1%, for example, which is therefore below the rate of population growth and reflects the 380 million people there, roughly half of Africa's population of 760 million, who are profoundly poor, surviving on less than US$1 a day (World Bank, *World Development Report*, 1997: 215). This was a depressing chapter to work on as the data and longer-term patterns emerged.

Earlier attempts to model economic growth and net population growth for Africa (e.g., Hazledine and Moreland, 1977) did not include human capital formation in either the production function or the infant mortality and population growth rate equations. This, however, is our main theme. Other studies that do include human capital formation (e.g. Crouch, Spratt, and Cubeddu, 1992) have not simulated outcomes with patterns that can be observed. Perhaps the closest to what follows is Barro (1991), Barro and Sala-I-Martin (1995: chap. 12), and Barro (1997). But none of these involve structural relationships programmed in a model for interactive simulation-type solutions to measure the outcomes, which is also an ultimate objective here.

Many of these problems in Africa have their roots in inadequate mass education in the rural areas and in the poorest countries, a point that will be developed below. This chapter anticipates two aspects of the complete interactive model developed for simulations, specifically the endogeneity of population growth and of political stability. Both are explored briefly here, but both are addressed more comprehensively in Chapters 6 and 11.

There is an optimistic aspect with respect to Africa, however. Even though falling per capita income, mass starvation that affects mostly children and the poorer families in rural areas, and turmoil seems the most probable scenario in many of the poorest countries, a major change in economic support for education and related education policies does show potential for turning this Malthusian scenario around. But it will require very large changes in policies, significantly larger than what has been happening in the past and larger than any of the relatively modest policy change scenarios developed in Chapter 12.

Current and Simulated Future Per Capita Economic Growth

Table 5.1 lists the 28 African nations included in the complete model. GNP per capita in 1985 is shown in column (1), GNP per capita in 1995 is shown in column (2), and the 1985–95 per capita real growth rate in column (3) in constant prices (1985 US dollars). The per capita growth rate varies from highs of 6.1% per year in Botswana and 5.4% in Mauritius to −5.4% in Rwanda and −3.2% in the Congo. An estimate of GNP per capita for 25 years hence is obtained on the assumption of a continuation of current policies using the complete model (which includes continuing to strengthen or weaken education at the same rate as in the past). The result is shown in column (4), and the per capita growth rate that this implies for each nation in 2020 is shown in column (5).

A few countries in Africa *continue* to grow relatively rapidly, such as Tunisia, Mauritius, and Botswana, whereas others, generally among the poorest, such as the Central African Republic, Madagascar, Rwanda, Sudan, and the Congo, get even poorer. Botswana, in addition to the advantages from mining and its proximity to South Africa, has invested very heavily in basic education. Botswana's per capita income rises to $6,353 by 2020 (in 1985 prices for comparison to column (1)). This is in spite of the fact that it is in the interior and landlocked, a negative factor stressed by Sachs (1997) and the HIID model. Mauritius also becomes relatively wealthy, with per capita income rising to $7,608 in 1985 prices.

On the other hand, in 10 countries per capita incomes fall to $170 or lower. As discussed below, these tend to be countries where net population growth rates are high, and sometimes rising. Female enrolments at the secondary education levels are generally low, and there is also a lack of adequate female primary education. So as the primary education of females expands it lowers infant mortality rates, raises longevity, and on balance raises net population growth rates, putting even more pressure on the schools to finance expansion just to stay even with the growing population. *The result is that human capital dilution in the form of less adequate education per capita occurs.* The advantages of lower fertility rates as females remain in school through ninth grade and beyond are not yet fully realized in most of these Sub-Saharan African economies within the next 25 to 40 years. This is compounded now by the crises back in the 1980s, when US deficits and interest rates were very high, forcing education and health investment cutbacks in debtor nations, and a lost generation in much of Sub-Saharan Africa (and Latin America) who now have fewer skills to contribute to economic growth. Furthermore, under these conditions political instability and civil wars in the poorest countries are likely to persist

Table 5.1 Current Growth Rates and Endogenous Growth Simulations Continuing Current Policies to 2020, Africa

	GNP per capita, 1985 (1985$) (1)	GNP per capita, 1995 (1995$) (2)	Per capita growth, 1985–95 (3)	Model estimates GNP per capita, 2020 (1985$) (4)	Growth rate per annum (5)
Algeria	2,550	1,600	−2.4%	943	−3.9%
Benin	260	370	−0.3%	190	−0.1%
Botswana	870	3,020	6.1%	6,353	6.1%
Burkina Faso	150	230	−0.2%	383	0.0%
Burundi	240	160	−1.3%	227	−1.4%
Central African Republic	280	340	−2.4%	120	−2.7%
Congo	1,070	680	−3.2%	613	−1.4%
Ethiopia	110	100	−0.3%	85	−0.5%
Ghana	370	390	1.4%	491	1.1%
Kenya	300	280	0.1%	334	0.2%
Liberia	480	NA	NA	352	−1.2%
Madagascar	240	230	−2.2%	157	−2.1%
Malawi	170	170	0.7%	134	−0.5%
Mali	150	250	0.8%	169	0.8%
Mauritania	410	460	0.5%	605	0.6%
Mauritius	1,100	3,380	5.4%	7,608	5.2%
Morocco	560	1,100	0.9%	819	0.9%
Nigeria	950	260	1.2%	1,372	1.3%
Rwanda	280	180	−5.4%	84	−3.7%
Senegal	370	600	0.0%	428	−0.5%
Somalia	270	270	−2.3%	74	−0.4%
Sudan	280	280	−0.2%	110	−2.6%
Tanzania	300	120	1.0%	382	1.0%
Togo	230	310	−2.7%	102	−2.5%
Tunisia	1,190	1,820	1.9%	2,690	2.5%
Zaïre	160	120	−1.0%	124	−1.7%
Zambia	410	400	−0.8%	339	−0.8%
Zimbabwe	640	540	−0.6%	767	2.9%

and perhaps to spread. In Chapter 7 the relation of secondary education to democratization and political stability is explored further, but here it is evident that political instability is not conducive to sustained per capita growth.

Within Africa, the rich get richer and the poor get poorer, as shown in Table 5.1. The endogenous development scenario essentially involving continuation of current policies produces no convergence of per capita incomes within this region.

Education and Per Capita Growth in Africa

There are three aspects to the growth process in Africa to be considered here. There is first the growth equation that contains education but also contains investment in physical capital and net population growth rates. Second, there are the determinants of the rates of investment in physical capital. And third, there are the determinants of net population growth rates.

The effects of education on pure economic growth through its effects on investment, on political stability, and on net population growth rates will be seen to be very important in Africa, even more important than the direct effects. There are additional effects from education on other aspects of development not included here that are considered in later chapters.

Economic Growth in Africa

The main determinants we found for real per capita economic growth based on data specific to the African nations are shown in Table 5.2 below. Rows (1) and (2) include primary and secondary gross enrolment rates, whereas row (3) is a similar specification using instead investment in education as a per cent of GDP. The latter reflects not just quantity but also an element of quality which is dependent on expenditure per pupil in the poor countries.

In all three rows investment in physical capital is highly significant, as are the negative effects of net population growth rates in rows (1) and (2). Both of these are highly dependent on education policies, which we will consider next.

The direct effects of education enrolments in rows (1) and (2) are less significant. But when the quality dimension is introduced through investment in primary and secondary education in Row (3) it is highly significant. Investment in higher education measured in such a way that it includes the investment made by donors in the education of African students abroad does not contribute positively. But when this same higher education term was lagged 10 years and added to the regression, its coefficient is positive with a *t*-statistic of 2.00 (see McMahon, 1987: 189).

Row (2) is the row selected for use in the complete model for simulations in Chapters 12 and 13. It is simpler, having dropped many of the control variables that are not significant, including *OIL*. The coefficients for the direct effects are quite small and will not have effects on the outcome as large as the indirect effects through investment in physical capital and population growth, which are considered next.

Investment in Physical Capital for Faster Growth

The determinants of investment in physical capital are shown in Table 5.3. Rows (4)–(6) are based on data specific to Africa in the 1970–94 and recent 1980–94 periods in work done by Arifa and McMahon (1997). The equation in row (7) is a

Table 5.2 Per Capita Economic Growth, Africa (t-statistics in parentheses)

Dependent variable	I_K/Y	GER1	GER2	n	OIL	Constant	R^2 (N)
(1) $y - n$	0.16	0.001	0.014	-1.25	0.12	0.810	0.52
	(3.72)	(0.08)	(0.32)	(-2.66)	(0.13)	(0.60)	29
(2) $y - n$	0.17	0.0016	0.0003	-1.25		0.787	0.51
	(3.92)	(0.08)	(0.30)	(-2.74)		(0.60)	29

Dependent variable	I_K/Y_{-5}	I_H/Y_{-5}	I_{HE}/Y_{-5}	n_{-5}	OIL	$(Y/N)_{70}$	$(y-n)_{-5}$	REC	AN	Constant	R^2
(3) $y - n$	0.65	1.62	-5.02	-0.35	-0.01	0.04	0.43	0.10	0.003	-0.05	0.44
	(3.06)	(2.19)	(-1.53)	(-0.75)	(-0.12)	(0.65)	(4.12)	(1.71)	(0.07)	(-0.70)	120

Note: Notation and data sources are the same as in Chaps. 3 and 4. Briefly, endogenous variables in the complete model with data sources are:

$y - n$ = growth of real GDP per capita, average for 1970–90 for rows (1) and (2) and for 5-year time periods from 1965–85 for row (3), all from World Bank, *World Tables* (1996) $(y - n)_{-5}$ = lagged 5 years);

I_K/Y = investment in physical capital as a per cent of GDP, average for 1970–90 for rows (1) and (2), and for 5-year time periods 1965–85 lagged 5 years for row (3), all from World Bank, *World Tables* (1996);

GER1 and GER2 = primary and secondary gross enrolment rates averaged for 1970–90, which is tantamount to about a 10-year lag, and which are partially endogenous;

I_H/Y_{-5} = investment in primary and secondary education as a per cent of GDP, lagged 5 years, from UNESCO (1995);

I_{HE}/Y_{-5} = investment in higher education as a per cent of GDP, lagged 5 years, from UNESCO (1995); and

n = net population growth rates averaged for 1970–90, from ILO (1996).

Controls for exogenous economic and cultural differences that were tested are:

OIL = dummy variable for oil-exporting nations;

$(Y/N)_{70}$ = initial GDP per capita in $US, from World Bank, *World Tables* (1996);

REC = recovery from recessions (1975–85 = 1); and

AN = Anglophone (1) or Francophone (0).

summary of the result obtained by Robert Barro (1991: 426, equation 20). The former show comparable but also illuminating complementary effects, whereas the latter has the benefit of a larger worldwide sample that reveals highly significant effects from education and political stability. The latter will be used in the complete model for simulations.

In general, with respect to the role of education in Table 5.3 both primary and secondary education enrolments lagged 20 years have a positive relation to the rate of investment in physical capital. Both are highly significant in row (7), and are also significant at the 0.05 level or nearly significant at the 0.20 level or better in rows (4)–(6). Political stability (*PS*) also has a strong positive relation to rates of investment in physical capital. Political stability will be shown in Chapter 7 to be dependent on past secondary education enrolment rates given that secondary education makes a major longer-run contribution to democratization, which in turn is conducive to greater stability. This is a meaningful point in Africa, since political and economic instability is widespread there and deters productive domestic and foreign investment.

Apart from education rates, political stability, and population growth, the other variables are controls for economic and cultural differences that were found to be significant among these and others that were explored. Briefly, those African countries that are growing faster (y is large) invest more. However, the higher rates of investment may be the cause, rather than the effect, and furthermore with investment rates dependent this is a non-homogeneous element that may be allowing growth rates to act as a proxy for other causal structural factors (such as political stability). So equations containing y are not used in the complete model. The level of interest rates (r) averaged over the same period as the dependent variable are not significant (e.g. row 6). Government support of consumption through social security, or through food subsidies and welfare (exclusive of defence and public investment in education), is related to lower rates of investment in physical capital, although it will be seen later to be related also to political stability.

But to return to our main theme, the role of education, the positive relation of primary and secondary education to private investment rates in all of the rows in Table 5.3 can be explained by the effect of human capital formation in offsetting diminishing returns to investment in physical capital that otherwise occurs. This bitter lesson has been learned through hard experience by international donors and lending agencies after many failed efforts with investment in physical infrastructure without an adequate education base in the society to sustain it (e.g. lending strategies; see World Bank, 1995: chap. 11). These coefficients also suggest that public investment in the expansion of education in Africa does not drive out private investment in physical capital, but instead attracts additional investment from abroad, as was discussed in Chapter 2, as well as inducing additional *total* saving and investment by families in the form of forgone earnings.

Education's influence on investment includes the lagged relation of secondary education to democratization and to political stability (discussed in Chapter 7 below), which in turn influences investment rates (see Table 5.3, row (7)). Finally,

Table 5.3 Investment in Physical Capital, Africa (t-statistics for rows 4–6 and standard errors for row 7 in parentheses)

Dependent variable	GER1 (/100)	GER2 (/100)	n	y	r	GDP60	PS (REV and AS)[b]	SSX	Constant	R^2(N)
(4) I_K/Y_{70-94}	0.058 (1.34)		−435 (−1.99)	266 (4.90)					14.3 (2.20)	0.44 33
(5) I_K/Y_{80-94}	0.103 (2.12)	2.05 (1.40)	−584 (−2.31)	251 (3.29)					10.15 (1.22)	0.36 33
(6) I_K/Y_{80-94}	0.103 (2.10)	2.35 (1.53)	−578 (−2.26)	246 (3.18)	−0.181 (−0.69)				12.5 (1.48)	0.34 33
(7) I_K/Y_{70-85}	0.079 (0.027)	0.131 (0.041)				−0.0098 (0.0048)	0.0055 (0.0021)	−0.12 (0.06)	0.175[a] (0.032)	0.58 76

Note: Notation here is the same as in Table 5.1 above, with the following changes and additions:

GER1 and *GER2* = gross enrolment rates, but scaled so that their coefficients must be divided by 100 for use in the complete model or when compared to other investment regressions;

y = rate of growth of real GDP, which tests for a non-linear accelerator effect, from World Bank, *World Tables* (1996);

r = the interest rate, averaged for the period, from World Bank, *World Tables* (1996);

*GDP*60 = real GDP per capita in US$ in the base year, from World Bank, *World Tables* (1996);

PS = Political Stability Index, from Coplin *et al.* (1995: table 2B, column 4) as used in Chapter 7 and in the complete model;[b] and

SSX = social security expenditures, similar to Barro's (1991) government consumption (exclusive of defence and education, both as a per cent of GDP).

[a] This constant term is the same as Barro's (1991: p. 426, eq. 20). But two variables in Barro's equation that are both related to the price index for capital goods are dropped from Table 5.3. They are PPI60, the 1960 value for the PPP investment deflator, with a coefficient of −0.065 (0.016), and PP160DEV, the deviation of PP160 from the mean, with a coefficient of 0.023 (0.023), which is not significant. This is because the ratio of investment to GDP already deflates to a pure number independent of international price level differences and exchange rates, and also these terms cannot be used in the simulations because the deletion of these terms does not affect the simulations, given that the intercept for each equation is adjusted in the programming of the model so that the value of the dependent variable in the initial year is set equal to the actual data for that country to avoid discontinuities as the simulation begins.

[b] Barro (1991) uses in his regressions *REV*, the number of revolutions and coups per year, and *AS*, the number of assassinations per million in the population per year, both between 1960 and 1985, to capture this effect. To approximate the coefficient for *PS* for use in the complete model, Barro's sign on the coefficient for *REV* is reversed and divided by 10 to reflect the difference from *PS* in means and standard deviations.

higher population growth has a significant negative relation to rates of investment in physical capital (rows (4)–(6)). It is quite possible that saving rates are lower as high population growth rates press families toward subsistence levels. But again, education has a very significant role on investment and growth in Africa through its influence on population growth, as will be discussed in the next section.

Population Growth, Capital Dilution, and Slower Growth

Using data that are specific to Africa, Table 5.4 summarizes the net effects on population growth of GDP per capita, of primary education, and of female secondary education. Underlying these reduced-form equations are structural relations. After controlling for GDP per capita the latter relate these levels of education to fertility rates, infant mortality, and longevity respectively, as will be considered in Chapter 6. The structural equations in Chapter 6 have the advantage of capturing the underlying cause-and-effect relationships and their related lag structures as well as of using a larger worldwide sample. These together result in much higher R^2s and coefficients that are all highly significant. So the structural equations from Chapter 6 are the ones that will later be used in the complete model to measure the time forms of these education impacts.

However, as a summary of these underlying structural relations, the equations in rows (8) and (9) of Table 5.4 are not misleading and they have the advantage of being based on data specific to Africa. So to complete our consideration of the relation of education to per capita growth in Africa it is appropriate to discuss them here.

Table 5.4 indicates that after controlling for per capita income (the positive Malthusian effect), primarily in order to measure the non-market returns to education without double counting, primary education has a positive but insignificant relation to population growth in both periods, probably because of its stronger positive structural effects in reducing infant mortality and increasing longevity, effects that are almost offset by the effects of female primary education in reducing fertility. The insignificance of these coefficients will disappear when these structural relations are specified in Chapter 6. But these overall adverse effects on population

Table 5.4 Population Growth, Africa (t-statistics in parentheses)

Dependent variable	GDP per capita, US$	$GER1_{70}$	$GER2_{70}$ (female)	Constant	R^2 (N)
(8) n_{70-94}	0.00004	0.0052	−0.056	2.82	0.17
	(0.26)	(1.10)	(−2.35)	(5.34)	33
(9) n_{70-80}	0.0008	0.0011	−0.057	2.70	0.27
	(2.75)	(0.19)	(−1.95)	(4.12)	33

Note: Variables and data sources as in Tables 5.2 and 5.3. GDP per capita is the average for the period indicated by the dependent variable on the left.

growth and hence on per capita economic growth remain for the poorest countries, where primary education is still limited. It can easily be observed that the population growth in each of the poorest countries with low levels of female primary education is still increasing (World Bank, 1996a: table 1-2, p. 7).

The secondary education of *females*, however, has a clearly significant negative relation to net population growth rates in 1970–94 (row (8)), and for the earlier period (1970–80 in row (9)) the size of the coefficient is very similar and nearly significant. This will be attributed in Chapter 6 to the fact that as the percentage of females reaching high school eventually exceeds roughly 30% their urban job prospects improve, their desired family size falls (Acsadi, Johnson-Acsadi, and Bulatao, 1990: 166), the number of years remaining in which they are fertile diminishes, and interaction with family planning programmes becomes more effective. Most females in the North African nations, in Botswana, and in South Africa have reached ninth grade and net population growth rates have all been falling there since 1975 (World Bank, 1996a: table 1-2, p. 7). But it will be some time before most of the nations in Sub-Saharan Africa reach this stage. This is the main reason the Malthusian scenario is expected to be dominant for the poorest nations in Table 5.1 for the foreseeable future.

Conclusions and Development Strategies

To summarize and apply the main conclusions that are emerging here (supported further in Chapters 6 and 7) to possible longer-run economic development strategies, it is useful to think in terms of four groups of countries that present different development challenges. Human resource development through education has a central role in the ultimate solution to the challenges within each. But there are long lags before basic education becomes widespread and can contribute significantly to political and economic stability, higher rates of investment, and reductions in population growth, and hence to sustained per capita economic growth. The countries' leaders need to know this, and not be discouraged, but instead take a longer view and get started immediately. Roughly, these groups are those dominated by:

- *Civil strife and economic collapse.* Nations in this group include the Sudan, Sierra Leone, and Somalia. As conditions worsen, they could also include Chad, Mali, and the Congo as well as others shown in Table 5.1 with falling per capita income. A longer-term strategy is needed, including immediate concrete steps, since keeping children in school now offers perhaps the best hope that conditions will not be the same or worse in these nations 25 years from now.
- *Little movement toward democratic political systems, with stagnant or regressing economies.* Nigeria (although its dictator died recently), Niger, Togo, and the Republic of Congo (formerly Zaïre) are examples of this group. Again, a longer-term strategy that turns on the relation of more widespread secondary education to democratization and the rule of law could be considered.

- *Emergence from conflict or dictatorial regimes and struggle for legitimacy and political stability.* Examples of this group are Rwanda, Burundi, and Liberia. Others, such as Ethiopia, Mali, and Malawi, are moving from dictatorial regimes toward more liberal governance. Many nations in Latin America also passed through this stage not very long ago. So there is hope, although aid is needed for strengthening political institutions and again major efforts are needed to improve the effectiveness of and access to basic education.
- *Promising economies making substantial progress toward more pluralistic political systems and experiencing faster per capita growth in the 90s.* This fourth group includes Botswana, Swaziland, Benin, South Africa, Namibia, Uganda, Tunisia, and some others. Together they are responsible for almost all of the faster 4.4% growth rate in Sub-Saharan Africa in the recent 1995–8 period (World Bank, *World Development Report*, 1998: World Development Indicators, pp. 214 and 220). The strategy of the United States, implemented by USAID (1998: 3), is to focus all US aid on these countries. It is also now the strategy of the African Development Bank, nearly all of whose loan approvals in 1997 were in four faster-growing countries (Tunisia, Morocco, South Africa, and Zimbabwe). This strategy is also recommended by the *Economist* (1997a) and based on the assumption that it will encourage reform elsewhere and that the benefits will trickle down.

The problems caused by rapid population growth and political instability in the poorest developing countries of Sub-Saharan Africa have long been recognized (e.g. World Bank, 1989, 1990, 1996a). What we have sought to do here that is new, however, is to trace systematically the effects on economic growth of expanding access to education of adequate quality at the primary and secondary levels via their effects on political stability (Chapter 7), population growth, and rates of investment in physical capital. As these are programmed into the simulation model the *indirect* structural effects of education on growth will be seen to be largest in the poorest countries.

The countries in the fourth group continue to do well in the endogenous growth scenario in Table 5.1 in spite of the 'lost generation' of the 80s. To anticipate the simulations in Chapters 12 and 13, explicit additional policy interventions that expand and improve basic education also help very significantly. That is the optimistic news. But on the other hand the poorest and most unstable nations in the other three groups will have to make a tremendous educational effort, significantly greater than the increments of 2 percentage points of GDP going to education that are simulated later, if they are to avert a Malthusian disaster.

Notes

1. Ali Arifa is Associate Professor of Economics at Lincoln University, Canterbury, New Zealand. Ali participated from the beginning in the development of this chapter, including the development of Eqs. 1 and 2 in Table 5.2, which are from Arifa and McMahon (1997: eqs. 3–5 and 7–8). The themes were also developed together as they emerged from his Ph.D. dissertation at the University of Illinois at Urbana-Champaign (Arifa, 1995) Row (2) in Table 5.2 has become part of the complete model used for the simulations.
2. The African countries that are included in the regressions are not identical to those included in the complete model. Specifically, countries in the complete model as listed in Table 5.1 that are not included in the regressions are Ethiopia, Liberia, Morocco, Tunisia, and the Congo. Countries included in the regressions that are not in the complete model are Cameroon, Chad, Côte d'Ivoire, Gabon, Guinea-Bissau, Lesotho, Niger, Sierra Leone, Gambia, Cape Verde, and South Africa. The latter group of countries cannot be shown in Table 5.1 because there are no model simulations for them.

PART III
Measuring the Non-monetary Benefits

6 Health and Net Population Growth

The effects of education on population growth are the net result of effects that improve health and effects that lower fertility rates.

The impacts of education on health are measured in what follows in terms of impacts on reductions in infant mortality rates and impacts on increases in longevity, because of their direct relationship to population growth. This leaves out the separate effects of education in reducing illness, which also contributes to productivity. But morbidity rates are correlated with longevity and therefore impacts on morbidity will include some of the non-market returns to education in reducing illness. The net effect, however, may be that the effects of education on economic productivity growth are somewhat underestimated due to errors in measurement of the dependent variable.

Fertility rates then are discussed, followed by analysis of the net effects on population growth rates. Health and population growth impacts are simulated in the interactive complete model in Chapters 12 and 13 using the empirical results reported here, together with the transmission of each of these effects to per capita growth. Other health and population impacts flow to poverty reduction and pollution.

The microanalytic foundations for recent advances in measuring the impacts of education on health and their valuation are developed by Wolfe and Zuvekas (1997) and Greenwood (1997) in a special issue of the *International Journal of Education Research*. In this same issue a conceptual framework article by McMahon (1997*a*) considers potential omitted-variable bias, including biases from measurement errors in the education and the dependent variables and the extent to which they offset bias from the omission of ability and family factors, and the effects of the omission of trends over time in the returns to education. These measurement-error and growth-over-time effects are assumed here to approximately offset ability and family factor effects for reasons discussed in McMahon (1997*a*), and Chapter 13 considers externalities explicitly. So these issues are not considered here.

However, one particular control is very important for purposes of measurement of the *non-monetary returns to education*. It is the need to control for per capita income in the regressions, to avoid double counting of the market returns to education that have been considered above in Chapters 2–5. There is a comprehensive survey of the microeconomic literature that does control for income by Grossman and Kaestner (1997), and therefore is relevant to the *non-market* health-related returns to education.

The analysis that follows of health and population impacts of education relates to this recent microeconomic literature. But it is focused on an attempt to distil the key net impacts of education for purposes of tracing its impacts on population growth nationwide, which then leads to interacting effects among sectors within the model of endogenous development. It is also focused on measuring the non-market returns to education in the form of better health and increased longevity more comprehensively.[1]

The Conceptual Framework: An Overview

There is consistent evidence in the worldwide literature that the education of women and female literacy *reduce fertility* (Michael, 1974, 1982; Caldwell, 1986; Cochrane, 1979, 1983; Kasarda, Billy, and West, 1986; LeVine, 1987; Moreland, 1982; Tan and Haines, 1984; Schultz, 1993; Greenwood, 1997).

There is also consistent evidence of an important positive relationship between the education of women and the health of children, which *reduces infant and child death rates* (Caldwell, 1986; Cochrane, Leslie, and O'Hara, 1982; Cochrane, O'Hara, and Leslie, 1980; D'Souza and Bhuiya, 1982; Grossman and Kaestner, 1997: sect. 4.4).

The *net effect* on population growth rates is important for our purposes since this has a major impact on *per capita* income and *per capita* economic growth rates, thereby determining living standards while also affecting poverty rates and inequality in distribution. The negative impact of high population growth rates occurs both in the short run (by simple division, as there are more mouths to feed) and in the medium term, since capital deepening (more physical capital, human capital, and knowledge per worker) is the primary determinant of productivity growth in politically stable environments.

In explaining the effects of education on fertility, researchers in economics have stressed that secondary education of females raises their capacity to enter the workforce, and other human-capital-intensive activities. Since their time is more valuable in these pursuits, time is shifted away from having more children, which is time-intensive. Children also become more of an economic liability when women enter the urban labour force. Demographers have also suggested that female education improves their understanding of biology, enhances acceptance and correct application of birth control methods, and delays marriage, all of which may be expected to reduce fertility rates. In addition, because educational participation tends to extend the length of the child's economic dependence on the family, it may shift attitudes toward reduced family size (Cochrane, 1979; Gomes, 1984). On the other hand, educated working women are more likely to breastfeed each child for fewer months, a practice which may contribute to shorter spacing between births and a potential increase in fertility.

Life expectancy and mortality are also important factors for net population growth. Findings in a number of developing countries have consistently shown an important relationship between education or literacy and life expectancy of the next generation, principally through improvements in infant and child survival rates (Caldwell, 1986; Cochrane, Leslie, and O'Hara, 1982; Cochrane, O'Hara, and

Leslie, 1980; D'Souza and Bhuiya, 1982; Hobcraft, McDonald, and Rutstein, 1984; Le Vine, 1987). Analysts have hypothesized that both the knowledge and the increased earnings potential gained through education enable parents to provide a healthier environment for their families, although the processes or mechanisms by which school-learned knowledge is translated into better health behaviours are still unclear (Eisemon, 1988; LeVine, 1987). Education may also have a different effect on child health and survival, to the extent that schools provide children with informal health care, immunizations, and dietary supplements (Caldwell and Caldwell, 1985; Eisemon, 1988; Greenwood, 1997).

Paternal education has been hypothesized to have a positive effect on children's life expectancy, principally through increased income and the 'market' value of education, allowing improvements in living standards and the use of health-promoting goods and services. Female education may have market effects on the child's life expectancy (which could sometimes be negative as well as positive, since formal labour may take mothers away from childrearing activities) and also non-market effects, through the influence of education on childrearing and household resource management (O'Hara, 1980).

When possible or relevant, both left-and right-hand variables have been gender-disaggregated in the model equations. For example, the data set does not include data on infant mortality, or age of marriage, by gender. The key dependent variables to disaggregate by gender were the educational variables, which were in turn used as independent variables in other equations. In some cases, due to data limitations, these latter equations were gender-disaggregated only to the extent that gender-specific independent variables were used, rather than having gender-specific dependent variables as well.

The net effects of education on population growth appear to be affected by levels of educational development (LeVine, 1987). In the early stages of development, developing countries first tend to exhibit the effects of education on improved health, infant survival, and life expectancy, and therefore may experience an increase in population growth. The fertility decline associated with education, on the other hand, tends to occur only at later stages of economic development and after more than a few years of education (Kasarda, Billy, and West, 1986; Wheeler, 1984a). In particular, it is only in those countries where women have achieved not just primary education (which improves health) but are completing secondary education and entering the labour force that the stronger effect on declining fertility rates begins to dominate.

Health Effects: Infant Mortality

The effects of education on better health include effects reducing infant mortality and increasing longevity. Both are related as well to morbidity.

The impact of female educational participation, lagged to approximate the period of time from beginning of schooling to child-bearing age, was considered in the presence of other potentially relevant factors, including GNP per capita, average female age at marriage, level of urbanization, male enrolment rates, and geographic region. The best-fitting equation is the following (*t*-statistics here in parentheses):

$$ln(IMR) = 5.863 - 0.00221GERF(t - 20) - 0.0289GER2F(t - 2) - 0.173ln(GNPPC).$$
$$\qquad\quad (24.08) \quad (1.55) \qquad\qquad (8.55) \qquad\qquad\quad (3.87)$$

$$(6.1)$$

Sample size = 77 $R^2 = 0.839$

ln (IMR)	Log of infant mortality rates, from World Bank, *World Tables* (1996).
GERF (*t* − 20)	Female gross enrolment rate, lagged 20 years; 1 = primary, 2 = secondary, F = female, and M = male, from UNESCO (1968, 1995).
ln (GNPPC)	Log of GNP per capita in US dollars, from World Bank, *World Tables* (1996).

Thus, both primary and secondary female enrolment rates lagged by 20 years, a rough proxy for level of maternal education, reduce the infant mortality rate. GNP per capita controls for the market returns to education so that the coefficients for female education measure a non-monetary marginal product of female education. Average female age at marriage, level of urbanization, and geographic region made negligible contributions to the equation and were removed. Log-linear specification of the model produced a fit superior to linear specification, suggesting that the effect of increasing female enrolments on infant mortality diminishes as relatively high rates of enrolment are achieved.

Male enrolment rates made a small contribution to reduced infant mortality when they replaced female enrolment in the equation, but their effects were much weaker than for female enrolment rates alone, and became negligible and insignificant when both male and female rates were included in the equation.

An alternative specification to which this can be compared is given by Barro and Sala-I-Martin (1995: 453). The standard errors are in parentheses.

$$ln(IMR) = 0.007GERIM - 0.003GER1F - 0.005GER2M + 0.003GER2F$$
$$\qquad\quad (0.003) \qquad\quad (0.003) \qquad\quad (0.005) \qquad\quad (0.005)$$
$$\qquad - 0.13ln(GNP) - 0.007ln(GNP)^2.$$
$$\qquad\quad (0.03) \qquad\qquad (0.002)$$

$$(6.2)$$

Sample size = 88 $R^2 = 0.73$

Variables are as defined under Equation (6.1) above. None of the coefficients for education are significant except for male primary education, which is also negative. But the insignificance is almost surely due to the inclusion of *ln* (GNP)^2, which dominates everything and captures unexplained effects at the higher income levels, including those due to the non-monetary returns to education.

The relation in Equation (6.1) of female gross enrolment rates at the secondary level to increases in infant mortality (and better child health) is therefore illustrated

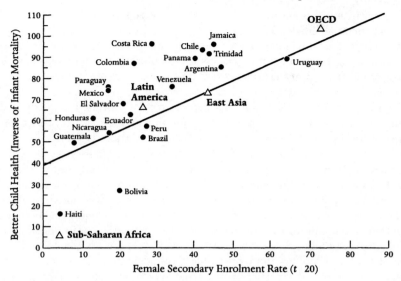

Figure 6.1 Better child health and female secondary education

in Figure 6.1. As shown, Latin America is far above Sub-Saharan Africa in this respect, but below the OECD nations.

Health Effects: Life Expectancy

Estimates of the determinants of life expectancy, *LEXP*, beyond the variables shown in Equation (6.3) below tried gender-disaggregated gross enrolment rates, lagged 20 years to represent maternal and paternal education, and GNP per capita as a proxy for living standards. Geographic region is included since it may reflect variation not only in per capita income but also in culture, health services, sanitation, and prevalence of disease. As *IMR* is in turn dependent on GNP per capita, the following equation was the best fit:

$$LEXP = 73.528 - 0.185IMR + 0.073GER2T(t - 20) - 2.932AFRICA - 2.464ASIA.$$
$$(83.19) \quad (26.24) \qquad (3.23) \qquad\qquad\qquad (6.45) \qquad\quad (4.88)$$

$$(6.3)$$

$$\text{Sample size} = 78 \quad R^2 = 0.973$$

The variables and sources other than those given above are:

LEXP	Life expectancy at birth in years, from World Bank (1997).
AFRICA, ASIA	Regional dummies: 1 = countries in these regions, and 0 = countries in OECD or LAC.

An overwhelming proportion of life expectancy is explained by *IMR*, and the indirect effects of female education and GNP per capita through *IMR*. Nevertheless, the coefficient for total male and female secondary enrolment rates is positive and significant, suggesting a net marginal contribution of education to longevity above and beyond these other factors. This is after controlling for cultural differences (diet, etc.) using the regional dummies.

The importance of education as a determinant of mortality is questioned by some, more than is its relation to infant mortality and fertility. But this question arises more in the industrialized OECD countries, and is related to mortality experience in the later years of life, rather than to the middle years or to infant mortality. Behrman *et al.* (1991), using a longitudinal Retirement History Survey in the US, challenge the finding by others of the importance of schooling as a determinant of illness and mortality. They find pension income and marital status, but not education, are significant predictors of the conditional probability of death. Menchik (1993) reports a similar finding for older US men. But as pointed out by Grossman and Kaestner (1997: sect. 4.2), birth studies include marital status, and 'the lack of a schooling effect may reflect causality from schooling to marital status'. Furthermore, Menchik includes net worth as well as earnings, which Grossman and Kaestner regard as not fully justified because it also interacts with lifestyle decisions and schooling in various ways. And finally, it is to be noted that Behrman *et al.* and Menchik exclude intergenerational effects of the parents' education on the health and longevity of children.

Barro and Sala-I-Martin (1995: 453) report results for their worldwide regression for life expectancy very comparable to those reported here. Although they again include log of GDP squared so that their results are hard to interpret, they nevertheless find not only per capita GDP but also female primary education (reflected through *IMR* in Equation (6.3)) and male secondary and higher education to be positive and significant net influences on life expectancy worldwide. Linear specification of the relationship among variables was superior to log specification, suggesting that for the levels of development represented in the sample, increases in educational participation remain important even for countries with relatively high enrolment rates.

Population Effects via Fertility Rates

Total births per female, as measured by the total fertility rate, are theoretically dependent on the persistence of females in school, which delays the age of marriage. Also, as suggested above, it depends on female choices to enter the labour force rather than remain in the home or work in agriculture. Availability of urban employment is also related to female secondary education. Finally, the resulting desire of educated women for smaller families could be expected to interact with the availability of family planning clinics. All three of these factors are present in what was found to be the best-fitting equation:

$$TFR = 6.128 - .00035[GER1F(t-20) + GER2F(t-20)]FP + 0.62AFRICA.$$
$$(29) \quad (9.8) \qquad\qquad\qquad\qquad\qquad (2.8) \qquad\qquad (6.4)$$
$$\text{Sample size} = 44 \quad R^2 = 0.787$$

Here *TFR* = total fertility rate, or births per woman, from World Bank (1997);

FP = family planning score, level of support for family planning, as developed by the Population Crisis Committee (1987). Including this variable reduces the sample size somewhat.

Other variables are as previously defined.

Primary and secondary female enrolment rates lagged 20 years in combination have a stronger effect than either alone. This is strengthened further when there is a higher level of government family planning support. To estimate this impact, an increase in the total female gross enrolment rate (primary plus secondary) from 50% to 100% reduces the fertility rate by 1.3 children on the average for women nationwide for a country that has a strong family planning program (*FP* = 75), whereas for a country with average family planning support (*FP* = 25) this same increase in female education reduces the fertility rate by 0.4 children. This is consistent with earlier work by Wheeler (1984*b*), who also finds that female education has its greatest impact on fertility when combined with support for family planning. Looked at from the other direction, high levels of female enrolment can more than triple the effectiveness of family planning efforts.

The *AFRICA* regional variable does reflect a complex of factors, but it does not dominate Equation (6.4), and it does perform a useful function in controlling for cultural factors. Fertility rates are significantly higher in Africa, as shown in Equation (6.4), but the variables for the other regions were not significant.

Other variables tried also had little impact, such as male education, female labour force participation, age of marriage, and level of urbanization. GNP per capita was also not significant. So for the control to be sure that only non-monetary impacts of education *on net population growth* are being measured (and to avoid doubling-up of controls), I depend on GNP per capita in Equation (6.1), which is a significant determinant of infant mortality rates and together with life expectancy (Equation 6.3) and this equation (6.4) for fertility will determine net population growth rates below.

The superiority of linear over log-linear specifications suggests that, for the levels of development represented in the sample, the effect of increasing female educational attainment on fertility remains just as important in countries with relatively high female educational attainment rates at the outset as in countries with low rates.

This relation of female gross enrolment rates in Latin America to total fertility rates is illustrated in Figure 6.2. Fertility rates in Sub-Saharan Africa remain well above those in the other regions. Fertility rates in Latin America, which are shown in more detail for the specific countries in this region (there are too many countries worldwide to show them all), remain consistently above those in East Asia (where per capita growth is fastest) as well as higher than those in OECD member nations.

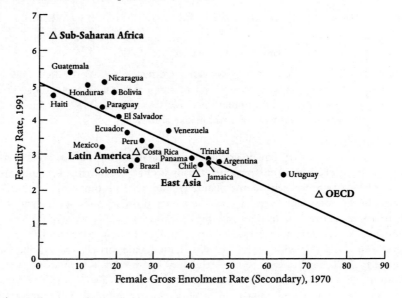

Figure 6.2 Female education and lower fertility rates

It is notable that the poorest countries (Haiti, Honduras, Guatemala, Nicaragua, and Bolivia) have the highest fertility rates, and also have among the very lowest lagged female enrolment rates.

Net Population Growth Rates

Lower infant mortality rates (Equation 6.1)) are a determinant of longevity (Equation (6.3)), which in turn affects the crude death rate (Equation (6.5)). The crude death rate (*CDR*) equation (with definitions and data sources given below Equation (6.7)) was estimated to be:

$$CDR = 10.09 + 0.452CDR(t-5) + 910.69/LEXP.$$
$$(-11.4)\ (10.8) \qquad\qquad (11.4)$$
$$\text{Sample size} = 151 \quad R^2 = 0.977$$

(6.5)

Simultaneously the fertility rate (Equation (6.4)) affects the crude birth rate (*CBR*) as follows:

$$CBR = 1.38 + 0.458CBR(t-5) + 3.58TFR.$$
$$(1.7)\ \ (8.3) \qquad\qquad (10.8)$$
$$\text{Sample size} = 160 \quad R^2 = 0.959$$

(6.6)

The net effect of the crude death rate and crude birth rate then determine the net population growth in the model:

$$n = \frac{POP - POP(t-1)}{POP(t-1)} = \frac{CBR - CDR}{1,000}. \tag{6.7}$$

n Net population growth rate, from World Bank (1997).

CDR Crude death rate, 1980 and 1985, from World Bank, *World Tables* (1976). ($t-5$) indicates CDR for 1975 and 1980.

CBR Crude birth rate, 1975, 1980, and 1985, from World Bank, *World Tables* (1997 and earlier years).

Life expectancy, *LEXP*, and fertility rates, *TFR*, are as previously defined in Equations (6.3) and (6.4). The sample size is larger because these equations have been estimated from 1980 and 1985 pooled data. Also, in the case of Equation (6.6) only, observations are not lost due to the unavailability of family planning data for some countries.

The combined effect of *improving health* via lower infant mortality and greater longevity and of *declining fertility* rates on *net population growth* is illustrated in Figure 6.3. This rather dramatizes two facts. First, net population growth rates are highest in Sub-Saharan Africa, and then fall monotonically as average female secondary enrolment rates rise and per capita earnings rise, as shown for Latin American, East Asian, and OECD countries. Second, Sub-Saharan Africa on average

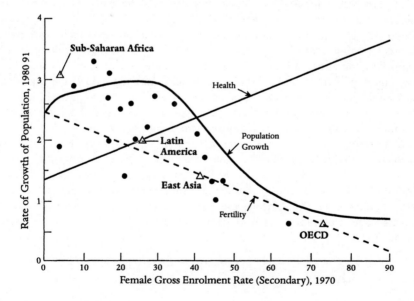

Figure 6.3 Education effects on health and fertility, and thereby on net population growth rates

has not yet reached the crossover point where the improved health of children which increases population growth rates is eventually counterbalanced by the declining fertility rates as more rural females enter secondary school. So net population growth can probably be expected to rise further, as shown, before the effects of female secondary education in lowering fertility rates, in some cases augmented by family planning, eventually begin to dominate. The round dots shown on the scatter diagram are for the countries in Latin America, most of which are at the in-between stages of this process of development.

Alternative Direct Estimates

There are two alternative approaches to the above structural approach, which does relate directly to the underlying logic of the causal relations between education and child health, education and longevity, and education and fertility and yet is relatively simple. They are the cohort-component method normally used by demographers, and estimating net population growth rates directly as a function of the education variables.

With respect to the former, standard cohort-component projections were made by Crouch *et al.* (1992) for Mali, Bolivia, Tunisia, Indonesia, and the Dominican Republic. The absolute error using these structural equations compared to the cohort-component method applied to these same countries for the same period was less than 2% after 40 years. Furthermore, projections made at later dates using the standard cohort-component method changed by more than 8% over a 4-year period due to changes in starting values and hence predicted values of critical parameters (see Crouch, 1991). Given that the standard cohort-component approach is often based on uncertain values of base-year data and on speculative projections of fertility and mortality rates, and does not utilize the underlying causal relationships contained in a structural approach (through which policy changes can be transmitted), the structural approach developed above is preferable, and most certainly preferable for my simulation purposes here.

With respect to the second alternative, that of estimating impacts on net population growth rates directly, again structural richness is lost by estimating a reduced-form equation instead, and there is nothing to be gained. To explore this, Ali Arifa together with the author estimated net population growth reduced-form equations for the African countries, as discussed in Chapter 5. One is repeated here from Table 5.4 to illustrate this point. The results for the 1970–4 period are:

$$n = 0.00004GNPPC + 0.0052GER1_{70} - 0.056GER2F_{70} + 2.82. \tag{6.8}$$
$$(.26) \qquad\qquad (1.1) \qquad\qquad (-2.35) \qquad\quad (5.34)$$

$$\text{Sample size} = 33 \quad R^2 = 0.17$$

All variables are as previously defined. With a low *t*-statistic for GNP per capita, and a low R^2, this shows that considerable richness is lost. Nevertheless the relation of initial primary education enrolment rates to net population growth is positive, although not reaching the 0.05 level of significance. The relation of female secondary education enrolment rates to net population growth is negative and clearly significant, as hypothesized, and as the reduced form computed from the structural model also indicates.

Conclusions

It can be concluded that there is considerably more logic and structural richness in relating the explanatory power of education to the underlying behavioural variables of infant mortality, longevity, and fertility rates than in using the education variables in a reduced-form equation to explain population growth rates directly. When the former is done, lagged female primary and secondary education rates account for substantial reductions in infant mortality (after controlling for per capita income), as well as significant increases in longevity worldwide. The costs of given increments to education enrolments can be calculated, and the value of these specific improvements to health due to education can be estimated, on the basis of the method described by Wolfe and Zuvekas (1997), by using the cost of obtaining these same health increments through expenditures on better medical care to estimate the cost-effectiveness of alternative strategies.

But this is not the end of the story. On the assumption that it is not totally reasonable to include GNP squared, which reflects unexplained factors in the regressions, it can also be concluded that lagged female enrolment rates operate from the outset to reduce female fertility rates. This is an effect that is strengthened by the availability of family planning clinics, although the education of females was seen to increase the effectiveness of family planning clinics threefold. This secondary education of females also eventually reduces net population growth rates, as has become most apparent in East Asia and the OECD member countries. This is an externality positively influencing per capita economic growth, but also, as will be discussed in more detail later in this book, it aids poverty reduction and makes a net contribution to reduced water pollution and reduced stress on forests and wildlife.

Note

1. The analysis in this chapter builds on the corresponding health sector in the Education Impacts Model in Crouch, Spratt, and Cubbeddu (1992: 14–18). Parts of this chapter are taken directly from that article; Luis Crouch was a co-principal investigator during earlier stages of this project. His help has also been acknowledged in the Preface, where I have assumed sole responsibility for the end result. Additional programming for Chaps 12 and 13 was done with the help of Ye Zhang at the University of Illinois, Urbana-Champaign.

7 Democracy, Human Rights, and Political Stability

The expansion of political rights, civil rights or human rights, and political stability are important aspects of general well-being. They involve a broader concept of development than just increases in per capita income. There are non-market final satisfactions that political freedoms, civil liberties, and reasonable economic stability provide to individuals over and above money earnings. But then there are also feedback effects to be discussed, from democratization to political stability to higher rates of investment and faster economic growth.

This chapter focuses on tracing the net impacts of education, controlling for its impacts on per capita income that influence democratization, human rights, and political stability. It also addresses the structural interaction among these sectors. With respect to human rights it should be made clear that the term is used here in the narrower way it is often used among Anglo-Saxon political scientists in the West to refer to 'civil rights' or 'civil liberties'. These are as defined by Freedom House (1996) as discussed below. Human rights in the Universal Declaration of Human Rights and in Article 13 of the Covenant on Economic, Social, and Cultural Rights (United Nations, 1966) include economic and social well-being, which is appropriate in some contexts but too broad to be consistent with the analysis here. This is because education is a 'human right' under the broader definition, which is not appropriate for our purposes since the objective is to trace the impact of education in giving rise to human rights (i.e. civil liberties), endogenous effects on the levels of education, and effects of education on per capita income (i.e., 'economic rights'). To define human rights more broadly merely settles these matters tautologically.

There are two main research traditions that have tackled the question of which social and economic traditions most favour democracy: cross-national quantitative studies and comparative historical research. Although this chapter is an instance of the former, it is also enriched by the latter. Furthermore, the two are not totally in conflict: both traditions generally agree that the level of economic development is causally related to the development of political democracy (e.g., Diamond, 1992; Huber, Rueschmeyer, and Stephens, 1993: 71–2, 83). I therefore take this as a starting point, which is also convenient in that it is necessary to control for per capita income when seeking to measure the portion of these non-market political-freedom benefits which can reasonably be attributed to education.

In the longer sweep of economic development, democracy and relative stability clearly have emerged in all of the OECD member nations, as well as in many respects in East Asia. Political rights, civil rights, and stability have begun to arrive in widespread ways in Latin America in recent years. These latter nations can perhaps best be described as in a *zone of transition*, with a hold on democracy that is both partial and fragile. Political and economic stability, freedom from coups and domination by the military, and human rights are enjoyed in a similarly tenuous fashion with democracy. In the newly independent countries of the ex-Soviet Union and some countries of Eastern Europe with less democratic experience, these political and civil rights appear to be emerging but are less well established. And in Sub-Saharan Africa, with the notable exception of South Africa, where democracy has emerged, as well as in parts of Central America, authoritarianism prevails.

From the comparative-historical perspective, some brief comments may help to illustrate what we mean by a *zone of transition* as applied to South America, since that continent is clearly in the middle of the process. Pervasive corruption in these fragile democracies is a continuing threat. So also is the tradition of rule based on raw power, violence, and decree that goes back to the pattern of the Spanish Conquest. There is little tradition of governance based on the rule of law, openness, and honesty. Corruption and tradition have often been the pretexts for a chequered history of military coups and rule by decree. In recent years, for example, President Carlos Menen in Argentina has ruled mostly by decree since 1991, limiting probes of official wrongdoing of the military during the 'dirty war'. Journalists continue to be intimidated in Argentina and killed in Latin America. Menen said, just prior to the summit on representative democracy in Madrid in July 1992, 'It doesn't bother me to govern by decree.'

Setbacks in Peru and Venezuela offer other examples of progress by fits and starts, and the fragile hold on partial democracy throughout this zone of transition. In Peru, President Fujimori, backed by the military, dissolved the Congress and suspended the constitution, putting corrupt politicians out of business and promising to eradicate the Shining Path guerrillas. In oil-rich Venezuela, where half the population lives in serious poverty, President Perez barely survived an attempted coup by mid-level officers in February 1992 and a second attempt in November. Again the military named corruption as the pretext for their attempted coups, and there was considerable sympathy in the population. But although Latin Americans of all classes believe their governments are steeped in corruption, as reported by polls cited by Payne (1993: 12), these same polls 'also indicate that most people do not want to forfeit their hard-won democratic freedoms'!

It is this theme that I wish to pursue in what follows. The hypothesis is that large-scale access to primary education, followed by secondary education especially, contributes both directly, in ways discussed below, but also indirectly, through the effects of per capita economic growth, to democratization, improved human rights, and greater political stability. After considering briefly the conceptual framework, each of these models and the empirical estimates used in the interactive policy simulations will then be discussed.

The Conceptual Framework

The conceptual framework suggests that economic growth and widespread access to primary education, and even more especially secondary education, enlarges the working and middle classes and facilitates their self-organization, thus making it more difficult for elites to exclude them politically. They value their improved economic status, their hard-won civil rights, and their democratic freedoms. Economic growth is also associated with the growing importance of manufacturing and service industries, creating additional centres of urban economic power that are independent of and counterbalance the power of rural landlords (see Kuznets, 1971). Educated citizens with access to modern media communications are able to be better informed about what is going on, to speak more articulately, and to some extent in co-operation with industrial interests to be more economically influential in strengthening their political rights. Human rights can often be a motivating force, and improvements in human rights can also follow as part of the process.

The feedback effects of democratization on economic growth and development are also very much a part of the conceptual framework. Some of them have been addressed in previous chapters, such as the feedback effects of democratization directly on economic growth, which I have concluded is negligible. De Haan and Siermann (1995) reach the same conclusion, and conclude that this feedback effect is 'not robust', as do Barro and Sala-I-Martin (1995: 439), who conclude that 'political freedoms and civil liberties . . . are individually and jointly insignificant . . . . Thus, once the other explanatory variables are held constant, [they] are not systematically related to economic growth.'

But the relation of democratization to political stability is considered below, which in turn I concluded in Chapters 2–6 above has a major relation to investment in physical capital and by this route to growth. Some of the feedback effects on *development*, however, are to be addressed within this chapter. These include the positive effects of political rights (democratization) on the progress of human rights, as well as on greater political stability. Feedback effects on other aspects of development, such as poverty reduction and environmental clean-up, will be considered in later chapters. The feedback effects from democratization are therefore very much a part of my structural approach to endogenous development; it is just that they operate through these other channels, and not directly.

Long-Run Adjustments

It is important to stress that this conceptual framework addresses a very long-run process, and addresses forces that affect all nations as pervasive influences. It does not deal with short-run year-to-year changes. The latter are the advances and retreats, fits and starts of which examples were cited above, and are characteristic of transitional factors within most of the individual Latin American countries. The predictions are therefore all subject to error margins, as suggested by the standard errors of the estimate.

These long-run influences can be assumed to move governmental units toward long-run equilibria typical of what is revealed by cross-section data. Households, firms, and governmental units are all normally assumed in cross-section data to have had sufficient time to adjust to the economic and educational/communications forces impinging on them. There can be factors such as a very long history of nothing but authoritarianism (e.g., Russia), or of strong military rule, that delay adjustments for long periods of course. But eventually, as in Latin America, some countries in Eastern Europe and the Caribbean, and in South Africa, the changes occasioned by these basic influences begin to show up.

In the other direction there are undoubtedly historical factors that have accelerated the process. In particular there are the traditions of parliamentary democracy, rule of law, and civil liberties associated with British emigration and British colonial history (see Clague *et al.*, 1996 for regressions testing these various traditions). Little else can explain the early democratization throughout the British Commonwealth, or the advanced levels of democratization relative to the much lower levels of economic growth in India, Sri Lanka, Bangladesh, and even Pakistan.

The strong probability that certain historical factors have accelerated the process of democratization and the rule of law (e.g., British history), and others have impeded it (e.g., Tsarist and Stalinist Russia, the Spanish Conquistadors), is not inconsistent with the causal forces operating through a longer-run structure considered here. This is because the effects of per capita economic growth and of the widespread dissemination of education are very long-run forces that are likely eventually to come to the fore.

Externalities

The benefits of education in the form of democratization, human rights, and political stability are not received by those who invest, but are instead externalities since they are largely received by others, and often in future generations. This is true of both the direct net contributions of education to democracy, and the indirect contributions (i.e., the cross-partial derivatives). Both of these will be measured and added up, even though it is much more difficult to estimate their economic value.

These externalities are an essential part of the conceptual framework. Parents who invest in the education of their children do not enjoy these benefits directly. The benefits are long delayed, and available to all free, so parents and students need not take these into account when they invest (Lucas, 1988 makes this point). To this extent education must therefore be supported publicly, as Jefferson clearly recognized. It is interesting that authoritarian regimes tend to be very reluctant to invest in education in political science, humanities, economics, or the law, which may have even more direct connections to democratization and the rule of law than the other disciplines. From the point of view of society as a whole, however, these are non-monetary returns to education which are also social-benefit externalities.

The Direction of Causation

In describing the conceptual framework, with the primary line of causation from per capita economic growth and education to democratization and not the other way around, my conclusion is in accord with the prevailing opinion of political scientists who specialize in research on this topic. They cite both the theory and the time lags involved. For example, Larry Diamond at Stanford University says, 'There are strong methodological and theoretical grounds for inferring that this relationship [from economic growth to democratization] is indeed causal' (1992: 469). Huber, Rueschmeyer, and Stephens (1993) at Princeton Univesity, citing their book *Capitalist Development and Democracy*, reach the same conclusion. They, and I, stress that this does not preclude the probability of a degree of reciprocal causation. There is no logical problem with a two-way causal flow; there are many instances of this in economics. And the feedback effects that we have been able to identify are in fact incorporated in the interactive model of endogenous development, as indicated above.

Determinants of Democracy

The concept of democracy that guides my research is quite conventional, at least in the West. It involves a relatively continuous range of variation from pure authoritarianism toward greater citizen participation and finally to considerable personal and political freedom.

Degrees of Democratization

The dimensions of the degree of democracy, the dependent variable, are closely though not perfectly captured by Freedom House's annual survey of political rights, referred to here as democratization, and of civil rights, referred to below as human rights.

The degree of democratization as measured by the Freedom House team includes:

- fair elections of legislative leaders and president with viable opposition candidates;
- competing political parties free of intimidation and with access to the press;
- limitations to authoritarian rule, including civilian control of the military, viable opposition parties with freedom from domination by totalitarian parties, religious hierarchies, or economic oligarchies; and
- a degree of decentralization of political power to provincial or local levels led by freely elected officials at those levels.

The dependent variable, degree of democracy, D, is measured on a scale of 1 to 7. The Freedom House Index (ibid.: 536–7) is inverted so that 7 represents the highest level of democracy, and 1 the lowest. As seen in Figure 7.1, most countries in the

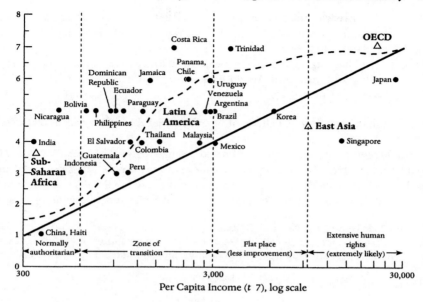

Figure 7.1 Democratization as a function of per capita income (straight line) and secondary education (increments above line)

OECD member nations have reached 7, those in Latin America 5 or 6, representing essentially 70 to 85 per cent political rights, and those in Sub-Saharan Africa on average 2 or 3. However, as indicated in the introduction to this chapter, this tends to be accompanied by considerable variation, with China, Haiti, and Indonesia at 1 or 2 and India at 5. In the Latin American countries, Africa, and Southern Asia there is also considerable corruption, fragility of democracy, and erratic changes. In Latin America, Costa Rica is the notable exception. Some countries are in fact dropping back toward the linear, visually estimated simple regression line in Figure 7.1.

Empirical Estimates of the Major Determinants

On the basis of the conceptual framework discussed above, democratization is hypothesized to be a function of lagged per capita income GNPPC, lagged secondary education, $GER2_{-12}$ or $LF2$, and military expenditure rates, $MILX$. Thus

$$D = \alpha_1 \ln GNPPC_{-7} + \alpha_2 GER2_{-12} + \alpha_3 MILX_{-1} + \mu_1, \qquad (7.1)$$

where $GNPPC_{-7}$ = log of Gross National Product per capita in US dollars, lagged 7 years, from World Bank (1997);

$GER2$ = gross enrolment rate in secondary education, lagged 12 years, from UNESCO (1997);

LF2   = per cent of the labour force with secondary education, lagged 5 years, substituted for GER2 in Model 2 in Table 7.1: from Psacharopoulos and Arriagadu (1992);

$MILX_{-1}$ = military expenditure as a per cent of total government expenditure, lagged 1 year, from World Bank (1997: 240); and

μ_1 = disturbances.

The disturbances include the effects of other variables that were tried, as discussed below.

These regressions have been estimated using cross-section data for the 75 countries for which data are available, with results shown as Models 1 and 2 in Table 7.1 below. The choice of lag structures in the case of GNPPC is to allow for the time delays necessary for the migration out of agriculture and working-class/

Table 7.1 Determinants of Democratization (dependent variable: $D =$ democratization, as measured by the Freedom House Index, inverted so that high values represent high degrees of democracy; t-statistics in parentheses)

	Model 1		Model 2	
	Coefficient	Significance level	Coefficient	Significance level
Per capita income				
(ln GNPPC$_{-7}$)	0.372	0.108	0.77	0.024
	(1.63)		(2.38)	
Secondary education				
GER2$_{-12}$	0.018	0.01		
	(2.60)			
LF2$_{-5}$			0.643	0.247
			(1.18)	
Military expenditure	−0.094		−0.003	
($MILX_{-1}$)	(−4.73)	0.0001	(−1.006)	0.995
Constant	−5.504		−1.52	
	(−4.99)	0.0001	(−0.72)	0.476
Adjusted R^2	0.494		0.449	
n	75		34	
F	23.16	0.0001	9.97	0.0001
MAE	1.21		1.25	
Standard error of the estimate		1.568		1.62

	Zero-Order Correlation Matrix, Model 1		
	ln GNPPC$_{-7}$	$MILX_{-1}$	GER2$_{-12}$
ln GNPPC$_{-7}$	1.00		
$MILX_{-1}$	0.08	1.00	
GER2$_{-12}$	0.78	−0.07	1.00

middle-class groups to build and coalitions to form. This lag could reasonably be regarded as even longer, but 7 years works pretty well. Secondary (and primary) education enrolment rates are lagged as in the growth equations because it takes 10 to 20 years for new entrants into the labour force to raise the overall level of the human capital stock significantly. *LF2* measures this stock directly, so a long lag is not justified but instead a 5-year lag that is in a logical relationship to GNPPC. *LF2* does not reach the 0.05 level of significance in Model 2 of Table 7.1 (which is not strictly comparable to Model 1 because the sample size is smaller due to the unavailability of data on *LF2* for all countries). Nevertheless, *LF2* does not do very well, and Model 2, although consistent, is inferior on statistical grounds to Model 1.

Other explanatory variables were tried but were not found to be independently significant in this multivariate context. They include the spread of mass basic education (*GER1*), urbanization (*URB*), and communication (*COM*). However, the first two are highly correlated with rising per capita income, and the use of communication media with the extent of secondary education. A dummy variable for *BRITISH* heritage was not tried. But when this was done by Clague *et al.* (1996) in a similar regression, whenever *LITERACY* was included, its OLS *t*-statistic is very high, *MUSLIM* remains negative but becomes insignificant, and *BRITISH* remains consistently positive but also becomes insignificant. It is possible that part of the British influence on democratization is being transmitted through education. The R^2 of 0.49, although highly significant, shows that there is variation that remains to be explained. But for now I conclude that the main effects are captured by the variables already included, which also represent the more basic forces on which urbanization, better communications, and articulate working-class, middle-class, and more urbanized business interests depend.

To test for non-linearity in the income effect, I also tried a quadratic relationship by introducing the log of GNP per capita squared. But in this multivariate context, when secondary education enrolment rates are included, it was not significant. There are also theoretical objections to excluding the unexplained factors captured by the log of GNP per capita squared. I also sorted by countries below and above $3,000 per year per capita income. But this also did not lead to significantly different results.

Major Determinants of Democratization

The most significant determinants of democratization as shown in Model 1, after dropping other potential determinants for which there was not clear evidence, therefore include:

Higher per capita income, one index of industrialization, the breakdown of rural elites, and the greater capacity for citizen exercise of political rights. Education contributes to democratization indirectly through these contributions to economic growth and to falling population growth rates. This effect is illustrated by the straight line in Figure 7.1.

Higher secondary education enrolments after a 12-year lag. Growing working and middle classes with more wide-scale participation in the growth process are likely to be desirous of defending hard-won individual rights, as indicated by the public opinion surveys in Latin America quoted above. Education also facilitates their self-organization, as stressed by Huber *et al.* (1993: 83). Education is also highly correlated with wider exposure to communications media. This effect is illustrated by the extent to which the curved line is above the straight line in Figure 7.1.

Lower military expenditure, as a per cent of total government expenditure. Perhaps with a smaller military, the capacity for military take-overs is reduced. With growing democracy, it is possible that the need for use of the military for internal authoritarian rule also subsides. The military also competes for public funds: in Figure 7.1, Singapore and Thailand both have relatively lower secondary education enrolment rates and a larger military.

The R^2 are quite respectable for cross-section data, and the t-statistics are highly significant, with the exception of the log of per capita income, which nonetheless reaches the 10% level of significance. It is noted at the bottom of Table 7.1 that the only place there is significant multicollinearity is between secondary education enrolment rates and per capita GNP. If secondary education is dropped, the log of per capita income becomes the most highly significant determinant.

Illustrative Discussion of these Determinants

As can be seen in Figure 7.1, the poorest countries worldwide start from an agrarian base with traditional forms of rule. *Those with per capita incomes below about $600 per year are normally authoritarian.* The economic lives of the farmers, as well as their political rights, are heavily influenced by the landlords, military budgets are often relatively large, and democracy is almost never observed to occur. Most of the countries of Sub-Saharan Africa, and some in Asia, are still in this range, with India and some nearby countries that also have a British heritage the notable exceptions. In the Caribbean, Haiti was in this range until very recently. China is at the top end of this range, but it has a relatively high secondary education enrolment rate, which was 54 per cent for females and 60 per cent for males in 1993 (World Bank, 1997: 226). After a lag of 12 years or so it will be interesting to see what happens in the years that follow.

Above about $600 and up to $3,000 per year, as shown in Figure 7.1, *there is a zone of transition*, with a growing middle class. These persons participate in the growth of earnings aided by the spread of mass basic education. I suggest that the traditional forms of rule become increasingly difficult to maintain.

Between $3,000 and $10,000 per year, as shown in Figure 7.1, *there is a flat range during continued industrialization*. It is characterized by substantial democratization, but further improvement is slow and erratic. Examples in Latin America of countries approaching this range include Argentina and Venezuela, as suggested at the beginning of this chapter.

Above $10,000 per year, democracy is extremely likely. This group includes the OECD European nations, Canada, the United States, Australia, New Zealand, and Japan, and is associated with high degrees of political stability, considered later. Singapore has more limited political and civil rights (and a larger military) and is the sole exception.

With respect to areas that were part of the former Soviet Union, Russia, the Ukraine, the Kyrgyz Republic, and Moldova are currently rated by Freedom House as 'partly free', 3 or 4 on my scale in Figure 7.1. They are in a zone of transition, somewhat delayed by a long history of authoritarianism and domination by the military. Further south, the lower per capita income, newly independent nations of Uzbekistan, Tajikistan, Turkmenistan, and Kazakhstan are all listed as 'not free', or 1 to 2.5 on the scale in Figure 7.1.

In addition to the net effects on democratization of the growth of per capita income and expansion of education, there is a highly significant negative relationship between militarization and meaningful democracy. This result is consistent with a number of multivariate studies surveyed by Diamond (1992: 466–7) which also find a negative effect of military expenditure on the chances for democracy.

In conclusion, I suggest that the dependence of democratization on the growth of per capita income is very robust. But the expansion of secondary education at the leading edge of this not only contributes to growth indirectly, but also makes a robust direct contribution to democratization. This is a social-benefit externality.

Human Rights

Human rights are defined as the protection of individual rights from arbitrary state action.

The Dimensions of Human Rights

Human rights are also measured by the Freedom House Index (1995: 536–7) in this case called Civil Liberties as indicated in the introduction to this chapter. We again invert the scale, so that 7 is the highest degree of civil liberties, and 1 the lowest.

The concept of human rights, and the index, includes ratings for the degree of:

- freedom of the press;
- freedom of assembly;
- an independent judiciary, so that there is no imprisonment without due process;
- free trade unions and religious institutions;
- gender equity;
- limited government corruption; and
- equal educational opportunity.

The composite index of human rights measured in this way is positively correlated with democratization. But they do not measure the same thing.

As with democratization, periods of significant civil liberties and human rights are rare indeed for countries in the zone of transition. In Latin America, for example, periods of clear civil liberties until recently were limited to:

Argentina (1912–30, 1946–51 and 1973–6),
Uruguay (1919–33 and 1942–73),
Chile (1970–3),
Bolivia (1952–64),
Venezuela (1945–8, and 1968–93), and
Costa Rica (all years),

according to Rueschmeyer, Stephens, and Stephens (1992: 305). The relative infrequency of clear democracy and well-protected civil liberties in Latin America prior to 1975, and China and Indonesia at present reflect the fact that these nations have been in the $600–$3,000 per capita income range, which is the zone of transition, and the fact that access to secondary education has been quite limited. However, since 1975, there has been a significant number of countries, especially in Latin America, that have moved dramatically toward full democratization and greater civil liberties.

Major Determinants of Human Rights

An analysis of influences on the expansion of human rights reveals the following are the major determinants, as shown in Table 7.2. The definition of all variables, data sources, and explanation of the reason for the lags are the same as those given for Equation (7.1) above. Other variables tested will be discussed shortly.

Higher Per Capita Income, lagged 7 years ($t = 2.01$).
Higher Secondary Education Enrolment Rates, lagged 12 years. Since this is correlated with per capita income and democratization (as shown at the bottom of Table 7.2), its standard error is larger and its t-statistic ($t = 1.39$) is lower.
Lower Military Expenditure as a per cent of total government expenditure ($t = -3.14$). This negative effect on human rights persists even after controlling for democratization, a relationship which may be particularly pertinent in Latin America given the relative lack of experience and commitment to rule by law there. It suggests that the sale and export of US arms is unlikely to be helpful to civil rights.
Democratization. The inference from the logic of the theory is that this is a causal influence on improved human rights. The lack of human rights may also be an important motivation for democratization as well. In any event, the effect is very highly significant ($t = 11.89$), to the point that it is somewhat surprising that the other explanatory variables are also highly significant.

Taken together, these four determinants explain 86% of the total variation in human rights. This is quite a remarkable explanation for cross-section data. The

Table 7.2 Determinants of Human Rights (dependent variable: *HR* = human rights, as measured by the Freedom House Index of Civil Liberties, inverted; *t*-statistics in parentheses)

	Model 1		Model 2	
	Coefficient	Significance level	Coefficient	Significance level
Per capita income	0.194		0.164	
(*In* GNPPC$_{-7}$)	(2.01)	0.048	(1.17)	0.250
Secondary education	0.006			
GER2$_{-12}$	(1.39)	0.166		
LF2$_{-5}$			0.209	
			(0.952)	0.349
Military expenditure	−0.030		−0.033	
(*MILX*$_{-1}$)	(−3.13)	0.002	(−1.49)	0.145
Democratization	0.588		0.632	
(*D*)	(11.88)	0.0001	(8.81)	0.00001
Constant	2.83		7.48	
	(4.48)	0.0001	(8.92)	0.00001
Adjusted R^2	0.87		0.87	
n	75		34	
F	119.4	0.0001	59.13	0.0001
Standard error of the estimate		0.654		0.638

Zero-Order Correlation Matrix, Model 1

	In GNPPC$_{-7}$	*MILX*$_{-1}$	GER2$_{-12}$	*D*
In GNPPC$_{-7}$	1.00			
MILX$_{-1}$	0.087	1.00		
GER2$_{-12}$	0.787	−0.073	1.00	
D	0.482	−0.419	0.577	1.000

simple correlations among the explanatory variables are low (see Table 7.2) except between secondary education and per capita income 5 years later. It is most logically a situation where each and both are contributing to human rights. Democratization is also correlated with each of these. But there are significant effects on human rights from income and education above and beyond the effects of democratization. The multicollinearity does not necessarily bias the coefficients but it does raise the standard errors, and hence lower the *t*-statistics.

Again, other explanatory variables were tried and performed less effectively. The human capital stock measures of secondary education in the labour force, *LF2* in Model 2 of Table 7.2, in the presence of democratization are once again far less significant than secondary enrolments were in the same sample, and also in Model 1. The urbanization and communications variables performed as expected but were not significant when the variables shown were included. However, their effects are once more embodied in the influences of the education variable and the democratization variable.

Human Rights Patterns Worldwide

Figure 7.2 illustrates the worldwide pattern of human rights. I have computed regional means for the countries included in my analysis, shown by triangles on Figure 7.2. Sub-Saharan African nations are low, with a mean of 3.5 or 'partly free' by the Freedom House ratings. The OECD is the highest. But it is interesting that East Asia excluding China is below the level that might be expected at their currently relatively high level of per capita income and education, pulled down by Singapore, Cambodia, and Indonesia. The Latin American average is somewhat higher than might be expected. The individual scatter dots illustrating primarily these transition countries in Latin America and the Caribbean show that Costa Rica and Trinidad have well-developed nationwide standards of human rights, and that Panama, Chile, Jamaica, and Uruguay are very close. India is also a shining example in the sense of being well above what might otherwise be expected at its level of development, whereas in relation to other Latin American countries, Guatemala and Peru lag behind. Human rights in Haiti have improved substantially, but it is too early to know if this is permanent.

But the regressions, and the curved line in Figure 7.2, both suggest that the progress of human rights is *also* dependent on democratization, which in turn is dependent on prior secondary education. This is consistent with the conclusion that there are very significant social-benefit externalities from education which have a direct impact on democratization and largely through this on human rights. It is also consistent with my major theme of endogenous development.

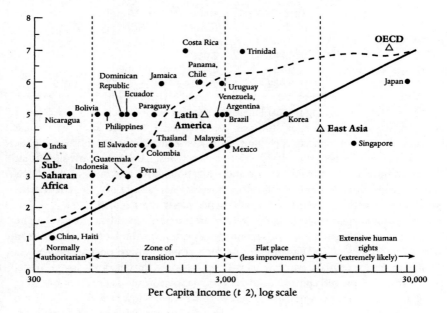

Figure 7.2 Human rights as a function of per capita income (f (education))

Political Stability

Democratization and human rights are important, but so is the stability of the political and economic system. This is necessary for the preservation of fragile democracies as well as the continuation of stable economic growth and development. This problem of instability and periodic throwbacks to authoritarianism following military coups has been particularly acute in Latin America and Africa; Mjumdar and Cambodia offer other examples.

The Concept of Political Stability

The measure of political stability used is that published regularly by Political Risk Services in the 'International Country Risk Guide'. (Coplin *et al.*, various years). It tends to reflect economic risk to some extent as well as political risk, since the latter is sometimes the source of the former. A risk assessment is made, based on the following 13 components (ibid., 1995: 41–2):

Economic expectations vs. reality	12 points
Economic planning failures	12
Political leadership	12
External conflict	10
Corruption	6
Military in politics	6
Organized religion in politics	6
Law and rule by law	6
Racial and ethnic tensions	6
Political terrorism	6
Civil war	6
Political party development	6
Quality of the bureaucracy	6
Maximum possible rating	100 points

The higher the rating, the lower the risk, or the higher the political stability, so that the risk rating for a particular country can be estimated from the following broad categories:

70–100 points	Very high political stability (low risk)
60–70 points	Moderate political stability
50–60 points	Low political stability
0–50 points	Political instability (high risk)

When financial risk (e.g., risk of loan default or expropriation) and economic risk (e.g., risk of inflation or devaluation) is included, a composite risk index is also calculated. These other measures of financial risk carry only half the weight of political risk in the composite risk index.

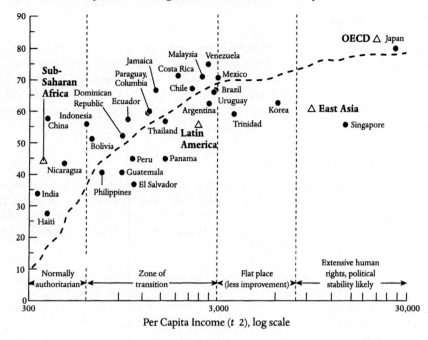

Figure 7.3 Political stability and per capita income

Perhaps not surprisingly, Sub-Saharan African nations tend to fall in the lowest political stability (i.e., highest-risk) category, as shown by the regional averages in Figure 7.3. Compared with the US and Sweden, rated at 81 in 1995, which is typical of the OECD member nations, Liberia is 29, Sierra Leone 27, Somalia 21, and Zaïre 33, all well below the Sub-Saharan average of 45 (Coplin *et al.*, 1995: 57–8). South Africa on the other hand is at 74, and Botswana, the fastest-growing economy on the continent, is at 73.

Latin American and Caribbean nations are on average now more politically stable, but fall into the high-risk and moderate-risk categories despite the decline of political instability in the last decade. Several nations with very high or high political risk as recently as 1993 have now moved toward somewhat greater stability (i.e., to the high or moderate-risk categories). These include Haiti (28 to 50), El Salvador (38 to 65), Guatemala (40 to 57), Panama (48 to 59), Nicaragua (42 to 63), and even Peru (45 to 52). But in others there has been some decrease in political stability, such as Venezuela (72 to 66), Mexico (70 to 64), and Brazil (70 to 64). Costa Rica has remained very stable throughout (74). Although there has been this short-term movement, it should be stressed that the regressions and the co-efficients to be used in the interactive model seek to capture primarily the longer-term basic trends.

Major Determinants of Political Stability

Determinants of political stability as shown in Table 7.3 have all been defined previously under Equation (7.1) above, where sources are given and the reasons for the lags explained, except for:

Table 7.3 Determinants of Political Stability (dependent variable: PS = political stability, as measured by Coplin *et al.*, 1997; t-statistics in parentheses)

	Model 1 Coefficient	Model 2 Coefficient	Model 3 Coefficient
Per capita income *In* (GNPPC$_{-7}$)	0.567 (5.29)	7.18 (5.54)	
GNPPC $_{-1}$			0.00025 (6.08)
Primary education (GER1$_{-12}$)	0.213 (3.32)		
Secondary education (GER2$_{-20}$)			0.0793 (1.62)
Military expenditure (MILX$_{-1}$)	−0.259 (−1.75)	−0.823 (−2.07)	−0.764 (−2.32)
Communications (COM$_{-2}$)	0.0006 (3.00)	0.00008 (1.84)	
Democratization (D)			0.965 (1.82)
Social security expenditure (SSX)	0.274 (2.27)	0.017 (0.072)	
Urbanization (URB$_{-1}$)	−0.146 (−1.95)	−0.075 (−0.519)	
Constant			48.69 (8.93)
Adjusted R^2	0.98	0.98	0.46
n	62	62	77
F	537.14	210.45	
Standard error of the estimate	0.654	9.16	

Zero-Order Correlation Matrix, Model 1

	In GNPPC$_{-7}$	MILX$_{-1}$	GER1$_{-12}$	SSX$_1$	COM	URB$_{-3}$	GER2$_{-12}$
In GNPPC$_{-7}$	1.00						
MILX$_{-1}$	−0.33	1.00					
GER1$_{-12}$	0.20	−0.18	1.00				
SSX$_{-1}$	0.68	−0.40	0.22	1.00			
COM	0.75	−0.13	0.14	0.59	1.00		
URB$_{-3}$	0.72	−0.13	0.31	0.67	0.59	1.00	
GER2$_{-12}$	0.85	−0.07	n.a.	0.72	0.50	0.75	1.00

n.a. = not available

COM   communications index: an unweighted average of newsprint consumption
      in kilograms per 1,000 persons and radios per 1,000 persons, lagged 2 years,
      from UNDP (1994: 160–1, 193);

SSX   social security expenditures as a per cent of the government budget (ibid.:
      164–5, 196);

URB   urbanization, the per cent of the population living in urban areas, lagged
      one year, from World Bank, *World Development Report* (1997: 230–1).

Social security expenditures are not conducive to economic growth directly but
can be stabilizing, whereas urbanization is expected to be destabilizing. The incidence of poverty did not prove to be significant. The constant was insignificant and
was dropped in Models 1 and 2. All regressions are corrected for heteroscedasticity.

The communication, secondary education, social security, and urbanization
variables are highly correlated with one another, as shown below in Table 7.3. In
a sense communications and social security expenditures are acting as proxies for
secondary education, which becomes significant in this regression when they are
removed. They are likely to be part of the same dynamic related to interest in
the dissemination of ideas and the capacity of individuals to become earning,
productive, and urbanized citizens. The major determinants of political stability
empirically significant in Table 7.3 are:

Per capita income. This is associated with greater political stability after about a 7-
year lag. It is highly significant in Model 1 ($t = 5.29$) and, even when GER1 is
dropped, in Models 2 and 3, suggesting that economic growth after a lag contributes to more politically stable regimes.

Primary enrolment rates are, very interestingly, significantly associated with greater
political stability after a 12-year lag ($t = 3.32$).

Secondary education is also associated with greater political stability but at a lower
significance level ($t = 1.62$) when democratization is included.

Military expenditure as a per cent of the government budget is strongly destabilizing.
This effect is more significant when primary education is dropped in Models 2
($t = -2.07$) and 3 ($t = -2.32$).

Communications, measured as the circulation of books and newspaper media and
incidence of radios, is significant in Model 1 ($t = 3.0$). But it is correlated with
prior secondary education, as seen in the zero-order correlation matrix. It is less
significant when primary education is dropped (Model 2) and when secondary
education is added (Model 3).

Social security expenditure are stabilizing (Model 2) but the relation is not robust
(Model 3), and they are highly correlated with secondary education ($r = 0.72$ in
the zero-order correlation matrix).

Urbanization, after controlling for per capita income and primary education, is not
conducive to political stability ($t = -1.95$). Again, however, urbanization is reflecting more basic causal factors. Where economic development in the agricultural
sector and secondary education have not accompanied industrialization, persons

with less education gravitate to the largest cities, which is a destabilizing influence (evident in Karachi, Rio de Janeiro, Cairo, and Chicago for example). It is probably better if persons leaving farms have better education and skills.

Democratization is positively associated with political stability but at only the 90% confidence level ($t = 1.62$) when there are controls for both per capita income and secondary education (Model 3).

Although the total per cent of variation explained in Table 7.3 is highest in Models 1 and 2 (98%), I do not have a structural explanation for social security expenditures or urbanization and I think there may be some spurious correlation. So these are dropped and communications is replaced with secondary education, which gets at much the same thing and is likely to be the more basic causal factor. Model 3 will therefore be used in the complete model in Chapters 11 to 13.

Illustration of Stability Patterns

Figure 7.3 illustrated the long-term process of movement toward greater political stability in a worldwide context. The regional means, located by triangles on the scatter diagram, suggest that political stability is greater among nations in the Latin American region than in Sub-Saharan Africa, where it is very low. It is higher in East Asia, although events in Indonesia suggest a temporary exception there. Stability in all three of these developing regions is lower, however, than that in the democratic OECD member nations.

Generally the higher per capita income nations such as Argentina, Chile, Costa Rica, Brazil, Uruguay, Mexico, Venezuela, and South Korea tend to be more politically stable. This is especially true when there is extensive primary education, communications, a social security system, and democracy, and a relatively smaller military.

Conclusions

Externality-type benefits for individuals aiding household production of final satisfactions arise from the freedoms associated with democracy, human rights, and political and economic stability. I have sought to trace the extent to which these benefits can reasonably be attributed to education, in a sense the marginal product of education. When per capita income is controlled, some of these non-monetary returns occur directly, reflecting not just the contributions of engineering and vocational education, but also perhaps disproportionately the contributions of the humanities, law, and the social sciences to human well-being. However, there are also contributions of education to economic growth, which I conclude from the analysis in this chapter also has a very significant impact in determining long-run movements toward democracy, greater human rights, and greater political and economic stability.

In my structural approach, there are also interactions and feedback effects that must be taken into account. Democratization appears to be a particularly strong determinant of human rights, as well as of political stability in the long run. It does not seem to have strong feedback effects on economic growth directly, but instead affects economic growth indirectly through political stability and its significant influences, favouring a stable environment that facilitates higher rates of investment in physical capital.

Finally, the benefits of education discussed in this chapter, monetary and non-monetary, are available in society to be enjoyed by all. They are therefore not taken into account by parents and students when they make their decisions about how much to invest in education. By the standard economic efficiency criteria, these individuals will under-invest, and to this extent efficiency will not be achieved. Many of the benefits, furthermore, are enjoyed by future generations. These are therefore clear instances of not just monetary and non-monetary private returns to the investment made in education, but also of social-benefit externalities, potentially measured in the ways suggested here.

8 Poverty and Inequality

This chapter considers the major factors that contribute to rural poverty, urban poverty, and inequality in the distribution of income. It does so with the purpose of isolating the direct and indirect impacts of human resource development through education. The focus is on the longer-run trends, although education also cushions the impacts of cyclical fluctuations on unemployment and poverty for those who have advanced education. After the indirect as well as the direct impacts of education on poverty are collected, the results are then used in Chapters 12 and 13 in the interactive model of endogenous development.

Poverty and income inequality both continue to be very serious problems worldwide. Fifty-six per cent of the people in the countries of Sub-Saharan Africa in countries for which there is data, as stressed in Chapter 5, are currently living in absolute poverty, on less than US$1 a day. In the Latin American countries for which there are data, 31 per cent are living in absolute poverty on less than $1 a day. Poverty is even worse in South Asia, e.g., Nepal 53 per cent, India 52 per cent (World Bank, 1997: 214). This $1 a day is close to the common measure of absolute poverty based on the cost of a basket of consumption goods in each country that includes enough food to maintain minimum daily caloric requirements for minimal health.

Many of the most poverty-stricken countries also exhibit a high degree of income inequality relative to other regions of the world. As measured by the GINI coefficient for all countries for which data is available, total income inequality is the worst in Brazil (GINI = 63). But inequality is also extremely high in Honduras (53), Guatemala (60), Nicaragua (50), Zimbabwe (57), and Kenya (57) (World Bank, 1997: 222). Only about 2 per cent of the total national income accrues to the poorest 20 per cent of the population in these countries, whereas 62 to 67 per cent accrues to the top 20 per cent (ibid.).

Poverty is known to be reduced by high per capita economic growth: this is a very robust relationship, both in worldwide data (see Sen, 1995) and in Latin America (see Psacharopoulos et al., 1993: 71). However, income inequality responds to different factors. The evidence for the Kuznets inverted U curve that implies that inequality rises first as growth occurs during the early stages of industrialization has been very seriously questioned in recent years. On the basis of, in part, the evidence from East Asia, it has largely been replaced with the widespread considered opinion that whether this happens or not depends heavily on what policies are followed.

The new hypotheses to be explored here, and quantified in a way that enables them to be used within the interactive model, seek to explain how inequality can *rise* with growth as in Brazil, *fall* with fast growth as in the East Asian economies, and rise in the 1980s and 1990s as has been noted above for the OECD countries (where the data are much better). The achievement of 'humane growth' (McMahon and Geske, 1983: 22) or 'growth with equity' (World Bank, 1993a), both defined as growth with falling inequality, is hypothesized to depend primarily on the early extension of junior secondary education to the rural areas after high completion of primary education has been achieved.

There are, however, other factors that contribute to the reduction of poverty and inequality not unrelated to education. Human resource development through secondary education, for example, has been found by others to be important to development of a skilled labour force essential to an export-oriented growth policy (Wood, 1994; Ito and Krueger, 1995). Prior secondary education is also seen to be important to agriculture (World Bank, 1993c), where many of the lowest-income persons are. Policies relating to the extension of access to and completion of secondary education contribute to productivity but also, especially for women, contribute to the eventual reduction of population growth rates. Fertility and health effects of education were considered in Chapter 7, but because they have been challenged vigorously by Behrman in connection with the reduction of poverty (Behrman, 1991) and inequality (Behrman, 1997), these issues will be considered further below. I will begin by considering the role of education in the reduction of absolute poverty; then I will examine the relation of education to the reduction of inequality.

Poverty Reduction: The Conceptual Framework

Poverty reduction has an income distribution dimension, not just an efficiency dimension. That is, it often involves not just raising the income of lower-income groups, such as education for poor rural farmers, which the evidence suggests has a very high rate of return, therefore making a significant contribution to allocative efficiency. But targeted policies can also involve some income distribution impacts. For example, targeted education programmes that build rural schools, train teachers, and pay teachers enough that they will work in the poorest districts may also tax higher-income groups to make this possible. The questions of distributive justice this raises are reserved for the next section. Attention here is largely on the economic, growth-related or efficiency aspects of poverty reduction.

Beginning with Chenery *et al.* (1974), and continuing in the issue on 'Poverty' of the *World Development Report* (1980), the World Bank's primary emphasis has been on poverty alleviation. This may be in part because it does not involve the more controversial distributional issues affecting non-poor groups. In the last fifteen years, the focus of international policy discussions has shifted almost entirely to poverty reduction, with the notable exception of the World Bank's attention to 'Growth with Equity' in its *East Asian Miracle* (World Bank, 1993a).

The reduction of absolute poverty as distinct from inequality is well known to occur as the result of economic growth. As indicated in the introduction to this chapter, this is a very robust relationship. Economic growth in Indonesia brought 37.9 million people out of absolute poverty from 1972 to 1982, and a larger number out of poverty from 1985–95 (World Bank, 1993a: 26, 1997: 214), although with the 1998–9 crisis, many are falling back. Incomes at the bottom can easily increase with more production even though the distribution of income remains as unequal as before, or even becomes more unequal. This failure of inequality to fall as absolute poverty is reduced has not occurred, however, in the fast-growing countries of East Asia.

With respect to the extent to which this growth effect is attributable to education, it has been shown in Chapters 2–5 that this will vary by level of education, by the quantity of schooling and investment in it (which includes an element of quality), and by region. But this only addresses the monetary returns to education. These are set aside in this chapter by controlling for per capita GNP, or in some cases growth of per capita GNP. This is to isolate the net additional non-market returns to education in the form of poverty reduction.

Some of the poverty alleviation effects of education (and later effects on the reduction of inequality) are related to lower population growth rates. Lower population growth not only puts less stress on public resources for public health and public education, but is also related to lower fertility rates and better health, which result in fewer dependents in poverty, as was noted in Chapter 7. In the regressions concerned with absolute poverty below, the effects via health and net population growth rates will be shown, but then they will also be replaced by a reduced form which seeks to trace the net direct impacts of education and education policies on poverty reduction.

Behrman (1991) offers the opinion that the impacts of education on poverty are generally overstated, on the same grounds discussed in Behrman (1997), namely, that there are unobserved factors which are correlated with the disturbances, such as ability, family factors, and community effects, that bias (upward) the education coefficients as they are used to estimate the true net marginal products of education. In his earlier paper concerned with the impacts of education on poverty he focuses on education's effect on health, mortality, and medical services (the latter are part of the monetary returns). We addressed this in Chapter 7 using a structural approach that addresses their interaction at different levels of development.

It takes different kinds of data, and data at the microeconomic level, to address the kinds of unobserved ability, family factors, and community effects identified by Behrman. However, education is included among the community effects that are externalities, both monetary and non-monetary, that I explicitly wish to include throughout this book and which his controls for community effects (which would include education in the environment, democracy, etc.) are likely to exclude. Similarly, controls for family factors will exclude the effects of parents' education, an intergenerational effect of education that is dramatically related to poverty. This intergenerational effect perhaps should not be excluded when the interest is in the impact of human capital production *by families* on economic development. There is also extensive research at the microeconomic level that provides a basis for the assumption on which my measures of the net benefits of education rest, namely that the upward bias in the estimates from unobserved ability, family factors, and remaining community effects is approximately cancelled out by the downward bias in the estimates that is caused by errors in measurement of the education variable. Educational attainment is often self-reported, and more important for the estimates reported in this book, enrolment rates normally reflect quantity and not quality. So education inputs are measured with error.

Specifically, there is now extensive research with genetically identical twins that is best able to control rigorously for ability, for family factors, and to some extent for the variation in community effects in the early years. Ashenfelter (the editor of *American Economic Review*) and Rouse (at Princeton), in particular, using a large sample of about 1,000 identical twins, find that the omitted-variable bias leads to about a 31% overestimate of the true returns to education (Ashenfelter and Rouse, 1998). There are many other studies of non-identical twins, siblings, father–son pairs, etc. that have been reviewed by Ashenfelter and Rouse (1997, 1998) and by Carnoy (1997), but none can control in such a rigorous fashion for ability and family factors as those studies based on individuals who have genetically identical IQs and other genetically and family-based personality traits.

At the same time there has been a wave of recent research that estimates the bias due to measurement error, recently surveyed by Carnoy (1997). Ashenfelter and Krueger (1994), using an earlier smaller sample of about 250 identical twins, estimate that this leads to about a 30% underestimate of the true returns to education, and Ashenfelter and Rouse (1998) to a 28% underestimate using their larger recent sample, again almost completely offsetting the ability bias. Other studies are consistent with this, as mentioned below. There are two main sources of measurement error in the education variable:

1. The quantity of schooling does not normally reflect quality. Since there is clearly a return to quality, as shown in studies by Behrman *et al.* (1983, 1997: 74–6), this would suggest that using the number of years of schooling, as in the gross enrolment rates used frequently in this book, would result in *underestimates* of the true return to investment in both the quantity and quality of human capital formation through education. In a special case that is perhaps an exception (see Carnoy, 1997), Behrman and Birdsall (1983) report that for a Brazilian sample (a place where rural school quality is low, as shown by Hanushek, Gomes-Neto, and Harbison, 1994), better school quality might induce proportionately more schooling attainment, in which case the measurement bias could run in the other direction.

2. Self-reported education is not reported accurately. Most researchers estimate this source of error to account for about 8–10% of the true schooling variance. This includes Behrman, Rosenzweig, and Taubman (1994, 1996), who in the earlier NAS–NRC study find it to be 8% but in the later study find it to be only 5.9%.

The preponderance of studies, reviewed by Carnoy (1997), going back to the well-known ones by Griliches and Mason (1988) and Griliches (1977) and including Becker (1993), reach conclusions consistent with the assumption on which the estimates in this book of the returns to education are based. To quote Ashenfelter and Krueger (1994: 1172), 'The results of our study, like the results of many of these studies, suggest that unobserved factors do not cause an upward bias in the simple estimates of the returns to schooling.' When interpreting this as also applying to the impacts of education on outcomes like better health and poverty reduction, this assumes that the relation of ability, family factors, and measurement errors to these non-market outcomes is similar to that on earnings. But there appear to be no studies of the impacts of measurement error in schooling attainment on these other non-market outcomes. In their absence, the assumption that they are similar would seem to be a reasonable first approximation.

Rural Poverty

The poor are primarily rural in developing countries, and often landless labourers. So this is perhaps the most important regression. These persons have been migrating to urban areas, especially in places like Pakistan and Brazil. In recent years Brazil has seen the largest increase in urban poverty in the Western Hemisphere.

Table 8.1 Determinants of Rural Poverty (*t*-statistics in parentheses)

	Model 1	Model 2	Model 3	Model 4
Growth of GNP per capita	−2.32		−3.20	
($y - n$), last 12-year average	(−1.37)		(−2.12)	
Per capita GNP (*ln* GNPPC)		−5.60		−0.870
		(−0.79)		(−2.00)
Primary enrolment ($GER1_{-20}$)	−0.11	−0.04	−0.212	
	(−0.64)	(−0.18)	(−1.20)	
Secondary enrolment ($GER2_{-20}$)	−1.77	−1.41	−0.467	
	(−3.16)	(−2.45)	(−1.04)	
Higher education enrolment	4.09	3.40	1.46	
($GER3_{-20}$)	(3.00)	(2.39)	(1.11)	
Military expenditure ($MILX_{-1}$)	0.65	0.63		
	(1.01)	(0.88)		
Human capital stock (*LF2*)				−21.75
				(−1.83)
Physical capital ($PHYSK_{-5}$)				8.47
				(2.08)
Democratization (*D*)				6.54
				(2.77)
Constant	69.39	90.59	73.98	53.90
	(5.87)	(2.68)	(8.25)	(3.15)
n	25	27	40	22
R^2	0.57	0.45	0.30	0.54
F	4.96	3.46	3.80	4.99
Significance	0.004	0.019	0.011	0.007
Standard error of estimate	15.01	17.11	20.15	17.10

Defining rural poverty as the per cent of rural households with incomes below the poverty level, the major determinants that I was able to isolate are shown in Table 8.1. The variables in Models 1–4 are defined briefly there, and the data sources and reasons for the lags are the same as those given in the preceding chapter. The dependent variable, rural poverty (*POVR*), is defined as the per cent of rural households with income below the poverty level in 1992, from World Bank (1996*c*), supplemented by UNDP (1994).

Per capita GNP is included in Model 2, where it is not significant when the education variables are included! It is also included in Model 4, where it is significant and has the expected sign: poverty is reduced at higher levels of average per capita income world-wide, as discussed above, but the expansion of basic education that reaches the lower rural income groups would appear to be a very major contributing factor.

Since per capita income was not significant in Model 2, it was dropped in Models 1 and 3, where all education enrolment rates are retained and GNPPC is replaced with the rate of growth of GNP. Now faster-growing countries are experiencing the lower levels of rural poverty, as is illustrated in Figure 8.1. There it can be seen that rural poverty remains very high in Jamaica, Brazil, and Bolivia in 1995, for example, but is remarkably low in China and South Korea. The slowest-growing countries are those in Sub-Saharan Africa (not shown), where in some cases growth has been negative and rural poverty is often the highest. But in many of these African nations artificially high exchange rates have burdened the rural sector and secondary education has not been expanded to the rural areas, a strategy that has not worked well for either growth or rural poverty reduction.

Increases in both primary and secondary enrolments after a 20-year lag are both associated with the reduction of rural poverty. Of the two, secondary enrolments are by far the most significant, largely because in many countries nearly universal primary enrolments had already been achieved.

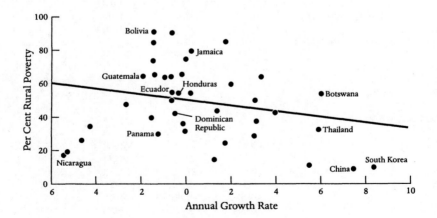

Figure 8.1 Rural poverty and economic growth

Higher education enrolments are associated with greater rural poverty. This is as expected and not surprising, since the rural poor do not have access to higher education and in fact are often taxed to pay for the nearly free tuition and food and housing subsidies that benefit the children of the elite. Greater rates of enrolment in higher education accompanied by poor quality were also found not to contribute to economic growth in any of the developing country regions in Chapters 2–5 above, although investment that raises quality (and includes study abroad and some R&D) was more often found to be positive and significant.

Military expenditure as a per cent of the government budget is associated with higher rural poverty, which is not surprising since it usually competes with rural schools for central governments' resources. But it is not significant, and when it is dropped as in Model 3, which because of data availability allows a larger sample size (which then is not strictly comparable), growth and primary education become relatively more significant.

Model 4 in Table 8.1 brings out some different and interesting effects. Education, measured here as the secondary-level human capital stocks in the labour force (*LF2*), is still associated with reduced rural poverty. Although higher per capita income is associated with less poverty, democratization is not. This is likely to be because many of the socialist command economies moved rigorously to reduce rural poverty (e.g., Nicaragua, China), but also because democratization often does not occur until the ruling elites recognize that their economic interests can be protected, as indicated in Chapter 7. And high rates of investment in physical capital are associated with more rural poverty, conceivably when the rural economy is drained to provide the necessary capital and because physical capital substitutes for raw unimproved labour.

Urban Poverty

Similar results are found for the per cent of urban households with income below the poverty level. Data sources are the same as above for this dependent variable (i.e., World Bank, 1996*b* and UNDP, 1995) and the other variables in Table 8.2. The model in Table 8.2 is the same as Model 3 in Table 8.1, with urban poverty now dependent.

Table 8.2 reveals that higher enrolment rates at both primary and secondary levels are also associated with lower urban poverty rates. Their significance reaches the 90% level, but it does not reach the 95% level. Secondary education is somewhat less significant than primary, however, as it was for the larger sample size in Model 3 of Table 8.1 for rural poverty. Growth of real GNP per capita is associated with lower urban poverty. But again, larger higher education enrolments in Table 8.2 are related to higher urban poverty since those in urban poverty also generally do not have access to higher education.

This relation of higher growth rates to urban poverty reduction is illustrated in Figure 8.2. Again, Brazil, where secondary education has not been extended to many rural areas, has the highest level of urban poverty.

Table 8.2 Urban Poverty (*t*-statistics in parentheses)

Growth of GNP per capita ($y - n$), last 12-year average	-2.02 (-1.52)
Primary enrolments ($GER1_{-20}$)	-0.238 (-1.70)
Secondary enrolments ($GER2_{-20}$)	-0.494 (-1.02)
Higher education enrolments ($GER3_{-20}$)	2.34 (1.77)
Constant	55.55 (7.58)
n	40
R^2	0.289
F	3.56
Significance	0.015
Standard error of estimate	16.13

Zero-Order Correlations

	GROWTH	$GER1_{-20}$	$GER2_{-20}$	$GER3_{-20}$
GROWTH	1.00			
$GER1_{-20}$	0.31	1.00		
$GER2_{-20}$	0.17	0.56	1.00	
$GER3_{-20}$	0.08	0.54	0.82	1.00

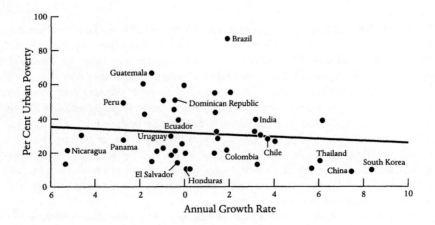

Figure 8.2 Urban poverty and economic growth

Income Inequality

The reduction of inequality does respond to appropriate human resource development policies. Distribution effects can be measured objectively, but changes in policy related to them contain political and normative elements.

The Conceptual Framework for Measurement

The main hypothesis that I seek to test is that the reduction of inequality does respond to rapid human capital accumulation policies, as advocated by Chenery *et al.* (1974) some 25 years ago. Land reform also undoubtedly has a role, as they indicate. But the focus here is on measuring the net contribution of education and related aspects of human resource development.

That is, the inverted Kuznets ∪ curve, which is sketched in Figure 8.3, where inequality is measured by the vertical axis, need not, and perhaps even does not, prevail when human capital accumulation policies are pursued *in place of* the unspecified factors captured by the income-squared term in the Kuznets inverted ∪ curve. That is, the inverted Kuznets ∪ suggests that as per capita income grows, inequality rises at first, as shown in Figure 8.3 for Brazil, as well as for Mexico and Argentina. Then, as economic development continues, income inequality falls. Kuznets (1955) originally suggested that since property income, composed of rent, interest, and profits, is more unequally distributed than earnings from human capital, as development occurs the latter eventually becomes proportionately more important relative to land rent and other income from property so that the average inequality in income which includes both eventually falls.

Although the latter scenario may well be true, the increase in inequality as industrialization begins is not inevitable. This has been demonstrated by the nations of East Asia, who have instead followed a path of rising per capita income, with fast growth as industrialization began accompanied by *falling inequality*. This straight-line, downward-sloping path is illustrated in Figure 8.3, along which lie Malaysia, Taiwan, South Korea, and Singapore. This has also been typical of Taiwan, and appears to be the path chosen more recently by Thailand and Indonesia. These countries demonstrate rather dramatically that there is not a trade-off between growth and equity—the two can and successfully do go hand in hand.

A second strong qualification to the Kuznets inverted ∪ curve, which follows in part from the above, is that it is not statistically robust when human capital investments are taken into account. Fishlow (1996) has recently surveyed the extensive literature on the Kuznets ∪ curve, but also presents his own regressions. Typical of this literature, he reports a significant predicted parabolic relationship with income in *GINI* coefficient regressions by Milanovic (1994) *when Asia is removed* by means of a dummy variable for Asia and *when secondary education is not included*. He then reports his own regressions that do *include average secondary education enrolments* over the preceding 25 years. They show that the income-squared term is then never significant and that its negative sign is not robust

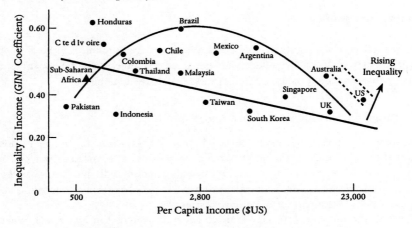

Figure 8.3 Inequality as a function of income per capita

(Fishlow, 1996: 29). I also estimated the Kuznets inverted U curve, this time with only *ln*GNPPC and *ln*GNPPC^2 included in the regression and nothing else, using the same data to be shown in Table 8.3, and got *t*-statistics of only 0.33 and −0.35 respectively, for example. There are of course other factors that also contribute to the reduction of inequality, such as land reform (see Fishlow, 1996: 29–30) and targeted institutional policies designed to reduce poverty, such as low-cost credit for poor farmers (e.g., Besley, 1997). But many of these policies are supported by the expansion of secondary education, such as the re-education of the children of farmers and the expansion of human-capital-intensive exports. As will be shown below, the rapid expansion of secondary education to the rural areas, which is also related to lower population growth rates, avoids the inverted Kuznets U curve's non-linear temporary increase in inequality as development occurs.

A second aspect of the conceptual framework as it relates to recent research on the distribution of earnings and of income in the advanced OECD countries requires comment. Since 1980, inequality in earnings, in personal income, and in disposable income has increased considerably in the United States and the United Kingdom, and to a lesser extent in almost all the other OECD countries, as shown in a recent extensive survey by Gottschalk and Smeeding (1997). This is as suggested by the dashed lines and arrow in Figure 8.3 indicating an upward shift in the hypothetical Kuznets U curve. Gottschalk and Smeeding conclude, as did Levy and Murnane (1992) earlier for the US, that the primary source of this is the increased earnings inequality among men related to the increasing demand for more educated and skilled workers. The effects of trade and increased competition of low-skill workers with low-skill workers in poorer countries have been contributing factors, as have regressive tax changes and transfer payment cuts, especially in the US and the UK, that have affected the after-tax and after-transfer-payment disposable income distributions. But as Gottschalk and Smeeding show, it is the greater inequality of *earnings* related to *differences in education among males* that have passed through to increases in the inequality of personal incomes and of disposable income that accounts for most of the difference.

This point is addressed further by Sullivan and Smeeding (1997), using a sample of OECD nations, as it relates to inequality of *earnings* as a function of education. Sullivan and Smeeding find that increases in what can be interpreted as roughly the average level of educational attainment does not reduce inequality of *earnings*. This is not inconsistent with Kuznets' rationale for the declining slope on the latter part of the Kuznets ∪ curve, because it relates only to shorter ranges of time (1989–94) and because it relates to the distribution of earnings and not the distribution of income.

The new Sullivan–Smeeding findings are also not inconsistent with the education effects on inequality to be discussed below, and as developed further by McMahon (1997a). Briefly, it is because, as is typical of other recent work in the same vein, these and other recent studies of the relation of education to inequality clean the data by removing part-time workers, younger workers, ageing workers, and the unemployed from the data. All of these are controls that operate to remove major sources of earnings inequality, such as health and employability, that depend especially heavily on education. These effects are discussed in the survey by Greenwood (1997). This is also because the education effects discussed below relate more directly to the *extension of access* to education to lower-income groups and not just increases in average educational attainment, which includes higher education that tends to increase inequality. This extension of access to basic education is what is happening primarily in the developing world. Increases in average levels of education, even at the primary and secondary level, that preserve the same degree of inequality in access and the same unequal quality among school districts cannot be expected to reduce the inequality of earnings. This point will be considered further in connection with discussion of the democratization variable below.

Empirical Determinants of Inequality

Table 8.3 shows the determinants of inequality in income distribution, most of which are significant at the 95 per cent level of confidence, but some at only the 90 per cent level. All variables have been defined previously and sources given except the dependent variable, *GINI* = the degree of income inequality, from World Bank (1997: 222).

Models 1 and 2 both show that reduced inequality is associated with faster growth of GNP per capita, as indicated earlier, even after controlling for education and population growth. This effect is significant in Model 1 at the 95 per cent confidence level, but does not quite reach this level of significance in Model 2.

Models 1 and 2 also show that the expansion of secondary education after a 20-year lag makes a significant net additional contribution to the reduction of inequality, even after controlling for net population growth. Model 1 indicates that

Table 8.3 Income Inequality (dependent variable: *GINI*; *t*-statistics in parentheses)

	Model 1	Model 2	Model 3	Model 4
Growth of GNP per capita	−0.011	−0.011		
($y - n$), last 12-year average	(−1.96)	(−1.76)		
Primary enrolments ($GER1_{-20}$)	0.0008			
	(1.36)			
Secondary enrolments ($GER2_{-20}$)	−0.001	−0.001		
	(−1.41)	(−1.94)		
Human capital stock (*LF2*)				−.067
				(−3.17)
Population growth (*POPGRO*)	0.037	0.034	0.058	0.034
	(1.96)	(1.79)	(4.69)	(1.40)
Physical capital/GNP (*K*/GNP)				55622
				(3.96)
Democratization (*D*)				0.018
				(1.79)
Constant	0.357	0.419	0.329	0.212
		(6.63)	(13.36)	(1.99)
(*n*)	42	42	30	21
R^2	0.42	0.384	0.44	0.68
Standard error of estimate	0.074	0.074	0.061	0.064

Zero-Order Correlations, Models 1 and 2

	GINI	GROWTH	$GER1_{-20}$	$GER2_{-20}$	POPGRO
GROWTH	−0.347	1.00			
$GER1_{-20}$	−0.249	0.226	1.00		
$GER2_{-20}$	−0.513	0.172	0.638	1.00	
POPGRO	0.565	−0.228	−0.563	−0.776	1.00

Zero-Order Correlations, Model 4

	D	K/Y	LF2	POPGRO
D	1.00			
K/Y	0.091	1.00		
LF2	0.655	0.166	1.00	
POPGRO	−0.714	−0.126	−0.747	1.00

primary education alone does not contribute with enough significance to the alleviation of inequality, although it can of course contribute to poverty reduction through economic growth. It is also needed as a basis if secondary education is to be expanded. Primary education is provided in villages throughout Africa, for example, but secondary education differences result in inequality since secondary education is available essentially only to those in the cities. This conclusion about the importance of the expansion of secondary education worldwide is consistent with the one reached by Knight and Sabot (1990) using microeconomic data and comparing the effects of secondary education in Kenya, where it was expanded, vs. Tanzania, where it was not.

Higher population growth rates are consistently related to greater inequality in Models 1–4. Population growth is endogenous in the complete model of endogenous development in Chapter 12 and is another way the secondary education of females operates to reduce inequality (see Chapter 6).

For effects on inequality, Model 2 is used in the complete model, and for the effects on rural and urban poverty, Model 3 from Table 8.1 and Model 1 from Table 8.2 are used; all three of these models have the larger sample size. However, Model 3 demonstrates the robustness of lower population growth rates as a determinant of reduced inequality even when they are taken in isolation. Model 4 shows that higher proportions of the labour force with secondary education are still very significantly related to reduced inequality, although the sample size is smaller. It also shows, as suggested above, that higher degrees of democratization after controlling for secondary education and for physical capital stocks are *not* related to reduced inequality. Democratization is *not* related to reduction in inequality. This is discussed further in the next section. As discussed in Chapter 7, democratization may not proceed until after the ruling elites are assured that their economic interests will be protected.

Distributive Justice

'Growth with equity' (World Bank, 1993) or 'humane growth' (McMahon and Geske, 1982: 22) is economic growth accompanied by the reduction of income inequality. Externalities are in principle part of efficiency considerations, not equity, although there can of course be some separate distributional impacts from particular externalities. The terms 'equity' and 'humane' involve normative value judgements that are outside the scope of pure economics and rooted instead in religious and philosophical values. This 'growth with equity' has occurred in East Asia, but also more broadly over time as OECD countries have moved from the low per capita income pre-industrialization stage to their current situation, where relative inequality is lower. In the OECD nations absolute earnings and absolute income differentials are larger, and more recent trends since 1980, especially in the US and UK, indicate rising inequality (as documented in Gottschalk and Smeeding, 1997). But this does not contradict the broad overall pattern.

In Western societies distributive justice is dispensed by the courts, who therefore address these philosophical values, but this alone also suggests how purely distributive questions involve a high degree of conflict. More to the point, when one considers the distributive aspects of education budgets, these are decided in democratic societies by majority vote in representative legislative bodies. This inevitably leaves some unhappy. They are usually those farthest away from the median income and median taste levels. There are, however, log-rolling and distortions by controlling elites or powerful special-interest pressure groups that take care of some of these outlier preferences. But these in turn can then also give undue weight to individuals in these groups and subvert one-person one-vote democratic principles.

Examples of education budget allocations that have important income distribution implications in OECD countries are state foundation levels for children in the poorest US school districts, and efforts through the courts in several states to get school finance reform that improves equity among children. In some developing countries there is the building of schools and provision of teachers and textbooks in the poorest rural areas.[1]

Because of the conflict that is involved and the resistance by ruling elites, allocations to primarily distributive activities (which some have argued government should confine itself to) tend to be severely limited. The result is that within democratic systems, dramatic inequality in the quality of education between rich and poor districts persists. The empirical results presented in Table 8.3 are also consistent with this hypothesis that greater degrees of democratization do not reduce inequality.

Conclusions

Poverty-reducing education policies in rural areas often have a very high rate of return, higher than the resources used for other purposes, and therefore have an efficiency dimension. Poverty reduction responds most significantly to the expansion of secondary education after a lag, over and above its clear response to economic growth. It does not respond to democratization, nor does the reduction of inequality, in contrast to popular belief.

The reduction of income inequality, however, has a different rationale. Inequality is also reduced with faster economic growth and by the rapid expansion of secondary education, but also by slower population growth. But since redistribution of either benefits or costs usually conflicts with the interests of ruling elites, especially in economies where economic growth is slow, the redistributional aspects involving children incur opposition and are limited.

Poverty and inequality next become endogenous in the complete model of endogenous development. Under my assumptions about the measurement of education's true marginal product, they constitute two additional dimensions of education's net impact on human welfare.

Note

1. For example, see Prescott *et al.* (1993) for an extensive analysis of pricing of public services and the poor in Indonesia. See also Chap. 13 for further analysis of optimal distribution and of the political decision process involving education budgets.

9 The Environment

Destruction of the environment reduces human welfare, both in the present and in the future. True economic development includes using some of the fruits of growth to improve the preservation of forests, animal, fish, and bird wildlife, ecosystems, soils, and air and water quality. If the benefits of rising money incomes are offset by implicit costs reducing health and the quality of life due to pollution, and if forests, soils, and ecosystems are destroyed and natural resources depleted, this cannot be called true economic development. Clean air, clean water, and well-maintained forests, land, and natural and recreational resources are part of the improvements in welfare that economic growth and true development brings.

Economic growth in the past has sometimes been associated with severe degradation of the natural world. But this need not occur if appropriate policies are followed. There are indirect structural effects from education to be discussed that can be part of these policies at different stages of development so that they relate to the different sources of degradation at these different stages. Poverty, rapid population growth, and extractive-type exports, which are all affected by education, are important sources of pollution, deforestation, and destruction of wildlife in the poor countries, for example. In contrast, factory emissions associated with industrialization and auto emissions can be relatively more important sources of air pollution, global warming, and the destruction of forests and wilderness areas as development occurs. But growth provides the economic capacity to eliminate or reverse these strains on the environment.

It is seldom realized how important human resource development through education is to reducing and reversing these environmental strains. This is partly because the role of education has not been studied explicitly. The World Bank has come the closest in its special issue of the *World Development Report, 1992* devoted to 'Development and the Environment'. (World Bank, *World Development Report*, 1993). But with notable exceptions such as Cropper and Oates (1992), most of the research has focused on technologies for limiting environmental degradation and on the effectiveness of various regulatory and tax-incentive policies. This can be seen in the World Bank's bibliography (*World Development Report*, 1993 182–91) and the *JEL* survey article by Cropper and Oates (1992).

Limited aspects of the role of education are considered by Smith (1997), who surveys the effectiveness of education in household decisions to avoid exposure to hazardous waste and similar behaviour-modifying activities, and in reacting to public policies. But he does not address the role of education in motivating democratic governments to take action in the first place, or the connections via poverty reduction.

In this chapter, the direct effects of education will be traced through reduced-form estimates that eliminate many of the structural effects (e.g., through poverty reduction or population growth). Net impacts of education that pass through to environmental quality are estimated directly, sometimes over and above, and sometimes in place of, these intervening channels through which some of the effects occur. Then a structural approach is implemented, and will be used later in Chapters 12 and 13 as education effects environmental quality through simulations of endogenous development. These structural effects occur as education reduces poverty and population growth, increases human-capital-intensive exports with less dependence on extractive exports, raises the economic capacity for installing pollution control devices, fosters democratization, and enables a more educated citizenry to secure recycling, effective regulations, and parks. The negative effects in the other direction must also be accounted for, such as those from educated robber-barons and from smokestacks. But the simulations of education policies include these and measure the net effects on the environment.

The first part of the chapter offers the conceptual framework and then focuses on deforestation. 'Deforestation' is an index for the destruction of forests but also for the destruction of animals and wildlife species and their habitats, with which deforestation is highly correlated. It is a proxy as well for the depletion of minerals and of arable land.

The second part of the chapter focuses on air pollution and water pollution. These are largely urban phenomena and measured by the urban air and urban river water quality indicators in each country as currently reported in World Bank, *World Development Report* (1992: 198–9). They reflect vehicle and industrial emissions into the air, and the dumping of sewage and industrial waste into the water.

The Conceptual Framework

The environment is a stock of environmental capital supplying inputs to production such as minerals, oil, timber, food, water, and air. Production, however, includes *household production* of final satisfactions or Becker commodities which utilize the environment as part of final satisfactions and the quality of life. There must be replenishment of the environment to cope with its deterioration if welfare is not to decline and if true development is to be sustainable in the long run.

Human capital created through investment in education is a separate argument in the production function internal to households and to firms. Just as with the environment, however, education is also available as an externality that benefits both forms of production. *Neither* of these—i.e., use of human capital by firms and by households to raise productivity—necessarily increases raw material use as production becomes more skill-intensive. There are also other indirect effects of education via lower fertility and population growth that can reduce certain strains on the environment. This gives rise to several key hypotheses to be explored further below.

The Environment as a Stock of Natural Capital

Optimal development goes back at its core to the concept of finding an optimal level of consumption (and hence production) that provides enough by way of saving and investing in the replenishment of the physical capital stock, human capital stock, and environmental capital stock to make this level of consumption 'sustainable'. John R. Hicks' *Value and Capital* (1946) defined income as the maximum amount that can be consumed while not consuming the capital stock, so that individuals remain as 'well off' in this respect in the future. To interpret this concept of income within the new social accounting system of Total Accounts, it must include the flow of non-monetary satisfactions from environmental capital. *Total investment* in this case includes not just investment in education and in R&D, as in Eisner (1989, 1997), but also investment in sustaining the quality of the environment.

This concept over time implies a dynamically sustainable or optimal consumption path of the type derived in the Ramsey (1928) growth model. Aronsson and Lofgren (1993) have recently incorporated environmental externalities in such a model and solved the Hamiltonian (which is merely the Lagrange multiplier of elementary calculus adapted to problems that incorporate dynamic rates of change over time) for the optimal trajectory. They have more recently also incorporated human capital that includes an externality (Aronsson and Lofgren, 1994). As such, these optimal growth models incorporating both environmental stocks and human capital stocks are very suggestive. Their opinion is that there is some discounting of the welfare of future generations by the current generation.

However, it is not clear that developing countries or industrial countries ever follow these optimal sustainable paths. It is clear that we know far too little that is concrete about feasible development paths involving both human capital and the environment. Although optimal steady-state solutions provide an overall context (see Figure 2.2), the focus of this chapter and of the simulations later is on generating feasible medium-term development paths involving education that are based on the data but that are not necessarily optimal.

The Main Overall Hypotheses

Skill intensity in production is productive and also substitutes for raw material intensity (as well as for raw unimproved labour), while education also generates externalities, both of which take pressure off the environment. Education also creates a demand for environmental regulation which is effective in democratic political systems.

The first hypothesis, that education contributes to per capita GNP growth (Chapters 3–5), means that this both uses environmental resources and generates the saving and investment necessary to finance water purification plants, clean air, and national parks. Rural education can also contribute to agricultural productivity and potentially less pressure to cut forests or wear out the land. To measure the non-monetary returns in the form of an improved environment, all regressions will control for GNP per capita.

The second hypothesis relates to a pure externality. It is that the education of women beyond the ninth year contributes to slower population growth, and hence less population pressure. Slower population growth in turn reduces the cutting of forests for fuel, the pressure on arable land, and the generation of urban sewage.

The third hypothesis is that education policies that lead to reduced poverty then also remove this source of pressure on the forests and water pollution. This variable, then, is removed from some of the regressions to test for the (reduced-form) direct effects.

Fourth, there are also net direct contributions of education to a better environment over and above these effects through population and poverty, so education enrolment variables will also be introduced directly. These include effects as education and skills help to expand manufacturing exports while at the same time relying less and less on the export of timber and other unprocessed raw materials, which eventually run out. This important relationship to successful exportation of manufactured goods relative to primary products has been tested extensively by Adrian Wood (1994). Consider, for example, that a few of the very highest per capita income countries in the world have very limited natural resources, such as Israel (US$13,220), the Netherlands ($20,480), Denmark ($26,000), Norway ($25,820), and Sweden ($27,010). They depend primarily on a highly educated and skilled population for the generation of these earnings. Most also have a well-protected and clean environment.

Beyond the structure of exports, another effect that the secondary and higher education variables are expected to reflect comes through democratization, which provides a channel through which citizens can express concerns about polluted water and air and get regulations that require environmental clean-up. Just as with population growth, democratization will be tested in some regressions, and then removed to allow the education variables to detect effects directly.

Deforestation and the Destruction of Wildlife

The percentage change in forests from 1970 through 1990, from World Bank (1992: 200, 1996b), is the dependent variable. Table 9.1 shows empirical tests for the hypotheses suggested above for the 76 nations worldwide for which data on all of the explanatory variables is available.

Table 9.2 focuses on the Latin American and Caribbean countries only, a region about which deforestation concerns have been widely expressed because of its pace there, earlier World Bank loans supporting it, the destruction of wildlife there, and the role of the Amazon forests in the creation of oxygen. There are 26 LAC nations with data for four 5-year periods for each country (1970–4, 1975–9, 1980–5, 1985–90). The absolute values within each of these 5-year periods were averaged, and then the percentage change over time computed between adjacent 5-year period

Table 9.1 Forestation Determinants Worldwide (dependent variable: $F =$ per cent annual change in forests (Worldwide mean $= -0.4\%$ per year); t-statistics in parentheses; all regressions corrected for heteroscedasticity)

	Model 1	Model 2	Model 3	Model 4
GNP per capita (GNPPC)	6.7E-07	5.7E-07	5.4E-07	5.3E-07
	(1.90)	(2.30)	(1.52)	(1.52)
Population growth (n)			−0.413	−0.400
			(−3.50)	(−3.31)
Primary education	−2.2E-05	−3.8E-05		
($GER1_{-20}$)	(−0.551)	(−1.32)		
Secondary education	9.9E-05		−0.0002	−0.0002
($GER2_{-20}$)	(1.56)		(−1.82)	(−1.92)
Higher education	−0.0002			
($GER3_{-20}$)	(−0.739)			
Rural poverty (POVR)		−6.5E-05		
		(−2.12)		
Change in agriculture				−0.053
(ΔAGA)				(−0.592)
Constant	−0.006	−0.006	0.009	0.009
	(−2.36)	(−1.32)	(1.85)	(1.86)
R^2	0.13	0.10	0.25	0.25
Sample size	75	76	75	75

averages. This results in 3 observations for each Latin American country for which there are data, or a sample size of 75. All explanatory variables in Tables 9.1 and 9.2 have been defined and the reasons for the lags explained previously in Chapters 7 and 8, where the data sources are also given except for ΔAGA = per cent changes in acres devoted to agriculture and ΔENG = per cent change in energy consumption, both from World Bank (1993: 200–1 and 226–7).

Determinants of Deforestation

The main determinants of 'Forestation' in Table 9.1, and therefore also of 'Deforestation', which measure the destruction of wildlife, ecosystems, and related depletion, are shown in Table 9.1. All models indicate that with higher levels of GNP per capita, the rate of deforestation is reduced.

Education. The net non-market effects of secondary education, controlling for GNP per capita in Model 1, also help to reduce the rate of deforestation (i.e., have a positive effect on forestation). It is only significant at the 85 per cent confidence level when there are no controls for population growth in Model 1, and primary and higher education are totally insignificant, as shown.

Secondary education, however, has a net positive effect on forestation when its effects in reducing population growth rates are considered. Secondary education of females reduces fertility and eventually net population growth rates, a point that

Table 9.2 Forestation: Latin America and Caribbean Only (dependent variable: F = per cent annual change in forests (mean is usually negative); t-statistics in parentheses; all regressions corrected for heteroscedasticity)

	Model 1	Model 2	Model 3	Model 4
Population growth (n)	−0.204	−0.196	−0.281	−0.176
	(−2.75)	(−2.73)	(−3.51)	(−2.46)
Clearing forests for agriculture (ΔAGF)	−0.4508	−0.432	−0.261[1]	−0.455
	(−7.10)	(−6.95)	(−3.66)	(−6.95)
Economic growth (y)	0.0619	0.062	0.011	0.039
	(9.07)	(9.74)	(5.43)	(3.98)
Initial level of GNP per capita (ℓn GNPPC$_{70}$)	0.0281	0.025	0.033	0.026
	(3.06)	(2.72)	(3.55)	(3.11)
Rural poverty ($POVR$)		−0.0002		
		(−2.13)		
Change in energy consumption (ENG)				0.018
				(2.32)
Constant	−0.183	−0.157	−0.214	−0.174
	(−2.91)	(−2.50)	(−3.41)	(−3.07)
R^2	0.724	0.76	0.55	0.65
Sample size	78	42	78	78
Standard error of the estimate (sigma)	0.996	0.999	0.980	0.991

[1] ΔAGA (not ΔAGF) in Model 3.

Zero-Order Correlation Matrix (LAC)

	ℓn GNPPC$_{70}$	y	n	ΔAGF
ℓ GNPPC$_{70}$	1.00			
y	−0.0250	1.00		
n	−0.1679	0.1671	1.00	
ΔAGF	−0.0650	0.1351	0.2448	1.00

was developed in Chapter 6. Employing this structural approach (in the way it is used for simulating education impacts in Chapter 12 below), a reduced-form equation can be obtained using Table 9.1, Model 3 for comparison with the impacts of education estimated directly in Model 1. Using the coefficients for female secondary education impacts on fertility and hence on population growth in Equations (6.3), (6.5), and (6.6), and assuming an average family planning score (FP = 60), the result can be inserted for population growth in Model 3. The net impact of secondary education after subtracting the −0.0002 effect shown is +11.0E-05. This is almost identical to the +9.9E-05 net positive effect on forestation obtained in Model 1 by direct estimation.

This structural approach is more precise for the simulations, since it specifies the causal flow through the population growth impacts of secondary education that are different at the different stages of economic development specific to each country. But the reduced-form equations obtained by substitution and alternatively by direct estimation from the data are useful for illustrating the significant direct impacts of secondary education on environmental quality.

Population Growth. Population growth in Models 3 and 4, as mentioned, is a very highly significant determinant of deforestation ($t = 3.3$ to 3.5). This extremely adverse effect of high population growth on the destruction of forests and wildlife persists during further in-depth examination of the data over time in Latin America. As shown in Table 9.2, under any permutation involving other key variables in addition to per capita income (the clearing of forest land for agriculture, growth rates, etc.), high population growth rates have a robust negative effect on the forests. The limited access by women to secondary education in the rural areas tends to keep fertility rates and population growth rates very high.

Poverty. Rural poverty appears to contribute significantly to deforestation, as shown in Table 9.1, Model 2 worldwide and in Table 9.2, Model 2 for Latin America and the Caribbean. However, in the latter case data on poverty is not available for some years in some of the LAC countries, so some observations are lost and the results are not strictly comparable. Questions can also be raised about the measures of rural poverty that are available. Nevertheless, by one estimate, 80 per cent of those below the poverty line in Latin America and the Caribbean live on marginal lands that are highly susceptible to environmental degradation.

Clearing of Forest Land for Agricultural Use also contributes in a major way to the reduction of forests in Latin America (Table 9.2), but it is not a significant factor worldwide (Table 9.1). This is measured in Table 9.2, Models 1, 2, and 4, as the change over time in the ratio of the area devoted to agriculture to the area devoted to forests, and in Table 9.2, Model 3 and Table 9.1, Model 4, as the total percentage change in agricultural area (ΔAGA). In Latin America this latter variant was also significant.

Other Effects Tested. A range of other effects was tested. Some of those intended as controls were significant, but many were never significant. Higher GNP per capita is significant in reducing the rate of deforestation, presumably as economies shift to more urbanized, human-capital-intensive modes of production. Higher economic growth rates are also good, not bad, for the forests, at least in Latin America (Table 9.2; $t = 3.98$ to 9.74). However, neither growth in GNP nor growth in GNP per capita were ever significant in any model worldwide. Lest this lead to complacency, however, the average rate of destruction of forests and wildlife habitat in Sub-Saharan Africa and also in Latin America is 6 per cent over the most recent 10 years for which data is available, and is much higher for the same decade in Bolivia (14.1 per cent), Indonesia (12.7 per cent), and the Philippines (44.4 per cent) (World Bank, 1997: 232). So generally speaking, the developing countries are not adding to their forests, but are destroying them less rapidly as growth occurs.

Increases in energy consumption (ΔENG) were also significant for Latin America, as shown in Table 9.2, Model 4. Since this is after controlling for per capita income and economic growth, this suggests that it may also reflect an increase in the use of alternative fuels such as oil which reduce reliance on wood for cooking and heating.

The percentage change in external debt was not significant at any reasonable confidence level for the Latin American countries. The structure of export growth and export levels were also found to be insignificant. The measures of exports which were tried included export growth, composition of exports (primary products and fuels as a percentage of total exports), and levels of exports, but not the specific ratio of manufacturing to primary exports used by Wood (1994).

For the worldwide data, democratization was also never significant, although its sign (positive) was always in the expected direction.

An Illustration of Deforestation

Figure 9.1 shows the annual per cent *reduction* in forest lands (i.e., deforestation) as a function of high population growth rates. Latin American and Caribbean nations are identified to illustrate the relationship more specifically, although the problem is equally acute in Sub-Saharan Africa, where population growth rates are even higher.

First, Figure 9.1 illustrates that all countries in Latin America and the Caribbean except Uruguay, Chile, Costa Rica, and Surinam are reducing their forest land. Second, those with the lowest per capita income and the slowest growth, all of which are in the circle except Bolivia, are reducing their forest land the most

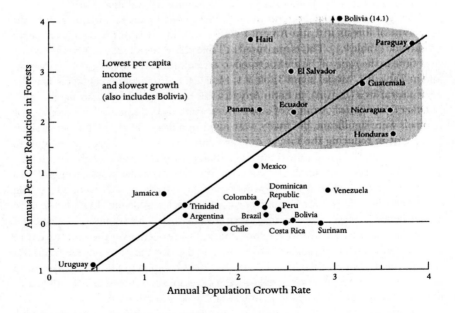

Figure 9.1 Deforestation and destruction of wildlife

rapidly. Third, higher population growth rates, as suggested by the linear regression line, are associated very significantly with the higher rates of deforestation.

Water Pollution

The measures of water quality that are available reflect primarily the deposition of sewage and of industrial and agricultural chemicals and waste in rivers near major cities in 27 countries.

The dependent variable chosen to be explained is sewage in rivers near urban areas. It is measured as the annual mean concentration of faecal coliform for the years 1983–6 for the given country, from World Bank, *World Development Report* (1993: 198). Many countries have observations for more than one river, so the average of the concentration rates for all cities in each country is used. All of the explanatory variables in Equation (9.1) below and in Table 9.3 are as defined in Chapters 7 and 8, where in addition the lags are explained and the data sources are given.

Determinants of Water Pollution

Per Capita Income. In Table 9.3 there are always controls for GNP per capita so that the non-monetary component of the net returns to education can be measured. Nevertheless, it is interesting that as per capita income rises, water pollution increases, at least at first. Later it diminishes, as illustrated in Figure 9.2, and shown by the following equation:

$$WATER = 267,710 lnGNPPC - 19,687 lnGNPPC^2 + 812 POVU - 917,860.$$
$$(3.82) \qquad (-3.74) \qquad (3.77) \quad (-3.90)$$
$$(9.1)$$
$$R^2 = 0.78 \quad n = 22$$

This in a sense is a pollution-(rather than inequality-) related Kuznets inverted U curve, with water pollution rising up to about \$3,000 per capita and then falling significantly, as shown by the negative coefficient of the $GNPPC^2$ term. The latter presumably occurs as the economic capacity for sewage treatment improves, but also as education and democratization increase. The latter are more fundamental causally related explanations than the $ln\ GNPPC^2$ term, which reflects unexplained influences. Water pollution is high in Latin America, and low in East Asia, where growth rates are high (see Figure 9.2).

The degrees of freedom are quite small because of the limited number of countries for which water pollution data are available, as indicated above. However, in a sense the sample size is really much larger. The individual cities rather than the nationwide averages could be used to increase the number of observations to 162. But then there would be a question about whether separate cities within

Table 9.3 Water Pollution (*t*-statistics in parentheses; all regressions corrected for heteroscedasticity)

	Model 1	Model 2	Model 3	Model 4	Model 5	Model 6
GNP per capita (GNPPC)	7.79	5.24	2.92	4.28	4.63	3.34
	(3.43)	(2.49)	(1.96)	(2.76)	(2.41)	(1.81)
Growth of GNPPC $(y - n)$	−209,080					
	(−1.49)					
Primary education	648			473	50.9	
$(GER1_{-20})$	(2.79)			(2.28)	(0.217)	
Secondary education	−196	−301		−401	−381	
$(GER2_{-20})$	(−1.00)	(−0.968)		(−2.12)	(−0.994)	
Higher education	−3,202	−2,800	−1,117		−2,674	−1,223
$(GER3_{-20})$	(−2.95)	(−3.04)	(−2.11)		(−3.26)	(−2.04)
Urban poverty (POVU)	1,627	773	557	1,202	711	696
	(4.09)	(2.88)	(2.15)	(2.17)	(3.11)	(1.62)
Democratization (D)	−8,769			−7,005		−1,697
	(−2.42)			(−1.57)		(−0.483)
Population growth (n)			70,704			573,480
			(2.08)			(2.51)
GNP per capita, 1960	−16.59			−16.86		
$(GNPPC_{60})$	(−2.55)			(−2.36)		
Political stability (PS)					331	
					(0.649)	
Constant	26,046	2,818	−23,051	−16,935	−19,293	−14,257
	(−1.06)	(0.300)	(−1.92)	(−0.576)	(−0.662)	(−0.825)
R^2	0.602	0.408	0.458	0.339	0.429	0.466
Sample size	22	22	22	22	22	22

Zero-Order Correlation Matrix

	GNPPC	D	n	POVU	$GER1_{-20}$	$GER2_{-20}$	$GER3_{-20}$	PS
GNPPC	1.00000							
D	−0.37863	1.00000						
n	−0.74034	0.16601	1.00000					
POVU	0.47460	−0.77197	−0.28524	1.00000				
$GER1_{-20}$	0.76977	−0.46328	−0.52793	0.55350	1.00000			
$GER2_{-20}$	−0.87601	0.06930	0.76409	−0.10345	−0.56922	1.00000		
$GER3_{-20}$	−0.41383	0.26094	0.55630	−0.58037	−0.47370	0.22020	1.00000	
PS	−0.70811	−0.16645	0.83153	−0.0035	−0.56244	0.78781	0.43528	1.00000

each country really constitute independent observations. Nevertheless the effects shown in Table 9.3 are very robust, including those in models with fewer variables and hence more degrees of freedom. So these are serious hypotheses, worthy of further testing. But this can only come in future years as more data on water pollution become available. In the meantime some tentative conclusions can be reached.

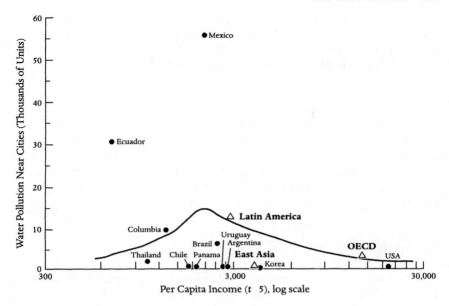

Figure 9.2 Water pollution, averages for regions

The suggestion is that even this initial increase in water pollution would not occur if more appropriate economic development policies were followed. Factors to which reduced water pollution appears to respond are the following:

Secondary and Higher Education Enrolments. In Table 9.3, primary enrolments alone are positively related to *more* water pollution, perhaps because more people remain in agriculture, use fertilizers, and are not politically active (Models 1 and 4; $t = 2.79$ and 2.28). However, secondary and higher education enrolments lagged 20 years are very significantly related to *reduced* water pollution. This is true for higher education in Models 1–3 and 5–6, and for secondary education in Model 4. These are non-monetary net impacts of education observable after controlling for per capita income and poverty in all models, and after controlling for population growth in Models 3 and 6.

Urban Poverty. The per cent of the urban population below the poverty line is a very significant determinant of higher water pollution in essentially all models in Table 9.3. High levels of urban poverty suggest that rivers are used as a means for waste disposal and that there are few alternative systems available to manage waste. This variable is also seen in Model 6 as a proxy for countries that have high population growth rates.

Democratization. Higher degrees of democratization are significantly related to *less* water pollution in Model 1, and in the same direction but with less significance in Models 4 and 6. This suggests that democratization provides a channel through which concerns about dirty water can be expressed and effective action taken.

Population Growth. High population growth rates are significantly related to high levels of water pollution. This effect comes through even after controlling for levels of urban poverty. But its introduction does appear to be associated with a smaller coefficient and somewhat lower level of significance for urban poverty. Population levels and population density, as distinguished from population growth rates, were both tried but neither was significant. Even population growth rates were seldom as significant as urban poverty.

Other Effects Tested. Variables measuring inequality in income distribution (income share going to the lowest 40% of the population and the ratio of income distribution of the highest 20% to the lowest 20%) were also tried in several models. The results showed an ambiguous sign of the coefficient and also insignificance at any meaningful confidence level. Measures of absolute poverty are relatively more effective determinants of water pollution.

Air Pollution

Air pollution results largely from industrial emissions and motor vehicle smog, but can also include agricultural dust-bowls and urban dumps. All of these can be generated by industrialization if the policies to curtail these externality spillover costs (e.g., effluent taxes) are inadequate. Global warming appears to be the ultimate externality in air pollution, pushing costs off on other countries rather than on to other people in the same country. But I have no good measures for it here.

The costs to the health, property, and future of children, and the appropriate types of remedies for these external spillover costs that are also consistent with allocative efficiency, have been well known since A. C. Pigou's *The Economics of Welfare* (1920). But there is always resistance by producers to bearing the full costs of production. Governments in democracies that respond to producer interests are therefore often slow to act.

The measure of pollution studied here, primarily because of the omission of global warming, is not fully comprehensive. It is the mean concentration of sulfur dioxide in the air for the 30 countries worldwide for which this datum is reported. The index is for 1983–6 as reported in World Bank, *World Development Report* (1993: 109), since this period contains more observations than the period 1987–90. For countries with reports for more than one city, the arithmetic average for all cities within that country is used again. All variables explaining air pollution in Table 9.4 are as previously defined in Chapters 7 and 8, with the explanation for the lags (when there are any) and the data sources as given there.

In Table 9.4 there is a control for GNP per capita in all models given the objective of measuring non-market returns to education, even if it is sometimes insignificant.

Net Effects of Education. Primary education is associated with *greater* air pollution in all models where it is included (Models 1–3). However, secondary education and

Table 9.4 Air Pollution (*t*-statistics in parentheses; all regressions corrected for heteroscedasticity)

	Model 1	Model 2	Model 3	Model 4	Model 5	Model 6
GNP per capita (GNPPC)	−0.0006	0.0005	0.0005	0.0054	0.0058	0.0041
	(−1.00)	(0.422)	(0.438)	(1.94)	(1.81)	(1.86)
GNP growth (*y*)	441.4					
	(2.33)					
Growth of GNPPC (*y* − *n*)				−1,218	−1,009	−865
				(−2.40)	(−2.60)	(−3.02)
Primary education	1.48	1.22	1.22			
(*GER*1$_{-20}$)	(3.09)	(3.94)	(3.52)			
Secondary education		−0.577	−0.566	−1.15	−0.644	−1.01
(*GER*2$_{-20}$)		(−1.65)	(−1.76)	(−2.15)	(−1.57)	(−2.11)
Higher education				−1.32	−2.26	−1.21
(*GER*3$_{-20}$)				(−1.96)	(−2.45)	(−1.94)
Democratization (*D*)	−6.53	−5.48	−5.48	−6.68		
	(−1.61)	(−1.99)	(−2.01)	(−1.26)		
Population growth (*n*)	−1,745	−1,482	−1,477	−1,738		−1,167
	(−2.26)	(−2.16)	(−2.22)	(−2.055)		(−2.11)
GNP per capita, 1960			−0.0009			
(GNPPC$_{60}$)			(−0.172)			
Political stability (*PS*)				−0.423	−0.403	−0.357
				(−2.01)	(−2.18)	(−1.58)
Constant	−61.7	−6.29	−7.35	204	111	140
	(−2.93)	(−0.305)	(−0.343)	(2.57)	(3.42)	(3.49)
R^2	0.507	0.552	0.553	0.495	0.301	0.455
Sample size	19	19	19	19	19	19

Zero-Order Correlation Matrix

	GNPPC	GNPPC$_{60}$	D	n	GER1$_{-20}$	GER2$_{-20}$	GER3$_{-20}$	PS
GNPPC	1.000							
GNPPC$_{60}$	−0.410	1.000						
D	−0.549	0.277	1.000					
n	−0.452	0.535	0.560	1.000				
GER1$_{-20}$	0.633	−0.171	−0.722	−0.432	1.000			
GER2$_{-20}$	−0.470	0.378	0.252	−0.841	−0.249	1.000		
GER3$_{-20}$	0.129	−0.787	−0.252	−0.629	−0.082	−0.527	1.000	
PS	−0.116	−0.630	−0.041	−0.017	−0.046	−0.013	0.569	1.000

higher education, both lagged 20 years, are consistently associated with *less* air pollution (Models 2–6). The latter is true even when per capita economic growth is included (Models 4–6). This suggests that as faster growth occurs, in part due to secondary education, and as technology improves, partly due to higher education, the economic and technological means for pollution abatement (both air and water) also increases.

Human capital accumulation at these more advanced levels also contributes to the use of greater skills in production, including service industries which are human-capital-intensive and non-polluting (e.g., health care, education, law, communications). Education level also contributes to democratization and greater environmental awareness.

Democratization. Again, as with water pollution, higher degrees of democratization are associated with air pollution abatement. This is a very robust relationship in all models (Models 1–4) even though it does not always reach the 95% confidence level. It is consistent with the original hypothesis that democracy provides a channel for implementing effective pollution control regulations or effluent taxes, and students in college and universities who are interested in their own future and become informed act as a catalyst. The latter also is consistent with casual observations.

Population Growth. High population growth rates are consistently and significantly related to less air pollution in all models (Models 1–4 and 6). This is the exact opposite of their relation to water pollution, suggesting strongly that air pollution is more a problem facing urbanizing industrializing economies than the agrarian economies of Sub-Saharan Africa, Central America, and the Caribbean, where birth rates tend to be the highest.

Political Stability. Political stability is significantly related to pollution abatement (Models 4 and 5), even more so when democratization is included (Model 4) than when it is not (Model 6).

Other Effects Tested. A dummy variable for command-economy socialist governments was tested and found to be positively related to high degrees of air pollution. However, there is only one socialist economy included in this air pollution sample (China), and the confidence level of its t-statistic is only at 80 per cent, so this regression is not shown. It is consistent, however, with casual observations of pollution levels in East Germany and some of the newly independent countries of the ex-Soviet Union, as well as with my hypothesis about democratization, so it may be worth further exploration.

The zero-order correlation matrix indicates that there is high multicollinearity between GER1 and GNPPC, as has been noted previously. This is the reason GER1 was dropped in Models 4–6. GER1 is also highly negatively correlated with democratization ($r = -0.72$). GER2 and GER3 are both negatively correlated with population growth ($r = -0.84$ and -0.62 respectively) so the latter is dropped in Model 5 to test the robustness of the education effects. The other levels of multicollinearity are not as high and therefore of less concern, although of course this is always a problem.

Urban poverty was tried in relation to air pollution, but it was never significant. Similarly, population density was not significant.

Per capita energy consumption, a dummy variable for OPEC, and income distribution measures were also tried. But each failed to elicit consistent signs for the coefficients, or significant results. The quadratic effect measured by ℓn GNPPC and ℓn GNPPC^2 also failed to yield significant results with respect to air pollution.

Illustration of Air Pollution Data.

Figure 9.3 illustrates averages of air pollution for those regions for which data are available. It is lowest in East Asia, which does include China, where it is quite high (see World Bank, 1993: 199). It is lower in the OECD member nations than in Latin America, where it is pulled up by relatively high air pollution rates in Chile and Brazil.

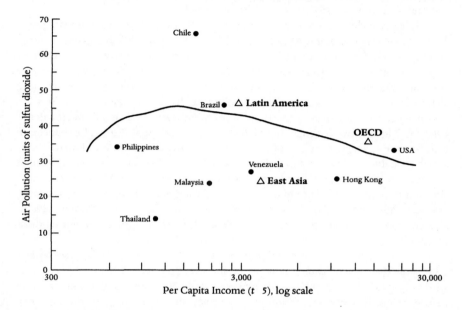

Figure 9.3 Air pollution, averages for cities

Conclusions

The inverted Kuznets ∪ curve for pollution (also sketched in Figure 9.3) emerges in non-linear regressions devoted to forestation, water pollution, and air pollution. But it is never a very significant relationship.

It is, however, a useful vehicle for calling attention by way of conclusions to the key theme of this chapter, and the analogy to the income distribution effects in Chapter 8. This theme is that the destruction of the environment via deforestation, the destruction of wildlife, water pollution, and air pollution need not occur as growth occurs if appropriate policies are put in place to avert this; the avoidance of destruction is conditional. Endogenous development paths considered in Chapters 12 and 13 that assume continuation of current policies do generate peaks in deforestation, water pollution, and air pollution in some countries *given their policies* (e.g., see Chile and Brazil in Figure 9.3), but not in others *given their policies* (e.g., see Malaysia, Venezuela, and Hong Kong in the same figure).

A third conclusion is that the potential for effective policies is illustrated by the fact that deforestation rates, water pollution, and air pollution all tend to be lower in the higher per capita income OECD countries. But this conclusion must be qualified by the fact that this chapter has not had adequate data to address global warming, which is an aspect of air pollution that involves externalities among nations, and to which high-income nations contribute most.

A fourth conclusion, or set of conclusions, is that explicit policies are suggested by the results reported in this chapter (and Chapters 12 and 13) that can be tailored to change the path of environmental destruction for different types of countries. Education policies, such as faster expansion of secondary education, sometimes have adverse effects on the environment at first but are later related to reduced deforestation and less water and air pollution. Expansion of higher education seems to contribute to the reduction of pollution but is less significant for deforestation. These show up when these effects are tested directly. But higher education also further reduces fertility and population growth rates that are destructive to forests, wildlife, and water purity. Basic education also has indirect effects, through the reduction of rural poverty, significant to preservation of the forests and, through the reduction of urban poverty, to reducing water pollution. Both secondary and higher education also contribute to democratization and through this to reduced water and air pollution, as well as directly to reduced water and air pollution.

There do seem to be some adverse direct effects from primary and secondary education on the environment as economic development begins to occur. But generally, with higher per capita income there are eventually lower rates of deforestation, lower water pollution, and lower air pollution (with the one qualification of global warming). There are also indirect effects of education through lower population growth and less poverty. These indirect structural effects will be shown to be clearly dominant, especially after some time passes, in Chapter 12.

10 Education and Crime

This chapter explores the relation of education to crime through a structural approach that considers not just the direct effects of the education of criminals on their behaviour but also the indirect community effects of education. Many of the latter (e.g. poverty rates) have been related to education in earlier chapters.

The focus is on the determinants of violent crime, as measured by homicides, for which the data are relatively clear-cut, and of property crime, used here to refer to the range of other standard crime categories. This chapter considers perspectives that can be brought to this issue based on the international crime data, which is also needed as the basis for simulations, together with some tests of the same effects using interstate US data.

Neither is a substitute for studies at the micro-level. But the latter are usually based on cross-section or longitudinal data covering the behaviour of individual *offenders* and do not pick up international perspectives, the effects on pre-offenders, or the structural effects of education. The crime literature has become very sophisticated in terms of statistical techniques. But it is also so specialized and so often focused only on offenders that have started a life of crime that it has not considered the more comprehensive structural role *of education* in preventing and controlling crime.

There are a few basic facts, some perhaps new, to which this analysis needs to relate. First, internationally, property crime increases as economic growth occurs. Second, and in contrast to this, violent crime and specifically homicide rates are lower in all of the higher-income OECD member countries except for the United States, where they are much higher. However, third, crime in the United States overall is lower now than in the late 1970s, in contrast to common perceptions.

To these must be added some basic facts from the standard crime literature. They are, fourth, that most crime is committed by young men in their teenage years and before age 25, most of whom are repeat offenders (Witte, 1997: 384). Among these offenders prone to crime, empirical studies show little impact from the school's primary educational activities or from years of schooling on the level of individual criminal activity. However, fifth, and very important, in communities with larger numbers of unsupervised teenagers, which also are likely to be those communities with the lowest gross enrolment rates and with little involvement by residents, there are very high crime rates (ibid.). And in the US, among young males who are not in school the murder rate has been increasing dramatically.

From another point of view all of these are symptoms. A more comprehensive rationale needs to be able to explain the sources of these basic facts, and thereby hopefully explain them all.

Background and Structural Rationale

In an excellent survey of the recent crime literature, Anne Witte (1997) suggests that economic models, starting with those by Becker (1968) and right up through those by his students in the present (e.g., Ehrlich, 1996), have focused on deterrence and on economic incentives for crime rather than theoretical models that systematically incorporate the role of education in preventing and controlling crime. One aspect of this, which Witte stresses, is that if a young man does not drop out, peer groups within schools are formed that play a larger role in his world and hence have larger potential effects in reducing crime. That is, although there may be no significant impacts from educational activities on crime, those schools with consistent and firm discipline that are oriented to the community, involve parents, and keep students busy and under supervision more hours each week also help constructive peer groups form, and reduce the preferences and opportunities for crime. A number of studies do find that more time spent at school or working are both associated with a significantly lower level of criminal activity (see Witte, 1997: 384). This certainly is consistent with the basic fact that communities with larger numbers of unsupervised teenagers have high crime rates.

Psychologists have found that early childhood education (as well as factors that have partial relations to education, such as good parenting and community education-related externalities) can overcome the effect of many influences that predispose some individuals to crime (see Rutter, 1985). Sociologists such as Shaw and McKay (1969) suggest that community disorganization associated with low economic status, minority social groups, and family disruption leads to increased levels of crime and delinquency. However, there does not appear to be much work that links this back to the inequality in expenditure per child in schools or to the inequality of earnings resulting from the quantity and quality of education. In the US inequality within public education often exceeds 8 times as much spent per child on average in the highest per capita income decile of school districts as those in the lowest-income decile, for example.

Direct Effects of Education

The structural rationale for the hypotheses tested in international data and in data for the US concerned with violent crime and property crime is that education may have net positive non-monetary direct effects (i.e., over and above income effects) on crime reduction as greater retention in secondary schools provides better supervision of teenagers and opportunities for more constructive peer-group formation. There are direct monetary effects of education as well. But these do not lead to clear hypotheses about the direction of the effects that are consistent with the basic facts about purely economic effects on crime rates (e.g., that *property* crime rates increase with higher average per capita incomes). Not all of the externality effects of education are necessarily positive.

Poverty and Unemployment

However, structurally there are hypothesized to be positive net effects of education on the reduction of poverty and on the reduction of unemployment that are expected to reduce both violent crime and property crime. Similarly, higher inequality in income distribution cannot be expected to have positive effects on either violent crime rates or property crime. As noted in Chapter 8, the net contribution of education to the reduction of inequality depends on what policies are followed with respect to the distribution of access to good education.

These structural impacts *of education* via poverty and unemployment are not considered by Witte (1997) or by the crime literature that tends to focus on the behaviour of individual criminals, even though it is generally recognized that community effects on criminal activity are very important.

The Determinants of Violent Crime

The dependent variables for 'crime' are split into two categories—'violent crime' (or homicide) and 'property crime', since their natures are so different from each other. The analysis of the international data will be accompanied by an exploration of the determinants of crime in the United States, where the data are more complete and well organized. A cross-sectional set of data for the 50 states of the United States plus the District of Columbia has been used for this latter purpose.

Violent crime technically consists of the following kinds of crime:

> murder,
> forcible rape,
> robbery, and
> aggravated assault.

Property crime is the sum of the following:

> burglary,
> larceny theft,
> motor vehicle theft, and
> arson (however, no data are available for this).

I first regressed these eight different kinds of crime separately against different explanatory variables, where an interesting observation emerges: the individual components of both violent crime and property crime behave broadly in the same way as their respective totals. This reinforces the reliability of the results reported below.

However, for the more narrowly defined categories there is an absence of well-defined measures of these crimes in the international data. So 'homicide' is used as a cleanly defined proxy for 'violent crime'. The difference of total crime minus 'homicide' will then be referred to here as 'property crime', some of which is violent.

The variables in Table 10.1 and their sources are:

HOMICIDE Homicides per 100,000 population, from United Nations (1998: table 34). For the US this includes wilful felonious homicides and manslaughter, but excludes attempts to kill, suicides, accidental deaths, justifiable homicides, and deaths caused by negligence. Not all are convictions, but all are offences as known to the police. US data from US Bureau of the Census, *Statistical Abstract* (1990: table 285).

U_{-2} Unemployment rate lagged 2 years, from US Bureau of the Census, *Statistical Abstract* (1990: table 658).

NARAD Narcotics addiction, i.e. number of persons addicted to any drug, from National Institute of Justice (1980, 1990).

POV Millions of persons in the US living below the poverty level, urban and rural, from US Bureau of the Census, *Statistical Abstract* (1992: table 722).

ln PERS-PCY Log of personal income per capita in constant (1982) dollars, from US Bureau of the Census, *Statistical Abstract* (1990: table 706).

All other variables in Table 10.1 are as defined previously, with sources given, in Chapter 8.

Table 10.1 Violent Crime: Homicide (t-statistics in parentheses; all models corrected for heteroscedasticity)

	Model 1	Model 2	Model 3	Model 4	Model 5	Model 6
GNP per capita GNPPC	−0.0004 (−2.82)	−0.0005 (−2.53)		−0.0005 (−2.35)		
In GNPPC			−1.15 (−1.21)			
In PERSYPC					1,735 (7.28)	1,447 (5.76)
Inequality or poverty GINI		14.9 (1.68)	16.0 (2.17)	13.6 (1.75)		
POV					54.1 (5.98)	
Secondary education (% completing)						−15.9 (−2.55)
Unemployment (U_2)						59.2 (3.05)
Narcotics addiction (NARAD)			0.0003 (0.406)	0.0002 (0.407)		
Constant	6.62 (7.01)	1.15 (0.267)	7.40 (0.904)	1.36 (0.339)	−1.65 (−7.11)	−1.23 (−5.20)
Sample size	55	30	30	30	51	51
Adjusted R^2	0.12	0.17	0.16	0.17	0.54	0.43

Per Capita Income

For homicide, Table 10.1 reveals that worldwide in Models 1–4, as per capita GNP rises, homicide rates fall! This pattern is highly significant in Models 1, 2, and 4. However, it is not a robust relationship among US states including the District of Columbia in Models 5–6. In fact, homicide rates are also higher in the US (where they are 9 per 100,000 persons) than in any other OECD country (where they are uniformly 1 or 2, except for Sweden and Denmark, where they are 5). A recent study published by the US Department of justice (Wintemute, 1998) attributes this in large part to the high availability of guns in the US compared to other OECD countries. Elsewhere, limits on handgun availability do not reduce crime rates but do shift them into the non-violent categories.

Narcotics

Table 10.1 also tests narcotics addiction, albeit demonstrating it to be insignificant internationally (Models 3 and 4). Narcotics addiction, however, is high in the US (234), Canada (308), and New Zealand (308), compared to 30 in the United Kingdom and other OECD countries, for example, where murder rates are all at a very low 1 or 2. Narcotics addiction is much higher in Jamaica, Mexico, Colombia, Bolivia, and Peru, and much lower in Chile but about the same as in the US. But only in Jamaica and Chile are the homicide rates higher than in the US.

Inequality

Significant effects, however, are found worldwide for inequality in income distribution *after* controlling for narcotics addiction in Model 3. Controlling for GNP per capita (rather than for *ln* GNPPC) in Model 4, the same effects of inequality in income distribution on crime persist. But now they are at the 92% confidence level ($t = 1.75$) rather than above the 95% level as in Model 3.

For the US data in Models 5 and 6, *GINI* coefficients are not available by state. But poverty rates emerge with a very robust relationship to violent crime, as shown in Model 5. Unemployment lagged 2 years is also highly significant (see Model 6). But when both are included, poverty emerges as by far the most significant effect, just as it does when large numbers of other variables (not shown) are tested.

Education

Secondary education gross enrolment rates could also be interpreted as closely related to smaller numbers of unsupervised teenagers in the community. It is very significant (at the 98 per cent confidence level) in its negative relationship to the homicide rate in the US. This is true even after controlling for higher unemployment rates, as shown in Model 6. It is not inconsistent with the findings cited by Witte (1997: 384) that the educational functions of schools do not seem to have much effect in changing the behaviour of individual criminals. But it certainly is consistent with the basic fact, and my hypothesis, that reducing the numbers of unsupervised teenagers in a community and providing more constructive channels for the formation of peer groups, both important roles of public education, are effective.

Both internationally and within the US, the structural effects of education in raising income per capita and in reducing poverty rates (and potentially inequality), however, would appear to be the most important. This is a hypothesis that warrants further exploration.

Figure 10.1 illustrates internationally and Figure 10.2 for the US that there is a *gross* relationship between lower homicide rates and higher secondary enrolment rates. This incorporates some of the above structural effects, since in Figures 10.1 and 10.2 there are no controls for these other effects.

By regions, the OECD nations have the lowest homicide rates in Figure 10.1. Latin America, where inequality and narcotics addiction are both relatively high, has the highest. Figure 10.1 also illustrates how the US is an outlier, with high homicide rates in relation to the OECD nations, how Jamaica and Chile are high in relation to Latin America, and how Thailand has high violent crime rates in relation to East Asia.

Nevertheless, if we look not at the reduced form, as in Figure 10.1, but at where the structural effects are sorted out, in Table 10.1, the effects of education are through growth and the reduction of poverty and inequality, and not above and beyond that. These occur as suggested by the micro-data, probably as unsupervised teenagers are kept off the streets.

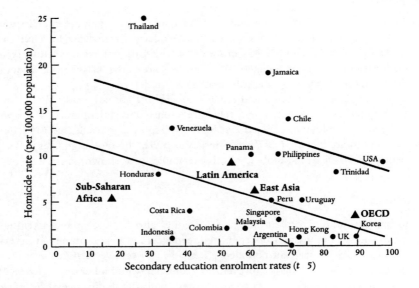

Figure 10.1 Homicide rates and education

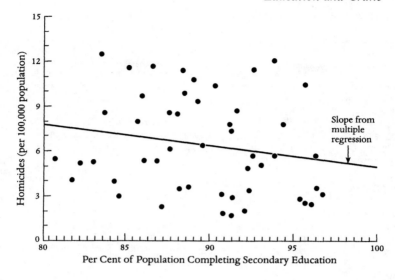

Figure 10.2 Homicide rates in the US, state by state

The Determinants of Property Crime

Property crime is responsive to many of the same forces, as indicated in Table 10.2, although there are some interesting differences.

The variables in Table 10.2 are all as defined previously in Chapters 7 and 8, or earlier in this chapter, except for the dependent variable:

CRIME   property crimes per 100,000 population, from United Nations (1998: table 34). This is the sum of burglary, larceny, theft, motor vehicle theft, arson, and the violent crimes of forcible rape, robbery, and aggravated assault, as known to the police. For the US the categories are the same; US figures from US Bureau of the Census, *Statistical Abstract* (1990: table 285).

GNP Per Capita

There is a dramatic difference for property crime in that rates increase as GNP per capita rises, rather than falling as they do for homicide. This effect can be seen to be significant internationally (Models 1–5) as well as within the US (Model 6). To the extent that these increases in income can be attributed to education, it is a negative externality. This might be why some of the micro-studies surveyed by Witte (1997) report no decrease in criminal activity, broadly defined, among individuals prone to crime as either education or earnings increase.

Table 10.2 Property Crime (*t*-statistics in parentheses; all models corrected for heteroscedasticity)

	Worldwide					US only	
	Model 1	Model 2	Model 3	Model 4	Model 5	Model 6	Model 7
GNP per capita							
GNPPC	1.04			6.13			
	(0.34)			(1.88)			
ln GNPPC	22,612	20,005	11,982		16,637	4,444	
	(2.15)	(2.14)	(2.07)		(1.81)	(3.47)	
ln PERSYPC							160,393
							(1.68)
ln(PERSYPC)^2							−8,283
							(−1.64)
Inequality or poverty							
GINI	93,893	57,780		82,451	64,936		
	(2.39)	(1.53)		(1.72)	(1.58)		
POVU	647		266				
	(1.79)		(0.85)				
POV						114	
						(2.35)	
Secondary education							
GER2	−974	−1,022	−530	−902	−955		
	(−2.11)	(−2.20)	(−1.66)	(−1.98)	(−2.16)		
LF2	2,255						
	(0.185)						
Unemployment (U_2)					−395		192
					(−0.94)		(2.02)
Constant (in	−188	−130	−71	−15	−107	−38.7	−772
thousands)	(−2.39)	(−2.10)	(−1.90)	(−1.02)	(−1.77)	(−3.10)	(−1.71)
Sample size	30	30	56	30	30	51	51
R^2	0.31	0.24	0.12	0.15	0.25	0.20	0.20

Inequality and Poverty

Again, after controlling for per capita GNP, higher inequality and higher poverty rates are both associated with a larger amount of property crime. This is true in the international data (Models 1–5) as well as within the US (Model 6). Generally, inequality as measured by the *GINI* coefficient is more significant than absolute poverty as a determinant of property crime rates. This can be seen in Model 1, as well as by comparing Model 3 to Models 2, 4, and 5. For the US, measures of inequality are not readily available for the 50 states plus the District of Columbia, but in the US absolute poverty is also clearly a significant determinant of property crime rates.

Unemployment lagged 2 years has a significant relationship to property crime in the US. Without a lag, no significant relationship could be found. When both poverty and unemployment are included, although this particular regression is not shown, poverty is clearly the most significant. Unemployment, also after a lag, becomes a rough proxy for poverty and near-poverty. But since unemployment rates among young males are about twice those at older ages, and among young black males are twice again the unemployment rates among young white males, unemployment rates are also measuring the numbers of unsupervised young males in the community who are on the streets.

Education

The net direct effects of secondary education, after controlling for all of the significant indirect effects, are consistently significant in reducing property crime rates in the international data at the 0.05 level in Models 1, 2, 4, and 5. That is, as economic growth occurs, property crime increases, but the expansion of secondary education enrolments to include lower-income groups, to the extent that this reduces inequality, poverty, and the numbers of unsupervised young males, has net effects in reducing crime rates to below what they would otherwise be.

I did test these GER2 (and LF2) effects using the US data but found them to be insignificant. Over half of the prisoners in US prisons have educational achievement at less than the sixth-grade level, and consistent with this, in the regressions poverty rates clearly have the most robust relationship to crime. But it is often not realized how very unequal the US education system is at the secondary level. As mentioned above, with its high degree of decentralization and heavy dependence on local wealth, expenditure per child varies widely, as do drop-out rates, and experiments are being tried that often tend to increase this inequality. The result is that secondary enrolment rates often do not have the same meaning as they do in poor countries, where the secondary education variable is measuring rapid expansion and expansion of access to the poorest groups in the population. There are also high degrees of inequality in the secondary education system in the United Kingdom, but for somewhat different reasons.

An Illustration

In the international data, the upswing in property crime rates as per capita income rises is sketched in Figure 10.3. The mean for the OECD member nations for property crime is shown high on the right, with the US and UK, as just mentioned, identified as no exception. The mean for the East Asian countries is remarkably low but their strong commitment to education and falling inequality have been discussed throughout this book. There are undoubtedly other, unknown factors that lead to property crime included in the disturbances, but my focus continues to be on the marginal direct and indirect contributions of education.

In Latin America the property crime rate average for the region is very high, given the per capita income level there. But as mentioned, inequality is high there. Chile is high, and Brazil (at 116,000 property crimes per year per 100,000 persons) is way off the top of Figure 10.3. It is remarkable how low the crime rate has been in Costa Rica, which is at a level of per capita income comparable to Brazil.

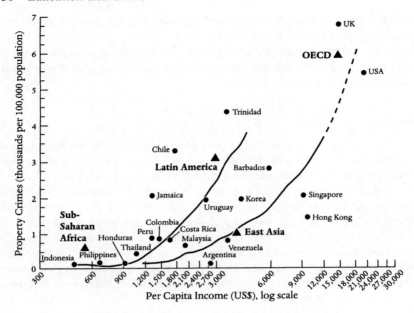

Figure 10.3 Property crime rates and growth

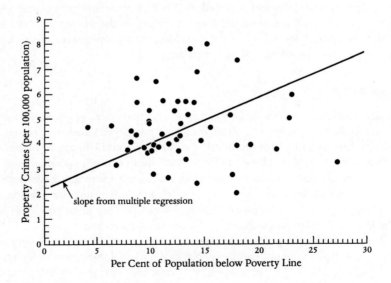

Figure 10.4 Property crime in the US and poverty (inequality), state by state

Summary and Conclusions

Overall, given the perspectives offered by the international data, both the direct and the net structural effects of education suggest some robust determinants of crime rates.

Homicide rates fall but property crime rates increase as economic growth occurs. However, after controlling for per capita income, when there are direct effects from higher percentages of teenagers under supervision in secondary schools, both violent and property crime measures are lower than they would otherwise be. This is consistent with the hypothesis that those enrolled have opportunities to form better peer-group relationships and are not unsupervised and out on the streets.

Additional effects from education also come structurally. Those countries that have been rapidly expanding secondary education have also reduced inequality, and this is associated with lower crime rates. Indirect effects also arise to the extent that public education reaches lower-income groups and reduces poverty, which in turn is also associated with lower crime rates.

There are of course other factors affecting crime rates, including good policing. But others are very particularistic. The efforts to trace the impacts of *education* in the crime literature have been somewhat limited and have also been narrow, in the sense that they have not normally sought to trace the net structural impacts of education after controlling for per capita income even in a preliminary way, as I have sought to do here. Nevertheless, the robust effects that I have found and have summarized in the preceding paragraph are consistent with hypotheses that reflect causal factors as they relate to crime rates in a community. They are also consistent with the basic facts summarized in the introduction to this chapter, some of which have emerged from the micro-studies in the literature.

PART IV
The Complete Model: Education and Economic Development

11 Tracing the Impacts of Education on Development: A Summary

This chapter is an overview of the main impacts of human resource development through education on development that appear in the complete model. It draws on the preceding chapters to summarize the conclusions reached and identifies the equations that were selected from those tested, which are then programmed as part of the final model for use in interactive simulations. It also describes the internal working of the education sector which is part of the complete model, and variables related to its efficiency, as well as other aspects that were not germane to the sectors but are necessary for the interactive simulations.

As indicated in prior chapters, two key criteria are used for the equations selected. First, the education impacts must be logical in terms of the underlying microeconomic theory, including the dynamic lag structure (either of production of final satisfactions and the theory of the household, or of production of economic outputs by the firm). The logic of the theory is important to the possibility of inferring causation from the theory, and not being limited to statistical correlations. Second, each impact, whether direct or indirect, must be empirically significant, and this after controlling for possible omitted-variable biases or other major disturbances that are known to be or found to be statistically significant. Although it is not always possible to implement these criteria perfectly, they are the necessary and sufficient conditions for finding a scientific truth. Simulations that employ the complete model to trace the total impacts, separate the direct from the indirect impacts, and consider cost-effectiveness are to be found in two later chapters.

The technical econometric aspects are not addressed in this chapter, since they have been extensively considered in the preceding chapters.

Measuring Market-Based Returns to Education in Growth Models

The market-based returns to education are both *direct* and *indirect*. Essentially all of the latter and some of the former are externalities, a point considered more specifically in Chapter 13. The *direct* effects raise skill levels and the productivity of time within firms and also within households, as human-capital-augmented time is used during leisure-time hours in household production of final satisfactions. These direct effects can include some externality-type benefits of education within firms, as firms with a concentration of well-educated employees provide incentives and share new knowledge. (For example, medical doctors are known to keep their knowledge more up to date when working in larger hospitals and modern clinics and sharing knowledge than when working as sole practitioners in isolation.) But there is a second tier of externality benefits as firms or households benefit from education external to the firm, largely through the *indirect effects* of education strengthening the rule of law and political stability and offsetting diminishing returns to investment in physical capital, which then feeds back along with other community effects on productivity within firms and households. Some of these community effects may even be due to education and knowledge disseminated by earlier generations.

This distinction between direct and indirect effects and between private and externality benefits is complex. But these are useful distinctions to keep in mind as endogenous growth models are characterized for the purpose of relating them to a summary of the conclusions from preceding chapters.

Knowledge-Based Economic Growth Models

When the process of dissemination of knowledge is considered, the purely competitive framework breaks down and elements of imperfect competition must be introduced to incorporate a localized theory of technical progress as well as externalities specific to the localized efforts made for disseminating it through education, as in Lucas (1988). The long-term growth rate thereby depends on governmental actions, such as investment in education, to reduce the monopoly elements in the possession of knowledge. It also depends on governmental actions related to taxation, maintenance of law and order, protection for intellectual property through patents and copyright, and provisions for freer international trade and investment, as well as the provision of other essential services. Actions to achieve conditional convergence are also required in the augmented Solow (1956) models extended to include human capital and government policies (Barro, 1997: 8–9; Mankiw, Romer, and Weil, 1992).

The economic growth model set out in Chapter 2 can be simplified and related generically to these long-run endogenous growth and augmented Solow models. In per capita terms the determinants of the rate of growth (which in this book is extended to become a rate of development using Becker's (1968) concept of full income, which includes final satisfactions) are expressed in the following equation:

$$\delta y/\delta t = f(y, y^*), \tag{11.1}$$

where y is the initial level of output per capita and y^* is the long-run steady-state level of output per capita. The latter depends on government policies with respect to education and its direct and indirect effects as well as other choice and environmental factors. The growth rate, $\delta y/\delta t$, diminishes in y for given $y*$, and rises in y^* for given y.

The sign of this initial per capita output term was found to be consistently negative for many empirical estimates of the growth equation using data specific to East Asia, Latin America, Sub-Saharan Africa, and the OECD nations in Chapters

3–5, as the first part of the preceding sentence suggests. The signs of education policies relating to investment in human capital and gross enrolment rates were also found to be consistently positive after controlling for *y* as above and for other environmental factors.

I have not suggested, however, that these education policies are the only thing producing conditional convergence, or alone are a sufficient condition for growth. I merely seek to isolate and study the effects of education after removing other disturbances. The Sachs (1998) Harvard Institute for International Development results shown in Chapter 12 identify other sources of growth and are another way (beyond the other elements in our growth equations) that we seek to put the contribution of education in perspective. It is important to notice that several of these 'other sources' of growth are partially indirect effects of education identified by my structural approach. The more appropriate conclusion is that there are both partial direct effects and indirect structural effects from education on economic growth, which are quite significant both individually and when combined into the total effects.

Generalizing across the four regions or groups of countries, indirect effects of education that are significant include:

1. *The effects of education on increased rates of investment in physical capital.* This arises as greater skills in the labour force help to offset diminishing returns to physical capital and as education contributes to political stability (Chapters 3, 4, and 5).
2. *The effects of government support for education on increased rates of total saving.* Education taxes force personal financial saving, defined in the standard fashion as refraining from consumption, and also induce larger forgone earnings which are a part of *and increase* total saving as more children stay longer in school (Chapter 2) and room and board costs are invested in human capital formation.
3. *The effects of education on fertility rates* with respect to the average education level of females in the community (i.e. the cross-partial derivatives), the effects on infant mortality rates, the effects on longevity, and *the net effects of these on population growth rates* (Chapter 6).
4. *The indirect effect of education via the rule of law, democratization, and political stability.* These are 'community effects' of education that contribute to economic growth but largely indirectly through their effects, as mentioned above, in facilitating higher rates of investment in physical capital (Chapter 7). Barro (1997) emphasizes the 'rule of law' but this is a major component of the political stability index as developed by Political Risk Services.
5. *New knowledge via investment in R&D* is important behind the scenes and was tested many times in the growth equations for the separate regions. But it was never found to be positive and significant as a separate factor when human capital accumulation is included in the growth equation, and therefore it is not included in the growth equations in the final complete model. Human capital formation clearly provides for the adaptation and diffusion of technology created originally by R&D, which is a conclusion also reached earlier for East

Asia by Kim and Lau (1996) and for Africa by McMahon (1987), as well as in new regressions in this book for East Asia, Latin America, and Africa. Kim and Lau conclude specifically that large amounts of human and physical capital accumulation account for growth in East Asia and that when there are controls for this, technical change contributes nothing to total factor productivity. My conclusion (although focusing on labour productivity) is consistent with this, although higher education, especially in the OECD nations, where basic education already exists, may have a strategic role in diffusing new advanced technologies and management techniques created primarily by R&D.

The five points above all deal with the constants in the original Solow (1956) model: the saving (and investment) rate; the rate of net population growth; the political environment, which includes the rule of law; and the rate of technical change, which in the Solow model is exogenous rather than being related to investment in R&D. These constants in particular, but also other significant inter-country differences, which have been included in the complete model as controls for cultural differences and various shocks are not constant across countries or over time. They are therefore what make the original Solow model, though inspired, so unsatisfactory.

Effects of Education on Economic Growth by Region

This sets the stage for summarizing the empirical relations of education to economic growth that we have found in Chapters 2–5 and that will be used in the complete model. The first part of this summary focuses on the growth equation, and on indirect effects through the investment equation (effects 1 and 2 in the preceding list) that have been selected in the preceding chapters for each region. Both the growth and investment functions are specific to each region, using time series data, generally in 5-year time periods from 1960 to the present for each nation, pooled with the cross-section data covering all of the countries within each region. The endogeneity of the other Solow constants (effects 3–5 above) and their relation to investment in education will be summarized later in this chapter (in the section titled 'Summary of the Non-Market Marginal Products of Education by Sector').

East Asian Growth and Investment

Since East Asia has experienced some traumatic financial shocks, it is necessary to stress again that the analysis in this book pertains to medium-and longer-term growth processes and not primarily to these more temporary cyclical deviations. The longer-term growth prospects have undoubtedly been somewhat impaired in East Asia, especially in Indonesia, in Thailand, and perhaps in India due to military tensions, and lower rates of investment will affect the simulations. But my conclusion is that long-term growth prospects in East Asia remain quite promising given the large prior accumulation of human and physical capital in some countries, the relative political stability in the region, the slow but steady progress of democratization (including Indonesia), the low and falling population growth rates compared to those in the poorest countries, and the steps that are being taken under IMF urging (steps that were taken in the US in the 30s prior to the IMF) to reform and fireproof the financial system in the countries most affected.

For medium-and longer-term growth in East Asia the complete model responds to increases in secondary enrolment rates in the growth equation that reflect policy decisions to increase public investment in human capital formation as a per cent of GNP and to maintain high rates of investment in physical capital. These were the key factors that emerged in the regressions in Chapter 3; they enter the complete model (from Table 3–6, Model 22). The direct effects from the expansion of junior secondary education are the most relevant in Indonesia, India, and Thailand, following the earlier pattern of Japan, South Korea, Taiwan, and others who deliberately created their larger human capital stocks at these levels through active expansion of education, first at junior and then at senior secondary levels (McMahon, 1994*b*). According to the robust results obtained by Adrian Wood (1994), this became a base for their export-oriented growth strategies. Wood finds that education facilitates growth of the more skill-intensive manufacturing exports, a finding that is consistent with the proposition that human-resource effects in development are conductive to export-oriented growth strategies. Domestic technical change fostered by higher public investment in R&D did not make a positive contribution; this is consistent with the conclusions reached by Kim and Lau (1996), which they explain in terms of new knowledge diffused through high rates of investment in human and physical capital (note the lack of a positive role for I_A/Y in any growth equation in Chapter 3 in which human capital is taken into account, such as Models 7, 7$'$, 16, and 22).

Apart from these direct effects, the *indirect effects of education* affect economic growth primarily through rates of investment in physical capital. In the complete model, greater primary, secondary, and higher education enrolment rates raise investment in physical capital by directly offsetting diminishing returns, but also through contributions to political stability (Table 3–6, Model 21; see also Model 22). Political stability is affected positively not only by higher investment in secondary education, but also by democratization (the function for PS used in the complete model appears in Table 7.3, Model 3). Democratization, is also positively affected after a 12-year lag by secondary education enrolments (D from Table 7.1, Model 1). Robert Barro (1997) refers to this complex of interactions as the significant effects of the rule of law on economic growth, a component of the index of political stability and also of democratization. Other things in the political stability index take into account the fact that some relatively authoritarian regimes in East Asia have been politically stable and have grown rapidly.

Latin American Growth and Investment

The Latin American growth equation (from Table 4.2, Model 3′) also responds to secondary enrolment rates after a 10-year lag and to rates of investment in physical capital. A variable to control for the differential impacts of oil shocks and their aftermath in the early 80s was necessary.

Indirect effects of education, some with considerable time lags, are of major significance in the Latin American region, where there has been greater political instability. Investment in physical capital as a per cent of GNP in the complete model is influenced by secondary education enrolments as they offset diminishing returns to physical capital, with a lag of 10 years, and as they influence political stability, in this case with a lag of 20 years (from Table 4.7, Model 5). Political stability is aided by the democratization that has been going on in Latin America, which in turn has been influenced by secondary education enrolments lagged 12 years (PS as above from Table 7.3, Model 3).

Sub-Saharan African Growth and Investment

In the African region, per capita growth rates are determined in a much more significant fashion by effects from primary education enrolment rates but also from secondary enrolment rates, both lagged 10 years. The rate of investment in physical capital is important, as it was in East Asia and Latin America. But in Africa the higher population growth rates, diluting the quality of education and leading to less capital per worker unless investment rates are very high, have very significant negative effects on per capita economic growth. The growth and investment equations for Africa for the complete model are shown in Table 5.1, Model 2 and Table 5.2 Model 7 with the population-growth equations from Chapter 6.

In Sub-Saharan Africa, universal primary education has not yet been achieved in many nations. So the effects of increased primary education enrolment rates can reasonably be expected to be more significant for growth, as the regressions suggest. The fast population growth rates, however, require rapid expansion of the education system just to stay even, and put severe pressures on the quality of basic and higher education alike. So the negative relation of population growth to per capita growth is logical in an augmented Solow model, above and beyond its negative relation to the growth rate in very-long-term steady-state solutions of the original Solow model. Secondary education exerts its delayed effects through reductions in population growth and greater political stability, but few Africans have secondary education and the institutions of democracy and political stability are not established in many African nations. Inequality in income distribution is relatively high, and violent *coups d'état* and civil wars remain endemic, which can be reduced by the indirect and dynamically delayed community effects of education that are so often overlooked.

These *indirect effects* of education on growth come through the effects of both primary and secondary education enrolments, lagged 20 years, on rates of investment in physical capital, but also as more widespread secondary education, also lagged 15–20 years, contributes to political stability and to democratization which, in turn, increase rates of investment in physical capital. (The investment function for Africa in the complete model in Table 5.3, Eq. (7), reflects political stability and democratization from Chapter 7).

Per capita growth rates have been negative in many nations in Africa during the period 1965–83, especially given the 1981–3 interest rate shocks resulting in a lost generation of investment in human capital. But since then there has been some recovery, prior to the 1998–9 downturn, just as in Latin America. There was a temporary restoration of growth prior to 1999 for many but by no means all African nations.

OECD Member Nation Growth and Investment

For the higher per capita income OECD countries, the growth and investment equations used in the complete model are as shown in Table 11.1. The growth equation now includes higher education enrolments, since these countries have had universal primary and nearly universal secondary education for some time. So further investment in education in these countries is more relevant to reducing secondary education drop-out rates and expanding higher education at the two-and four-year college levels. All education measures are lagged 15 years to allow the new knowledge embodied by the education of graduates entering the labour force to gradually become effective as they gain experience and use their new knowledge and capacities to learn on the job to raise economic productivity.

The growth equation is from prior work by the author on the relation of education to productivity growth in 15 OECD nations (McMahon, 1984a: table 1, p. 306). Since the variables are scaled differently there, the coefficients are re-scaled to relate to the complete model. So the t-statistics are not appropriate and are therefore not shown. The investment function is based on worldwide data as estimated by Barro (1991: table III, p. 426). It is adapted as explained specifically in Table 5.3, row (7). To refine the precision of the measurement of impacts of

Table 11.1 Growth and Investment in OECD Nations

Growth equation (15 OECD nations):

$$y - n = 0.19\ I_K / Y + 0.0002\ (GER1\,T_{-15} + GER2\,T_{-15} + GER3\,T_{-15})$$
$$-\ 0.1076\ GNPPC_{-15}\ -\ 0.5\ (U\ /100)\ +\ 1.6$$
$$R^2 \simeq 0.57 \quad n = 45$$

Investment equation (worldwide data):

$$I_K / Y = -\ 0.0098\ GNPPC_{60} + 0.0007\ GER2_{-20} + 0.0004\ PS - 0.12\,(SSX/100) + 0.175$$
$$\quad\ (0.0048) \qquad\qquad (0.00033) \qquad\quad (0.00021) \qquad\quad (0.06)\quad\ (0.032)$$
$$R^2 \simeq 0.58 \quad n = 76$$

education on economic growth in the OECD nations, the coefficients could be re-estimated, although 1997 estimates by Petrakis and Stamatakis (1999) are similar. So Table 11.1 seems to offer a reasonable first approximation, a workable methodology, and an estimate of approximate impacts in the simulations.

There is other work as well that further documents the nature of the significance of secondary and higher education and R&D for economic growth in the OECD nations and in the US. For example, estimates of nested CES and translog production functions for the US, and other regressions for the five largest OECD nations, reveal the complementarity of higher education with R&D (see McMahon, 1992*a*: table 5–1, p. 115, and pp. 119–21). Using a different approach that employs microanalytic estimates of rates of return to higher education and to R&D, as well as rates of return to basic education and to physical capital, and that converts these into generalized Cobb–Douglas production function parameters for use in simulations as part of a comprehensive macroeconometric model of the growing economy for the US from 1948 to the present, shows quite interesting implications for the growth rate (see McMahon, forthcoming). In both cases the complementarity of higher education with R&D probably leads to overestimates of the rates of return to each, but these results do stress the importance of the diffusion of new knowledge as graduates enter the labour force, which is necessary before technology is effective. This complementarity of higher education with R&D (within a nested CES production function) turns out to explain about 19% of the growth rate in the US under simplifying assumptions (McMahon, 1992a: table 5–2, p. 119).

Rates of investment in physical capital also make an important contribution to growth in the OECD growth equation as well, which is consistent with other studies. The control for the unemployment rate is to remove shorter-term cyclical effects. The control for initial GNP per capita, and in particular its negative sign, is consistent with diminishing returns to physical capital that would otherwise occur and with conditional convergence, just as within East Asia and LAC. *The indirect effects* of education on growth appear through the investment function as secondary education offsets diminishing returns to physical capital, and as political stability (*PS*) contributes to higher rates of investment in physical capital. Political stability in turn depends partly on democratization, and both depend on education as community effects that feed back on the growth process. Social security expenditures as a per cent of the public budget, since they support consumption, are again negatively related to the rates of investment in physical capital (Barro 1991: 426; Barro and Sala-I-Martin, 1995: table 12.2, p. 451).

The Education Sector in the Complete Model

The internal structure of the education sector must be specified in order to show how policy simulations, such as changes in the rate of investment in education as a per cent of GNP or direct changes in secondary enrolment rates (in Chs. 12 and 13), operate through it to affect education outcomes. For these the internal efficiency of the education sector, however low or high it may be, is assumed to be constant (or changing at current rates). Nevertheless the structural reforms relevant to internal efficiency that can be implemented within the model will also be identified, and simulated outcomes that are not country-specific will be briefly described.

Enrolments and Investment in Education

Primary, secondary, and higher education enrolments are each broken down by gender and included in the complete model by means of the equations specifying the education sector as shown below. Direct changes in primary, secondary, or higher education *enrolments* are educational policies of the type that are often the focus of planning decisions by the ministries of education or by schools and colleges, whereas changes in the level of expenditure on education are economic decisions outside the control of the education sector. The latter decision is usually made by the economic planning agencies, the chief executive and the Cabinet, and the national or sub-national legislative bodies.

Gross enrolment rates are used rather than net enrolment rates because they are what is relevant to the financing. They include over-age students due to repetition and drop-outs and to part-time and older returning students. They reflect some internal inefficiency (e.g. poor attendance, or students that do not finish college expeditiously). But they are the basis for actual budgets, which is what is meaningful here, and for the financing of lifelong learning.

The rates of investment in education as a per cent of GNP (I_H/Y) is assumed to be constant in all simulations unless it changes explicitly. This means that absolute investment in education will grow, but not as a per cent of GNP, which is a reasonable assumption, as will be discussed later. If this rate of investment is changed, this term, shown in bold in each equation below, in turn affects gross enrolment rates. Examples of these kinds of changes in financial support (deriving from the demand for education outputs expressed through legislative bodies) include the building of schools and the provision of teachers and textbooks in rural areas. This is extremely relevant in developing countries (or in the OECD countries—for example, the building of two-year community colleges), as is the financing of teacher training and other improvements in quality that make good education more accessible in the lower-income districts so that enrolments increase.

If, alternatively, secondary education enrolments are increased directly by the ministry of education (or state department of education) then the effect on the simulations comes through a shift in the constant term in the relevant gross enrolment rate equations. This increases *GER2* by the amount of the increase (e.g. + 20 percentage points). Actual enrolments will increase slightly more than + 20, however, because of the other terms in the enrolment equations, such as GNP per capita and others that are endogenous and generate feedback effects.

Primary, Secondary, and Higher Education Enrolments

The equations, shown below, determining primary, secondary, and higher gross enrolment rates (*GER1*, *GER2*, and *GER3* respectively, with postscripts F = female and M = male) can be thought of as reduced forms. They each contain factors that are related to the effective demand for education outputs (coming from legislatures and political leaders) and factors related to the unit costs of education. The demand-related factors are education's share of GNP (I_H/Y), the per cent of this share devoted to primary education (*PEXP*), urbanization (the inverse of *LAGRI*, the labour force in agriculture), and GNP per capita (GNPPC in constant 1985 US dollars). The supply-side factors in each equation relating to the unit costs of producing graduates are expenditure per pupil as a per cent of GNP per capita (*XPSP*) and (for secondary education only) the grade 5 completion rate (*PEDCF* and *PEDCM*).

This analysis of the education sector, involving the underlying structural demand and supply equations leading to the reduced forms, is similar to that set out earlier and explained in greater depth in McMahon (1970). The empirical estimates are made by Crouch *et al.* (1992: 12–14), the co-principal investigator in the basic research underlying this and the health sector, as indicated in the Preface. The empirical estimates use the EIM data base, with most of the data and detailed sources for each variable given in Crouch *et al.* (1992: 33–6).

With the variables as defined above, and *t*-statistics in parentheses, female and male gross enrolment rates at each level are determined as follows:

$$GER1F = 119.9 - 0.362LAGRI_{-5} + 1,858(I_H/Y)PEXP - 324.8XPSP$$
$$(15.1) \qquad (-3.03) \qquad\qquad (5.50) \qquad\qquad (8.06) \qquad\qquad (11.2)$$
$$R^2 = 0.686 \quad (n = 44)$$

$$GER1M = 119.3 - 0.205LAGRI_{-5} + 1,600(I_H/Y)PEXP - 291.6XPSP$$
$$(19.0) \qquad (-2.18) \qquad\qquad (6.02) \qquad\qquad (9.19) \qquad\qquad (11.3)$$
$$R^2 = 0.715 \quad (n = 44)$$

$$GER2F = 42.9 - 0.40LAGRI_{-5} + 0.0033GER1F_{-5}(PEDCF)_{-5} + 929(I_H/Y) + 44.9EMENA + 8.51LAC$$
$$(5.02) \quad (-5.73) \qquad\qquad (5.27) \qquad\qquad\qquad (2.83) \qquad\quad (5.73)$$
$$R^2 = 0.798 \quad (n = 52)$$
$$(11.4)$$

$$GER2M = 54.5 - 0.40LAGRI_{-5} + 0.0025GER1M_{-5}(PEDCM)_{-5} + 800(I_H/Y) + 44.3EMENA$$
$$(6.24) \quad (-6.15) \qquad\qquad (3.48) \qquad\qquad\qquad (2.97) \qquad\quad (5.60)$$
$$R^2 = 0.665 \quad (n = 52)$$
$$(11.5)$$

$$GER3' = -29.123 + 0.0005GNPPC.$$
$$(na^1) \qquad (3.23)$$
$$R^2 = 0.993 \quad (n = 22)$$
$$(11.6)$$

EMENA is a dummy variable for the European, Middle East, and North African countries. To test for the stability of these relationships, Equations (11.2)–(11.5) were re-estimated for various years, first at time t, then $t - 5$, $t - 10$, and finally $t - 15$. These results were compared and the stability of the relation, parsimony, and goodness of fit were tested to select the best prediction equation, which is then shown above and used in the final model.[2] The simulations for a subset of countries were also examined to assess the model's capacity to produce realistic results.

These equations show that enrolments respond positively to the availability of financial resources (I_H/Y, GNPPC), better quality as reflected in completion rates (*PEDCF*), and to cultural factors reflected in urbanization (*LAGRI*) and region (*EMENA*). Enrolments respond negatively to higher unit costs (*XPSP*). Gross enrolment rates at primary and secondary levels are the average of female and male gross enrolment rates (i.e., $GER1 = (GER1F + GER1M)/2$, and $GER2 = (GER2F + GER2M)/2$), which are definitional identities in the complete model. Using population weights to get this average would require a projection of age-specific population groups in each nation, which would increase the computation costs beyond the benefit of any marginal increases in accuracy. Reducing the inefficiencies in gross enrolment rates requires structural reforms, as discussed below. These typically occur in developing countries over a longer period of time as a nation develops and the education system matures.

Costs per Student

On the supply side, cost per student as a per cent of GNP per capita (*XPSP*) reflects quality but also inefficiency, as shown below. It is essentially the supply price of educational opportunities and facilities as supplied by the education system in each nation. Empirically it is overwhelmingly dependent on average teacher salaries in most countries (*TSALRT*). The latter is also expressed as a multiple of GNP per capita to allow cross-country comparisons free of exchange rate issues. Cost per student also depends on the student–teacher ratio (*STRP*), expressed as an inverse since lower student–teacher ratios obviously mean higher cost:

$$XPSP = 0.024 + 0.922TSALRT(1/STRP).$$

$$(3.19) \qquad (15.81) \tag{11.7}$$

$$R^2 = 0.865 \quad (n = 40)$$

This says that costs per student will be higher when teachers' salaries are higher and also when class sizes are smaller. Lowering class sizes therefore raises costs, but can also increase individual attention given to the student and thereby raise quality, especially in the poorest countries, where class sizes tend to be very large. Raising teachers' salaries also raises costs, but also can increase quality as more able people are attracted into the profession and given the rewards necessary to get more advanced training and stay up to date in their fields. This cost per student *as a per cent of GNP per capita* does *not* respond significantly to higher GNP per capita in either linear or log specifications. The latter is consistent with the relatively well-known fact that to retain a teaching force of approximately constant quality, the effective demand for basic education has an approximately unitary income elasticity (e.g., McMahon, 1970 for the US).

In addition to higher quality, higher unit costs can also reflect inefficiency. Expenditure on teaching materials and libraries (and on teacher training) are well known to be cost-effective means of achieving better learning outcomes and better quality (Fuller and Clarke, 1994: table 1, lines 5–8, and World Bank 1995: chap. 4 and figure 4.1). So expenditure per student on teaching materials and school libraries, both as a per cent of GNP per capita, were tried as a determinant of unit cost but found to be insignificant in the presence of the term shown measuring teachers' salary times class size. So a reasonable inference (based on the other studies cited) is that shifts in the budget toward larger percentages for teaching materials and libraries do improve quality and internal efficiency, but do so at essentially the same cost per student since they are not significant in determining cost per student. No consistent measure of test scores exists which covers the countries in the complete model. So I rely on the other studies surveyed in Fuller and Clarke (1994), fifth-grade completion rates, and my measures of ultimate outcomes in Chapter 12.

Fifth-Grade Completion Rates

Fifth-grade completion rates for males and females (*PEDCF* and *PEDCM*) are important, especially in the developing countries, because they are an index of the success of the school system in producing graduates. Hence they are an index of the school system's efficiency in this regard. They are positively influenced in Equations (11.8) and (11.9) by the cost per student (*EPSP*) times GNP per capita (GNPPC). Completion rates for females in Equation (11.8) are also positively influenced by higher female gross enrolment rates in the past ($GER1F_{-5}$), which could reflect cultural factors. Fifth-grade completion rates are abnormally low in Latin America and Caribbean countries, as indicated by the significant negative coefficient for this regional dummy variable ($- LAC$):

$$PEDCF = 24.6 + 0.165GER1F_{-5} + 19.91ln[XPSP(GNPPC)] - 27.52LAC$$
$$(2.50) \qquad (2.31) \qquad\qquad (8.28) \qquad\qquad\qquad (5.58) \qquad\qquad (11.8)$$
$$R^2 = 0.664 \quad n = 49$$

$$PEDCM = 18.1 + 21.29ln[XPSP(GNPPC)] - 27.80LAC.$$
$$(1.79) \qquad (8.97) \qquad\qquad (5.58) \qquad\qquad\qquad (11.9)$$
$$R^2 = 0.645 \quad n = 50$$

These cost and completion rate equations were also checked for stability, parsimony, and goodness of fit. It can be noticed that all these relations are recursive with significant lags between cause and effect, which permits use of single-equation estimating methods.

Interpreting these completion rates as one index of internal efficiency in the schools, their significant positive dependence on higher expenditure per pupil (*XPSP* times GNPPC in Equations (11.8) and (11.9)) is consistent with the hypothesis that higher expenditure per pupil provides for better quality, and that this higher quality is conducive to higher completion rates. Behrman and Birdsall (1983) certainly found the latter to be true in Brazil. These higher costs per student, however, also are associated with smaller increases in primary enrolment rates, as seen in Equations (11.2) and (11.3), as per pupil costs rise. The inefficiency in the primary schools in Latin America, where absenteeism and drop-out rates are often very high, shows up in the significantly negative coefficient for *LAC*.

Higher primary completion rates, then, indicate in turn a higher proportion of children who are eligible to enter the secondary schools, and are associated with higher secondary gross enrolment rates in Equations (11.4) and (11.5), as would be expected.

Finally, in the specification of the education sector, the proportion of the labour force in agriculture, *LAGRI*, which enters the gross enrolment rate equations must be treated as endogenous if it is to be possible to simulate the effects of education policy changes in the future. As shown in Equation (11.10), it declines as economic growth occurs (see $- \ln$ GNPPC) and it also declines further as secondary education enrolment rates increase (see $- GER2T$):

$$LAGRI = -0.12 \ln \text{GNPPC}_{-10} - 3.0\ GER2T_{-20}.$$
$$n = 75$$

(11.10)

No standard errors are shown because this equation was re-estimated with the constant term deleted and then *LAGRI* set equal to the actual value of *LAGRI* in each country in the initial period. (The original equation in Crouch *et al.*, 1992: 18, has the same variables but it causes *LAGRI* to become negative in many countries.) The result does produce stable and reasonable predictions of the proportion of the labour force in agriculture in all of the countries for which it was tried, and therefore is used successfully for the simulations. But it does not have ideal econometric properties; it could be re-estimated, but the refinements in the estimated outcomes would likely be very modest, given the accuracy with which Equation (11.10) predicts *LAGRI* for many countries. The association of higher secondary education enrolments with lower percentages of the labour force remaining in agriculture can be interpreted as reflecting the role of secondary education in the transition to an industrializing economy as many with secondary education take industrial jobs, mostly in the provincial cities.

Investment in Education, Access, and Education Reforms

A distinction must be made here between policy simulations that change the level of investment in education or access at different levels, and structural reforms within the education sector, since the latter focus more explicitly on internal efficiency. With the structure of the education sector now in view in Equation (11.2)–(11.9), what follows indicates briefly the extent to which policy simulations using the complete model can trace the impacts of investment and reforms.

Investment and Access

Although a change that increases or decreases *investment* in education as a per cent of GNP (I_H/Y) will affect access, in the simulations most of the other terms in the education sector remain constant. Cost per pupil (*XPSP*), pupils per teacher (*STRP*), and teachers' salaries as a ratio to GNP per capita (*TSALRT*) specifically remain constant, although they can be changed by making simultaneous changes in other policies.

However, if economic growth is occurring for whatever reasons, then GNP per capita (GNPPC) will grow endogenously, the proportion of the labour force in agriculture ($LAGRI_{-5}$) will decline, and enrolment will grow for reasons quite apart from the policy change.

If instead secondary enrolments are the only thing changed in the policy simulations, as GNP grows some additional resources are available to all levels of education given that education's share of GNP remains constant. But the per cent of the education budget going to secondary education increases and the other levels of education are squeezed by this shift within the education budget. The other endogenous variables in the equations, such as GNPPC and *LAGRI*, continue to affect gross enrolment rates as before as part of endogenous development.

Education Reforms

The impacts of several structural reforms within the education sector that are listed below can be simulated by employing the complete model. Brief remarks follow about each, because internal efficiency is a difficult aspect frequently studied (e.g. Boedions, MacMahon, and Adams 1992; Hanushek *et al.* 1996).

Reform 1. Greater gender equity: changing female enrolments (GERF). If the enrolment rates of females are far below those of males, as they are in much of Sub-Saharan Africa, and especially in North Africa and Nepal, it is possible and useful to simulate the impacts of increases in the enrolment rates of females only, or of increases at different rates than those for males.

Many of the impacts come through non-market effects. For example, differential impacts of female education on lower fertility and lower net population growth rates (feeding back eventually on per capita economic growth rates), and less poverty and inequality, are noticeable.

Reform 2. Rationalizing the allocation of education budgets among levels: changing the per cent allocated to primary (PEXPT), secondary (GER2T), or higher education (using combinations with total enrolments of GER1T, GER2T, and GER3T). Each of these variables in Equations (11.2)–(11.10) above can be changed by any amount, although no single gross enrolment rate is allowed within the model to go above 115 per cent, which allows for over-age students. This means that when universal primary education is achieved, additional funds are channelled to secondary education, and so forth. In those nations that have not achieved universal primary education with high primary completion rates it is meaningful to simulate the impacts of deliberate increases in primary enrolments and a relative shifting of funds to this level, as has been decided recently in India.

Reform 3. Changes in teachers' salaries (TSLAT). In some nations teachers' salaries are extremely low relative to average GNP per capita; in others they are very high. In the former nations, moonlighting by teachers, the lack of ability to attract and hold the better teachers, and pupil absenteeism contribute to low completion rates (Equations (11.8) and (11.9)), and hence to lower contributions by primary and secondary education (via *GER1T* and *GER2T*) to economic growth and development. On the other hand, in nations where teachers' salaries are high relative to GNP per capita, higher unit costs, once they have achieved high completion rates, then limit access (Equations (11.2) and (11.3)).

Reform 4. Changes in the student–teacher ratio (STRP). The student–teacher ratio is very high at the primary level in some countries, again often where student absenteeism and drop-out rates are high and primary completion rates are low, so that reducing class size is cost-effective. In others where it is low, increasing class sizes (or no further reductions in class size) are likely to be more cost-effective.

Simulations making these changes in isolation, or any combination of them in concert, are possible. It is not possible, however, to simulate privatization of the public schools beyond the public–private mix currently existing in each country. The efficiency effects of doing this become involved with the inherent lack of comparability of the public-pupil mix with the private-pupil mix, suggesting the formidable research tasks involved, not to speak of the inadequacies in the data for econometric estimation.

The kinds of structural changes that are considered here also give primary attention to the developing countries. So although there are some insights to be gained for the OECD nations, further econometric estimation focused on the more advanced education levels using data for these nations would be desirable, and in the meantime caution should be used in making inferences within the OECD.

As a final qualification, it would be extremely desirable to have internationally comparable test scores or other measures of learning outcomes as measures of school and college quality. But they simply are not available for a wide enough range of nations to be able to be used meaningfully. However, quality is not ignored; I have used what is perhaps the next best measure of quality, albeit an incomplete one, in the form of school completion rates as a measure of the success of the school system in producing graduates. I have also measured the ultimate productivity of education in the form of its contribution to economic growth and to non-market private and social benefits, since these are measures of the quality of education in terms of final outcomes.

Summary of the Non-market Marginal Products of Education by Sector

To measure the non-market returns to education, controls have been imposed throughout for per capita income in order to isolate the non-market net marginal products of education and thereby avoid double-counting the monetary returns. These non-market returns, therefore, are over and above the returns measured by markets in economic growth, and some are pure externalities (see McMahon, 1999). Because of the other controls in each equation, they should also be net of other empirically significant non-education impacts on the growth and development process. These non-market returns are the result of human capital being used in household production of final satisfactions during non-market or leisure-time hours. The equations summarized here rather informally continue to identify those used in the complete model.

Population and Health

Population growth rates are the net result of falling fertility rates, better health of children (as measured by falling infant mortality rates), and better health in general (as measured by greater longevity) (Chapter 6, Eqns. (5)–(7)). Each of these in turn are determined by a separate equation that depends on the behaviour of households as they respond to primary and secondary education levels, or both, after controlling for per capita income (Chapter 6, Eqns. (1) and (3) and Chapter 6, Eqn. (4) are in the complete model).

The net effect of all three of these elements over time is that population growth rates are *higher* at first as females attain basic education up through about grade 9. Primary education contributes to improved child health, lower infant mortality, and greater longevity, all of which increase the population size. This phase can be expected to continue for some time in Sub-Saharan Africa, Nepal, India, and Pakistan and other places where most females are not yet completing ninth grade. Then, above about grade 9 the sustained one-way effect of further female education on falling fertility rates begins to swamp the population-increasing effects of female education on better health, causing net population growth rates to begin to fall.

This stage of falling net population growth rates has been reached in the fast-growing East Asian nations. There, most females are now educated well into the secondary level and education at both the primary and secondary levels is for the most part gender-neutral. In some Latin American countries where female secondary enrolment rates were very low (given the 20-year lags) in 1970, such as Nicaragua (13 per cent), Honduras (9 per cent), and Peru (21 per cent), net population growth rates are currently still very high (Nicaragua 3.4 per cent, Honduras 3.5 per cent) and moderately high (Peru 2.3 per cent). These compare to female secondary enrolment rates in 1970 in Japan of 81 per cent, Korea 25 per cent, and Singapore 41 per cent. In the future, net population growth rates in these Latin American countries with low female secondary enrolment can be expected to remain relatively high. However, Uruguay, which had a high female secondary enrolment rate 20 years ago of 46%, now has a population growth rate that is very low (0.7%), and a per capita economic growth rate that is significantly higher than most other Latin American nations.

The female enrolment rate variables in the fertility rate equation contain an interaction term with investment in family planning clinics, an effect that is positive and highly significant. This suggests that female education alone is highly significant in reducing fertility and net population growth rates, but that it also interacts with and can be augmented by infant-health and family planning programmes where they exist. Making use of both female secondary education and this interaction is perhaps the best and perhaps the only hope for Sub-Saharan Africa and some of the other poorest countries. There high and rising net population growth rates, poverty, civil wars as the poor in the countryside join against those in the cities (in a sense repeating the French Revolution, but sometimes with an additional ethnic dimension), and Malthusian mass starvation are on the increase. This interaction between female education and family planning clinics also has a cost-effectiveness dimension (which could be further explored) in contributing both to better health and slower population growth.

Democratization

One of the important non-monetary direct contributions of education to human welfare is the net contribution it makes to democratization. Democratization in turn was found in Chapter 7 to contribute to political stability. Since political stability contributes to higher rates of investment and hence to economic growth, there is also a structural feedback effect from education through democratization to economic growth.

In particular, after controlling for rising per capita income, to which education contributes (included in the monetary returns), higher secondary education enrolment rates and lower military expenditure as a per cent of total government expenditure are very important key determinants of democratization (as in Table 7.1, Model 1, which is in the complete model). Democratization is measured here by the Freedom House (1997) political rights index and is not a dichotomous variable, but moves from lower levels of democratization to intermediate levels of the effectiveness of political institutions, and eventually after long delays to full rights and freedoms.

The positive relationship of rising per capita income to higher levels of democratization, including the main direction of the causal flow from income to democratization, has been stressed by most political scientists who have studied this, such as Diamond (1992), and is consistent with my results here. But the gross relationship is not a simple linear one. In particular, countries with per capita income below about US$400 per year are almost without exception agrarian and authoritarian. Those between $400 and $2,000 have increasing degrees of political rights but are in a zone of rapid transition. Those from about $2,000 to $6,000 have reached a plateau, with perhaps 80% of the political rights typical of full democracies. Finally, those above $6,000 are in a zone where democracy is extremely likely and virtually universal.

China is on the bottom rung of the zone of transition, and only now showing the beginnings of a bit of movement. Indonesia was a bit higher before the resignation of Suharto, and has since shown erratic movement toward more widespread political participation. Most Latin American and Caribbean countries are in the middle of this zone of transition, although Haiti at $310, Bolivia at $470, and Honduras at $720 are near the lowest threshold. The upper-middle-income countries, such as Brazil, Mexico, Panama, Argentina, and Venezuela, are in the $2,000–$4,000 range and far into the zone of transition, although still experiencing fragile and less than full democracy. All of the OECD nations are full democracies. There are only isolated exceptions from this pattern, such as India, where there is a strong tradition of British parliamentary democracy associated with Nehru (but with roots in the British heritage), and Hitler's Germany at the other extreme, which has since reverted to democracy. From our long-run perspective, the higher per capita income and education levels in Germany and now the transition environment in the Newly Independent Countries could be viewed as delayed adjustments.

The net contribution of secondary education to this process apparently occurs as larger percentages of the population are no longer under the control of rural landlords, enjoy rising urban earnings as they become part of a growing middle class, and seek political rights. The relevance of this secondary educational attainment shows up significantly in the regressions.

Many have suggested that the author try the direct feedback of democratization on economic growth. But I do not find this effect to be significant. Nor does Barro (1997). Democratization and the rule of law instead appear to operate through effects on political stability, and through this in turn on higher rates of investment in physical capital and hence on economic growth.

Human Rights

The story with respect to human rights is very similar to that of democratization. Human rights as measured by the Freedom House index include freedom of speech, freedom of the press, freedom of assembly, and civil rights and protections in legal proceedings.

Human rights do not increase as rapidly with per capita income growth as does democratization. Military expenditure as a per cent of the government budget again has a highly significant and very negative impact on human rights. Again, secondary education enrolment rates, with a 10-year lag, have a highly significant positive relationship to human rights. When democratization is included as an explanatory variable, its significance is very high ($t = 11.8$) and the percentage of variation in human rights that is explained by these factors rises to 87%. (This is a brief summary of the equation from Table 7.2, Model 1, used in the complete model.)

Overall there are *direct non-monetary impacts* from the expansion of secondary education on human rights. But there are also *indirect* structural impacts of secondary education on human rights that come from its relation to democratization, as measured by the cross-partial derivatives. There is an additional contribution of education to human rights made by growing per capita income, but this has already been counted as part of the monetary returns to education and is therefore removed by the control for per capita income to avoid double-counting.

Political Stability

Political stability is measured by the 'composite index' in the 'International Country Risk Guide' (Coplin *et al.*, 1997) and is close to but not identical with Barro's (1997) 'rule of law'. It can largely be explained statistically by rising per capita income, lower military expenditure as a per cent of total government expenditure, higher secondary education enrolment rates, and democratization, as in Table 7.3, Model 3, which is chosen for the complete model. Other factors that I show to make positive contributions to political stability are more widespread newspaper communications (this is also correlated with secondary education enrolments), urbanization (with a negative effect on political stability), and social security expenditures as a per cent of the government budget (positive relation to stability).

It is interesting that higher secondary enrolment rates have a *direct* positive relation to greater political stability as well as an *indirect* contribution through democratization. It is not secondary education that is destabilizing, as some authoritarian leaders fear. Instead it is large numbers of uneducated poverty-striken people in rural areas (the fuel for civil wars in Rwanda, Chad, Mali, and throughout Sub-Saharan Africa where junior secondary education has not been extended to the rural areas). This can be accompanied by urbanization, such as in the large rings of uneducated, largely unemployable people from the countryside who have migrated to urban slums around Rio de Janeiro, Karachi, or the Chicago and Los Angeles ghettos. The indirect contribution of education to economic growth via political stability has already been counted as part of the economic returns to education in the first section of this chapter.

Poverty Reduction

Absolute poverty in the rural areas, defined as the per cent of rural families living in poverty on about US$1 a day or less, is reduced by per capita economic growth (as in Table 8.1, Model 3, which is used in the complete model). This is a very robust relationship, as is well known. But poverty is also found to be lower when there are higher primary, but more significantly higher secondary, education enrolment rates, both lagged 20 years. This is after controlling for per capita income (as in Table 8.1 Models 2 and 4), so I interpret it as a non-market effect of secondary education on distribution over and above this estimate of its efficiency-related effects on earnings. In all regressions, however, larger enrolments in higher education are directly associated with *more* rural poverty, not less. One possible explanation of this is that it reflects pressures from higher-income ruling elites and military regimes in poor countries to keep higher education tuition very low, which benefits them (and expands higher education enrolments) but does not significantly benefit rural families.

The pattern in urban areas with respect to the variables to which urban poverty responds is identical to that for rural poverty (see Table 8.2, Model 1).

Inequality in the Distribution of Income

Inequality in income distribution, as measured by the *GINI* coefficient, is a different matter from the per cent of either rural or urban households in absolute poverty. Inequality is also measured in terms of the distribution of personal income, which includes rent, interest, and profits, and not the distribution of earnings.

I conclude that when the non-linear growth term that generates the inverted Kuznets U is removed, and secondary education enrolment rates are added, this largely explains the reduction in inequality as growth occurs (as in Table 8.3, Model 2, used in the complete model). The inverted Kuznets U, is thereby left to apply only to those economies where growth-with-equity policies are not being pursued, which could explain its lack of significance in the larger data set. This result is the conditional 'growth with equity' typical of the policies followed in East Asia as identified in World Bank (1993a). These policies have not been followed in Brazil and some other Latin American countries since the 1960s and in these places inequality remains extremely high, as Kuznets predicted.

In Africa, the rise in inequality as development proceeds, as predicted by the inverted Kuznets U, occurs, I conclude, because the 'growth with equity' path is conditional. There are of course other policies that are also relevant to reducing inequality (such as abandoning overpriced exchange rates, supporting agricultural development and land reform, and providing for the availability of agricultural credit). But with respect to education policies, Knight and Sabot (1990) earlier found a similar result when comparing Kenya and Tanzania. They concluded that expanded secondary enrolments in Kenya reduced the scarcity rents earned at the secondary level, while also contributing to productivity growth, thereby reducing inequality in earnings, an outcome that did not occur in Tanzania, where access to secondary education had not been expanded earlier.

The *indirect* structural effects of education on the reduction of inequality are almost as large. Female education slows population growth rates (reducing the size of families), thereby reducing inequality. Lack of female education increases inequality in the model (see also Table 8.3, First and Fourth rows). This is consistent with T. W. Schultz's and Simon Kuznets' earlier observations that as earnings due to human capital formation loom more important than property income from rent, interest, and profits (which is more unequally distributed), this lowers inequality in income distribution toward the levels typical in the OECD member countries.

The Environment and Sustainable Development

Economic development is not true development if in the process the environment, which is important to the quality of life, is destroyed. Three of the major aspects of maintaining a sustainable environment are considered, namely deforestation accompanied by destruction of wildlife as it loses its habitat, water pollution, and air pollution. The fourth, global warming, is not addressed directly, although to some extent it can be subsumed under economic effects that also drive deforestation and air pollution.

Much of the economics and environmentalist literature concerning the environment focuses on the design and implementation of effective regulations. Here I use a more distinctive approach by considering underlying factors that contribute to environmentally destructive activities as well as to the forces contributing to democratization that press governments to permit or to regulate deforestation and pollution.

Forests and Wildlife

After controlling for per capita income, lower population growth rates and *lower* secondary education enrolment rates, lagged 20 years, reduce the rate of deforestation (as in Table 9.1, Model 3, used in the complete model). However, there are *indirect* effects of secondary education that work in the other direction and, as will be seen in the simulations later, eventually dominate to reverse the bad effects on the environment. As secondary education lowers rural poverty, this reduces deforestation. It also contributes to urbanization and to economic growth, which provide the political base for regulation of those aspects of lumbering and agriculture that are destructive, as well as the economic capacity to support national parks.

This structural process also can be illustrated by substituting the population, poverty, and growth equations into those relating to the environment in Chapter 9 and then tracing the net dependence of environmental quality on education levels. This net dependence turns out to be positive, but after significant lags, as in the simulations that follow. This reduced form is also consistent with the earlier hypotheses (that demands for environmental preservation are made effective through democratic governments, that the preservation of forests and wildlife depends on better economic capacity, and that less rural poverty reduces the need to cut firewood and poach animals).

Although not developed originally from the data in this book, a fourth interesting effect can be derived from the work by Wood (1994), who finds that as skill levels of the labour force improve there is a shift away from (extractive) primary exports. This shift toward human-capital-intensive manufacturing and services can potentially help to reduce the strain on the environment.

Reduced Water and Air Pollution

Water pollution is measured by selected river water samplings near major cities in each nation for developing countries worldwide, and air pollution by particles in the air reflecting air quality.

Water pollution increases as development begins, but then it responds significantly to reductions in the rate of population growth (a function of education) and to reductions in the amount of urban poverty (also a function of education), as in Table 9.3, Model 3, used in the complete model. These are purely non-market indirect effects of education, since there is a control for per capita income to avoid double-counting the market returns. Demands for effective regulation of pollution are more effective as democratization proceeds (which is also a function of education), another indirect effect. (The latter appears in Table 9.1, Models 1 and 4.)

Air pollution follows a somewhat different pattern on the supply side from either deforestation or water pollution. Since air pollution is supplied largely from industrial emissions, motor vehicle emissions, and urban heating and cooling, it is *consistently and positively* related to rising per capita income and hence positively related to economic growth (see the growth term in Table 9.4, Model 1, which is used in the complete model). It also responds in the opposite fashion to population growth (faster population growth means less air pollution, presumably because most of the population is rural), and poverty is not a significant factor. The reduced-form correlations of secondary and higher education with air pollution (in Table 9.4, Models 5 and 6, which were not programmed into the complete model) do relate more education to less air pollution. I tentatively conclude that education effects on air pollution come indirectly, however, through democratization and slower population growth (as in Table 9.4, Model 1). The possible exception may be in the negative relation of higher education to air pollution, with university-educated citizens demanding more effective regulation, but again probably through democratic political systems.

Violent Crime

Violent crime as measured by homicide rates worldwide is lower when inequality in income distribution is lower, after controlling for GNP per capita (as in Table 10.1, Model 2, used in the complete model). The relation of homicide to per capita income is negative, so the *indirect* structural effects of secondary education through higher per capita income and less inequality (or less poverty, as in Table 10.1, Model 5) both operate to reduce violent crime.

This is consistent with the hypothesis suggested by Ehrlick's theory and by the criminology literature surveyed in Chapter 10. Both suggest that secondary school (and community college) attendance, which since they keep young people off the streets and under supervision in school or in jobs and aid formation of positive peer-group relationships, reduce crime rates. I did try a reduced-form version of Chapter 10's Model 2, using data for the US, where homicide rates (and the prevalence of handguns) are dramatically higher than in other OECD nations. With secondary education and unemployment rates (the latter after a two-year lag) used directly in the homicide equation, and controlling for per capita income as before, these education-related terms are both significant and act in a direction that is consistent with this hypothesis. Tax exemptions for tuition at secondary and associate-degree levels (as proposed by the US Congress in 1998) support propriet-ary schools that cherry-pick the best students, and do not address the serious crime problem caused by drop-outs.

Property Crime and Drugs

Property crime more generally (measured as all other reported crime per 100,000 in the population) increases dramatically with economic growth, in sharp contrast to homicide.

It is true that education can contribute to some kinds of crime, such as embezzlement and computer hacking, which are therefore negative externalities. Education also has negative indirect effects on property crime to the extent that it contributes to economic growth. But after controlling for per capita income, the most robust relationship in the international and US data alike is the strong negative relation of community-wide secondary education gross enrolment rates to lower property crime rates (Table 10.2, Models 1–5).

Inequality in income distribution and urban poverty are both significantly related to increases in property crime (all as shown in Table 10.2, Model 1, which is used in the complete model). But here also education has indirect effects on property crime rates as it reduces inequality and urban poverty, as discussed above.

The worldwide and US crime regressions suggest, overall, that education reforms directed at increasing gross enrolment rates, which keeps young people off the streets and aids in forming more positive peer-group relationships (e.g. reducing the number of high school drop-outs, lengthening the school day, increas-ing community college enrolments, etc.), do reduce crime directly. Even though education for those who have already chosen a life of crime may not work very well, the evidence indicates that broadening the base of community education reduces poverty, inequality, and structural unemployment, and hence homicide and property crime rates.

Conclusions

Microeconomic research underlies each of the sectors summarized above. It has been examined in each of the preceding chapters, but also in detail in articles recently published by the author and others in a special issue of the *International Journal of Education Research* devoted to recent advances in measuring the benefits of education (McMahon, 1997b). There are also specialized recent survey articles on health by Grossman and Kaestner (1997), and on crime by Witte (1997). All of this microeconomic research is surveyed in an article on measuring total returns to in *Education Economics* (McMahon, 1998b). Most of the individual studies at the micro-level are narrow and piecemeal, and virtually none addresses structural impacts. Therefore, no overall measurement of the outcomes of education is achieved, although pioneering efforts have been made by Haveman and Wolfe (1984) and Wolfe and Zuvekas (1997).

The conclusion can be reached that although a few negative externalities from education have been found, a point consistent with Mark Blaug's impression mentioned earlier, the empirical evidence is overwhelming that the net *direct* and net *indirect structural* effects are positive.

The next two chapters turn to a systematic effort to measure these direct and structural outcomes, and then relate them to the costs.

Notes

1. This equation cannot be estimated from data available in the OIM model. GER3 is used only in the production function for the OECD nations (and in the urban and rural poverty equations, which are not presented as part of the simulations). It was taken from the estimates of income elasticities of the public effective demand for higher education in the US in McMahon (1974: p. 86, equation 4) with the other explanatory variables taken at their mean and collapsed into the constant term. This equation is therefore a rough approximation and would need to be re-estimated when refining the simulations involving higher education in the OECD nations.
2. Stability was checked by comparing the predicted outcomes in 1970 with those in 1980, and those for 1980 with 1985 and 1990. Parsimony was resolved by backward deletion, where variables making no significant independent contribution were removed individually, the equation re-estimated, and the process repeated until all remaining variables are significant at trend level or better (suggesting removal of chance effects) with minimal reduction on the adjusted R^2. Goodness of fit was assessed through examination of the adjusted R^2. For further details see Crouch *et al.* (1992: 11).

12 Measuring the Total Social Benefits of Education: The Complete Model

By bringing together the direct and indirect effects of human resource development through education on each of the market and non-market outcomes, this chapter uses the complete interactive model to estimate the total social benefits of education. In the case of benefits to pure economic growth, these include the private returns plus externalities associated with increasing returns in the spirit of the new endogenous growth models. In the case of the non-market impacts, there are again both private benefits and externalities, but in this case they are the result of household production of final satisfactions and lead to impacts that are part of endogenous development.

Estimates are made by means of strategic policy simulations that generate time paths using data specific to each country through 2035 AD. This is done for a base solution involving a continuation of past policies, which will be referred to as the 'endogenous development scenario', and then for two specific education and economic policy interventions that generate 'policy change scenarios'. The difference between these time paths for each endogenous variable is then the measure of the total social benefits of education. These total social benefits are later broken down into direct partial benefits and indirect structural benefits; the latter are externalities. It will be noticed that there are time lags, and quite different time lags, as the direct and indirect structural benefits phase in. So this is an exercise in comparative dynamics.

The empirical estimates of total social benefits are shown for a few selected countries in each region (simply because to show them for all of the 78 countries in the complete model would consume too much space) and for a period from the present usually through 2035 (although occasionally through 2020). In addition to the two kinds of strategically chosen policy changes shown, 8 other types of policy changes, including those reforms discussed in Chapter 11, can be simulated using the complete model, and for any of the 78 countries in Latin America, Asia, Africa, or the OECD. Occasional regional overviews or comparisons between poor developing countries and advanced industrialized countries are also presented.

The first section of this chapter considers the no-new-policy-change endogenous development scenario. It is this time path which will be compared with the time paths after an explicit change in education policy. This section includes comparisons to econometric results in other recent models that are sufficiently comparable in their structure to permit meaningful comparisons.

The second section presents the estimates of the total social benefits of education as measured in 13 nations, 3 in each region but 4 in Asia. These estimates focus in the first 8 panels for each nation on measures of the net effects of education changes alone on economic growth, poverty reduction, and inequality, and in the next 8 panels on the non-market impacts on democratization, human rights, health, the environment, crime, and other aspects of the quality of life. Chapter 13 separates the total effects on each into direct effects and indirect impacts which are externalities.

Since this is a new approach to measurement of the direct and indirect outcomes over time, a few qualifications are important. The marginal products of education, on which rest all of the measures of the net outcomes of education, depend on the econometric estimates discussed in depth in the preceding chapters. All of these are subject to standard errors of the estimates as well as to possible continuing refinement of the specification by future investigators. So although this qualification is not constantly repeated throughout, it should be constantly kept in mind. It implies that the measurement of the returns to education should not be interpreted, and are never intended, as point estimates at each date for each country. Instead they are indicative of levels for which there is a standard error that cannot be shown on each graph, and suggestive of a range or relative magnitude and direction for each effect. Sometimes forces build up in particular countries until there are dichotomous jumps, so that these effects do not follow the smooth continuous trends given by the regression coefficients based on larger numbers of countries. But there is nevertheless an indication of what is likely to happen eventually, and a first approximation of its relative magnitude.

Endogenous Development: Continuing Current Policies

The base-line scenario to which the impacts of increments to education are to be compared will be referred to in the case of pure economic growth as the 'endogenous growth scenario', or in the case of broader development goals as the 'endogenous development scenario', since the latter goes beyond purely market-measured effects.

After I have considered the base-line scenarios, the effects of two explicit policy interventions involving different kinds of increments to education will then be considered. The policy changes chosen are generally consistent with strategies recommended by the World Bank (1996) in their education-sector policy paper, which are not unlike those usually recommended by other international agencies and specialists in this field, for achieving overall efficiency in the allocation of resources as a means to faster per capita growth as well as poverty reduction.

The Endogenous Development Scenario

The base-line endogenous growth or endogenous development scenarios cannot be strictly a 'no policy change' solution of the model with past expenditure levels and enrolment rates absolutely fixed. For one thing, as per capita economic growth occurs, even if it is slow, private households spend more on education, firms spend more on education, and governmental units at all levels also spend more on education and R&D, even though political rhetoric does not always recognize this natural endogenous growth process. Therefore gross enrolment rates gradually increase, perhaps slowly as in most of Sub-Saharan Africa, or much more rapidly as in East Asia. As this process occurs, there are constant budget debates within households, firms, and governmental units. The process reflects the fact that education is a 'normal good' in economic terms. These expenditure and gross enrolment rate increases, therefore, are endogenous or internally determined as economic growth occurs over time in this broader political-economy context. (For specific development of this point see McMahon, 1971, 1974, 1975, 1987, and Forthcoming, and the other literature cited in these articles.) Similar statements can be made about the partial endogeneity of policies in each of the other sectors.

The more meaningful question, therefore, must be what would happen not if all public and private expenditure levels were constant, but instead if there were a continuation of existing policy adaptations within each country which have involved iterative changes over time and are reflected in any regression coefficients estimated from data for 1960 to the present. With controls for cultural differences, this permits comparisons to the net effects from explicit additional policy interventions.

The endogenous development path that involves no explicit new major policy change is shown in Tables 12.1, 12.2, and 12.3 for all African, Asian, Latin American, and OECD nations in the complete model, (also shown for Africa in Table 5.1). This path is the result of setting the constants for all equations equal to the starting data for each country and solving the complete model for each year from the present to 2035 AD. Only the endogenous growth path for GNP per capita is shown; the development paths for the other endogenous variables will be considered later.

Tables 12.1a, 12.1b, 12.2, and 12.3 also serve to list the nations for which the complete model is operational. GNP per capita is shown for 1985 (in 1985 prices) in column (1) and for 1995 (in 1995 prices) (Table 12.2 in 1985 prices) in column (2) for each country. The per capita growth rate from 1985–95 (in constant prices) from World Bank, *World Development Report* (1997) is shown in column (3). Then column (4) estimates what GNP per capita will be by 2020 under continuation of existing policies. This is not by simple extrapolation of the current economic growth rate but instead by use of the production function and the other interactive development processes under existing policies. Column (5) shows the longer-term per capita growth rates prevailing up to 2020.

The results are interesting but sometimes very depressing. All East Asian economies re-establish at least some positive growth by 2020 (Table 12.1b). All Latin American economies in the complete model experience positive per capita growth under these conditions except El Salvador (Table 12.2), and all OECD member nations also experience positive per capita growth (Table 12.3). But many of the nations of Sub-Saharan Africa exhibit negative per capita growth rates by

Table 12.1a Africa: Current Growth Rates and Future Endogenous Growth, Simulations to 2020 (Under Continuation of Current Policies)

	GNP/CAP 1985 (US$)	GNP/CAP 1995 (1995 $)	Per capita growth, 85–95	Model estimates	
				GNP/CAP 2020 (1985$)	Growth rate (%)
Algeria	2,550	1,600	−2.4	943	−3.9
Benin	260	370	−0.3	190	−0.1
Botswana	870	3,020	6.1	6,353	6.1
Burkina Faso	150	230	−0.2	383	0
Burundi	240	160	−1.3	227	−1.4
Cent. African Rep.	280	340	−2.4	120	−2.7
Congo	1,070	680	−3.2	613	−1.4
Ethiopia	110	100	−0.3	85	−0.5
Ghana	370	390	1.4	491	1.1
Kenya	300	280	0.1	334	0.2
Liberia	480	n.a.	n.a.	352	−1.2
Madagascar	240	230	−2.2	157	−2.1
Malawi	170	170	0.7	134	−0.5
Mali	150	250	0.8	169	0.8
Mauritania	410	460	0.5	605	0.6
Mauritius	1,100	3,380	5.4	7,608	5.2
Morocco	560	1,100	0.9	819	0.9
Nigeria	950	260	1.2	1,372	1.3
Rwanda	280	180	−5.4	84	−3.7
Senegal	370	600	0	428	−0.5
Somalia	270	270	−2.3	74	−0.4
Sudan	280	280	−0.2	110	−2.6
Tanzania	300	120	1.0	382	1.0
Togo	230	310	−2.7	102	−2.5
Tunisia	1,190	1,820	1.9	2,690	2.5
Zaire	160	120	−1.0	124	−1.7
Zambia	410	400	−0.8	339	−0.8
Zimbabwe	640	540	−0.6	767	2.9

Table 12.1b Asia: Current Growth Rates and Future Endogenous Growth, Simulations to 2020 (Under Continuation of Current Policies)

	GNP/CAP 1985 (US$)	GNP/CAP 1995 (1995 $)	Per capita growth, 85–95	Model estimates	
				GNP/CAP 2020 (1985$)	Growth rate (%)
India	290	340	3.2	931	1.5
Indonesia	520	980	2.3	1,419	1.5
Japan	11,240	39,640	2.9	32,227	2.4
S. Korea	2,160	9,700	2.2	6,951	1.7
Malaysia	1,970	3,890	2.54	5,893	2.5
Nepal	170	200	2.4	441	2.3
Philippines	570	1,050	0.6	740	0.6
Singapore	7,600	26,730	6.2	74,484	5.2
Sri Lanka	380	700	2.6	1,249	1.7
Thailand	810	2,740	4.9	4,510	4.4

Table 12.2 Latin America: Current Growth Rates and Future Endogenous Growth, Simulations to 2020 (Under Continuation of Current Policies)

	GNP/CAP 1985 (US$)	GNP/CAP 1995 (1985 $)	Per capita growth, 85–95 (real terms)	Model estimates	
				GNP/CAP 2020 (1985$)	Growth rate (%)
Argentina	2,120	2,590	1.8	5,869	2.5
Bolivia	490	492	1.8	674	0.4
Brazil	1,670	2,182	−0.8	4,498	2.7
Chile	1,450	1,857	6.1	5,028	3.6
Colombia	1,350	1,837	2.6	6,329	5.7
Costa Rica	1,400	1,722	2.8	2,313	1.9
Dominican Republic	760	785	2.1	1,105	1.0
Ecuador	1,150	1,424	0.8	4,016	3.2
El Salvador	830	704	2.8	457	−0.2
Guatemala	1,190	1,250	0.3	1,750	1.0
Haiti	310	312	−5.2	466	0.4
Honduras	740	865	0.1	1,860	3.6
Jamaica	920	1,056	3.6	1,417	1.6
Mexico	2,200	2,609	0.1	5,627	2.5
Nicaragua	770	902	−5.4	1,656	1.6
Panama	2,100	2,510	−0.4	3,983	2.1
Paraguay	1,190	1,291	1.2	2,093	1.2
Peru	1,010	1,040	−1.6	1,453	1.0
Uruguay	1,730	2,336	3.1	7,239	3.9

2020, and per capita incomes fall far below subsistence levels in some economies, as was noted earlier (Table 12.1a and Ch. 5). There is a lack of convergence under endogenous development; many of the poor nations get even poorer, especially in Africa, and the rich get richer.

In Asia the current slowdown is temporary, given the more basic forces at work in these endogenous development scenarios, although not without a cost. The fundamentals are strong in most East Asian nations, especially those along the Pacific Rim that possess a large modern physical capital stock and a well-educated labour force. Indonesia, Thailand, and Malaysia are not as far along in this regard, but they also have open, market-oriented economies and governments that are interested in sustaining economic growth, and most are moving aggressively under IMF prodding to correct the financial instabilities and crony capitalism in their banking systems. India was not affected much by this, and was doing better, but now may be caught up in a nuclear arms race devoting resources to the military that it can ill afford. The fundamentals in Sri Lanka and Nepal are also less strong than on the Pacific Rim. Only time will tell, but the current slowdown may have taken 1 or more percentage points off the 25-year per capita growth rates in that region as they absorb loss of skills due to unemployment and have lower capital accumulation as they institute the kinds of reforms and financial safeguards that

Table 12.3 The OECD Industrialized Economies: Current Growth Rates and Future Endogenous Growth, Simulations to 2020 (Under Continuation of Current Policies)

	GNP/CAP 1995 1985 (US$)	GNP/CAP 1995 (1995 $)	Per capita growth, 85–95	Model estimates GNP/CAP 2020 (1985$)	Growth rate (%)
Australia	10,284	18,720	1.4	17,615	1.3
Austria	9,100	26,890	1.9	18,305	1.9
Belgium	8,290	24,710	2.2	19,924	2.2
Canada	13,623	19,380	0.4	17,361	0.3
Denmark	11,380	29,890	1.5	20,300	1.5
Finland	11,026	20,580	1.5	19,635	0.9
France	9,810	24,990	1.5	17,992	1.6
Germany	10,980	27,510	2.1	23,374	2.1
Greece	3,700	8,210	1.3	6,372	1.2
Ireland	4,940	14,710	5.2	29,579	4.6
Italy	7,750	19,020	1.8	16,456	2.5
Japan	11,430	39,640	2.9	30,404	2.7
Netherlands	9,660	24,000	1.9	20,756	2.3
New Zealand	6,940	14,340	0.8	9,412	0.8
Norway	14,560	31,250	1.9	26,851	1.8
Portugal	1,980	9,740	3.6	7,033	3.2
Spain	4,370	13,580	2.6	11,973	2.3
Sweden	12,020	23,750	1.3	19,232	1.2
Switzerland	16,370	40,630	0.2	17,847	0.4
Turkey	1,080	2,780	2.2	2,557	1.6
United Kingdom	8,530	18,700	1.4	14,754	1.6
United States	16,930	26,980	1.3	28,392	1.0

were faced in earlier stages of development by the US and European economies. With this qualification all East Asian economies in Table 12.1b still show positive per capita growth rates through 2020, much higher than in Africa. Singapore and Japan are unique in achieving higher per capita incomes by 2020 than are found in the OECD nations by that time. But Nepal, with its largely illiterate labour force, remains very poor.

These are not predictions, but instead are the generation of a base-line scenario that assumes the continuation of current policies, against which increments or decrements will be measured as education policies are changed. As mentioned, only growth in GNP per capita is shown but there are 41 other endogenous variables and hence 41 additional base-line scenarios for the other sectors in each of these 78 countries. Each of these is under the same hypothetical conditions, involving no further policy changes or major exogenous shocks.

In Latin America and the Caribbean region (Table 12.2), just as in Africa as mentioned in Chapter 5, there is a whole 'lost generation' of young people whose education and health were impaired by cutbacks in the education and health systems resulting from high interest rates in the US (that spread), large debt burdens, inflation, unemployment, and related political instabilities in the 1980s. These bore down particularly hard on many economies on these two continents. But as shown in Table 12.2, economic recovery then began. Although the average annual per capita growth rate for this region was only 0.3 per cent for 1985–95 as compared to −1.1 per cent for Sub-Saharan Africa as computed by the World Bank (1997: 215), greater political stability has also been achieved. Growth was somewhat faster until 1998. The endogenous development scenario which does not focus on temporary recessions suggests that under current policies this will generally be sustained up through 2020. The IMF (1998: 65–8) has also observed this resiliency and potential for longer-term growth in Latin America if the current contraction is not too protracted.

Nowhere is it implied that education is the largest single source of growth, or that education policies are the only kind of policies that are important, only that they are available and may be cost-effective. To put other sources of growth in perspective, the recent Harvard Institute for Economic Development study by Radelet, Sachs, and Lee (1996), for example, attributes the lower growth rates in Sub-Saharan Africa, South Asia, and Latin America when compared to East Asia in part to the *direct* effects of less adequate schooling policies (resulting in 0.4, 0.2, and 0.1 per cent lower growth rates respectively). But beyond this, some of the growth differences in their study are due to demographic effects, such as lower life expectancy and faster total population growth in these non-Asian regions (accounting for 1.9, 0.9, and 0.2 per cent lower growth rates respectively), effects which I treat here as partly *indirect effects* of the difference in education policies. Similarly some of the other effects on growth in the Harvard regressions include indirect effects from education, such as export-oriented growth effects and institutional quality effects (1.7, 2.1, and 1.8 per cent respectively). For example, an educated skilled labour force is essential to the success of manufacturing exports and to the success of export-oriented trade policies. Also, education has been shown to be conducive to the rule of law and political stability. In the HIID model as cited by Sachs (1997: 20), this leaves only 1.0, 0.2, and 0.6 per cent differences below growth rates in East Asia that are due to limitations of natural resources and landlocked geography. This does not suggest that education is all-important, but that it is more important than suggested by the HIID model when the indirect structural effects are taken into account.

Education Policy Changes and Measurement of Net Effects

Explicit change scenarios are compared to these base endogenous development scenarios in the Figures below for Argentina, Bolivia, and Brazil (representative of the LAC region), India, Indonesia, Malaysia, and Singapore (East and South Asia), Kenya, Tanzania, and Tunisia (Africa), and the United States, United Kingdom, and Canada (OECD).

Policy Changes Chosen for the Simulations.

The dynamic time paths compared in each panel are Scenario 1, the base endogenous development Scenario; Scenario 2, a 2 percentage-point increase in public investment in education as a per cent of GNP, representing a political/economic policy decision; and Scenario 3, a 20 percentage-point increase in male and female secondary education enrolment rates, representing a Ministry of Education decision. Other policy options are available but these are chosen to reflect the following priorities for policy reforms suggested by the World Bank (1996):

1. *A higher priority for education.* This can be defended on efficiency grounds in that the social rates of return to education, especially at the primary and secondary levels, are relatively high in these countries (as they normally are) even though they do not include non-market returns estimated by Wolfe and Zuvekas (1997) to be roughly equal to the monetary returns.
2. *Greater attention to outcomes.* This is implicit in the entire approach.
3. *Public investment focused on basic education.* Both changes do this. Increased expenditure on education, as in Scenario 2, in nations where primary education is not yet universal (e.g. India) tends to increase primary enrolments more rapidly first in the model.
4. *More household involvement.* It is not possible to model this important reform directly within this model. However, as public elementary and secondary schools are extended to rural areas, with teachers and books provided, parents are induced to leave their children in school longer, to save in the form of forgone consumption (and forgone real earnings), and to invest more household time and resources in human capital formation. This is an extremely important way of increasing parents' *total* saving and investment rates, even in the poorest countries.
5. *Greater attention to equity.* Expansion of access to basic education through ninth or tenth grades, at least to poor farmers, is certainly consistent with this. The complete model also traces the impacts of education policy changes on inequality in the distribution of income (and can trace the impacts of greater gender equity in those nations where this is a serious problem).

The first 8 panels for each nation show the impacts of these policies on per capita economic growth, population growth, and equity (as represented here by income inequality and poverty rates), and the last 8 panels for each nation simulate non-market impacts on human rights, political stability, health, and other non-market returns.

Latin America

Brazil (Figure 12.1)

In Brazil, the increase in investment in human capital as a per cent of GNP by 2 percentage-points $(I_H/Y = +2)$ and of secondary education enrolment rates by 20 $(GER2M$ and $GER2F = +20)$ in 1995 both increase secondary enrolment rates by about the same amount up through 2035, or for females from about 35 per cent to 55 per cent in 1995, as shown in panel 2. Gross Domestic Investment as a per cent of GNP gradually increases, according to regressions that use data for Latin America as shown in panel 4. This is partly because greater skills in the labour force both attract investment and offset diminishing returns to physical capital. But it is also because the education contributes after a lag to democratization and political stability (panels 10 and 11).

Other indirect effects of this increased education on growth (panel 3) come after a lag of 15–20 years through lower fertility (panel 6) and lower net population growth rates (panel 5).

The effects on income inequality are important because the income distribution in Brazil is one of the most unequal in the world. The *GINI* coefficient of inequality, discussed in Chapter 8, falls very slightly under no-policy-change endogenous development (panel 8), but falls much more sharply by 2015 with explicit expansion of basic education that involves more and better education extended to rural areas. This inequality is also reduced after a 20-year lag as net population growth rates and family size fall (panel 5). A *GINI* coefficient for Brazil of 0.54 by 2035 under these policy change scenarios still compares, however, to much lower ones of 0.30–0.40 at present in the fastest-growing countries of East Asia. The effects on poverty reduction are also as expected; not only rural poverty (panel 12) but also urban poverty (panel 7) fall considerably. This is due to faster per capita growth and lower net population growth rates, in what is known to be a robust relation.

Among other non-market impacts on the quality of life, democratization (panel 10) rises to its upper bound in the index and human rights (panel 9) improve steadily but more significantly as broader percentages of the population enter the middle class and participate meaningfully in the development process. The improved health of the population is apparent from the 2- to 3-year increase in life expectancy by 2035 (panel 14) and 2 per cent reduction in the infant mortality rate below what it is estimated to become under continuation of existing policies in the endogenous development scenario (panel 13). Homicide rates fall (panel 16) as larger percentages of young people remain under supervision in secondary schools (panel 10), although property crime rates behave differently, as will be shown later.

With respect to stresses on the environment in Brazil, the rates of deforestation and collateral destruction of wildlife is enormous, with 11,196 square miles of forest land destroyed, an area larger than the state of New Jersey, in 1994–5. This is 3 times as much as in 1990–1, just before Brazil hosted the Earth Summit. Brazil's Congress passed an environmental crimes bill in 1998 that provided for effective enforcement by making companies that damage the environment liable for cleaning up the problem and compensating victims, as well as requiring precautions to keep burning from getting out of control. However, this was strongly opposed by lawmakers representing rural and industrial interests. They pressured President Cardoso to veto these provisions, which he did when he signed the bill (*New York Times*, 1998). Brazil has long enshrined in its constitution one of the most sophisticated environmental laws in the world, but it is not enforced. Under continuation of current policies in the endogenous development scenario, forest and wildlife destruction continues at the current 2 per cent per year for the next 20 years, but then

Figure 12.1 Brazil: Estimated Policy Impacts on Economic Growth Equity

Scenarios:

1. Endogeneous development;   2. $I_H/Y = +2$;   3. $GER2T = +20$

1. Gross secondary enrolment rate: Male

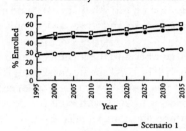

2. Gross secondary enrolment rate: Female

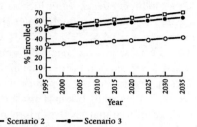

—○— Scenario 1   —□— Scenario 2   —●— Scenario 3

3. GNP Per Capita

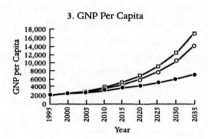

4. Gross Domestic Investment/GNP

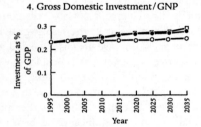

5. Population Growth

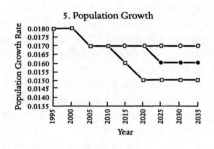

6. Total Fertility Rate

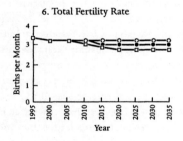

7. Urban Poverty

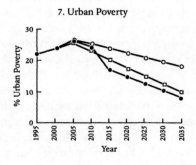

8. Income Inequality

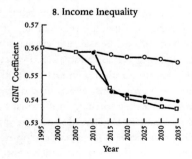

Brazil: Non-market Impacts on Economic Development

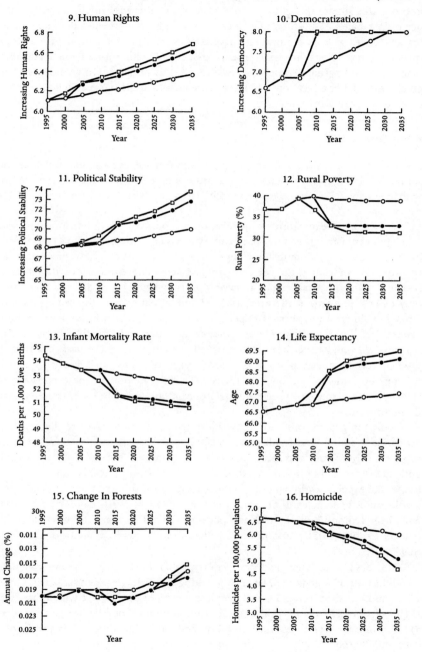

gradually improves. If education policies are changed, the net effects begin to improve this situation slightly in 2015 over what otherwise might be expected to occur (see panel 15). These effects come through strengthened democratization (panel 10) as well as continuing urbanization, slower population growth rates (panel 5), reductions in rural poverty associated with more female education (panel 12), and perhaps some positive direct effects of education as more students go on with higher education. All of these are factors in the regression equation that predicts deforestation rates.

Bolivia (Figure 12.2)

Bolivia is chosen as the second country in Latin America for a similar policy change simulation because it provides some contrasts as a much lower-income country, with per capita income about one-fourth that of Brazil, and one-tenth that of Argentina.

The increase in expenditure on education as a per cent of GNP from 4.2 per cent to 6.2 per cent can be seen to raise primary gross enrolment rates to 111.1 per cent by 2035 (panel 2), including 106.7 per cent for females. Secondary enrolment rates rise to 74.3 per cent (71.3 per cent for females). The endogenous development scenario with no special policy intervention suggests they would rise for females only to 84.4 per cent at the primary level and 45 per cent at the secondary level. Gross enrolment rates above 100 per cent like those at the primary level are to be expected at first, especially in Latin America, due to internal inefficiency as over-age students who may have dropped out or failed some time in the past return to the grade levels in question. Raising secondary enrolments directly does not raise primary enrolments, or, since in this case education remains as a constant per cent of GNP, it does not raise secondary enrolments as far in the later years given limited resources.

Population growth rates are not reduced (panel 5) but in fact rise slightly under Scenarios 1 and 3. The fertility rate falls most rapidly as enrolment expansion is supported by additional resources (Scenario 2, panel 6). But this does not keep up with the effect on improvements in health (lower infant mortality in panel 13, and longer life expectancy in panel 14), which is typical of countries starting with lower involvement of females in education at the secondary level. Labour productivity and Gross Domestic Investment as a per cent of GNP rise, as does GNP per capita (panels 4 and 3). But by 2035 per capita income still remains at about one-fourth of that in Brazil.

With these policy changes, rural poverty, urban poverty, and income inequality all fall farther in Bolivia than under the endogenous development scenario (panels 12, 7, and 8 respectively). The rate of destruction of forests and wildlife increases slightly (panel 15), driven primarily by continuing high population growth (panel 5). But human rights, political stability, and homicide rates all improve more substantially (panels 9, 11, and 16 respectively).

Figure 12.2 Bolivia: Estimated Policy Impacts on Economic Growth and Equity

Scenarios:

1. Endogeneous development; 2. $I_H/Y = +2$; 3. $GER2T = +20$

1. Gross secondary enrolment rate: Total

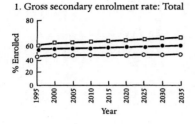

2. Gross primary enrolment rate: Total

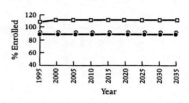

—o— Scenario 1   —□— Scenario 2   —•— Scenario 3

3. GNP Per Capita

4. Gross Domestic Investment/GNP

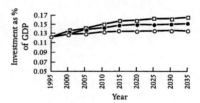

5. Population Growth

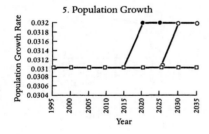

6. Total Fertility Rate

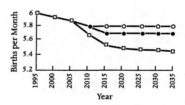

7. Urban Poverty

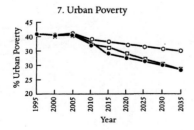

8. Income Inequality

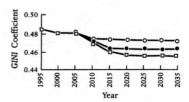

Bolivia: Non-market Impacts on Economic Development

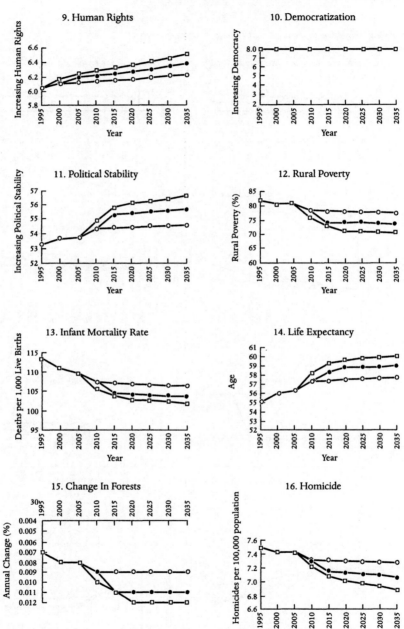

Argentina (Figure 12.3)

Argentina starts with higher primary and secondary enrolment rates in 1995 than Bolivia, as well as greater gender equity. Since it has had universal primary education for some time, both policies raise secondary education enrolment rates toward 100 per cent by 2035 (panels 1 and 2). Physical capital investment, the capacity to export manufactured goods (e.g. Wood, 1994b), and GNP per capita, are all higher after either policy change, whereas the total fertility rate, population growth, urban poverty, rural poverty, and income inequality are all lower (panels 3–8 and 12). Some of these have indirect feedback effects that improve political stability, which has been a real problem in Argentina, as well as human rights (panels 11 and 9). Property crime increases in absolute terms with economic growth, and more rapidly with faster economic growth (panel 15). But water pollution stabilizes and health improves under both scenarios (panels 16, 13, and 14).

East and South Asia

Using the production functions and investment functions specific to Asia, I next explore the potential direct and indirect effects of education policies in India, Indonesia, Malaysia, and Singapore. It is tempting to consider Nepal, one of the very poorest countries, and Japan, one of the richest, but Sub-Saharan African and OECD nations will better represent these groups. There is also great interest in economic development that might benefit the enormous population and stagnant economy of India, which is now showing some life. There is also interest in the economic development of the emerging but unstable economy of Indonesia, in comparing it to the larger education efforts in Malaysia, and comparing both to Singapore's remarkable success.

India (Figure 12.4)

Here 487.9 million people currently live on less than US$1 a day, i.e. 52.5 per cent of its population are below the poverty line (World Bank, 1997: 214); this is larger than India's entire population of 360 million at the time of independence from Britain in 1947. Although the average annual growth rate of its GNP has been around 3.5 per cent, after subtracting population growth rates of 2.1 per cent (compared to lower population growth rates of 1.8 per cent in Indonesia and 1.7 per cent in Singapore; ibid.: 220), the resulting per capita economic growth rate has been slow rather than fast in relation to the rest of East Asia.

There are a number of reasons for this relatively slow development. The rejection by Nehru and his followers of a market-based, export-oriented growth strategy based on a skilled labour force, large subsidized industrial parastatals protected against trade, agriculture relatively unprotected and thereby taxed to support these, and a jungle of controls on production, prices, and employment are a few (*Economist*, 1997c: 17). But unlike the Asian tigers, Nehru's India neglected

Figure 12.3 Argentina: Estimated Policy Impacts on Economic Growth and Equity

Scenarios:

1. Endogeneous development;   2. $I_H/Y = +2$;   3. $GER2T = +20$

1. Gross secondary enrolment rate: Total
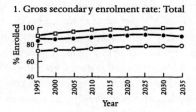

2. Gross primary enrolment rate: Total
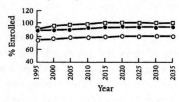

———o——— Scenario 1   ———□——— Scenario 2   ———●——— Scenario 3

3. GNP Per Capita
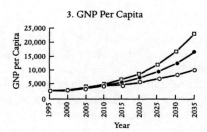

4. Gross Domestic Investment/GNP
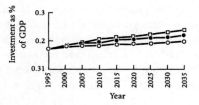

5. Population Growth
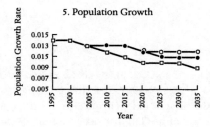

6. Total Fertility Rate
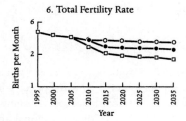

7. Urban Poverty
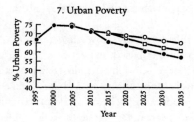

8. Income Inequality
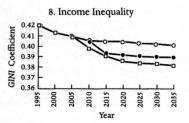

Argentina: Non-market Impacts on Economic Development

9. Human Rights

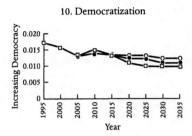

10. Democratization

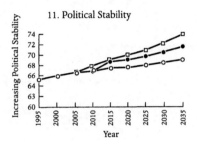

11. Political Stability

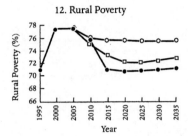

12. Rural Poverty

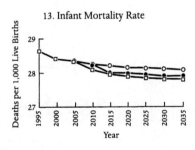

13. Infant Mortality Rate

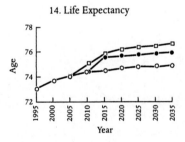

14. Life Expectancy

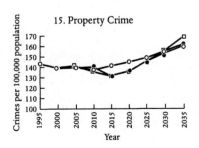

15. Property Crime

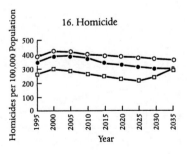

16. Homicide

Figure 12.4 India: Estimated Policy Impacts on Economic Growth and Equity

Scenarios:

1. Endogeneous development; 2. $I_H/Y = +2$; 3. $GER2T = +20$

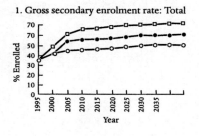

1. Gross secondary enrolment rate: Total

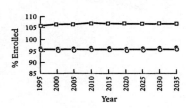

2. Gross primary enrolment rate: Total

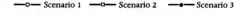

3. GNP Per Capita

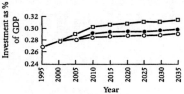

4. Gross Domestic Investment/GNP

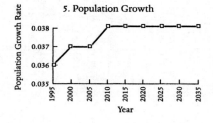

5. Population Growth

6. Total Fertility Rate

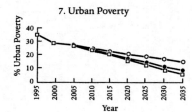

7. Urban Poverty

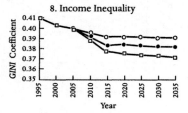

8. Income Inequality

India: Non-market Impacts on Economic Development

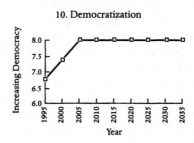

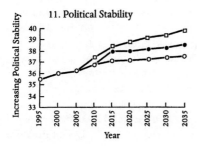

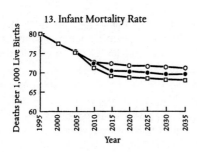

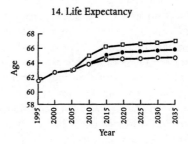

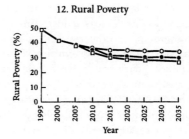

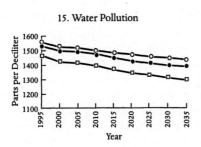

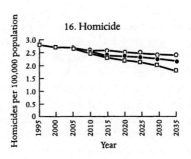

primary education, as did Pakistan, Bangladesh, and Nepal, considering it a social welfare programme for families, as it is still treated in these government budgets, rather than an essential investment in India's future. Instead there was wasteful over-investment in higher and technical education (as in Pakistan), fostering both emigration and unemployment of college graduates. Meanwhile 48 per cent of India's population remains illiterate, worse than the 43 per cent in Sub-Saharan Africa (World Bank, 1997: 215).

These conditions have changed recently and India's per capita growth has accelerated to 4.2 per cent for 1988–97. So the per capita growth paths in Scenarios 2 and 3 shown on the graphs for India (panel 3) should be interpreted in a way that take these increases in primary and secondary education, some of which have already occurred, into account. The endogenous development Scenario 1 is a baseline that estimates what might have happened if these (and further) shifts had not occurred. The increased investment as a per cent of GNP supports more rapid achievement of universal and adequate primary education but also significant increases in secondary enrolment rates, higher than even the more direct 20-point secondary enrolment rate increase (which with education resources remaining a constant per cent of GNP does result in expanding secondary expenditure as a per cent of GNP, but squeezes primary education especially).

Investment is attracted, with the more highly educated labour force (panel 4), GNP per capita rises under Scenario 2 to about twice what it would presumably have been otherwise, and fertility rates fall (panels 3 and 6). But with improvements in health (panels 13 and 14), due primarily to extensions of female primary education and to rising per capita incomes, net population growth rates rise a bit. This is the same dilemma faced by Sub-Saharan Africa, where insufficient numbers of females have reached secondary education levels to depress fertility rates even to 3 or 4 (they are down to 1.5 in Singapore).

The success story to date in India, however, has been that of establishing and sustaining a stable democracy and a high level of human rights (panels 9 and 10). This is in sharp contrast to all other countries with the same or lower per capita income worldwide (see Chapter 7) and to most of Sub-Saharan Africa, and in spite of India's great diversity (19 languages), Hindu–Muslim violence (half a million have been killed), and the break-off of Muslim Pakistan and Bangladesh. Much of it is probably attributable to the unique combination of familiarity with British institutions plus the efforts of Pandit Nehru, and not economic growth or the expansion of education. But growth and education should both contribute to continued improvements in human rights and democracy (panels 9 and 10) in the long run, based on the worldwide patterns observed in Chapter 7.

Political stability is enhanced after a lag of 15 years or so by this expansion of access to primary and secondary education, as larger percentages of the population have skills that enable them to participate in the fruits of economic growth (panel 11) and as rural poverty is reduced by this policy (panel 12). Health improves significantly, showing up both in a net additional reduction by 2020 in the infant mortality rate by about 4 per cent (panel 13) and an additional increase in life expectancy of 2–3 years (panel 14). This has adverse effects on population growth rates in the short run, raising them to 3.8 per cent (panel 5), since the net additional reduction in fertility rates (panel 6) is not yet large enough to offset the effects on population growth in the opposite direction that come from better health. India needs to look seriously at Indonesia's experience with family planning clinics and the interaction term between secondary education of females and family planning efforts that strengthen their effectiveness, as was shown in Chapter 6.

Finally, water pollution, a serious problem in India, diminishes at a much faster rate with this education policy intervention (panel 15), as do homicide rates (panel 16).

Indonesia (Figure 12.5)

Indonesia has experienced considerable economic instability, related primarily to problems in the banking system, tariffs, and parastatal investment, but also to the spread of the financial crisis affecting Thailand, South Korea, and some other Asian economies. This has led to political instability as prices have risen rapidly and interest rate increases designed to curb excessive real estate speculation and raise the value of the rupiah have caused high unemployment. Other IMF-imposed reforms in the financial structure have contributed to this in the short run, but are intended, of course, to stabilize the economy and restore growth after the transition. I am concerned here, however, with longer-term growth prospects and the development process, abstracting to some extent from these partially temporary disturbances.

Following independence from the Dutch, Indonesia achieved universal primary education relatively rapidly with a major national effort. But then it did not follow up with expansion of secondary education, as did all of the East Asian nations on the Pacific Rim. In my policy simulations illustrated in the figures for Indonesia, an increase in education expenditure by 2 percentage points from the current, relatively low 3.2 per cent is automatically channelled almost entirely into the expansion of secondary education as shown, expanding it more rapidly to the rural areas. This was what was very strongly recommended in all of the work for Indonesia's Second 25-Year Plan, in which Indonesia made human resource development through education the nation's number one priority (see Boediono, McMahon, and Adams, 1992: table 1.2). There has been gender equity, for the most part, in Indonesian education, as is shown in panels 1 and 2. Compared to Indonesia's Second 25-Year Plan, which called for achieving secondary enrolment rates of 80 per cent by 2020, these new simulations produce almost precisely this. But thus far at least, the government has not put the necessary resources into this effort and for this reason it seems unlikely that this target will be achieved. The 1998 financial crisis is likely to have delayed it further, although the IMF urges nations to sustain their investment in education while cutting public consumption-type expenditures.

Nevertheless, under Scenarios 2 and 3, it would appear that diminishing returns to investment in physical capital *are* offset, and rates of investment in physical capital (hopefully not all real estate) are increased over a medium-term period by

Figure 12.5 Indonesia: Estimated Policy Impacts on Economic Growth and Equity

Scenarios:

1. Endogeneous development;   2. $I_H/Y = +2$;   3. $GER2T = +20$

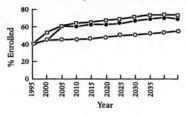

1. Gross secondary enrolment rate: Male

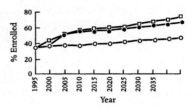

2. Gross secondary enrolment rate: Female

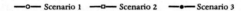

—○— Scenario 1   —□— Scenario 2   —●— Scenario 3

3. GNP Per Capita

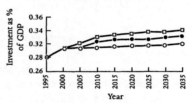

4. Gross Domestic Investment/GNP

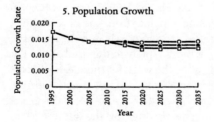

5. Population Growth

6. Total Fertility Rate

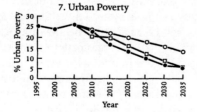

7. Urban Poverty

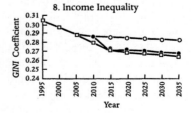

8. Income Inequality

Indonesia: Non-Market Impacts on Economic Development

9. Human Rights

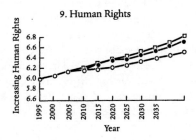

10. Democratization

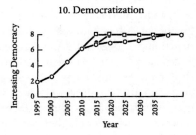

11. Political Stability

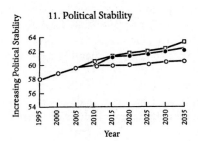

12. Rural Poverty

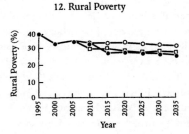

13. Infant Mortality Rate

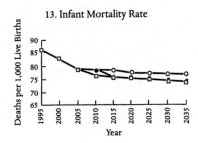

14. Life Expectancy

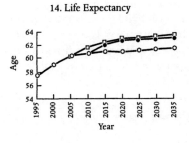

15. Change in Forests

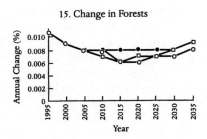

16. Property Crime

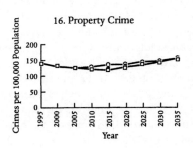

this policy of investing more in education (panel 4). Indonesia has previously been committed to an export-oriented growth policy, so the domestic saving rate has not been and is not likely to become the only source of money capital. (As mentioned, Indonesian investment has been excessively channelled into real estate, with construction that does not depend as heavily as might be supposed on a skilled labour force, since skilled construction workers are often brought in from abroad.) Fertility rates and net population growth rates fall further with this education intervention. This provides a very interesting illustration of the difference with India, which, unlike Indonesia, did not invest earlier in achieving universal primary education, and where higher population growth rates are therefore still to come.

GNP per capita rises, with the qualifications mentioned on p. 180, higher than it would otherwise be by 2035 (see panels 4, 6, 5, and 3). The 'growth with equity' path to which Indonesia has been committed is significantly aided by means of this special education policy intervention, as income inequality falls further than it would be expected to otherwise (panel 8). Urban poverty and rural poverty both fall faster as well under both scenarios (panels 7 and 12), augmenting the effects on poverty reduction from per capita economic growth.

It is notable, given the 1998 developments in Indonesia, that democratization, human rights, and political stability all increase under endogenous development with no special education policy intervention. But they all increase even more rapidly under these relatively modest increments to the education system (see panels 9, 10, and 11). There are further benefits observed previously from education in the same pattern, in the form of better health as measured by lower infant mortality and greater longevity (panels 13 and 14). Property crime does increase, but very slightly, after 2015 as growth occurs, and is not significantly affected by this education policy. The serious destruction of forests and wildlife that is occurring, however, is eventually turned around, presumably because it becomes possible for exports to become more skill-intensive (Wood, 1994) but also as rural poverty is decreased (panel 15).

Malaysia (Figure 12.6)

Malaysia has achieved higher secondary education enrolment rates than either Indonesia or Thailand, with an endogenous development path relatively constant at around 60% (panels 1 and 2) and wider extension of basic education than India at both the primary and secondary levels. *Ceteris paribus* (in this case assuming stabilization of the currency etc. following short-run shocks), the policy of increasing investment in education as a per cent of GNP by an additional 2 percentage points (Scenario 2), or alternatively gross enrolment rates at the secondary level only by 20 percentage points (Scenario 3), can be seen to attract even higher rates of investment (panel 4), to reduce fertility rates (panel 6) and net population growth (panel 5, in contrast to India), and together to contribute significantly to higher per capita economic growth (panel 3). By 2030, per capita income is higher under Scenario 2 (see qualifications, p. 180), which provides for investment

Figure 12.6 Malaysia: Estimated Policy Impacts on Economic Growth and Equity

Scenarios:

1. Endogeneous development; 2. $I_H/Y = +2$; 3. $GER2T = +20$

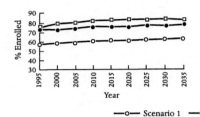

1. Gross secondary enrolment rate: Male

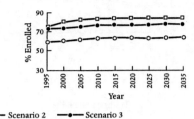

2. Gross secondary enrolment rate: Female

—○— Scenario 1   —□— Scenario 2   —●— Scenario 3

3. GNP Per Capita

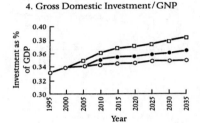

4. Gross Domestic Investment/GNP

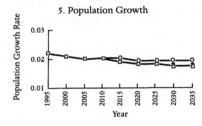

5. Population Growth

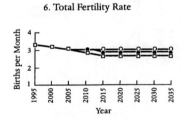

6. Total Fertility Rate

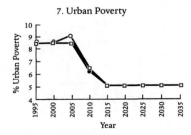

7. Urban Poverty

8. Income Inequality

Malaysia: Non-Market Impacts on Economic Development

9. Human Rights

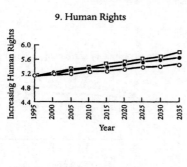

10. Democratization

11. Political Stability

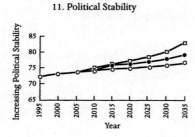

12. Rural Poverty

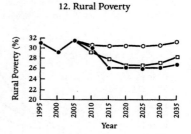

13. Infant Mortality Rate

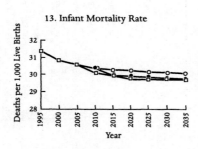

14. Life Expectancy

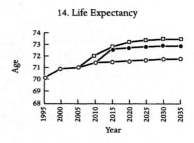

15. Change In Forests

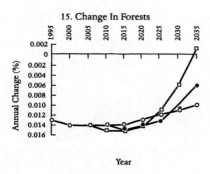

16. Homicide

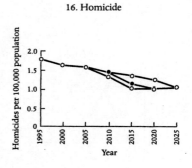

in both primary and higher education as well as secondary. The new policy does not seem to lower urban poverty below the effects from policies already in place (panel 7), but it does lower rural poverty considerably by 2015 (panel 12) and the effect in lowering inequality is dramatic (panel 8). The latter effect is due, within the context of the *GINI* equation estimated and discussed in Chapter 8, not only to the higher secondary education enrolment rates but also to faster economic growth and slower population growth. This policy intervention is clearly conducive to sustaining 'humane growth' (McMahon and Geske, 1982: 22–5) or 'rapid growth with equity' (World Bank, 1993: 7).

Additional non-market impacts from this increment to existing policies suggest a further contribution to democratization (panel 10) and also to human rights (panel 9) as time passes in Malaysia. These, in turn, contribute to greater political stability and/or rule of law (panel 11), which in turn feeds back on faster growth. Both the education and high per capita income that result contribute to better health through lower infant mortality (panel 13) and to substantial additional increases of 2 to 3 years in longevity (panel 14). The negative rates of annual change in forest land and wildlife habitat are dramatically reduced after 2025, due primarily to lower rural poverty, more manufactured relative to primary material exports, and more persons with higher education (see the equations in Chapter 9), but homicide rates, which are low (1.8 compared to 9.3 in the United States) and falling anyway, are not much affected (panel 16).

Singapore (Figure 12.7)

Singapore will be considered for comparison as an example of the highest per capita income economies in the world but still within East Asia.

In spite of the rapid per capita growth in Singapore, secondary education is not universal by any means, with a gross enrolment rate of only about 70 per cent for both males and females (panels 1 and 2). Tertiary education has remained very restricted, to about 7–11 per cent of the population, which was typical of the UK prior to the Robbins Report. As investment in education as a per cent of GNP and/or access is expanded, rapid growth rates of GNP per capita, which are already high, are raised further and the still slower population growth, somewhat higher investment, education-productivity effects, and simple compounding effect, brings living standards to remarkable levels (panels 5, 6, 4, and 3). The financial disturbances throughout East Asia are likely to reduce this somewhat, however. Urban poverty is low and unaffected but income inequality is significantly reduced by 2 percentage points on the *GINI* index below what it is otherwise likely to be (panel 8).

It is interesting that human rights improve faster (panel 9), as does democratization (panel 10). Political stability is already very high, although Singapore has been relatively authoritarian as measured by the Freedom House Index (Freedom House, 1997). This suggests that growth is sometimes fast in relatively authoritarian regimes, somewhat more consistent with my hypothesis about political stability being dependent only partially on the rule of law than with Barro's (1997) emphasis

Figure 12.7 Singapore: Estimated Policy Impacts on Economic Growth and Equity

Scenarios:

1. Endogeneous development; 2. $I_H/Y = +2$; 3. $GER2T = +20$

1. Gross secondary enrolment rate: Male

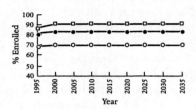

2. Gross primary enrolment rate: Female

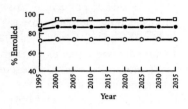

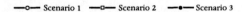
—o— Scenario 1   —□— Scenario 2   —●— Scenario 3

3. GNP Per Capita

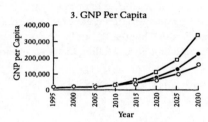

4. Gross Domestic Investment/GNP

5. Population Growth

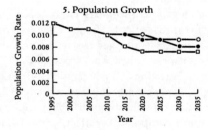

6. Total Fertility Rate

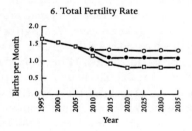

7. Urban Poverty

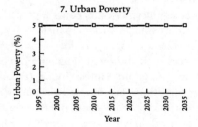

8. Income Inequality

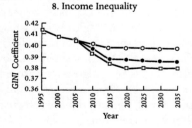

Singapore: Non-Market Impacts on Economic Development

9. Human Rights

10. Democratization

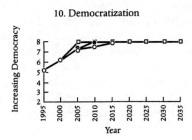

11. Political Stability

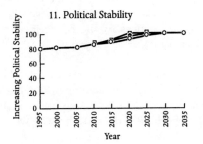

12. Worker Output Ratio

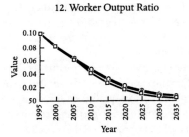

13. Infant Mortality Rate

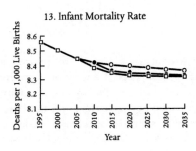

14. Life Expectancy

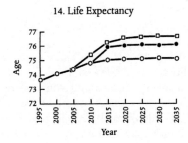

15. Water Pollution

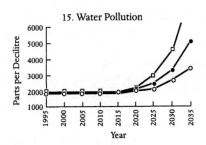

16. Homicide

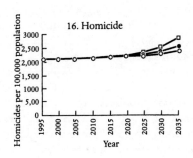

on only the rule of law. Labour productivity continues to rise in Singapore under all scenarios, as shown by the worker–output ratio, an inverted measure of the output–labour ratio measuring labour productivity (panel 12). Health continues to improve as part of endogenous development without the policy change. But with the further extension of secondary education to disadvantaged groups, average infant mortality rates fall about one-tenth of a percentage point faster in Singapore and average life expectancy increases by about 2 years more than otherwise (panels 13 and 14). The water pollution equation did not have a GNPPC-squared term (with presumably a negative sign) to control for the non-linearity of outliers like Singapore, with the very highest growth rate in the world. This in retrospect was probably a mistake, since the other factors in the equation (more democracy, less population growth, less poverty, more higher education) all operate to reduce water pollution (panel 15). Property crime is affected by conflicting forces; it is increased by economic growth, but reduced by the falling inequality, with the result that there is little net effect on crime in Singapore (Chapter 10 and panel 16).

On balance, although some of the additional positive crime and political stability effects are negligible, there are 'growth with equity' and additional non-market benefits to the quality of life to be realized even in Singapore, one of the higher-income and fastest-growing countries in the world. It remains to be seen whether this will generalize to the OECD member countries.

Africa

Tanzania (Figure 12.8) and Kenya (Figure 12.9)

Turning now to Sub-Saharan Africa, which contains many of the poorest and politically unstable economies in the world, the impacts of education investment policies in Tanzania and Kenya were compared earlier in the well-known natural experiment studied by Knight and Sabot (1990). They concluded, on the basis of largely microeconomic data, that the more rapid expansion of secondary education in Kenya than in Tanzania (partially by private financing), in countries that had about equal per capita income in 1960, was conducive to more rapid economic growth in Kenya than in Tanzania. It was also associated with greater reductions of inequality due to the reduction of secondary education scarcity rents in the labour market. Shortly after the publication of their book, Tanzania's policy was announced to have changed.

However, primary gross enrolment rates remain low in Tanzania (60 per cent compared to 97 per cent in Kenya, shown in panel 2 in both cases), and secondary education enrolment rates remain at disastrously low levels (under 5 per cent in Tanzania, but 15% for Kenya, shown in panel 1 in both cases). The increase of 2 percentage points in investment in education as a per cent of GNP raises *primary gross* enrolment rates by about 20 percentage points above what they would otherwise be in both countries, but also raises gross secondary enrolment rates eventually by about the same amount. Scenario 3 raises only secondary education enrolment rates by 20 percentage points.

The estimated net effects of this change are interesting and somewhat dramatic. More external investment is attracted (panel 4 in both countries), a major objective of current USAID policy. Political stability improves, which is badly needed in Kenya given the recent crises (panel 11). Within the model, these indirect effects of education, as well as the direct effects on labour skills and productivity, produce real per capita growth, which otherwise, under current policies, is estimated to be low or essentially zero in both nations (panel 2). Scenario 2, involving increased resources invested in education, which in these countries would help to build rural schools and hire teachers for them, not just at the secondary but also at the primary level (panels 1 and 2), contributes the most to economic growth. This government action induces additional saving and investment in education by parents, since saving is defined here to include forgone earnings, as discussed in Chapter 2. This increase in total saving (and investment) in turn raises the steady-state level of output per effective worker and thereby raises the growth rate for any starting level of GNP, the effect that shows up in panel 3. GNP per capita is estimated to reach US$1,000 (in 1985 prices) or triple the current level in Tanzania by 2035, and $1,600 in Kenya, which quadruples current living standards.

Rural poverty declines with this change in policy, especially in Kenya, given that within the model the extension of secondary education to the rural areas, where most of the people are, is a major determinant of rural poverty reduction (panel 12). Income inequality also declines significantly, or by about 2 percentage points on the *GINI* index in both countries. But inequality is still high in Tanzania (*GINI* = 0.48) and even higher in Kenya (0.51), even after the change.

Disturbing aspects arise because population growth in Tanzania continues to rise after 2015 in spite of reductions in the fertility rate (panels 5 and 6). Population growth rates stabilize in Kenya, but at a very high rate of 4 per cent per year, more than is likely to be reduced much by AIDS. This pattern of lower infant mortality and higher life expectancy dominating at first is the same as that found above for India. This is a significant point at which our complete model deviates from Barro's (1997: 23–5), since he examines the effects of fertility rate declines on per capita growth directly rather than the time form of the lagged response through structural infant mortality and longevity effects on net population growth.

Impacts on democratization and human rights of this expansion of primary and secondary education are clearly positive, but only after a lag of about 15 years, when graduates have entered an urbanizing labour force (panels 10 and 9). This is interesting because the degree of democracy as evaluated by Freedom House (1997) index is currently very low in Tanzania (2) and in Kenya (4, both in panel 9). The provisions for human rights are not much better (panel 10). Many of these 'easy' gains from earlier expansion and improvement of basic education have already been realized in the industrialized OECD member countries, who are at the top of the democratization and human rights index. This is one dramatic example of this difference.

Figure 12.8 Tanzania: Estimated Policy Impacts on Economic Growth and Equity

Scenarios:

1. Endogeneous development;   2. $I_H/Y = +2$;   3. $GER2T = +20$

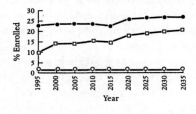
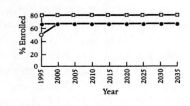

1. Gross secondary enrolment rate: Total

2. Gross primary enrolment rate: Total

—o— Scenario 1   —□— Scenario 2   —•— Scenario 3

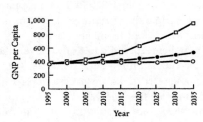
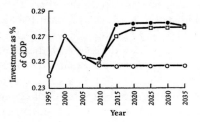

3. GNP Per Capita

4. Gross Domestic Investment/GNP

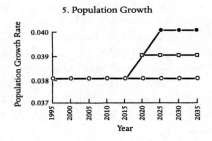
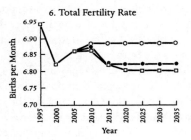

5. Population Growth

6. Total Fertility Rate

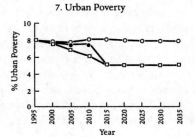
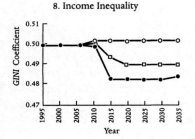

7. Urban Poverty

8. Income Inequality

Tanzania: Non-Market Impacts on Economic Development

9. Human Rights

10. Democratization

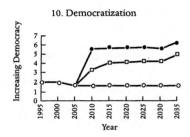

11. Political Stability

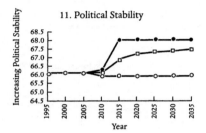

12. Rural Poverty

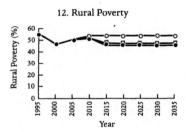

13. Infant Mortality Rate

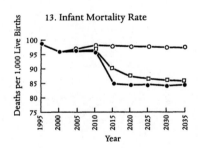

14. Life Expectancy

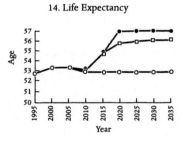

15. Change In Forests

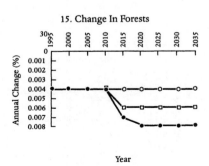

16. Homicide

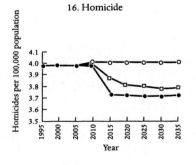

Figure 12.9　Kenya: Estimated Policy Impacts on Economic Growth and Equity

Scenarios:

1. Endogeneous development;　2. $I_H/Y = +2$;　3. $GER2T = +20$

1. Gross secondary enrolment rate: Total

2. Gross primary enrolment rate: Total

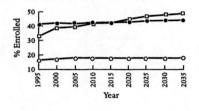
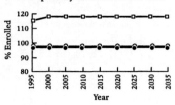

—○— Scenario 1　—□— Scenario 2　—●— Scenario 3

3. GNP Per Capita

4. Gross Domestic Investment/GNP

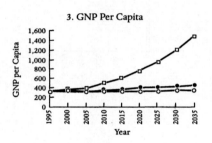
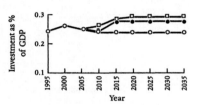

5. Population Growth

6. Total Fertility Rate

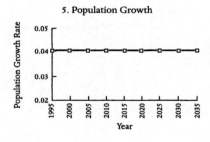
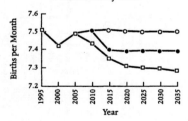

7. Urban Poverty

8. Income Inequality

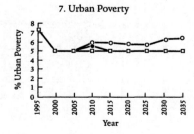
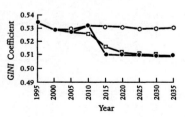

Kenya: Non-Market Impacts on Economic Development

9. Human Rights

10. Democratization

11. Political Stability

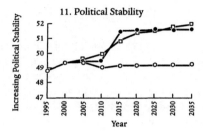

12. Rural Poverty

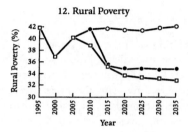

13. Infant Mortality Rate

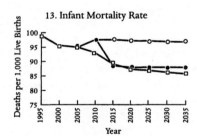

14. Life Expectancy

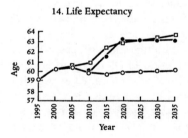

15. Change In Forests

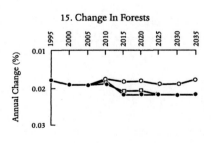

16. Homicide

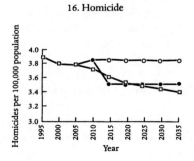

Deforestation rates and the destruction of wildlife, which are related, get worse in Tanzania and in Kenya (panel 15), largely due to the population growth effects in the equation (so hurry and see the elephants, giraffes, lions, and gazelles on the Serengeti before they are all gone). But these environmental impact equations warrant continuing refinement, and other policies that will limit this destruction may be changed more aggressively than they have been in the past.

Homicide rates (panel 16) are not high in either country by US standards (4 in Tanzania and Kenya, compared to 9.2 in the US). But they fall further in both scenarios, rising with urbanization but falling largely in response to the reduction in inequality in the equation used in the model.

Congo (formerly Zaïre) (Figure 12.10)

Starting with the data under the prior regime, GNP per capita is projected by the endogenous development scenario to continue to decline. The 2 percentage point increase in investment in primary and secondary education as a per cent of GNP (panels 1 and 2) is the most successful option for arresting this decline (panel 3), largely through its contributions to political stability (panel 11) after a 20-year lag. This improves the climate for higher rates of investment (panel 4), and the direct effects of education on labour productivity aid export capabilities. Again, population growth rates do not fall but continue to rise until 2035 (panel 5) in spite of the reduction in fertility rates (panel 6) because of the positive direct and indirect effects of education on better health, as evidenced by lower infant mortality rates (panel 13) and greater life expectancy (panel 14).

Although there is not much positive growth, rural poverty is reduced with this extension of education to farmers, where it is so badly needed (panel 12). Also, inequality as measured by the *GINI* coefficient is reduced (panel 8), perhaps putting 'growth with equity' in a new light. There is no per capita growth, and *the reduced inequality neither aids nor impedes growth except for its relation to political stability.* Perhaps the education of farmers deters civil wars and what essentially happened in the French Revolution from being repeated over and over throughout Africa. At least the new education policy enables the decline in per capita income to be arrested, even though desirable net population growth effects are delayed for about 35 years. High net population growth (3.8 per cent) can be expected to be a continuing problem for a long time.

OECD Member Countries

France, the UK, and the US illustrate the measurement of the outcomes of education at the more advanced stages of economic and political development. The complete model can be run for any of the 22 OECD member countries that are listed in Table 12.3, however.

Figure 12.10 Congo: Estimated Policy Impacts on Economic Growth and Equity

Scenarios:

1. Endogeneous development; 2. $I_H/Y = +2$; 3. $GER2T = +20$

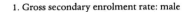

1. Gross secondary enrolment rate: male

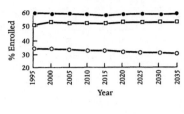

2. Gross secondary enrolment rate: female

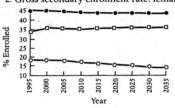

—o— Scenario 1   —□— Scenario 2   —•— Scenario 3

3. GNP Per Capita

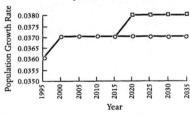

4. Gross Domestic Investment/GNP

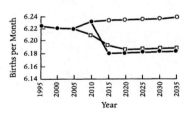

5. Population Growth

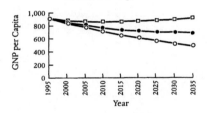

6. Total Fertility Rate

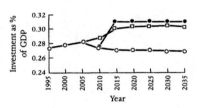

7. Urban Poverty

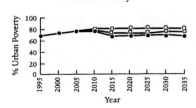

8. Income Inequality

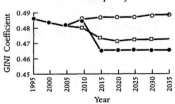

Congo: Non-Market Impacts on Economic Development

9. Human Rights

10. Democratization

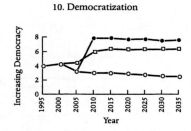

11. Political Stability

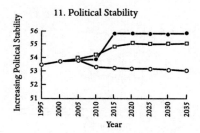

12. Rural Poverty

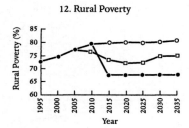

13. Infant Mortality Rate

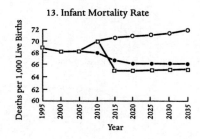

14. Life Expectancy

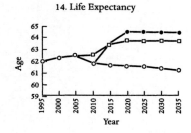

15. Water Pollution

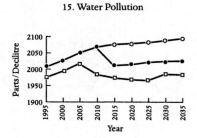

16. Homicide

It should be kept in mind that except for the production and investment functions, which are specific to data over time for the 22 OECD nations, the other functional relations are estimated on the basis of data for all 78 economies in the worldwide sample. So the non-market return estimates reflect patterns in the developing countries as well and are not fine-tuned to the smaller and more sophisticated gradations in the non-market aspects of the quality of life in the OECD member countries. For example, there is a ceiling on the democratization index of 8 in the way the Freedom House (1997) index has been inverted, a level which all of the OECD countries have essentially attained. It will be seen that these three countries all hit this ceiling, even though it is apparent that there are many ways that the legislative and governmental processes do not work perfectly anywhere. Similarly, the effect of female secondary education on fertility rates may be larger when the total number of children born to the average female is 7 to 8, as it is in Tanzania and Kenya, but much smaller where it is 1 to 2, as it is in France, the UK, and the US. A separate analysis specific to the OECD countries with an extended index (as in the case of democratization) would be needed to get more refined measures of the non-market returns to education in the more advanced societies. Nevertheless, if some allowance is made for lack of detail in the magnitudes at the limits of the ranges, a general indication of the direction and pattern of the expected non-market outcomes in OECD member nations can be obtained.

In principle a new way is being suggested for measuring the externalities, including the contributions of education and research in liberal arts fields. Measurement of the returns to research has generally been limited to engineering, physical science, and life science fields using patents secured in the past. But with the definitions of non-market benefits and structural effects here, perhaps other basic and applied fields can be linked more closely to new outcomes (e.g. research and graduate education in law and political science to the rule of law and to political stability, with feedback effects on growth) as a better basis for estimating their contribution.

France (Figure 12.11)

In France, higher education has been expanded significantly in recent years, but tuition is still relatively low. The increase in investment in education from 5.7 per cent of GNP to 7.7 per cent raises total secondary education gross enrolment rates from their current 90 per cent (male) and 95 per cent (female) to 110 per cent, which allows some over-age students to finish as well, and also raises higher education enrolments from their current 31 per cent to 42 per cent by 2035 (panel 1).

The total effects in scenario 2 are to raise per capita income about US$5,000 (in 1985 prices) above where it would otherwise be (panel 3). Part of this is through indirect externality effects through higher Gross Domestic Investment rates (panel 4), which in turn is aided by the strengthening of political stability (or rule of law) (panel 11). The effects on improvement in the effectiveness of democracy are harder to pick up because of the index-number problem mentioned previously

Figure 12.11 France: Estimated Policy Impacts on Economic Growth and Equity

Scenarios:

1. Endogeneous development; 2. $I_H/Y = +2$; 3. $GER2T = +20$

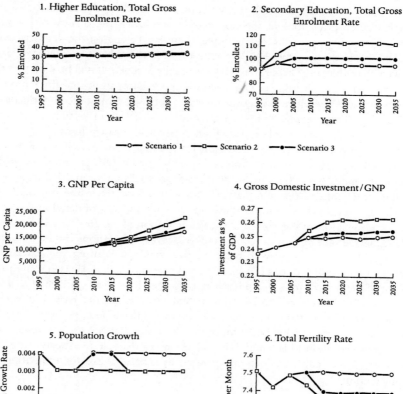

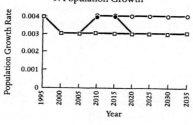

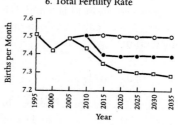

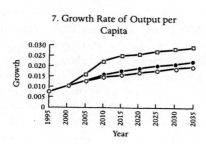

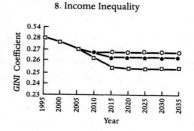

France: Non-Market Impacts on Economic Development

9. Human Rights

10. Democratization

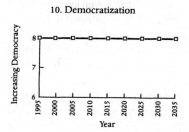

11. Political Stability

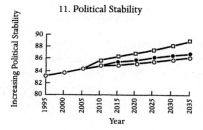

12. Rural Poverty

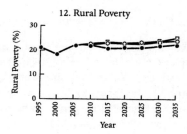

13. Infant Mortality Rate

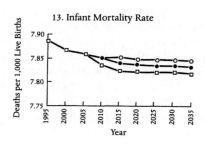

14. Life Expectancy

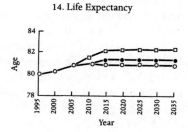

15. Change In Forests

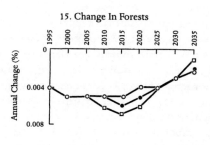

16. Property Crime

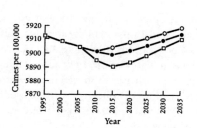

(panel 10). But further improvements in human rights are implied (panel 9), as are further improvements in infant mortality and 1 to 2 additional years of life expectancy beyond what it would otherwise be (panels 13 and 14). Homicide rates, already low at 1.2, fall further (not shown), and property crime rates rise less than would be expected under the base endogenous development scenario (panel 16). These net improvements over the development that would have occurred anyway are measures of the non-market returns to education.

Income inequality, which in poor countries is increased by more expenditure on higher education, is instead decreased by the balanced increase in France (panel 8). There is a reduction of high school drop-outs (panel 2) and the increase in higher education enrollments to 41 per cent (panel 1) is not highly elitist.

The United Kingdom (Figure 12.12) and the United States (Figure 12.13)

The effects in the UK and the US are somewhat similar to those in France. Per capita GNP increases beyond where it would otherwise be without this increased investment, due to both direct and indirect effects of education in both countries (both Figures, panel 3). Some of this can be seen to arise due to higher output per worker (Figure 12.12, panel 5) and some through higher labour force participation rates (both figures, panel 7).

Particularly noteworthy are the net reductions in income inequality that are achieved in both countries (see panel 8 for both countries). Under an increase in investment in human capital, larger percentages finish high school (panel 2 for both countries), and higher education enrolments, including 2-year community colleges, expand from 22 per cent to 35 per cent in the UK and from 56 per cent to 68 per cent in the US under Scenario 2 (both figures, panel 1). The effect on inequality is important to note because inequality has been rising in both the US and the UK, as documented by Gottschalk and Smeeding (1997). Under this change in policy, the effects are somewhat different than in poor countries that do not have universal primary and junior secondary education. In the UK and US there is expansion of access to high school drop-outs and to those not now going on to higher education. As their skills are improved they can compete better as technical change and globalization proceed; the trend toward rising inequality is reversed in both of these scenarios.

With respect to the efficiency of these investments in human capital, the current monetary social rates of return in the US, which include both the direct and indirect effects on per capita income but not the non-monetary returns, are 12 per cent for males and 18 per cent for females finishing 2-year community college degrees and 13.4 per cent for males and 13.2 per cent for females for a 4-year college education (Arias and McMahon, 1998: table 3 and footnote 15). The latter are expected rates of return which are computed to take into account the upward trends since 1980 in the net earnings of college graduates over high school graduates within each successive age group as graduates age. There are no trend-adjusted rates available for the UK, but the standard static cross-section rate of return for the secondary level is 10 per cent for males and 8 per cent for females, and at the university level is 8 per cent for males and 12 per cent for females (Psacharopoulos, 1994: table A-3). The true dynamic rates actually experienced would be about 3 per cent higher than that, or 11 per cent and 15 per cent for a 4-year college education in the UK, if the US trend adjustment is any guide. These rates of return apply to expansion of access at the current levels of quality. Problems with improving internal inefficiency at the secondary level in the US have been much discussed (e.g. Heckman, 1996). If these problems could be overcome, the rate of return would be even higher.

Even at current levels of quality these *real* rates of return are all high relative to the average *real* rate of return on investment in corporate bonds, and slightly lower than the inflation-adjusted total return on smaller company stocks. The inflation-adjusted total return on long-term corporate bonds in the US averaged 7.04 per cent for 1993–7; in 1997 it was 11.06 per cent (Ibbsotson and Associates, 1998: table 4–1) and was not much different in the UK. Total returns averaged 16.6 per cent on small company stocks during the same period (ibid.). The investment in secondary and higher education considered here is therefore a better investment than in corporate bonds, and as good or better than in small company stocks on purely efficiency grounds given that the non-market direct and indirect returns are not included (panel 3). Even for the more focused investment in secondary education designed to prevent high school drop-outs, which Heckman (1998*a*, 1998*b*) estimates to cost US$25,000 per student in 1998 prices, the rates of return if males *complete* high school average a high 12.4 per cent if the current trends in labour markets are taken into account (Arias and McMahon, 1998: table 3). There are significant non-market returns to this kind of investment in expanding retention in high schools that Heckman has de-emphasized because of a lack of measures.

With respect to the non-market returns, the measures generated by both scenarios contribute, first, quite significantly to better health. There are net additional reductions in infant mortality rates as females finish high school, and also increases in life expectancy after 2015 in the US and UK, that may help to make the policy quite cost-effective (panels 13 and 14). There may also be other positive effects on health (reduced smoking, better awareness of low-cholesterol diets, etc.) that this model takes only partially into account through its measure of effects on longevity. Second, minor improvements in the working of democracy are apparent in the US only (Figure 12.13, panel 10) but there are improvements in human rights (e.g. more equitable access to legal services) and to political and economic stability in both nations (both Figures, panels 9 and 11). Third, rural poverty is not reduced by this policy (both Figures, panel 12) and property crime rates rise (panel 16 for both countries). But what is important is that property crime rates are lower than they would have been otherwise.

Fourth, homicide rates are also lowered in the US by this policy (Figure 12–13, panel 16). This is a significant thing to consider, since the incarceration of a single prisoner costs about $40,000 per year in the US. If, using Heckman's (1998*b*) estimate, it costs $25,000 per year for all 4 years to keep a high school drop-out in school, after which he earns $8,000–10,000 per year more than the average eighth-grade graduate for the 40 years or so he is in the labour force, the net

Figure 12.12 United Kingdom: Estimated Policy Impacts on Economic Growth and Equity

Scenarios:

1. Endogeneous development; 2. $I_H/Y = +2$; 3. $GER2T = +20$

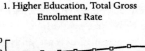

1. Higher Education, Total Gross Enrolment Rate

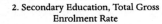

2. Secondary Education, Total Gross Enrolment Rate

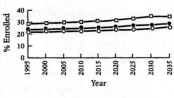

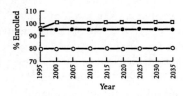

——o—— Scenario 1   ——□—— Scenario 2   ——•—— Scenario 3

3. GNP Per Capita

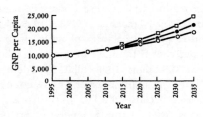

4. Gross Domestic Investment/GNP

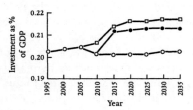

5. Growth Rate of Output per Capita

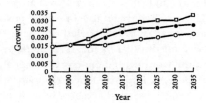

6. Total Fertility Rate

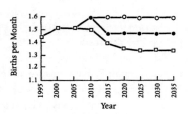

7. Labour Force Participation Rate

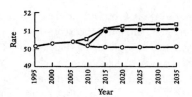

8. Income Inequality

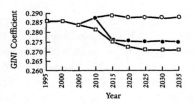

United Kingdom: Non-Market Impacts on Economic Development

9. Human Rights

10. Democratization

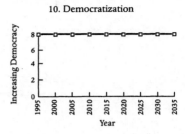

11. Political Stability

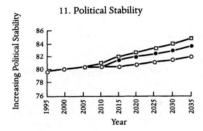

12. Rural Poverty

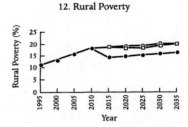

13. Infant Mortality Rate

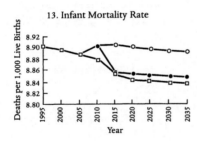

14. Life Expectancy

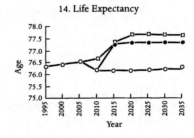

15. Change In Forests

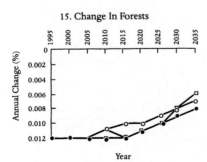

16. Property Crime

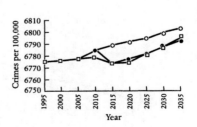

Figure 12.13 United States: Estimated Policy Impacts on Economic Growth and Equity

Scenarios:

1. Endogeneous development;　2. $I_H/Y = +2$;　3. $GER2T = +20$

1. Higher Education, Total Gross
Enrolment Rate

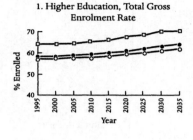

2. Secondary Education, Total Gross
Enrolment Rate

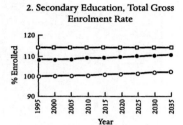

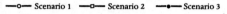

3. GNP Per Capita

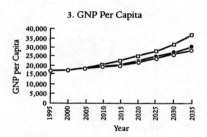

4. Gross Domestic Investment/GNP

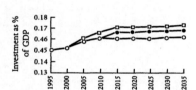

5. Population Growth

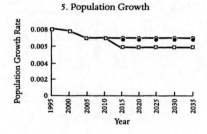

6. Total Fertility Rate

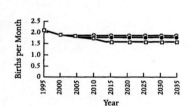

7. Growth Rate of Output per
Capita

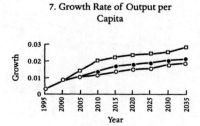

8. Income Inequality

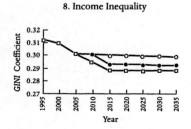

United States: Non-Market Impacts on Economic Development

9. Human Rights

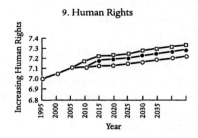

10. Democratization

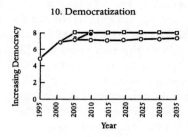

11. Political Stability

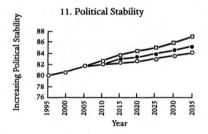

12. Rural Poverty

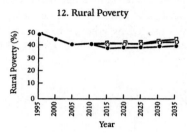

13. Infant Mortality Rate

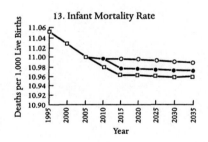

14. Life Expectancy

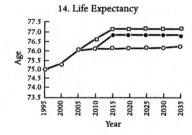

15. Change in Forests

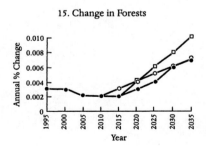

16. Homicide

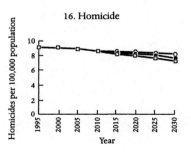

benefits to society are considerable. Finally, deforestation rates are eventually reversed in both countries as they gradually respond to the economic capacity to finance parks and preserves, to the slower population growth, and to the wider education in the electorate (both Figures, panel 15).

Overall, these measures are a first approximation of the various market and non-market returns to education in OECD member nations, both direct and indirect. They can continue to be refined in various ways; one is by separating the direct from the indirect returns, as is done in the next chapter. But perhaps they could also eventually be broken down further by college or even by discipline, including the liberal arts and sciences, to get more comprehensive measures of the contributions from the diffusion of new knowledge.

If we live in knowledge-based economies with education central to the growth process, and with the new knowledge created largely by R&D in the OECD nations disseminated by education, there surely are not just market but also many non-market direct and indirect effects on human welfare and the quality of life worthy of systematic measurement.

13 Separating and Valuing the Direct and Indirect Effects of Education

The total benefits of education to be discussed will be separated in this chapter into measures of the direct or partial effects and the indirect structural effects. Indirect effects, which are also externalities, will then be expressed as a per cent of the total benefits. One or two countries from each region worldwide are chosen to illustrate this separation: Brazil, India, Kenya, the United Kingdom, and the United States; but the same could be done for any of the 78 countries in the complete model.

The investment costs (e.g. 2 per cent of Gross National Product in each nation) can then be related to these direct, indirect, and total returns on the investment within each nation. When the outcome of concern is economic growth, the benefits for computing a social rate of return are the total increments to GNP over future years attributable to the additional education, which are then discounted back to their present value by the internal rate of return. Valuation of the non-market efficiency-related benefits and the distributive justice impacts are more complex, but these will also be considered. For non-market returns, unless one uses the Wolfe–Zuvekas (1997) method (which politicians do not normally do), or assumes a Bergson-type welfare function with explicit value weights, or uses politically determined education budgets increased to include the interest, profits, and forgone earnings costs of educational investments, it will usually be necessary to settle for cost-effectiveness types of measures. The latter do not place an economic value on the measures of the outcomes when evaluating the cost-effectiveness of the non-market and distributional outcomes.

The Conceptual Framework for Separation of Direct and Indirect Effects

The concepts of direct and indirect effects, or alternatively partial and structural effects, and how they have been separated in the model will be considered before their measurement.

Direct Partial and Indirect Externality Effects

The direct (or partial) benefits of education are the marginal products of education, outcome by outcome, after controlling for 'other things'. They are closely analogous to those isolated by standard partial equilibrium analysis in economics, which assumes other things do not change (i.e. *ceteris paribus* conditions, or 'other things being equal'). Empirically partial effects have been measured in multiple regressions after controlling for other things that could logically affect the outcomes, holding them constant by statistical means. There has to be some limit to the other things controlled for, and the limit is therefore those other things for which there is evidence of empirical significance. Remaining weak effects are collected in the disturbances. Hopefully there are no *significant* variables omitted which would then bias the results. The direct effects are then given by the direct partial derivative of the outcome in question with respect to education. Empirically this is the slope coefficient for the education input(s) in each multiple regression equation.

The indirect benefits can only be measured by means of the structural feedback interactions within the complete model. They are impacts of education on these other things in the community, which in turn feed back effects on the outcome in question, often felt significantly only after considerable lags. They are, therefore, the cross-partial derivatives, summed up using the weights that represent the effects of these other things on the outcome in question. For example, education has a direct marginal impact on health. But there are also additional indirect effects of education on health that come though its *incremental* effect on per capita GNP, which improves nutrition and increases expenditure on health care. The total effects on health are the sum of these direct partial effects on health plus the indirect effects via increments to per capita income and other community environment measures that affect health. The model does not profess to have captured all of the indirect effects, but I have sought to capture the significant ones.

The term 'benefits' is used here to mean net benefits, since there can be some negative social costs. Most of these negative effects are smaller and net out as the regressions are run. If net negative effects still persist, most of these are cancelled out by other positive effects in the feedback process as simulations are run. In the rare case where negative direct or indirect effects still predominate, they will be shown in the tables that follow as negative benefits or costs.

Indirect Effects as Externalities

It would be nice to have a clean measure of externalities. But direct effects, although they are partial, are not precisely the same as private benefits. Benefits realized privately clearly include some effects from externalities. However, the indirect effects of education are predominantly externalities. The units that produce them, such as private schools and households, are unable to obtain private payment for all of the benefits to others in the community (such as lower crime rates, or democracy that benefits future generations, or better public health), benefits whose collective importance is undeniable.

The indirect effects are education-related public goods, which are largely 'non-rivalrous' in Romer's (1990) terms, and, like new ideas, use by one does not preclude use by others. This is not to say that those with more education do not benefit more from some of these (e.g. the less well educated make less use of the Internet, or of public broadcasting, or of new knowledge that is available, and have less effective access to the courts). But those with little or no education nevertheless benefit substantially from most of these community effects due in part to education, such as human rights, democracy, public libraries, community knowledge about illnesses, and democratic enactments such as the minimum wage. Immigrants from poor countries also benefit from earnings higher than those available at home, due in part to political stability, new R&D knowledge available from co-workers, and other education-related environmental factors. The fact that there is not a perfectly even distribution of all of the benefits from all externalities among persons with different education levels is not sufficient to establish that they are insubstantial or do not exist. Returning a high school drop-out to school may be seen by the student as not a large enough private benefit to induce him or her to invest the full cost that is involved, but there may nevertheless be a significant benefit to others in the community in the form of lower costs in the criminal justice system, lower public assistance costs, and higher tax revenues, none of which the student realizes privately.

Since the level of these community effects is largely unaffected by the individual's decision to invest in education, there is no reason for these non-rivalrous goods to be taken fully into account by households and firms when they decide how much to invest. This lack of private incentive to invest is the key, not whether individual benefits arise to free riders from these externalities, as they clearly do.

These types of externalities from basic primary and secondary education, like the externalities from research, are widely recognized although seldom measured. But the question has been raised by some as to whether there are externalities from higher education, primarily because graduates, especially from some institutions, are paid so well. However, this ignores the indirect structural effects from higher education discussed throughout the last chapter.

It is the non-rivalrous nature of almost all of the indirect effects, together with the inability to apply the exclusion principle so that those who invest privately in education are able to obtain payment, that leads to under-investment. Steps must be taken publicly, therefore, to remedy this market failure.

Direct effects, in contrast to the indirect effects, are largely private benefits. But they can include benefits from some externalities. This is because I am measuring direct benefits by means of multiple regression methods, in which case the education term picks up not just internal benefits deriving from the actions of the firm or household, but also externality benefits at two levels: within the firm as workers learn from one another and their earnings are thereby enhanced, and community effects external to the firm, attributable to the level of education in the community that benefits the productivity of the firm. Again, there are insufficient private incentives to invest enough in education to receive these education-generated 'non-rivalrous' benefits that exist in the firm and the community and are available without larger investments.

The measures of direct and indirect effects of education below arise with monetary market benefits, but both also occur as non-market benefits that arise from production by households of final satisfactions during leisure-time hours.

Production by Firms and Households with Externalities

It helps to be more specific about externalities in production by firms and by households and their relation to indirect effects.

For production by firms leading to market outputs, the reduced-form production function in Equation (13.1) below attributed to Lucas (1988) contains human capital used on the job, μH, and external effects from human capital, H^α (using the same notation as in Chapter 2):

$$Y = Y(K, \mu H, N, A)H^\alpha. \tag{13.1}$$

As before, H^α is the average level of education in the community.

H^α is not only the direct effects of the average level of education in the community on productivity but also the indirect effects of education coming through to the rule of law and political stability. There may also be additional indirect effects via lower crime rates, contributions of education to R&D, and other community effects for which I have been less able to show separate empirical significance. So they are picked up by μH or in the disturbances.

The externalities that can be measured are the indirect effects or cross-partial derivatives: $\delta Y / \delta X_i \delta X_i / \delta (H^\alpha)$. Here $\delta X_i / \delta (H^\alpha)$ are the significant *community effects* of education, such as the effects of education on political stability (X_i) or the rule of law, and hence on rates of investment in physical capital.

For households, measurement of externality effects of education in the production of non-monetary satisfactions uses Becker's (1964) household production function, extended to include external effects:

$$Z = Z(Y, (1 - \mu)H)H^\beta. \tag{13.2}$$

Here Y represents the sum of all market goods, or per capita income, for which statistical controls are imposed in order to measure the non-market returns. The direct effects are the partial derivatives of Z with respect to $(1 - \mu)H$ and with respect to H^β. The external indirect effects are the same kind of *cross*-partial derivatives as before, or in this case $\delta Z / \delta X_i \delta X_i / \delta (H^\beta)$. The latter term is again the effect of the average level of education in the community operating indirectly through human rights, democracy, health, crime, and the environment, all of which are quite important to the quality of human life (Z). The separate non-market effects of education on each Z_i are the respective marginal products of education from the empirical estimates, but the Z_is must be valued before they have a common denominator and can be summed up.

The direct effects have been estimated first by regression methods holding the indirect effects constant, including Y in Equation (13.2) when seeking to measure the non-monetary returns. Then, to estimate the non-direct effects, the complete model was reprogrammed to allow only for direct effects, and a separate set of simulations was run for these. To get the direct effects, all of the other endogenous variables in each equation in this simulation were programmed to take on the same values as in the base-line endogenous development scenario generated by running the model with no new education policy change. The direct impact of education on each outcome, therefore, is the increment above the endogenous development growth path. It is the partial impact of education, which is the direct effect only with 'other things the same' as they would have been without this special policy intervention.

The indirect benefits can then be measured simply by subtracting these direct benefits from the total benefits as given in the preceding chapter. The total benefits must also be expressed net of the endogenous development scenario values. Then the indirect benefits can be expressed as a per cent of the total benefits.

Empirical Measures of Direct and Indirect Effects on Growth by Region

The total effects, the direct effects, and the indirect effects as a per cent of the total effects from an education policy change are shown in Tables 13.1–13.5 for each year up through 2035 AD. These are for Brazil, India, Kenya, the United Kingdom, and the United States respectively, and are roughly representative of differences in the patterns among LAC, Asian, African, and OECD nations. Total, direct, and indirect effects are all net of the endogenous development values and are generated by simulations for Scenarios 2 and 3. Primary attention, however, will be given to Scenario 2, the policy change involving an increase of 2 percentage points in investment in education as a per cent of GNP. This scenario is the one that gives the investment costs which are the basis on which total social rates of return to education can be computed. Also, this policy does not simply squeeze the other levels of education in order to increase secondary enrolments, but instead channels most of the additional resources to primary education first in countries where adequacy at that level has not yet been achieved, then most of the additional resources to secondary, and finally most to higher education where secondary education is closer to being universal, as in the OECD countries. This therefore also permits more meaningful comparisons of returns to similar relative efforts among economies at widely different levels of development.

Economic Growth: Total, Direct, and Externality Effects

As shown in Table 13.1, panel 1, the investment of 2 percentage points more of GNP in education in Brazil raises per capita income by about US$9,801 in 1985 prices by 2035 (the same as in Figure 12.1). Column (5) shows that about 40.97 per cent of this is due to indirect effects, almost all of which can be regarded as externality benefits of education. These externalities are a smaller per cent of the total effects in the earlier years and build as time passes because individuals are in the labour force for about 40 years, or up to 2040, and also new cohorts benefit from this policy change, so it takes time before the community effects feed back on production. Most of these indirect effects in Brazil arise in the regressions because of the

Table 13.1 Total, Direct, and Indirect Effects of Education: BRAZIL

Year	Total Effects		Direct Effects		Indirect Effects as % of Total	
	Scenario 2: $I_H/Y + 2$ (1)	Scenario 3: GER2 + 20 (2)	Scenario 2: $I_H/Y + 2$ (3)	Scenario 3: GER2 + 20 (4)	Scenario 2: $I_H/Y + 2$ (5)	Scenario 3: GER2 + 20 (6)
GNP Per Capita						
1995	0.00	0.00	0.00	0.00	0.00%	0.00%
2000	45.98	0.00	41.86	0.00	8.97%	0.00%
2005	256.38	55.80	220.62	50.46	13.95%	9.58%
2010	699.27	407.15	560.16	365.67	19.89%	10.19%
2015	1391.35	918.49	1039.23	814.40	25.31%	11.33%
2020	2428.58	1685.41	1714.65	1459.40	29.40%	13.41%
2025	3969.51	2793.13	2655.07	2373.84	33.11%	15.01%
2030	6288.18	4418.10	3965.33	3661.53	36.94%	17.12%
2035	9801.26	6838.48	5785.33	5470.10	40.97%	20.01%
Inequality in Income Distribution						
1995	0	0	0	0	0.00%	0.00%
2000	0	0	0	0	0.00%	0.00%
2005	0	0	0	0	0.00%	0.00%
2010	−0.006	0	−0.005	0	16.67%	0.00%
2015	−0.014	−0.015	−0.013	−0.015	7.14%	0.00%
2020	−0.017	−0.015	−0.014	−0.015	17.65%	0.00%
2025	−0.018	−0.016	−0.015	−0.016	16.67%	0.00%
2030	−0.019	−0.016	−0.014	−0.015	26.32%	6.25%
2035	−0.019	−0.016	−0.014	−0.015	26.32%	6.25%
Political Stability						
1995	0	0	0	0	0.00%	0.00%
2000	0.004	0	0	0	0.00%	0.00%
2005	0.145	0	0	0	0.00%	0.00%
2010	0.749	0.139	0.549	0	26.70%	0.00%
2015	1.669	1.693	1.234	1.461	26.06%	13.70%
2020	2.17	1.838	1.371	1.462	36.82%	20.46%
2025	2.539	2.057	1.371	1.462	46.00%	28.93%
2030	3.061	2.386	1.371	1.462	55.21%	38.73%
2035	3.891	2.946	1.372	1.462	64.74%	50.37%
Democratization						
1995	0	0	0	0	0.00%	0.00%
2000	0	0	0	0	0.00%	0.00%
2005	1.145	0	0.868	0	24.19%	0.00%
2010	0.812	0.812	0.548	0.548	32.51%	32.51%
2015	0.62	0.62	0.372	0.372	40.00%	40.00%
2020	0.422	0.422	0.189	0.189	55.21%	55.21%
2025	0.216	0.216	3.89E-16	3.89E-16	100.00%	100.00%
Change in Forests						
1995	0	0	0	0	0.00%	0.00%
2000	0	0	0	0	0.00%	0.00%
2005	0	0	0	0	0.00%	0.00%
2010	−0.001	0	−0.001	0	0.00%	0.00%
2015	−0.001	−0.001	−0.002	−0.003	−100.00%	−200.00%
2020	−0.001	−0.001	−0.002	−0.002	−100.00%	−100.00%
2025	−0.001	−0.001	−0.003	−0.003	−200.00%	−200.00%
2030	0.001	0.001	−0.003	−0.003	400.00%	400.00%
2035	0.002	0.001	−0.003	−0.003	250.00%	400.00%

Table 13.1 (Contd.)

Air Pollution						
1995	0	0	0	0	0.00%	0.00%
2000	−0.912	0	0	0	0.00%	0.00%
2005	−2.922	−2.454	0	0	0.00%	0.00%
2010	−3.98	−2.824	−0.795	0	80.03%	0.00%
2015	−4.995	−4.931	−1.789	−2.119	64.18%	57.03%
2020	−4.867	−4.352	−1.987	−2.118	59.17%	51.33%
2025	−4.143	−3.679	−1.988	−2.118	52.02%	42.43%
2030	−3.059	−2.862	−1.988	−2.119	35.01%	25.96%
2035	−1.569	−1.776	−1.988	−2.119	−26.70%	−19.31%
Property Crime						
1995	0	0	0	0	0.00%	0.00%
2000	0.445	0	0	0	0.00%	0.00%
2005	2.141	0.461	0	0	0.00%	0.00%
2010	−2.383	2.953	−6.742	0	−182.92%	0.00%
2015	−9.609	−14.055	−15.164	−17.961	−57.81%	−27.79%
2020	−9.805	−10.953	−16.851	−17.961	−71.86%	−63.98%
2025	−6.179	−7.461	−16.859	−17.969	−172.84%	−140.84%
2030	−1.375	−3.305	−16.851	−17.961	−1125.5%	−443.45%
2035	4.328	1.219	−16.851	−17.961	489.35%	1573.42%
Homicide						
1995	0	0	0	0	0.00%	0.00%
2000	−0.006	0	0	0	100.00%	0.00%
2005	−0.029	−0.009	0	0	100.00%	100.00%
2010	−0.159	−0.044	0	0	100.00%	100.00%
2015	−0.353	−0.323	0	0	100.00%	100.00%
2020	−0.504	−0.4	0	0	100.00%	100.00%
2025	−0.668	−0.512	0	0	100.00%	100.00%
2030	−0.908	−0.675	0	0	100.00%	100.00%
2035	−1.273	−0.924	0	0	100.00%	100.00%

contribution of education to democracy and political stability (or the rule of law) and through these to higher rates of saving and investment in physical capital. The indirect effects from increasing secondary education enrolments only in Scenario 3 are only about half this, or about 20 per cent of the total, partly because the benefits from better primary education are missing.

In India, the indirect effects of the increased investment in education on per capita economic growth are about 38 per cent of the total by 2035 (Table 13.2, panel 1), very similar to the 40 per cent indirect effects in Brazil. These effects again come through increased investment in the model, presumably largely attracted from abroad as investment benefits from a skilled labour force but also in part from increased stability. For political/economic stability, in turn, the indirect effects are 40.76 per cent of the total (Table 13.2, panel 3, Scenario 2).

Kenya provides some interesting contrasts. With roughly the same level of per capita income as India but a more limited degree of democracy and political stability (see Figure 12.9), the relative importance of increases in political and economic stability in Kenya is greater (Table 13.3, panel 3). Political stability, in turn, benefits from the effects of education on democratization (panel 4). These

Table 13.2 Total, Direct, and Indirect Effects of Education: INDIA

Year	Total Effects		Direct Effects		Indirect as % of Total	
	Scenario 2: $I_H/Y + 2$ (1)	Scenario 3: GER2 + 20 (2)	Scenario 2: $I_H/Y + 2$ (3)	Scenario 3: GER2 + 20 (4)	Scenario 2: $I_H/Y + 2$ (5)	Scenario 3: GER2 + 20 (6)
GNP Per Capita						
1995	0.00	0.00	0.00	0.00	0.00%	0.00%
2000	1.53	0.00	0.00	0.00	0.00%	0.00%
2005	15.51	0.30	7.23	0.00	53.39%	0.00%
2010	73.57	7.36	48.13	5.04	34.57%	31.60%
2015	222.73	50.21	156.19	43.71	29.87%	12.95%
2020	505.10	148.86	349.38	134.42	30.83%	9.70%
2025	975.75	301.31	651.78	272.88	33.20%	9.44%
2030	1749.80	534.52	1121.08	482.03	35.93%	9.82%
2035	3019.53	891.76	1846.58	796.33	38.85%	10.70%
Inequality in Income Distribution						
1995	0	0	0	0	0.00%	0.00%
2000	0	0	0	0	0.00%	0.00%
2005	−0.001	−0.001	0	0	0.00%	0.00%
2010	−0.006	−0.001	−0.006	0	0.00%	0.00%
2015	−0.014	−0.008	−0.013	−0.008	7.14%	0.00%
2020	−0.017	−0.009	−0.014	−0.009	17.65%	0.00%
2025	−0.017	−0.008	−0.014	−0.008	17.65%	0.00%
2030	−0.018	−0.009	−0.015	−0.009	16.67%	0.00%
2035	−0.019	−0.009	−0.015	−0.009	21.05%	0.00%
Political Stability						
1995	0	0	0	0	0.00%	0.00%
2000	0	0	0	0	0.00%	0.00%
2005	0.002	0	0	0	0.00%	0.00%
2010	0.559	0.001	0.549	0.001	1.79%	0.00%
2015	1.376	0.824	1.235	0.817	10.25%	0.85%
2020	1.695	0.843	1.371	0.816	19.12%	3.20%
2025	1.826	0.875	1.371	0.817	24.92%	6.63%
2030	2.004	0.924	1.371	0.817	31.59%	11.58%
2035	2.316	1.001	1.372	0.817	40.76%	18.38%
Human Rights						
1995	0	0	0	0	0.00%	0.00%
2000	0.045	0	0.045	0	0.00%	0.00%
2005	0.112	0.068	0.103	0.068	8.04%	0.00%
2010	0.139	0.068	0.114	0.068	17.99%	0.00%
2015	0.158	0.07	0.115	0.068	27.22%	2.86%
2020	0.187	0.08	0.114	0.068	39.04%	15.00%
2025	0.227	0.097	0.114	0.068	49.78%	29.90%
2030	0.259	0.115	0.114	0.068	55.98%	40.87%
2035	0.295	0.132	0.114	0.068	61.36%	48.48%
Air Pollution						
1995	0	0	0	0	0.00%	0.00%
2000	−0.161	0	0	0	0.00%	0.00%
2005	−1.145	−0.075	0	0	0.00%	0.00%
2010	−3.987	−1.167	−0.795	0	80.06%	0.00%
2015	−6.815	−3.533	−1.789	−1.184	73.75%	66.49%
2020	−7.528	−3.508	−1.988	−1.184	73.59%	66.25%
2025	−7.44	−3.441	−1.988	−1.184	73.28%	65.59%

Table 13.2 (Contd.)

2030	−7.17	−3.328	−1.987	−1.183	72.29%	64.45%
2035	−6.633	−3.182	−1.988	−1.184	70.03%	62.79%
Water Pollution						
1995	−86.303	−16.145	0	0	100.00%	100.00%
2000	−95.385	−16.145	0	0	100.00%	100.00%
2005	−98.589	−16.179	0	0	100.00%	100.00%
2010	−103.626	−16.8	0	0	100.00%	100.00%
2015	−111.791	−34.696	0	0	100.00%	100.00%
2020	−122.782	−38.088	0	0	100.00%	100.00%
2025	−131.004	−41.459	0	0	100.00%	100.00%
2030	−138.812	−45.12	0	0	100.00%	100.00%
2035	−143.612	−48.707	0	0	100.00%	100.00%
Change in Forests						
1995	0	0	0	0	0.00%	0.00%
2000	0	0	0	0	0.00%	0.00%
2005	0	0	0	0	0.00%	0.00%
2010	−0.001	0	−0.001	0	0.00%	0.00%
2015	−0.003	−0.002	−0.003	−0.002	0.00%	0.00%
2020	−0.002	−0.001	−0.002	−0.001	0.00%	0.00%
2025	−0.002	−0.001	−0.002	−0.001	0.00%	0.00%
2030	−0.002	−0.001	−0.002	−0.001	0.00%	0.00%
2035	−0.001	−0.001	−0.002	−0.001	100.00%	0.00%
Homicide						
1995	0	0	0	0	0.00%	0.00%
2000	0	0	0	0	0.00%	0.00%
2005	−0.003	0	0	0	100.00%	100.00%
2010	−0.097	−0.002	0	0	100.00%	100.00%
2015	−0.238	−0.136	0	0	100.00%	100.00%
2020	−0.307	−0.145	0	0	100.00%	100.00%
2025	−0.36	−0.161	0	0	100.00%	100.00%
2030	−0.44	−0.184	0	0	100.00%	100.00%
2035	−0.575	−0.22	0	0	100.00%	100.00%

indirect effects account for a much larger 95 per cent of the total effects of education on per capita economic growth in Kenya (Table 13.3, panel 1, Scenario 2).

In the UK and the US the indirect externalities from the increased investment in education on per capita economic growth are again substantial, but lower. They are 59.34 per cent in the UK by 2035 (Table 13.4, panel 1, Scenario 2) and 37 per cent in the US (Table 13.5, panel 1, Scenarios 2 and 3). The increments to political stability in both the US and UK and to continuing improvements in democracy that were shown in Figures 12.12 and 12.13 are smaller than in the African countries, since the initial level of political stability is much greater. Nevertheless, there are indirect effects that come through higher rates of investment in physical capital, which might be interpreted in part as the effect of education in offsetting diminishing returns to physical capital and making such investments more profitable than they would otherwise be. But there are also major indirect effects through R&D, since in the OECD countries higher education is strongly complementary to new knowledge created by R&D, with higher education embodying the new ideas and acting as

Table 13.3 Total, Direct, and Indirect Effects of Education: KENYA

Year	Total Effects		Direct Effects		Indirect as % of Total	
	Scenario 2: $I_H/Y + 2$ (1)	Scenario 3: GER2 + 20 (2)	Scenario 2: $I_H/Y + 2$ (3)	Scenario 3: GER2 + 20 (4)	Scenario 2: $I_H/Y + 2$ (5)	Scenario 3: GER2 + 20 (6)
GNP Per Capita						
1995	0.00	0.00	0.00	0.00	0.00%	0.00%
2000	12.50	0.00	1.67	0.00	86.63%	0.00%
2005	60.54	2.36	7.62	2.36	87.41%	0.04%
2010	144.82	14.45	16.26	14.41	88.77%	0.30%
2015	258.37	29.19	25.01	26.82	90.32%	8.11%
2020	408.96	52.38	33.93	39.58	91.70%	24.42%
2025	601.39	76.78	43.03	52.75	92.85%	31.29%
2030	847.64	102.82	52.33	66.36	93.83%	35.46%
2035	1164.35	131.22	61.85	80.41	94.69%	38.72%
Inequality in Income Distribution						
1995	0	0	0	0	0.00%	0.00%
2000	0	0	0	0	0.00%	0.00%
2005	−0.001	0	0	0	100.00%	0.00%
2010	−0.006	0	−0.006	0	100.00%	0.00%
2015	−0.015	−0.02	−0.013	−0.02	13.33%	0.00%
2020	−0.018	−0.02	−0.015	−0.02	16.67%	0.00%
2025	−0.019	−0.02	−0.014	−0.02	26.32%	0.00%
2030	−0.02	−0.02	−0.014	−0.02	30.00%	0.00%
2035	−0.021	−0.02	−0.014	−0.02	33.33%	0.00%
Political Stability						
1995	0	0	0	0	0.00%	0.00%
2000	0.001	0	0	0	100.00%	0.00%
2005	0.129	0	0	0	100.00%	0.00%
2010	0.878	0.424	0.548	0	37.59%	100.00%
2015	1.81	2.357	1.235	1.93	31.77%	18.12%
2020	2.21	2.364	1.372	1.93	37.92%	18.36%
2025	2.352	2.37	1.371	1.929	41.71%	18.61%
2030	2.486	2.382	1.371	1.929	44.85%	19.02%
2035	2.696	2.41	1.371	1.929	49.15%	19.96%
Democratization						
1995	0	0	0	0	0.00%	0.00%
2000	0	0	0	0	0.00%	0.00%
2005	1.267	0	1.267	0	0.00%	0.00%
2010	3.192	4.457	2.851	4.456	10.68%	0.02%
2015	4.023	4.459	3.168	4.457	21.25%	0.04%
2020	4.26	4.469	3.168	4.457	25.63%	0.27%
2025	4.48	4.481	3.167	4.456	29.31%	0.56%
2030	4.598	4.537	3.167	4.456	31.12%	1.79%
2035	4.595	4.595	3.168	4.457	31.06%	3.00%
Human Rights						
1995	0	0	0	0	0.00%	0.00%
2000	0.045	0	0.045	0	0.00%	0.00%
2005	0.122	0.161	0.103	0.161	15.57%	0.00%
2010	0.175	0.161	0.114	0.16	34.86%	0.62%
2015	0.219	0.168	0.114	0.16	47.95%	4.76%
2020	0.267	0.177	0.114	0.16	57.30%	9.60%
2025	0.322	0.19	0.114	0.16	64.60%	15.79%

Table 13.3 (Contd.)

Human Rights						
2030	0.379	0.21	0.114	0.16	69.92%	23.81%
2035	0.436	0.225	0.114	0.16	73.85%	28.89%
Life Expectancy						
1995	0	0	0	0	0.00%	0.00%
2000	0.01	0	0	0	0.00%	0.00%
2005	0.055	0	0	0	0.00%	0.00%
2010	1.021	0.017	0.505	0	50.54%	0.00%
2015	2.433	1.81	1.136	1.775	53.31%	1.93%
2020	3.027	3.153	1.262	1.775	58.31%	43.70%
2025	3.177	3.142	1.262	1.775	60.28%	43.51%
2030	3.296	3.145	1.262	1.776	61.71%	43.53%
2035	3.516	3.189	1.262	1.776	64.11%	44.31%
Total Fertility Rate						
1995	0	0	0	0	0.00%	0.00%
2000	0	0	0	0	0.00%	0.00%
2005	0	0	0	0	0.00%	0.00%
2010	−0.069	0	−0.029	0	57.97%	0.00%
2015	−0.165	−0.11	−0.065	−0.11	60.61%	0.00%
2020	−0.198	−0.11	−0.072	−0.11	63.64%	0.00%
2025	−0.204	−0.109	−0.072	−0.109	64.71%	0.00%
2030	−0.209	−0.11	−0.072	−0.11	65.55%	0.00%
2035	−0.217	−0.111	−0.072	−0.11	66.82%	0.90%
Infant Mortality Rate						
1995	0	0	0	0	0.00%	0.00%
2000	−0.084	0	0	0	0.00%	0.00%
2005	−0.375	−0.017	0	0	0.00%	0.00%
2010	−3.551	−0.113	−2.58	0	27.34%	0.00%
2015	−6.872	−7.554	−5.107	−7.456	25.68%	1.30%
2020	−7.952	−7.433	−5.395	−7.266	32.16%	2.25%
2025	−8.283	−7.377	−5.304	−7.145	35.97%	3.14%
2030	−8.604	−7.411	−5.279	−7.112	38.64%	4.03%
2035	−9.152	−7.6	−5.338	−7.19	41.67%	5.39%

a major vehicle for their transmission to firms as graduates are employed. But part of the indirect effects come through higher education itself, since the increased investment in higher education is partly the direct effect of the policy change but also partly the result of an endogenous feedback in the model, as investment in higher education is also a function of faster per capita economic growth. The latter is part of the *social demand for higher education*; it rises as per capita income rises.

The other side of the coin is that the contribution of higher education itself to economic growth in the OECD countries reflects this same complementarity between higher education and R&D and therefore the effects of the new knowledge created by R&D. It is hard to know whether this should be counted as a contribution of higher education or of R&D; this question has been explored in estimates of nested CED production functions for the US (McMahon, 1992*a*). I have been unable to include in this model direct effects from investment in R&D. It is important in Romer's (1990) theoretical work and generally recognized as

Table 13.4 Total, Direct, and Indirect Effects of Education: UNITED KINGDOM

Year	Total Effects		Direct Effects		Indirect Effects as % of Total	
	Scenario 2: $I_H/Y + 2$ (1)	Scenario 3: $GER2 + 20$ (2)	Scenario 2: $I_H/Y + 2$ (3)	Scenario 3: $GER2 + 20$ (4)	Scenario 2: $I_H/Y + 2$ (5)	Scenario 3: $GER2 + 20$ (6)
GNP Per Capita						
1995	0.00	0.00	0.00	0.00	0.00%	0.00%
2000	0.00	0.00	0.00	0.00	0.00%	0.00%
2005	71.64	0.00	0.00	0.00	0.00%	0.00%
2010	381.73	65.10	54.93	0.00	85.61%	0.00%
2015	991.39	475.81	271.27	57.54	72.64%	87.91%
2020	1831.45	1198.11	641.15	379.06	64.99%	68.36%
2025	2887.56	2094.77	1105.89	808.74	61.70%	61.39%
2030	4212.24	3218.62	1682.56	1355.15	60.06%	57.90%
2035	5890.41	4638.39	2394.91	2038.86	59.34%	56.04%
Inequality in Income Distribution						
1995	0	0	0	0	0.00%	0.00%
2000	0	0	0	0	0.00%	0.00%
2005	0	0	0	0	0.00%	0.00%
2010	−0.006	0	−0.006	0	0.00%	0.00%
2015	−0.014	−0.021	−0.013	−0.021	7.14%	0.00%
2020	−0.016	−0.021	−0.014	−0.021	12.50%	0.00%
2025	−0.017	−0.021	−0.014	−0.021	17.65%	0.00%
2030	−0.017	−0.021	−0.014	−0.021	17.65%	0.00%
2035	−0.017	−0.021	−0.014	−0.021	17.65%	0.00%
Political Stability						
1995	0	0	0	0	0.00%	0.00%
2000	0	0	0	0	0.00%	0.00%
2005	0.005	0	0	0	0.00%	0.00%
2010	0.603	0	0.548	0	9.12%	0.00%
2015	1.493	2.07	1.234	2.001	17.35%	3.33%
2020	1.928	2.225	1.371	2.001	28.89%	10.07%
2025	2.189	2.43	1.372	2.002	37.32%	17.61%
2030	2.485	2.686	1.372	2.002	44.79%	25.47%
2035	2.875	3.009	1.371	2.001	52.31%	33.50%
Life Expectancy						
1995	0.00	0.00	0.00	0.00	0.00%	0.00%
2000	0.00	0.00	0.00	0.00	0.00%	0.00%
2005	0.00	0.00	0.00	0.00	0.00%	0.00%
2010	0.51	0.00	0.51	0.00	0.59%	0.00%
2015	1.22	1.84	1.14	1.84	6.66%	0.00%
2020	1.45	1.86	1.26	1.84	12.79%	0.70%
2025	1.46	1.85	1.26	1.84	13.80%	0.65%
2030	1.46	1.85	1.26	1.84	13.50%	0.65%
2035	1.47	1.85	1.26	1.84	13.92%	0.65%
Infant Mortality Rate						
1995	0	0	0	0	0.00%	0.00%
2000	0	0	0	0	0.00%	0.00%
2005	0	0	0	0	0.00%	0.00%
2010	−0.023	0	−0.022	0	4.35%	0.00%
2015	−0.05	−0.068	−0.044	−0.067	12.00%	1.47%
2020	−0.057	−0.067	−0.047	−0.066	17.54%	1.49%
2025	−0.056	−0.065	−0.047	−0.065	16.07%	0.00%

Table 13.4 (Contd.)

Infant Mortality Rate						
2030	−0.055	−0.064	−0.046	−0.064	16.36%	0.00%
2035	−0.055	−0.063	−0.045	−0.063	18.18%	0.00%
Total Fertility Rate						
1995	0	0	0	0	0.00%	0.00%
2000	0	0	0	0	0.00%	0.00%
2005	0	0	0	0	0.00%	0.00%
2010	−0.092	0	−0.058	0	36.96%	0.00%
2015	−0.216	−0.227	−0.13	−0.227	39.81%	0.00%
2020	−0.255	−0.227	−0.144	−0.227	43.53%	0.00%
2025	−0.257	−0.227	−0.144	−0.226	43.97%	0.44%
2030	−0.256	−0.227	−0.144	−0.227	43.75%	0.00%
2035	−0.257	−0.227	−0.144	−0.227	43.97%	0.00%
Air Pollution						
1995	0	0	0	0	0.00%	0.00%
2000	0	0	0	0	0.00%	0.00%
2005	−0.285	0	0	0	0.00%	0.00%
2010	−1.828	−0.664	−0.795	0	56.51%	0.00%
2015	−3.322	−4.309	−1.789	−2.901	46.15%	32.68%
2020	−3.316	−3.828	−1.988	−2.901	40.05%	24.22%
2025	−2.768	−3.306	−1.988	−2.902	28.18%	12.22%
Property Crime						
1995	0	0	0	0	0.00%	0.00%
2000	0	0	0	0	0.00%	0.00%
2005	0.219	0	0	0	0.00%	0.00%
2010	−6.024	0.186	−6.742	0	−11.92%	0.00%
2015	−14.417	−25.505	−15.169	−24.599	−5.22%	3.55%
2020	−15.746	−23.731	−16.854	−24.599	−7.04%	−3.66%
2025	−13.818	−21.784	−16.854	−24.599	−21.97%	−12.92%
2030	−11.259	−19.598	−16.854	−24.6	−49.69%	−25.52%
2035	−8.486	−17.082	−16.854	−24.599	−98.61%	−44.01%

possessing major externalities with particular relevance in the industrialized countries (and hence worldwide), offsetting diminishing returns to both human and physical capital. But it was not possible, using data from OECD member countries, to establish significant direct effects from the rate of investment in R&D by regression methods once both basic and higher education were included in the production function (see also McMahon, 1984a). This leads to the conclusion that most of the practical effect from R&D comes only after it is embodied through investment in higher education and in physical capital and hence through the complementarity between higher education and R&D.

However, in a macro-econometric model estimated from US time series data, knowledge-capital stocks created through investment in R&D are included in the production function, as are stocks of human and physical capital (McMahon, forthcoming). Here exponents for higher education in the production function are restricted to those deduced from microeconomic rates of return, and the exponents for R&D stocks to those implied by Mansfield's (1995) microeconomic rates of return to investment in R&D. Then, by means of simulations, the total effects from investment in R&D and investment in human capital are traced. But even here the

Table 13.5 Total, Direct, and Indirect Effects of Education. UNITED STATES

Year	Total Effects		Direct Effects		Indirect Effects as % of Total	
	Scenario 2: $I_H / Y + 2$ (1)	Scenario 3: GER2 + 20 (2)	Scenario 2: $I_H / Y + 2$ (3)	Scenario 3: GER2 + 20 (4)	Scenario 2: $I_H / Y + 2$ (5)	Scenario 3: GER2 + 20 (6)
GNP Per Capita						
1995	0	0	0	0	0.00%	0.00%
2000	0	0	0	0	0.00%	0.00%
2005	143	0	108	0	24.68%	0.00%
2010	713	58	512	53	28.09%	8.03%
2015	1675	423	1130	340	32.55%	19.60%
2020	2851	1034	1865	697	34.58%	32.63%
2025	4251	1742	2749	1132	35.33%	35.04%
2030	5945	2576	3801	1646	36.05%	36.12%
2035	8008	3571	5051	2249	36.92%	37.03%
Inequality in Income Distribution						
1995	0	0	0	0	0.00%	0.00%
2000	0	0	0	0	0.00%	0.00%
2005	0	0	0	0	0.00%	0.00%
2010	−0.006	0	−0.006	0	0.00%	0.00%
2015	−0.012	−0.012	−0.012	−0.012	0.00%	0.00%
2020	−0.012	−0.012	−0.012	−0.012	0.00%	0.00%
2025	−0.011	−0.011	−0.011	−0.011	0.00%	0.00%
2030	−0.011	−0.011	−0.011	−0.011	0.00%	0.00%
2035	−0.011	−0.011	−0.011	−0.011	0.00%	0.00%
Political Stability						
1995	0	0	0	0	0.00%	0.00%
2000	0	0	0	0	0.00%	0.00%
2005	0.105	0	0	0	0.00%	0.00%
2010	0.745	0	0.549	0	26.31%	0.00%
2015	1.496	1.244	1.09	1.09	27.14%	12.38%
2020	1.781	1.387	1.104	1.104	38.01%	20.40%
2025	2.083	1.53	1.089	1.089	47.72%	28.82%
2030	2.438	1.687	1.059	1.059	56.56%	37.23%
2035	2.876	1.881	0.956	0.956	66.76%	49.18%
Life Expectancy						
1995	0	0	0	0	0.00%	0.00%
2000	0	0	0	0	0.00%	0.00%
2005	0	0	0	0	0.00%	0.00%
2010	0.508	0	0.505	0	0.59%	0.00%
2015	1.008	1.003	1.003	1.003	0.50%	0.00%
2020	1.023	1.022	1.017	1.017	0.59%	0.49%
2025	1.008	1.007	1.002	1.002	0.60%	0.50%
2030	0.98	0.98	0.974	0.974	0.61%	0.61%
2035	0.954	0.954	0.949	0.949	0.52%	0.52%
Change in Forests						
1995	0	0	0	0	0.00%	0.00%
2000	0	0	0	0	0.00%	0.00%
2005	0	0	0	0	0.00%	0.00%
2010	0	0	−0.001	0	0.00%	0.00%
2015	−0.001	−0.002	−0.002	−0.002	−100.00%	0.00%
2020	0	−0.001	−0.002	−0.002	0.00%	−100.00%
2025	0.001	−0.001	−0.002	−0.002	300.00%	−100.00%

Table 13.5 (Contd.)

2030	0.002	0	−0.002	−0.002	200.00%	−100.00%
2035	0.003	0	−0.002	−0.002	166.67%	−100.00%
Narcotics Addiction						
1995	0	0	0	0	0.00%	0.00%
2000	0	0	0	0	0.00%	0.00%
2005	0.003	0	0	0	100.00%	0.00%
2010	0.015	0.001	0	0	100.00%	100.00%
2015	0.033	0.009	0	0	100.00%	100.00%
2020	0.05	0.019	0	0	100.00%	100.00%
2025	0.069	0.03	0	0	100.00%	100.00%
2030	0.086	0.04	0	0	100.00%	100.00%
2035	0.104	0.049	0	0	100.00%	100.00%
Homicide						
1995	0	0	0	0	0.00%	0.00%
2000	0	0	0	0	0.00%	0.00%
2005	−0.015	0	0	0	100.00%	0.00%
2010	−0.159	−0.007	0	0	100.00%	100.00%
2015	−0.34	−0.214	0	0	100.00%	100.00%
2020	−0.459	−0.277	0	0	100.00%	100.00%
2025	−0.598	−0.346	0	0	100.00%	100.00%
2030	−0.762	−0.425	0	0	100.00%	100.00%
2035	−0.964	−0.519	0	0	100.00%	100.00%
Property Crime						
1995	0	0	0	0	0.00%	0.00%
2000	0	0	0	0	0.00%	0.00%
2005	0	0	0	0	0.00%	0.00%
2010	−5.559	0.123	−6.742	0	−21.28%	0.00%
2015	−10.592	−13.73	−13.393	−13.393	−26.44%	2.45%
2020	−8.61	−12.73	−13.571	−13.571	−57.62%	−6.61%
2025	−6.005	−11.246	−13.386	−13.386	−122.91%	−19.03%
2030	−2.875	−9.434	−13.014	−13.014	−352.66%	−37.95%
Water Pollution						
1995	−150.074	−38.367	0	0	100.00%	100.00%
2000	−150.585	−38.879	0	0	100.00%	100.00%
2005	−150.309	−38.349	0	0	100.00%	100.00%
2010	−135.413	−37.389	0	0	100.00%	100.00%
2015	−119.849	−49.929	0	0	100.00%	100.00%
2020	−122.152	−51.736	0	0	100.00%	100.00%
2025	−121.872	−51.786	0	0	100.00%	100.00%
2030	−114.937	−50.571	0	0	100.00%	100.00%
2035	−68.912	−47.603	0	0	100.00%	100.00%
Democratization						
1995	0	0	0	0	0.00%	0.00%
2000	0	0	0	0	0.00%	0.00%
2005	0.992	0	0.369	0	62.80%	0.00%
2010	0.959	0.959	0.343	0.343	64.23%	64.23%
2015	0.978	0.978	0.371	0.371	62.07%	62.07%
2020	0.926	0.926	0.326	0.326	64.79%	64.79%
2025	0.837	0.837	0.245	0.245	70.73%	70.73%
2030	0.75	0.75	0.167	0.167	77.73%	77.73%
2035	0.657	0.657	0.084	0.084	87.21%	87.21%

separate micro-returns to R&D and higher education are likely to include these complementarities and therefore to overlap.

Overall, the indirect effects on growth are about 40 per cent of the total. In the OECD countries this is likely to be partially due to diffusion of new knowledge created by R&D, since higher education is in the growth equation there. But they are largest proportionately in the poor countries, where political stability is a major problem (e.g. Kenya, 94 per cent), and after population growth starts to fall.

Direct and Indirect Effects on Non-market Outcomes

Inequality

Inequality in the income distribution is reduced in Brazil (Table 13.1, panel 2) by about 0.019 percentage points, or from 0.56 to about 0.54 on the *GINI* index, by 2035. About 26 per cent of this is attributable to externalities via indirect effects (column (5)). These indirect effects arise in the model largely because of the effects of education in slowing population growth there (see the *GINI* equation in Chapter 8). The direct effects operate largely through the greater direct access to primary and secondary education in the rural areas that this policy provides (given that primary and secondary enrolment rates are increased and urban enrolment rates are already relatively high). But there are additional indirect effects through the feedback from faster economic growth, since Brazil appears to have reached the peak on the inverted Kuznets U curve. Democratization, however, was not significant as an independent factor in the *GINI* equations.

Income inequality is also reduced in India by this policy (Table 13.2, panel 2, Scenario 2) by about 4.5 per cent by 2035, or from 0.415 to 0.37 on the *GINI* index. Only 21 per cent of this is due to indirect effects, compared to 26 per cent in Brazil, largely because net population growth rates in India do not start to fall earlier (see Figure 12.4).

In higher-income nations such as the UK and US, reductions in inequality occur almost entirely through direct effects as the results of higher retention rates in the secondary schools (see Tables 13.4 and 13.5, panel 2). The indirect effects are larger in developing countries.

Political Stability and Democratization

Political stability increases in Brazil by 2035 (Table 13.1, panel 3) with either increased investment in education or with increased secondary education. In column (5) about 64 per cent of the total effects on political stability can be seen to be due to the indirect effects of education. Almost all of these indirect effects are attributable to the strengthening of democracy (see panel 4 and Chapter 7). If military expenditure as a per cent of the government budget were endogenous, instead of just being a constant for Brazil (as it is in the equations in Chapter 7), this indirect effect via democratization might be even larger.

For democratization itself in Brazil (panel 4) the direct effects of more wide-spread education are substantial at first but then give way to the indirect effects that come largely through economic growth (see the regressions in Chapter 7, including this equation for the complete model).

In India, although democracy and human rights are remarkably strong given the low per capita income, human rights do continue to improve. About 61 per cent of the improvement that follows this investment in basic education via Scenario 2 is the result of the indirect effects of education via economic growth (see Table 13.2, panel 4).

In Kenya the improvement in human rights is over 73 per cent, due to the indirect effects coming through democratization and economic growth (Table 13.3, panel 5). The significant but delayed increases in political stability are about 49 per cent, attributable to indirect effects via democratization, which then helps invest-ment rates and growth.

In OECD countries, there are some increases in the degree of democracy in the US, in spite of the upper bound on the Freedom House democratization index (whose upper bound was raised by one point). These improvements are consistent with reductions in the large majority who do not vote among those who do not finish high school or college. This problem with voting is considered further below in connection with the representativeness of political processes.

Health and Population Growth

Life expectancy is lower in Kenya than in India, and infant mortality rates are higher. Under these conditions the indirect effects of education due to improve-ments in health in reducing income inequality are also relatively larger in Kenya (33 per cent, vs. 21 per cent in India; see Tables 13.2 and 13.3, panel 2). In Kenya the indirect effects of education on lower infant mortality rates (panel 8), greater life expectancy (panel 6), and lower fertility rates (panel 7) are 41 per cent, 64 per cent, and 66 per cent respectively. Some of these indirect effects on health and family size are attributable to faster economic growth and some to the interaction of female education with family planning programmes in Kenya.

In the OECD countries this investment in education also has significant effects on better health. This is revealed by greater life expectancy, increasing 1.26 years in the UK and 0.949 years in the US, for example, by 2035, and by lower infant mortality, decreasing by 0.045 per cent in the UK (as shown in Table 13.4, panels 4 and 5 and Table 13.5, panel 4). The proportion of these effects on health that are indirect is small (13.9 per cent for life expectancy in the UK and 0.52 per cent in the US, for example). But this is an under-estimate, because these health equations contain some regional dummies that pick up indirect community effects (but whose effects are reported here as part of the direct effects). For the reduction in infant mortality, the 18 per cent of the total effects that are indirect in the UK is more meaningful, since there are no regional dummies. But a very small propor-tion of the total contribution of education to reduced infant mortality in the UK is due to the indirect effect from rising per capita income and most (82 per cent) to the direct effects from more advanced education for the mother.

The Environment

The current rate of destruction of forests in Brazil (Table 13.1, panel 5) at about 2 per cent a year continues up to 2025, a rate that is made slightly worse (0.1 per cent) by the direct effect of increases in secondary education as more land is cleared (panel 5, Scenario 3). The indirect effects are delayed, but begin to dominate by 2030, rising to 400 per cent of the net total effect. These indirect effects are what eventually slow down the decline in forest land in both scenarios (see panel 5). These indirect effects are due to slower population growth, related to the education of females in the equation used from Chapter 9, and the urbanization associated with increased growth.

In India, there are also total effects of education that contribute to reduced air pollution, 70 per cent of which are indirect due to advancing democratization and rising economic capacities (panel 5). For reduced water pollution 100 per cent are indirect (Table 13.2, panel 6), and for reduced destruction of forests and wildlife eventually 400 per cent are indirect, since some of the direct effects are negative as junior secondary education of farmers expands (see panel 7, Scenario 2).

In the OECD nations, the effects of education on the environment are long-delayed and again overwhelmingly indirect. This is shown for the US, where eventually the rate of destruction of forests and wildlife is reversed. Forest land and wildlife are currently declining at 0.5 per cent per year, and only after 2025 do the indirect effects from this increment to investments in education start to slow this down in the rough estimates produced by the simulations (Table 13.5, panel 5). Expansion of access to higher education is likely to be a significant factor here, since although it is not in the final forest and wildlife equation used in the model, it was significant in some earlier regressions reported in Chapter 9. The significant education effects in reducing air pollution (e.g. Table 13.4, panel 7) and water pollution (Table 13.5, panel 9) are mostly from GNP growth, less poverty, slower population growth, and larger percentages with higher education, almost all of which are indirect externality effects of education.

Crime

In Brazil property crime and homicide rates are again dominated by indirect effects (Table 13.1, panels 7 and 8). All of these aspects of development improve with increased investment in education, but the improvements are very significantly due to indirect effects in the equations from slower population growth, less poverty, and, in the case of property crime rates and homicide rates, less income inequality.

In India, 100 per cent of the effects of education on lower homicide rates are indirect (Table 13.2, panel 8). Most of these indirect effects of education are again due to less rural and urban poverty, less inequality, delayed effects on population growth, and delayed effects from economic growth.

Property crime rates fall community-wide in the UK and US with higher secondary education enrolment rates, as might be expected, as young people stay in high school. This direct effect is even larger than the total effects of education, which include negative indirect effects from economic growth (Tables 13.4 and 13.5, panel 8). The indirect effects are because property crime increases with economic growth according to the worldwide data, which explains the net negative indirect effects. These negative indirect effects are small at first (-5 per cent to -26 per cent in Tables 13.4 and 13.5, panel 8) but rise sharply (to -98.61 per cent in the UK and -352 per cent in the US by 2035; see Tables 13.4 and 13.5, panel 8, Scenario 2). There are positive indirect effects on crime from the reduction in inequality (Tables 13.4 and 13.5, panel 2) and poverty, however.

In the US, where homicide rates are higher (compare Figures 12.12 and 12.13), the indirect effect of economic growth on homicide rates is insignificant (in contrast to its positive relation to property crime rates). But 100 per cent of the significant effects of education in reducing homicide rates are indirect (see Table 13.5, panel 7). Narcotics addiction is a positive function of GNP per capita in worldwide cross-section data, but is lowered by reduced narcotics production (importation), and by lower unemployment (see panel 6). Indirect effects of increased education in lowering the homicide rate in these simulations come through its contribution to lower structural unemployment and to lower inequality (panel 7).

Overall

If it is possible to generalize, the externality indirect effects of education on pure economic growth are positive and account for around 40 to 45 per cent of the total in most countries. This is a substantial fraction, and since the direct-effect coefficients might also pick up some externalities, it is most likely to be a conservative estimate. Indirect-effect externalities are a much smaller fraction of some of the non-market outcomes, such as reductions in inequality and life expectancy, but a much larger fraction, up to 100 per cent or above, in others, such as the indirect impacts of education on crime and the environment. So, as is often the case, the conclusion cannot be one single ratio. Instead there is a wide range of direct effects and of externality indirect effects, different for each specific outcome, and different depending on the time-frame considered.

A second general conclusion is that although some externalities of education are negative, most of these tend to be the indirect effects of education in increasing economic growth (such as the relation of growth in the data to higher property crime rates, higher narcotics addiction, and greater air pollution). But these are isolated situations, since there are other indirect effects that appear to be positive. There are also positive direct effects of education on these same outcomes, plus the range of other indirect effects of education improving the quality of life that have been discussed above and in MacMahon (1999).

A third conclusion is that each direct or indirect impact of education is more or less important depending on the level of economic development. The net impacts on democratization, political stability, and net population growth rates, for example, appear to be larger in the poorest developing countries, where instability and rapid population growth are endemic. Other effects loom relatively more important in economies with higher per capita income.

Fourth, *some* non-market benefits are nearly 100% externalities by definition— e.g. democratization, political stability, and effects on crime rates.

Fifth, and finally, there are two levels of externalities or free rider benefits picked up in the *direct* effects of education given the way the education coefficients in the regression equations are estimated. These include knowledge gained from co-workers and benefits to the knowledge base embodied by the education system itself that have been produced by earlier generations.

Valuing the Impacts of Education

There are four methods for valuing the net marginal products of education to be discussed in the final part of this chapter. They are:

- *market-based valuations using micro-economic earnings data* and/or economic growth increments in the GDP national accounts;
- *cost-based valuation of the non-monetary quality-of-life returns to education*, both direct and indirect, based on the cost of producing the same outcome by methods other than by education. This is the Haveman–Wolfe (1984) and Wolfe–Zuvekas (1997) approach;
- *assuming weights for a social welfare function*, such as the Bergson Welfare Function, to weight the various outcomes. These outcomes can then enter into an optimization, and also the economic value of the solution values for the outcomes can be added up, as in Wolfe and Zuvekas (1997);
- *valuation of outcomes by the political decision process* as education budgets are determined. This also has its limitations, as will be considered.

The pros and cons of each of these methods will be compared briefly. Then each basis for valuation of the externalities and non-market effects will be considered specifically, since they are complements rather than substitutes for one another. None of these methods is ideal, but each contributes meaningful insights.

Market-Based Valuations

The first method of valuing outcomes, by using microeconomic earnings, has the merit that education-developed skills are valued automatically and relatively precisely by the labour market. The problem is, however, that it covers only the monetary returns, leaving out the non-market productivity of these human capital skills used during leisure-time hours. At the aggregate level, the Gross National Product Accounts have the advantages that they are market-based, as are earnings, and also do seek to separate out the value of public goods, including education, based on factor costs. These include the perceived value to society of the externalities and of the income distribution effects. But there are major problems in that the cost-based valuation of public education outcomes in the national accounts does not include the forgone earnings costs of education to families, which are a major part of the total. Standard social rates of return based on earnings data that use taxes paid as the basis for valuing social benefits are subject to this same criticism.

The second major problem is that factor costs in government budgets that are based on the cost of the raw materials and labour used in the government processes involved in providing them do not include either interest costs or profits as part of the costs, so these are therefore not included as part of the value of the final outcomes on the product side of the accounts. Valuation on the basis of original costs also ignores the estimated future values of education outcomes, which in turn could be higher when trends in rates of return are upward, as they are now, or lower when they are downward.

The third problem is that government budgets in the national accounts are determined by political decision processes, and in authoritarian regimes these political processes sometimes introduce major distortions.

The distributional impacts produce special problems. But there may be no other practical way of valuing these.

Cost-Based Valuations of Non-market Returns

The second basic method for valuation of education's non-market outcomes is through cost-based valuations, the cost of producing the same outcome by other means. This has the great merit that it is rooted in efficiency considerations (and therefore appealing to economists). It has the related merit that the provision of more cost-based valuations to legislators enables them to see what the cost–benefit ratios are, as well as the relation to the cost-effectiveness of alternative methods of securing similar outcomes. This would have the effect of making political decision-making more rational. This is fine as far as it goes, and likely to help.

One problem is that the method is laborious, so such estimates have not generally been available to legislators. A second problem is that legislators will often ignore cost-based valuations, and hence ignore efficiency. Kenneth Arrow (1997: 26) says, 'although this comparative cost analysis has been made repeatedly, it often has not had much effect, I regret to say'. I suggest that this is most likely to occur where income distribution impacts are involved. Pure income distribution effects cannot be valued exclusively on a cost basis, because valuation involves questions of equity, and these questions often cannot be clearly separated from efficiency considerations. Equity is not part of pure Pareto efficiency. Legislators, therefore, are reasonable if they sometimes consider equity, which results in decisions not based purely on efficiency. In principle, therefore, and not just in practice, the value of income distribution (including intergenerational equity) effects can be resolved only by political decision processes.

Philosophical Valuations

The third method for valuation assumes weights for use in a Bergson Social Welfare Function that come from the utility function of a beneficent dictator or an omniscient ethical observer. This has the considerable merit of including value weights for externalities and income distribution effects. It also has the merit that in principle it leads to a determinate solution for optimal levels of taxation and the maximization of social welfare.

The problem is that in academic solutions these weights are inherently philosophical values. They would normally have to be determined by the economist representing the dictator, or assumed by the economist on the basis of his or her view of the political process, or based on the economist's view of the values of the omniscient ethical observer, or merely ignored, with such values implicit rather than explicit. If the weights come from authoritarian political leaders, dictators are frequently not beneficient. So although this solution may realistically represent how education is valued in a number of countries in the world (consider North Korea, Mujumdar, Congo, Somalia, or the Sudan), merely using the weights in the leader's utility function is not a satisfactory basis for valuation of the outcomes of education.

The problem with assuming the weights assigned by an omniscient ethical observer is that these weights are impossible to know empirically. Sometimes attention is focused by economists only on the efficiency aspects. But this ignores distributional effects (and hence assumes commutative equity), or lets the results of the market prevail. Distribution effects are important in the case of education, which involves different generations and also children who start out from an unequal basis. When the weights include distribution or are implicit, they are philosophically or religiously based, which can mean they are in the eye of the beholder. One result of this is that the solutions are abstract and do not describe a process that has much of an empirical counterpart.

Valuation by Political Decisions

The fourth method is to accept the budget outcomes produced by the political decision process. This has the advantage of being empirically based. But there are major problems with it. Apart from the problem with authoritarian valuations in some countries—which is not insurmountable, since it is possible to choose the valuations of nations where the political processes are reasonably democratic as measured by the Freedom House index (Freedom House, 1997: 536–7)—many of the true non-market marginal products of education are not very well known to legislators. A second problem is that special-interest groups of various types frequently have an undue capacity to prevent action or to accelerate actions to their liking and thereby distort budget-based valuations of education. Nonetheless, this political decision process for valuation of externalities and income distribution effects will be considered later below, since it is basically the one used in practice.

Social Rates of Return

New social rates of return can be computed which reflect the total direct and indirect effects of education on per capita GNP. The basis for valuing these returns to education is the cost to the government (in the cases of public education or subsidized private education) in the factor markets for organizing education to produce these outcomes. The purpose of this section is to describe and illustrate briefly how these new social rates of return can be computed.

Using *rates* of return as a way of valuing outcomes (rather than returns alone) has among other advantages the fact that it is relatively independent of the budget decisions of authoritarian governments, since it includes their actual factor costs in the calculation. Even if the level of investment in education is very low in an authoritarian regime, the *rate* of return on that investment may nevertheless be very high, and vice versa. Also, this basis for valuation does not value education highly only when the costs are high. If the education system is internally inefficient in producing effective increments to learning outcomes, a question currently being debated in connection with the public k-12 education system in the US by Hanushek *et al.* (1996) and others, this will show up in lower rates of return and hence a lower relative value of the actual outcomes.

The Investment Costs

On the cost side, the *increment* to the direct investment costs of education is the per cent of GNP for any nation, expressed in per capita terms. To this must be added the forgone earnings costs per capita borne largely by parents, but these are specific to each nation. These direct and forgone earnings costs, shown in the calculation in Table 13.6, continue into the future for 40 years through 2035 (just as do the net returns). This time period was chosen in part because 35–40 years is approximately the average amount of time that persons are in the labour force, at least in the higher-income economies. A timing problem arises, however, because the returns phase in only after a lag and continue after 2035 whereas the costs continue up through 2035, even though most of the returns from investments in education made in the later years are not realized until after 2035.

To solve this problem, on the cost side in Table 13.6 I use for direct costs 2% of GNP per capita summed up over a 5-year period to 2000, plus a declining fraction of the annual costs after that time that phase down to zero on a straight-line basis by 2040. This is because graduating students in each successive cohort after 2000 have not completed their time in the labour force before 2040 and therefore their contributions are not fully included in the returns prior to that time. The 5-year period for the initial investment costs is based on the assumption that it is this long on average before the additional new students benefiting from this investment complete high school or college and get located productively in the labour force. This 5-year gestation period is also a major part of the reason for the lag in increments to the returns observable in all of the Figures and in Table 13.6. Forgone earnings costs are handled in the same way. They are multiplied by 0.75 to remove the portion of the year that students are not in the school.

Table 13.6 Social Rates of Return to Education in the UK and US (all returns and costs in US$, constant 1985 prices)

	2000	2005	2010	2015	2020	2025	2030	2035	2040
United Kingdom									
Growth in GNP per capita (from Table 13.4)	0	72	382	991	1,831	2,887	4,212	5,890	5,890
Direct + forgone earnings cost[a]	1,156	220	189	158	126	95	63	38	0

UK social rate of return (pure internal rate of return, in real terms): 15%

	2000	2005	2010	2015	2020	2025	2030	2035	2040
United States									
Growth in GNP per capita (from Table 13.5)	0	143	713	1,675	2,851	4,251	5,945	8,008	8,008
Direct + forgone earnings cost[a]	2,178	410	351	292	233	174	115	56	0

US social rate of return (pure internal rate of return in real terms): 14%

[a] In addition to the explanation above, forgone earnings costs are based on mean earnings of all persons in the labour force age 18–24 in 1995, from the *Current Population Reports* (US Bureau of the Census, 1996: table 16) converted to 1985 prices. For increments in high school enrolments this is average earnings of males and females with 9–12 years of education but no diploma, and for college level it is earnings of high school graduates.

   These totals must be converted from a per student basis to a per capita basis, since the increments to earnings and the increments to direct costs are in these terms. So to reflect the increment in enrolments, 0.20 times high school enrolments and 0.20 times college enrolments from NCES (1996: 16) are divided by the total population and used as adjustment factors at each education level.

Benefits

On the benefits side of the computation, the total returns to education are the increments in GNP per capita for each country which are net of GNP per capita in the base scenario. The latter controls for the other determinants of economic growth that are in the model, such as population growth, rates of investment in physical capital, and other policies, since only the rate of investment in education, with its net direct and indirect effects which phase in, is allowed to change.

   Using the net increments to GNP per capita as computed above for the measure of the private and externality benefits of education, however, still does not cover all of the non-market benefits. It could be said that the public sector expenditures on education estimate the value of the final non-market outcomes of education, or at least society's current evaluation of them, which to some extent is true. But private sector non-market outcomes (and forgone earnings costs) are not included, and public sector budgets (which are used for a cost-based valuation of the outcomes) do not include any imputation for forgone earnings, interest or profits. (For a recent discussion of these issues in the valuation of education outcomes in the Total Accounts, see Eisner, 1997: 527–8.) The omitted forgone earnings costs alone, for example, are about 56.4 per cent of the total costs for males at the bachelor's level and 54 per cent of the total costs for female public university students in the US (McMahon, 1998c, appendix B, p. B-3). This plus interest and profits suggests that over half of the value of education outcomes is omitted in the standard GNP accounts. Forgone earnings costs are smaller at the primary and junior secondary levels in the OECD countries, but are larger in Latin American, East Asia, and Africa.

So using GNP measures to estimate the total returns to education understates the true social benefits of education, due to the omission of profits, interest, and forgone earnings costs on the product side of the accounts. A truly comprehensive measure would have to add imputations for these to the total benefits.

A question may arise about the reason for using GNP per capita (or GDP per capita when the latter is available) rather than Denison's National Income Per Person Employed (Denison, 1974: 13–16). First, Gross National Product is essentially equal to National Income, apart from four relatively small reconciliation elements which include indirect business taxes (i.e. sales taxes) that finance education at the state level and are a logical part of the value of cost-based government output. And second, I use GNP *per capita* rather than per person employed because the framework of this book has stressed that there are non-monetary private benefits of education generated by *household* production during time not spent in the labour market and available to the entire population on a per capita basis, not just to members of the labour force, as in the NIPPE measure. Human capital leads to productivity improvements in the non-market time of homemakers and of activities leading to rents, interest, and profits, not just to labour income.

Empirical Estimates of Social Rates of Return

Social rates of return are estimated for the United Kingdom and the United States on the basis of the increments to GNP per capita attributable to increments in investment in education. These are shown in Table 13.6, and are to be regarded as a first approximation. The same calculation can be done for any of the 78 countries in the complete model.

For the US this 14 per cent social rate of return is to be compared to 11.3 per cent at the high school level and 13.3 per cent at the bachelor's level for 1995, using micro-earnings data (Arias and McMahon, 1998: table 3). These take dynamic trends within each age cohort into account. Turning to the UK and assuming the dynamic trends are roughly similar so that the static cross-section social rates of return for 1985 can be adjusted by the same percentage-point difference, then according to micro-data the real social rate of return at the secondary level is 13 per cent and the real social rate of return to higher education is 11 per cent (Psacharopoulos, 1994: table A-1). These can be compared to the 15 per cent social rate of return in the UK based on the model simulations above.

It can be tentatively concluded that this new method leads to social rates of return that are close to but about 2 or 3 percentage points above those found in microeconomic data based on earnings alone. I caution again that they are intended only as a preliminary first approximation in OECD nations designed to illustrate a new approach to the estimation of social rates of return.

Cost-Based Valuation of Non-monetary Benefits

The above must be supplemented to arrive at a more comprehensive valuation that covers non-monetary education outcomes. Micro-earnings relate only to market time and this new GNP estimate is also based only on market time. Both include appropriations to public education budgets designed to pay for non-market benefits. But these appropriations do not include the sizeable forgone earnings costs of education (or interest or profits). Hence the factor cost basis for valuing both monetary and non-monetary outputs of education misses these pieces.

Pioneering work on the valuation of non-monetary returns, both private and externalities, has been done by Haveman and Wolfe (1984), now updated by Wolfe and Zuvekas (1997). A brief summary of their technique follows.

It starts by estimating the marginal product of education of producing a given outcome (e.g., lower poverty followed by lower crime rates), using a household production function, as has already been shown as Equation (13.2), with the control for money income to eliminate the monetary returns to education, which would otherwise be double-counted. Controls for ability and family factors are appropriate when the objective is to estimate the value added by a single educational institution. But for most purposes, when estimating the non-monetary returns to education the upward bias in returns due to ability and family factors is assumed to be offset by the downward bias due to measurement error in the education variable resulting from self-reporting error and the omission of quality.

Haveman, Wolfe, and Zuvekas then assume that households will equate the *ratio* of schooling's marginal product over its price (i.e., MP_{SCH}/P_{SCH}) to a similar *ratio* of the marginal product of other inputs in producing similar outcomes relative to their prices (i.e., MP_X/P_X). This is a rather standard assumption about household behaviour that relates to all market goods. But here an implicit value, or price, of a unit of schooling, P_{SCH}, is involved. It can be equated to the other terms that can be measured. After rearranging the above, this equation is:

$$P_{SCH} = MP_{SCH}/MP_X P_X \qquad (13.3)$$

The terms on the right are known, or can be determined. So third, the marginal product of other inputs (i.e., MP_X) that can be purchased on the market to produce this same education outcome must be estimated. Since the outcomes are equal (i.e., another year of longevity), the willingness to pay for education to accomplish this objective (P_{SCH}) will be equal to the cost of the other inputs such as health care. Or, to offer another example, if the expenditure on policing times the ratio of their marginal products necessary to lower the local crime rate can be estimated (i.e., P_X), then the local citizens should be willing to pay this amount times the ratio of the marginal products for increases in the local secondary school retention rate that would accomplish this same result.

In this latter example, since there are indirect effects of education, several marginal products must be estimated. The indirect effects require valuing the cross-partial derivatives of crime with respect to poverty reduction times their partial derivatives with respect to education, to which must be added the value of the direct effect of education in reducing the number of unsupervised teenagers on the streets.[1]

This cost-based valuation of the benefits of education is appropriate for the non-market private returns as well as for externalities. These include the direct and indirect impacts that relate to efficiency, but not the valuation of poverty reduction or income redistribution effects. In principle the alternative costs of producing all of the 15 non-market outcomes in this book by other means for each of the 78 countries could be estimated. Until this is done, Wolfe and Zuvekas (1997) have offered a rough overall estimate which suggests that their value is approximately equal to the value of the monetary returns. This may be conservative, in the sense that Grossman (1997) puts the health benefits of education alone at 40 per cent of the monetary benefits. But it is a useful way to think about it, because it means that if the monetary rate of return, based on microeconomic data, is, say, 13 per cent, then the total rate of return, including the non-monetary private and externality benefits, is really 26 per cent!

As legislators see what the costs of the alternatives are for producing each of the 15 outcomes they should be able to make more rational choices and public decision-making could be improved. Although political decision-makers will frequently ignore these guides to greater efficiency, perhaps inefficiency can be reduced to the extent that income distribution impacts are treated separately. Information on the costs of achieving non-market education outcomes by alternative means is also information that would be helpful in planning cost-effective economic development strategies in the developing nations.

Optimal Efficiency in Expenditure/Taxation Levels

The usual criterion for economic efficiency is that total private plus public investment in education should be expanded up to the point where the *total social rate of return*, which would include the value of both the monetary and the non-monetary returns as well as the value of externalities, is just equal to the interest rate. The interest rate is taken as an overall average of the opportunity cost to society of the funds involved. When adjusted for inflation, it is about 10 per cent in developing countries and currently about 7 per cent on long-term corporate bonds in the US and other OECD nations, where money capital is relatively cheaper (Ibbsotson and Associates, 1998: 95).

However, for optimal levels of taxation for education it must be recognized that there are imperfect capital markets and it is not possible for families in any country to borrow easily in private capital markets to finance human capital formation. Those students and families most in need are least likely to be able to provide the collateral that banks or other lenders require, even though the total private rate of return might be very high. So it is not just economic growth-related market and non-market externalities that governments must subsidize, but also private investment in education, where there are high private returns but the capacity to borrow is limited if there is not to be under-investment. Therefore the optimal level of expenditure and taxation must include a correction for imperfect capital markets.

Valuing Distributional Effects via a Bergson Welfare Function

Issues relating to distribution and distributive justice are above and beyond these efficiency-based non-monetary returns and externalities. They are often ignored by economists when focusing on efficiency. Yet they are inherently part of the maximization of human welfare (see, e.g., Samuelson, 1955: chart 5, p. 352). Income distribution effects also need to be considered if the results of any analysis of human resource development strategies are to be relevant to policy and to actual outcomes.

Optimal Distribution in Pure Theory

The degree of redistribution that is optimal still requires a welfare function, such as that given by Samuelson's (1955) 'omniscient ethical observer', to achieve a determinate solution. The weights for benefits going to each income group can be specified in a Bergson (1938) Welfare Function, with income distribution weights as set out comprehensively by Eckstein (1961: 446–8). This involves a normative value judgement, usually made by the economist on behalf of some (hopefully) beneficent dictator, as indicated above. Such values inherently have a religious basis (e.g., the New Testament, or the Koran) or a philosophical basis (e.g., Rawls, 1977), and although important are outside of pure economics.

There are, however, ways of measuring conceptually the efficiency gain from a change in income distribution. This was originally developed by Atkinson (1970) and is applied to education in McMahon (1982: 24–5). But even here the location of the (ordinal) welfare function that specifies the optimal distribution and hence the 'value' of the redistribution involves interpersonal comparisons of utility, which puts it outside pure economics.

Education budgets nevertheless allocate resources among children which dramatically affect their earning capacities later. Income distribution effects arise because of the access to quality education and its effects on the future distribution of income. So distributional impacts inevitably enter the political debate and are a part of actual budgets. The distribution issues take the form of debates about horizontal equity, or equal treatment of equals, and also of vertical equity among families with great differences in family income and assets and/or school districts with great differences in property wealth. Family income is the primary determinant of where children live and hence the value of housing, which largely determines the revenues available to the schools and the quality of education they receive; it also is a major determinant of who attends college (see, e.g., McMahon,

1984*c*). Since the quality of education received largely determines scores on achievement tests, family income and 'ability' measures are very highly correlated.

There is a literature in pure economic theory dealing with optimal taxation that takes income distribution and hence vertical equity into account (see Diamond and Mirrlees, 1971). But it has largely ignored this correlation and therefore has not yet faced the main issue in a way that yields results that are empirically very relevant. It has not dealt with income redistribution through education policies, apart from Mirrlees (1974), who considers only differences in ability levels. Ulph (1977) advances a theoretical solution that relates to education, but he rules out by assumption the central vertical equity issue, which is the connection of parents' wealth to the expenditures on education that distribute the earning power. He says, 'individuals are assumed to be equal in all respects other than innate ability' (*ibid.*: 343).

Optimal Distribution in Empirical Research

The more empirically related research on education finance is nearly dominated by this equity issue, however.[2] This literature brings in normative concepts of equity, which is usually justified on the grounds that where inequality is extreme, as in the poorest countries or in unequal local funding of schools, then a large majority of the readers and any democratic electorate would view steps toward some reduction of this inequality as 'equitable'.

How much reduction, however? Degrees of vertical equity in the distribution of future real income-earning capacities (or utilities) among children range all the way from 'commutative equity', which holds that the 'market results should prevail' and hence that any redistribution is evil or should be ignored, toward Rawlsian 'positivism', which would maximize the welfare of the least-advantaged members of society (Rawls, 1977). The latter is more highly redistributive. The in-between gradations of vertical equity are discussed by Alexander (1982) and McMahon (1982: 14–25).

No nation among the OECD member countries, and perhaps none of the 78 nations included in the complete model, goes to either of these ethical extremes of commutative equity or Rawlsian positivism in their education policies. More common is to aspire to 'equality of educational opportunity', which goes beyond commutative equity and minimal provision (i.e. foundation levels), but does not more fully correct the wrongs of society as in Rawls (1977). Empirically, however, most nations achieve something considerably less than equality of educational opportunity. This includes the US, where the education system is highly decentralized in its financing and hence heavily dependent on differences in local parental wealth, as well as the UK, where access to the best schools and colleges has traditionally been unequal. At the higher education level, however, it is increasingly widely accepted that quality can be protected by creating a hierarchy of institutions that cater to different sectors of the market, but that this can be augmented by means-tested financial grants to help provide for better equality of opportunity.

The income distribution effects of education depend primarily on *who gets the education* (e.g. Psacharopoulos 1977; Harbison and Hanushek, 1992: 192–9), and not on increasing the average level of education while essentially preserving inequality of access (e.g. Sullivan and Smeeding, 1997). Deliberate policies to extend quality education to the rural areas, for example, can contribute to achieving a path of *growth with equity* (World Bank, 1993), defined as growth accompanied by falling inequality.[3] Examples of education policies conducive to growth with equity in the OECD countries, where inequality has been rising (Gottschalk and Smeeding, 1997), are Project Head Start in the US, means-tested higher education grants to students in the US, UK, and most other OECD countries, programmes to reduce high school drop-outs in poor neighbourhoods and rural areas, and recent expansion of access to community colleges in the US and UK. The budgets for these policies have a targeted distributional objective, some more than others, so some positive value is placed on the distributional outcomes of education. But they also have an important efficiency component (their rates of return are generally high, even ignoring externalities), so this is not a 'pure' valuation of only distributional outcomes.

Normally this *humane growth* or *growth with equity* dynamic time-path is polit-ically much more feasible, since it reduces the intensity of the conflict that is inherent whenever changes in income distribution are involved. Fast growth rates accompanied by reductions in poverty and inequality is the path achieved by all eight of the world's fastest growing countries in East Asia (see World Bank, 1993 and Chapter 8).

In conclusion, the *optimal distribution* solutions as they pertain to the valuation of the distributional outcomes of education remain relatively abstract and without very much of an empirical counterpart. An exception may be the literature on 'growth with equity', but even here the value placed on 'equity' is not always clear because it may be based in part on the values placed on efficiency.

Valuation of Outcomes by Political Decision Processes

Optimal solutions for efficiency and equity to one side, both the efficiency and distribution outcomes of education are valued in practice by political decision processes as education budgets are determined. This means that the political process decides on the value of the externalities (which, therefore, some people have an incentive to minimize and others to exaggerate) which are a part of the efficiency criteria, as well as deciding on the value of the distributional impacts which relate to equity. There are different philosophical views of what constitutes equity or distributive justice. There are also political distortions from over-repres-ented special interests or under-represented groups. The valuations that this results in are not necessarily optimal, either in being efficient or in the sense of maximiz-ing social welfare by being both efficient and equitable.

Actual budget decisions made empirically through a political decision process reflect the economic interests of the stakeholders. This is a responsive process which is also usually appropriate if there are no distortions. For example, as average family income rises, parents want more and better education for their children, so the effective demand for both basic public education and higher education rises (e.g. McMahon, 1970, 1984c, 1992b). The overall income elasticity of demand for public education is about 1.0 (McMahon, 1970). But higher education has a higher income elasticity, which may be higher in part because of dynamic trends that are giving increasing advantages to those with more advanced education (Arias and McMahon, 1998).

Translating these dynamic trends and distributional issues into the language of majority-voting models, this becomes a matter of how the median voter is affected. The large literature with applications to education goes back to Bowen (1943, 1948: 180–1, 1977). A formal exposition of Arrow's impossibility theorem, and how it does not apply if preferences are single-peaked, appears in Musgrave (1959: chap. 6). More recently Stiglitz (1974: 362–6), in this majority-voting vein, has touched on the central issue of public education budgets where both abilities and wealth differ. He essentially concludes that the income redistribution effects of education get largely washed out. He says, 'the wealthier professionals often seem to be among those who are the most ardent supporters of [public higher] education; this is perhaps because the belief in a high private rate of return to education leads them to be relatively high demanders, [eliminating any] redistributive effects' (ibid.: 362).

Most of the majority-voting literature still makes unrealistic assumptions, however, about one-man, one-vote and ignores the effects of differences in wealth. Ignoring wealth differences is often closely related to pressures to keep the financing localized. The result is that much of the literature arrives at unrealistic conclusions, suggesting that public education is more egalitarian than it really is, and that more inequality in wealth can lead to higher investment in public education (e.g., Stiglitz, 1974: 361–2). Most of the majority-voting literature is abstract, not subject to empirical tests, and often without an empirical analogue. (See for example all seven of the articles in Shapiro 1995.) Frequently the majority do not vote, and furthermore those who vote and how they vote are heavily influenced by special interests, wealth, and financial contributions to candidates. Contributions under the control of legislative leaders are used to influence Congressional and state legislative votes that affect public education budget levels, tax levels, and allocations. This almost equates money with votes, endorsed recently by the Supreme Court in the US for example as 'free speech'.

Recent significant work by political scientists addresses this issue. Huber, Rueschemeyer, and Stephens (1993: 75) conclude that 'the economically dominant classes [and also the bourgeoisie] accept democracy only where their interests are effectively [provided for].' This is consistent with the empirical finding in Chapter 8 that according to the worldwide data, democratization, as measured by the Freedom House index, has no significant relation to reduced inequality in income distribution. This is after controlling for per capita income, and is limited to the 64 countries for which data on *GINI* coefficients is available from the World Bank

(1997: 222–3). This is somewhat surprising given the popular connotation of democracy as egalitarian, and an hypothesis that merits continuing testing.

With a new *qualified median* calculated after deletions for those who do not vote and after weights for special-interest influences, those who pay more taxes and receive fewer benefits pay a higher 'tax price' and generally want smaller education budgets. They can be expected on average to be less favourable to valuation of externalities and of distributional effects in education budgets, whereas those with children in the schools and from families with lower property wealth can be expected to favour larger resources for the schools. These forces are not likely to balance out with budgets just equal to cost-based valuations and the efficiency criteria they imply. Furthermore, when it comes to the valuation of the distributional equity impacts, those from high-income suburbs have incentives to try to reduce their taxes (and hence public expenditure), and also to reduce public support for redistributive aid to the poorer schools. This can be observed in the repeated opposition from the higher-income suburbs to those aspects of school finance reform that would reduce the large inequality in expenditure per child in states where there is a lot of inequality (e.g., Texas, Ohio, and Illinois) and where reforms of this nature were largely defeated recently, although they did pass in Mississippi, the latter being a remarkable exception. Surveys of voters in local school elections find that most of those opposed to higher school district budgets are generally not parents with children in school, but tend to be those who are older and pay property taxes and, where they exist, state income taxes. With respect to support for externalities, some housing compounds for high-income retired persons in Florida, Arizona, and Southern California admit no children and refuse to pay *any* taxes in support of public education, irrespective of what the implications may be for efficiency or distributional equity.

The even more basic problem in using public budgets as the basis for valuation of the distributional and indirect impacts of education is that many persons who benefit from the indirect effects of education do not know what they are and do not vote. In the 1994 Congressional elections, as reported by Mortinson (1997) based on US Census Bureau reports, where turn-out was higher than in state-level or local school elections, 63.8 per cent of those with bachelor's degrees voted, but only 31.3 per cent of those with only "some high school" voted. For those with less than a sixth grade education, it was even lower (21.9 per cent).

In the developing countries, East Asian countries apparently value the income distribution and externality effects of education highly. Most expanded access to secondary education rapidly after universal primary education was achieved. In the regressions in Chapter 8 this was associated with significant reductions in inequality in income distribution after a 20-year lag (as distinguished from reductions in absolute poverty). This evidence is consistent with the strong positive relation between inequality in access to education and inequality in income distribution found by Psacharopoulos (1977). More generally, the failure to expand access to the next-highest level of education after universal education at the next-lowest level is achieved may be a very significant source of the failure of inequality to fall in places like Brazil, or in Sub-Saharan Africa. Delays in expanding junior secondary education to the rural areas in Thailand is another example. All of these delays may reflect low valuation placed on lower population growth rates and on education for poor farmers in regimes within which poor rural groups are under-represented.

Conclusions

Separating the direct and indirect effects of education, most of which in the latter instance are externalities, the simulations suggest that about 40 per cent of the impacts of education on pure per capita economic growth are through indirect community effects. For the non-monetary outcomes not included in GNP the direct effects of education on some (e.g. democratization) are almost purely externalities. After appropriate lags, indirect effects rise to 20–30 per cent for reductions in inequality, political stability, and democratization for the countries in my sample; to 40–66 per cent for effects on fertility rates and infant mortality; and to 100 per cent or even above (if there are negative effects from growth) on homicide, the environment, and property crime.

Although these estimates can undoubtedly be refined as research proceeds, I think that they are useful as a first approximation. They also define a new approach to measuring the direct and social benefits of education. The result shows that sweeping generalizations about the effects of education and about externalities are not possible. The total effects of education and the proportion that is indirect vary both among countries and among levels of economic development, although some patterns can be observed.

Turning to valuation of these outcomes which goes beyond these quantitative measurement of the impacts, new social rates of return suggest a real overall rate of about 14 per cent in the US (where higher education is largest) to 15 per cent in the UK (where secondary education is largest). Improvements in internal efficiency have not been studied here (although the model can do this in limited ways). If there were such improvements, these rates of return would be higher.

The omission of interest, profit, and forgone earnings costs suggests how these budget-based valuations of education outcomes are still incomplete. They can also be distorted by special interests, as suggested in my consideration of the qualified median voter. So cost-based valuations of the non-market returns are therefore considered. On the basis of recent work by Wolfe and Zuvekas (1997), these are about equal in value to the market-based returns. With respect to the value of distributional impacts, it is obvious that the political decision process places some positive value on these. But most also have an efficiency component, and the value placed on the purely distributional component alone appears to be quite small.

If, however, the non-market private and externality benefits of education are roughly equal in value to the market-based returns, this roughly doubles all rates of return to education in OECD-type economies. And for some kinds of returns, such as the contribution of education to slower population growth, reduction of inequality, and political stability, the value of the non-market social benefits may be even larger in the developing economies.

Notes

1. Other aspects of the formal solution applicable to this situation include the relation to the household production of human capital of the time constraint, the full-income budget constraint, and the formation of the Hamiltonian leading to optimization. These formalities are set out in McMahon (1997: 26–7) and in even greater detail in Heckman (1976).
2. See, for example, any issue of the *Journal of Education Finance*; the special issue of the University of Michigan *Journal of Law Reform*, Spring 1995, which focuses on this topic; World Bank (1993), which stresses growth with equity.
3. This has been defined in more technical terms as humane growth (McMahon, 1982: 22–5), which starts at points below the grand utility-possibility frontier and simultaneously improves efficiency while also reducing inequality. Everybody is 'better off', although inequality also falls.

14 Summary of Conclusions: Measuring the Social Benefits, Convergence, and Policy Dialogue

The rich nations are continuing to get richer, and the poorest nations are getting poorer. This concluding chapter reflects on this lack of absolute convergence worldwide, and also within Africa. It then appraises what has been achieved by way of systematic measurement of the net outcomes of education and their cost-effectiveness. Finally, it considers the use of policy dialogue simulations as a possible strategy for achieving cost-effective economic development. Hopefully, the latter may contribute to better understanding of the full scope of the central role of education as an investment in the diffusion of knowledge for knowledge-based growth and development.

The possibilities for policy dialogue are not unique to the poorer developing countries; they are also relevant in the industrialized OECD nations, including the United States and the United Kingdom. Governments and economic and education policy agencies are normally interested in cost-effective development strategies. Also, students, families, faculty, education administrators, and legislative leaders in OECD and developing nations need to be engaged in a continuing dialogue about education that is informed by more comprehensive measurement of education outcomes.

Endogenous Development in Retrospect

As indicated in the Preface and Chapter 1, this book is inspired in part by the resurgence of interest in growth and development models that are extended into more realistic settings. In particular, the causal role of education is consistent with the fact that individual technologies spread only very gradually to other producers and other countries, and not through frictionless, purely competitive settings. The importance of this lack of perfect information has been noted very forcefully by Joseph Stiglitz (1998: 12), who says, 'And when you plugged in [imperfect information] you found markets to be almost always inefficient', a point that has important implications for the dissemination of knowledge by education for economic development. As one visits poor countries in Sub-Saharan Africa or South Asia, for example, one is struck by the fact that the simplest early technologies, such as the steam engine for pumping water, small electric motors for grinding grain, or in rural Africa even bicycle transport, which have often been around for hundreds of years and would make life far easier for poor rural families, have not been disseminated effectively into areas where there is little or no communication and education. The same is true economy-wide in poor countries for the more recent advanced techniques in all fields that are often available in thousands of research journals in research libraries in industrial countries or even available locally over the Internet. These techniques are critically important to knowledge-based growth, but are not widely disseminated and are inaccessible where the education-created skills necessary to utilize them are limited.

The Meaning of Endogenous Development Reconsidered

'Endogenous development' has been proposed as a new term with a very specific meaning. It is analogous to endogenous growth, but includes improvements in the non-market aspects of the quality of life, which endogenous growth does not. It also differs in that it does not refer to long-run steady-state analytic solutions, but instead to a medium-term process in comparative dynamics. Policy-makers are more concerned with shorter-run dynamic impacts and the time-form of the lagged responses that occur within or shortly after their tenure in office, and often realize that there can be further policy changes in the future that will further revise steady-state growth outcomes.

More specifically, the term 'endogenous' is used in three standard ways, but *not* in the fourth (i.e., long-run steady-state solutions are not developed here). Endogenous development means, first, that the 22 key variables related to economic development are determined econometrically by the data, and are not taken as given constants or exogenous variables, as they are in the Solow model. There is also joint dependence in some sub-sectors where there is no recursiveness. Second, the values of each of these 22 variables are determined endogenously as the model is solved for their values within each time period as part of simulations that run from the present for 40 years into the future, thereby generating a dynamic time-path for each variable. Third, as in endogenous growth models, the term does imply that the time-paths of the endogenous variables are primarily determined by internal domestic decisions by firms, households, and governmental units, but not necessarily without input from the world community. For example, the rate of investment in physical capital might increase as the result of improved skills in the labour force and greater political stability which is partially brought about by internal domestic education policy decisions, even though some of the new money capital invested is attracted from abroad. The same is true for population growth rates, influenced largely by domestic decisions but also by the transmission of new knowledge from abroad. Creation of the capacity to use the new technologies and the new management ideas are largely domestic decisions. And fourth, since investment in R&D involves deliberate decisions by governments and by firms and since, philosophically, it is unlikely that there is any limit to the number of new ideas, there can be increasing returns from the benefits of education in production by firms *and production by households* (Romer 1987, 1990; Lucas, 1988; and our extension of Becker, 1964). By analogy with endogenous growth solutions, development could go on indefinitely without bounds.

Conditional Convergence?

If all nations on average can continue to grow and develop, at least over the next 40 years, what is the likelihood of conditional convergence under endogenous development, and if it is not occurring, what are some policy options?

Certainly the time it takes to double income per capita has fallen dramatically. Britain needed about 60 years to do it after 1780, the US nearly 50 years after 1840, and Japan about 35 years after 1885. Turkey achieved the same feat in 20 years after 1957, Brazil in 18 years after 1961, South Korea in 11 years after 1966, and China in 10 years from 1977 (World Bank, *World Development Report*, 1991; *Economist*, 1991). But are the very poor likely to get relatively poorer in per capita terms as the rich get richer? A range of policy changes will help prevent this, but can changes in *government policies for human resource development through education* alone eventually reverse this distressing trend?

There is evidence of some conditional convergence within the East Asian region, within the Latin American region, and within the OECD member group. Significant and robust negative coefficients for the initial GNP per capita term in the production functions, estimated from data specific to Asia in Chapter 3 and to Latin America in Chapter 4 after controlling for determinants of the long-run steady-state target growth rate, are evidence. But this may apply to countries within a grouping which contains more communication and/or common denominators of language. Convergence is not benefiting Nepal, Afghanistan, Mjumdar, or Pakistan, for example, or most of the nations within Sub-Saharan Africa. Here divergence and not convergence is more typical.

Yet some of the poorest nations worldwide and within Sub-Saharan Africa have some of the greatest natural resources. The Democratic Republic of the Congo (formally Zaïre) is a case in point. The Congo boasts vast wealth in the form of the world's largest deposits of diamonds and cobalt, and some of the richest supplies of copper. But, in combination with corruption and disastrous development policies, this has brought only trouble and extreme poverty to the people. In cases where there are rich oil deposits, such as in the Middle East, the capacity to produce and export non-oil-related manufactured goods and services that require skilled human resources is very limited, and development also does not extend to many of the non-market aspects considered in this book. Many other examples could be cited.

At the same time, many of the world's highest per capita income nations have few or no natural resources: nations such as Denmark, Switzerland, the United Kingdom, the Netherlands, and Israel, for example. One thing that characterizes this group is that they have much more highly developed human resources, which also helps to increase the number of creative people. Education has also contributed there to the rule of law, political stability, democratization, human rights, and reduced inequality compared to the poorest countries. When these indirect externality effects of human resource development through education are fully considered, T. W. Schultz's (1990) original observation that the significance of natural resources (including landlocked geography; see Sachs, 1998) are vastly overrated, and human resources are vastly underrated, takes on even greater significance.

In the poorest nations in particular, where the current rates of investment in education as a per cent of GNP are often low, the social rates of return for investment in basic education are very high: 24 per cent for primary education and 18% for secondary education in Sub-Saharan Africa, and 18 per cent for primary education and 13 per cent for secondary education in Latin America, for example (Psacharopoulos, 1994: table 1). Chapter 13 estimates new social rates of return based on increased investment in education in the US and UK of 14 per cent and 15 per cent, respectively.

When the cost-effectiveness that includes the non-market returns to education of such investments in the poor countries is considered as a means of narrowing the gap between the richest and the poorest nations, the potential for starting to close this gap is greater. The increase in political stability (and the rule of law) in Tanzania and Kenya, for example, *after a lag of about 20 years*, is related to a problem that is endemic throughout much of Africa. Gains via political stability are not available to the same degree in the OECD nations. There are also significant gains from the impacts of education on increased life expectancy.

This much suggests that there are unutilized and cost-effective policies that would contribute to conditional convergence. However, there are problems, given the late start. In these Sub-Saharan African countries as well as in Bolivia and India, as was noted in Chapter 12, the extension of education to more females contributes to sharp drops in infant mortality rates, a plus for health except for the fact that this is not fully offset in these poorer countries by the decline in the fertility rates. The result is that population growth rates can be expected to increase. This slows *per capita* economic growth rates and severely limits the possibilities for convergence.

But this same limitation does not hold for countries who have achieved relatively co-equal education of the majority of both males and females up through about ninth grade, as is shown in the simulations for Indonesia and Malaysia. In these countries the effects on the fertility rate dominate, population growth rates (one of the Solow constants) decline, and the spurt in GNP per capita is larger. The outlook for their achieving conditional convergence is more promising.

Finally, a word must be said about the relative impacts of this change in human resource development policies on other aspects of development. The effectiveness of the policy for achieving reductions in poverty and in income inequality is considerable. In the poorest nations, where the inequality is higher to start with, it contributes to greater equity. But overall, unless the action is faster and more dramatic than what has been simulated here, the very poorest nations in each region have relatively limited capacities to begin to achieve conditional convergence within the next 40 years. There is a demographic bulge to overcome first.

Also, are increases in investment in education of this larger 3 to 4 percentage points of GNP realistic? If this could be accompanied by family planning and if part of the increase could come from reduced government support of consumption (which is high in the Middle East and in Pakistan, for example, which Barro, 1997 reports to have a negative relation to per capita growth), 2 percentage points lower might be effective in getting faster per capita development. This is apart from nations which have achieved higher junior secondary education rates already, for whom the outlook for conditional convergence is most promising.

Measurement of the Social Benefits of Education

With respect to the returns to measured economic growth, a new approach has been suggested for measuring social rates of return. It may be useful in offering evidence supplementing micro-studies, or in making estimates in the many countries where microeconomic rate-of-return studies do not exist. The total net benefits of education in the form of increments to GNP per capita can be discounted back to their present value and set equal to the incremental investment costs (2% of GNP here) plus forgone earnings costs for any of the 78 nations in the model. This assumes current levels of internal efficiency in the education system and current rates of improvement. The discount rate that equates these is the social rate of return to education.

These include those externalities that are market-related, not including, for example, externalities in the household production of non-market returns or the value of forgone earnings in the valuation of outputs of education. On this basis the 14 per cent and 15 per cent rates computed for the US and UK for illustrative purposes are slightly higher than social rates of return computed from microeconomic earnings data adjusted for dynamic upward trends in net earnings differentials at the college levels.[1] It is reasonable that this approach should result in estimates that are a bit higher, since the indirect effects of education on investment and the direct effects on rent, interest, and profit income are included, and not just the direct effects on labour earnings, as in micro-estimates.

Overall, the estimates of social rates of return and of non-market impacts based on the complete model, the equations for which are identified in Chapter 11, should not be interpreted by the reader as precise point estimates applicable to each country and have not been so described. There have been controls for the degree of political stability, military budget differences, cultural/legal differences, and differential impacts of oil shocks, but the coefficients in the production functions and other equations reflect basic underlying forces that are typical region-wide or worldwide, and therefore reflect what is likely to happen in that country in terms of the general direction and relative magnitude over a longer period.[2] The reader should therefore not use the results to try to make specific point predictions for a particular country using the smooth percentage changes on the graphs, but should instead view the prediction equation as indicating when key forces are building up, and should expect discontinuous jumps when the pressure induces change.

The effects of innate ability differences and family factors can reasonably be assumed to be offset by measurement-error effects from the education variable due to systematic errors in self-reporting, as well as from quality, which is not included in measures of enrolment.[3] This compensating offset of ability and measurement-error biases is assumed to apply to production of both the monetary and the non-market outcomes of education, based in part on the recent studies by Ashenfelter and Rouse (1997, 1998) of identical twins. This view is very widely held by education and labour economists, although this opinion is not unanimous. (See Ashenfelter and Krueger, 1994: 1172; McMahon, 1997a; and Arias and McMahon, 1998 for details.)

The Cost-Effectiveness of Non-market Returns

Another accomplishment is the capacity to calculate and to trace over time the cost-effectiveness of investing an additional percentage of GNP in education as a means of achieving given percentage changes in various indicators: in health via increased longevity and reduced infant mortality, in net population growth rates, in human rights, in crime reduction, or in most of the 22 measures of outcomes in each of the 78 nations in the complete model.

Beyond this, patterns can be observed among nations at different levels of per capita income and development, as shown in Chapters 12 and 13. For example, the gains from education, such as slower population growth, the rule of law, and greater political stability, are larger in Sub-Saharan Africa; but these particular gains are smaller in the more advanced industrialized countries because most of these have already been realized. Other outcomes are relatively greater in the industrial countries, such as the gains from higher education given the new technologies, gains from higher labour force participation rates, and net indirect contributions to less inequality, lower crime rates, better health, greater longevity, and a sustainable environment.

Valuation of Non-market Outcomes

Cost-based valuation using the Wolfe–Zuvekas (1997) technique discussed in Chapter 13 would seem to hold great promise, since otherwise the various non-market outcomes do not have a common denominator and their value cannot be computed or added up. This comment does not apply to the distributional impacts of education, although many poverty-reduction programmes contain a major efficiency component which can be valued by these means. As this is done for each of the identified non-market education outcomes, the cost-based value of this outcome is best expressed as a percentage of the monetary return to education, for which there are more common measures, so in this way the results can be used more widely.

Haveman and Wolfe (1984) and Wolfe and Zuvekas (1997) have done this relatively comprehensively on the basis of microeconomic studies, although they do not consider all of the outcomes covered in this book. On this basis they arrived at the first comprehensive estimate ever made of the total non-market outcomes, placing them as roughly equal to or slightly greater than the value of the increments to earnings attributable to education. The result is that these non-market returns approximately double standard rates of return based on earnings, by their estimate roughly doubling the 14 per cent and 15 per cent social rates of return I computed for the US and UK.

A possible next step would be to estimate the value of the non-market outcomes of education generated by simulations of the complete model in Chapter 12 based on the alternative costs of producing these same outcomes by other means. These could then be added up.

Measurement of Externalities and Distributional Effects

The structural measure of indirect effects of education, almost all of which are externalities, explicitly identifies a range of indirect community effects of education and measures them in a way that they have not been previously studied. These include the feedback effects, after appropriate lags, on economic growth, but also non-market impacts on health, democratization, poverty reduction, crime, and other outcomes tested specifically and in their simulated impacts over time in Chapters 2–13.

There also has been a valuation of these indirect structural effects, but only as they relate to pure economic growth. Within the GNP market-based measures they are estimated to have the value of about 40 per cent of the total effects of education on GNP per capita in most countries. This percentage emerges only after appropriate lags, and is considerably higher than 40 per cent in the more politically unstable, high-population-growth Sub-Saharan-African countries. This measure of indirect structural effects is more likely to understate than to overstate the true value of externalities, because some externality impacts are included in the way the direct effects of education are measured, and also because forgone earnings and some other costs are omitted from the way outcomes of public education are valued in the GNP accounts.[4]

Cause and Effect or Correlations?

The inference of causation rather than only co-variation in the case of these indirect-effect externalities and distributional impacts depends on the structural specification of these, including the lags between education and its delayed impacts in ways that follow the logic of the process of the underlying cause-and-effect relationships. The basic cause-and-effect logic is often at the level of the basic multi-period life-cycle theory of the household. Just as for earnings outcomes, it also requires that there be appropriate controls (and not an excess of inappropriate controls) when significant empirical correlations are found. When the attention to outcomes is limited to earnings, Card (1998) offers an excellent survey focusing on this point, which includes the offset of factors affecting the choice of education and measurement error, and recent advances. The inferences of cause-and-effect relationships, when made in this book, depend in part on economic theory developed and tested in microanalytic research, as summarized in each chapter of this book and in other published surveys by McMahon (1997*a*, 1998*b*) and Card (1998).

Typical of all of the recent work on endogenous growth models, the effects I seek, however, can only be seen in aggregate data that reveal overall total nation-wide effects. The hundreds of micro-studies are very particularistic, studying specialized aspects of each effect which partially cancel each other out. To gain this substantial advantage and new insights there is a cost, since the aggregate parameters are not necessarily the simple means of the corresponding micro-para-meters but can be biased by cross-effects from non-corresponding micro-parameters and from aggregation over simultaneous sets of micro-relations, for example. But most other disciplines have their micro and aggregate branches (e.g., atomic physics and mechanics, or microbiology and the physiology of body systems), none are able to derive aggregate properties mathematically and rigor-ously from the microanalytic foundations or vice versa, and solving this pervasive 'aggregation problem' has not been the objective here. Instead it is wiser to recognize that aggregation biases can affect the precision of the cause-and-effect connections in 'predictions', that whole new insights can be gained by looking at the nationwide effects, insights that might otherwise pass unnoticed, and that patterns that are logical at aggregate or prototype-micro levels for which there are consistent correlations can reveal effects that are worth further study at the micro-level, a pattern very common in many other disciplines.

Policy Dialogue as a Development Strategy

Discussion with economic and financial policy decision-makers regarding the contributions of education to economic development and the cost-based value of these contributions is likely to make them more aware of what these outcomes of education are and of alternative means of achieving their objectives.

There are also persons in economic development missions in the developing countries and in international agencies who have overall responsibility for development strategies, and yet relate to specialists who are often very compart-mentalized; specialists in health or in population, or in crime, for example. A common thread can be systematic evidence which traces the direct and indirect impacts of education on each of these specialties in a consistent way that can contribute to the overall design and cost-effectiveness of alternative development strategies.

Are Explicit Policy Changes Needed?

The evidence developed here suggests that convergence will not occur under an endogenous development scenario which allows for additional efforts, including education efforts, typical of the recent past. Considerably more dramatic policy interventions will be needed in these countries.

In fast-growing countries under the endogenous development scenario, which assumes a unitary income elasticity of the effective demand for education (investment in education as a per cent of GDP which determines enrolments is held constant), development proceeds rapidly.

In the poorest countries the rates of return to investment in primary and junior secondary education are often very high. This is especially true for the education of young females as this interacts with family planning efforts. But government policy-makers have not responded adequately to this. Governments sometimes continue to view basic education as a social welfare benefit and not as an investment essential to economic growth and development. India, Nepal, and Pakistan are examples of this, as is the gender inequity throughout much of the Middle East and North Africa. A second reason may be political factors, as suggested by the fact that governments sometimes take public credit at the beginning of the year for education budgets that are then quietly cut back later in the year behind the scenes by the ministry of finance. As a result, the total saving rate is low, with the political decision-makers and economic planners not realizing the potential stimulus to household *total saving and investment*. This occurs as forgone earnings are saved and invested by parents while children are fed, clothed, and housed and allowed to stay longer in school. These decisions are influenced by government decisions to build schools in rural areas, hire teachers, provide textbooks, and improve quality (as was done throughout East Asia; see Chapter 3).

Cost-Effective Development Strategies

Perhaps a policy dialogue strategy that makes the economic decision-makers aware of the systematic evidence that is available about the full range of returns to investments in basic education will help to instigate the kinds of dramatic change in policies that are necessary in some of the very poorest and unstable countries. Often loans and aid to these countries are very limited, and conditionality in loan and aid programmes is often resented (or ignored) when understanding is lacking. In the process of this policy dialogue, the priorities to be assigned to the relative value of each education outcome, and hence the weights to be applied, must be ascertained from the leaders within each nation so the policy can be custom-made and not imposed by outsiders. The goals will change somewhat over time as new policy-makers are selected and the key people in each ministry change. But then the process can be repeated.

A second approach is to try to place a value on each outcome of education using the Wolfe–Zuvekas (1997) cost-based valuation method suggested, supplemented by alternative valuations of the distributional outcomes. The result would be a prototype outcome that could then be presented to legislators or policy-makers, but not on an interactive basis.

Conclusion

Kenneth Arrow (1997), and T. W. Schultz (1973) before him, have suggested that there may be a tendency to underestimate the true non-market impacts of education because no good measures exist. I agree and have sought to develop a method for *systematic identification and estimation* of these impacts. In this sense it might be seen as carrying 'knowledge for development' (World Bank, 1998) an additional step forward, advancing ideas that the author discussed at the World Bank in July 1994. The method addresses not just the *direct* marginal products of education (the partial impacts), but also the *indirect* structural impacts as measured by the cross-partial derivatives.

Pursuit of the theme of measurement of the returns from the diffusion of new knowledge through education leads not just to reduction of imperfect information in markets but also to the concept of endogenous development, which traces the non-market returns to education and knowledge as well. Whether the pursuit of this theme contributes to a reconstruction of the theory and empirics of economic development is an issue that will have to be left for others to judge and to extend. But it does have significant implications for measurement of the more ultimate outcomes of education, and for economic development in the developing countries.

So hopefully there has been some progress. What would seem to be needed is not so much to hypothesize about possible limitations, given that I have gone to great lengths to set out explicitly the conditions under which the measures apply and the conditions under which they do not, but instead to refine the theory and the measurements. The goal is worth seeking: I have sought to show how continuing improvement in systematic measurement of the private and social benefits of education should help in finding cost-effective ways for increasing the diffusion of knowledge as a key means for achieving knowledge-based economic growth, reduction of poverty and inequality, better health and alleviation of population pressures, more effective democracy and political stability, lower crime rates, and sustainable environmental quality. All are vital aspects of true development. All are also fundamental to the quality of life for individual families and hence to human welfare.

Notes

1. All of the data for this calculation are available in the 'expert' version of the model, except the local wage rate for computing forgone earnings.
2. It is not possible to estimate the equations using data that is specific to each country, because the necessary data do not exist over sufficient periods of time or across a large

enough number of regions within each country. Even where such data exists the variation may be too small for meaningful coefficients to be estimated. It might be possible in a few instances to re-estimate particular equations with data that is specific to a single country, using cross-section data across provinces, but this would be very costly and laborious.

Note also that the production and investment functions for Africa and for the OECD nations have been estimated with data specific to those regions, but not with the same degree of precision as for the production functions specific to East Asia and Africa.

3. Quality differences normally lead to understatement of the true returns to education, although perhaps not in rural Brazil, where better quality in the schools induces sustained enrolments, according to Behrman and Birdsall (1983).

4. The Coase (1993) theorem, which suggests that there can sometimes be privately negotiated transactions to correct market failures due to externalities, is not relevant here. This is because the primary issue here is measurement of the scope of externalities, and not who should correct the implicit market failure. However, under imperfect information, which education is intended to correct, there are unlikely to be negotiated private settlements that are efficient.

Bibliography

Acsadi, George, G. Johnson-Acsadi, and R. A. Bulatao (1990), *Population Growth and Repro-duction in Sub-Saharan Africa: Technical Analyses of Fertility and Its Consequences*, Washington, DC: World Bank.

Alexander, Kern (1982), 'Concepts of Equity', in McMahon and Geske (1982), 193–214.

Arias, Omar, and Walter McMahon (1998), 'Dynamic Rates of Return to Education in the US', working paper, Department of Economics, University of Illinois at Urbana-Champaign.

—— and W. McMahon (1997), 'The Relation of Population Growth to Per Capita Economic Growth in Sub-Saharan Africa', mimeo, Lincoln University, Canterbury, NZ.

Arifa, Ali (1996), 'Investigation of the Relationship between Population Growth and Income per Capita', unpub. Ph.D. dissertation, University of Illinois at Urbana-Champaign.

Aronsson, Thomas and Karl-Gustaf Lofgren (1993), 'Welfare Measurement of Technological and Environmental Externalities in the Ramsey Growth Model', *Natural Resource Modeling*, 7: 1–14.

—— —— (1994), 'Social Accounting and Welfare Measurement in a Growth Model with Human Capital', working paper, University of Umea Department of Economics, Umea, Sweden.

Arrow, Kenneth (1997), 'The Benefits of Education and the Formation of Preferences', in Behrman and Stacey (1997), chap. 2.

Ashenfelter, Orley, and Alan Krueger (1994), 'Estimates of the Economic Returns to Schooling from a New Sample of Twins', *American Economic Review*, 84: 1157–73.

—— and Cecilia Rouse (1997), 'How Convincing is the Evidence Linking Education and Income?', in Orley Ashenfelter and Cecilia Rouse, *Cracks in the Bell Curve: Schooling, Intelligence, and Income*, mimeo, Princeton, NJ: Princeton University Department of Economics.

—— —— (1998), 'Income, Schooling, and Ability: Evidence from a New Sample of Identical Twins', *Quarterly Journal of Economics*, 113: 253–84.

Atkinson, A. B. (1970), 'On the Measurement of Inequality', *Journal of Economic Theory*, 2: 244–63.

Baltagi, Badi H., and Qi Li (1991), 'A Joint Test for Serial Correlation and Random Individual Effects', *Statistics and Probability Letters*, 13: 277–80.

Barro, Robert J. (1991), 'Economic Growth in a Cross-Section of Countries', *Quarterly Journal of Economics*, 106: 407–44.

—— (1997), 'Economic Growth and Convergence', in Robert Barro, *The Determinants of Economic Growth: A Cross-Country Empirical Study*, Lionel Robbins Memorial Lectures, London School of Economics, Cambridge, Mass.: MIT Press.

—— and Jong-Wha Lee (1993), 'International Comparisons of Educational Attainment', *Journal of Monetary Economics*, 32: 363–94.

—— and Xavier Sala-I-Martin (1995), *Economic Growth*, New York: McGraw-Hill.

Becker, Gary (1968), 'Crime and Punishment: An Economic Approach', *Journal of Political Economy*, 76: 169–217.

Becker, Gary (1976), *The Economic Approach to Human Behavior*, Chicago: University of Chicago Press.

—— (1981), *A Treatise on the Family*, Cambridge, Mass.: Harvard University Press.

—— (1988), 'Family Economics and Macro Behavior', Presidential Address, AEA, *AER*, Mar. 1–12.

—— (1993), *Human Capital*, 3rd edn., Chicago: University of Chicago Press.

Behrman, Jere R. (1990), *Human Resource Led Development? Review of Issues and Evidence*, Geneva: Asian Regional Team for Employment Promotion, ILO-ARTEP.

—— (1991), *The Action of Human Resources and Poverty on One Another: What We Have Yet to Learn*, LSMS Working Paper No. 74, Washington, DC: World Bank.

—— (1993), *Human Resources in Latin America and the Caribbean*, background paper for the Inter-American Development Bank, Washington, DC.

—— (1997), 'Conceptual and Measurement Issues', in Behrman and Stacey (1997), chap. 1.

—— and N. Birdsall (1983), 'The Quality of Schooling: Quantity Alone is Misleading', *American Economic Review*, 73: 928–46.

—— and Nevzer Stacey (1997), *The Social Benefits of Education*, Ann Arbor: University of Michigan Press.

Behrman, J. R., M. R. Rosenzweig, and P. Taubman (1994), 'Endowments and the Allocation of Schooling in the Marriage Market: The Twins Experiment', *Journal of Political Economy*, 102: 1131–74.

—— —— —— (1996), 'College Choice and Wages: Estimates Using Data on Female Twins', *Review of Economics and Statistics*, 78: 672.

—— R. T. Sickles, P. Taubman, and Abdo Yazbeck (1991), 'Black–White Mortality Inequalities', *Journal of Econometrics*, 50: 183–203.

Ben Porath, Yoram (1967), 'Production of Human Capital and the Life Cycle of Earnings', *Journal of Political Economy*, 75: 352–65.

Benson, Charles (1982), 'Household Production of Human Capital: Time Uses of Parents and Children as Inputs', in McMahon and Geske (1982), 52–77.

Bergson, A. (1938), 'A Reformulation of Certain Aspects of Welfare Economics', *Quarterly Journal of Economics*.

Besley, Timothy (1997), 'Political Economy of Alleviating Poverty: Theory and Institutions', in Michael Bruno and Boris Pleskovic (eds.), *Annual World Bank Conference on Development Economics 1996*, Washington, DC: World Bank, 117–34.

Birdsall, Nancy, and Richard Sabot (1993), 'Virtuous Circles: Human Capital Growth and Equity in East Asia', background paper for the Asian Miracle, Washington, DC: World Bank, Policy Research Dept.

Boedino, Walter McMahon, and Don Adams (1992), *Education, Economic, and Social Development*, Jakarta: Ministry of Education, and Tallahassee: EPP, Florida State University.

Bowen, H. R. (1943), 'The Interpretation of Voting in the Allocation of Economic Resources', *Quarterly Journal of Economics*, 58: 27–48.

—— (1948), *Toward Social Economy*, New York: Rinehart and Co.

—— (1977), *Investment in Learning: The Individual and Social Value of American Higher Education*, San Francisco: Jossey-Bass.

Breusch, T. S., and A. R. Pagan (1979), 'A Simple Test for Heteroscedasticity and Random Coefficient Variations', *Econometrica*, 47: 1287–94.

Burton, Vernon, Terence Finnegan, and David Herr (forthcoming), *Frontiers in Social Science Computing*, Urbana-Champaign, Ill.: University of Illinois Press.

Caldwell, J. C. (1982), *Theory of Fertility Decline*, New York: Academic Press.

—— (1986), 'Routes to Low Mortality in Poor Countries', *Population and Development Review*, 12: 171–214.

—— and P. Caldwell (1985), 'Education and Literacy as Factors in Health', in S. P. Halstead, J. A. Walsh, and K. S. Warre (eds.), *Good Health at Low Cost*, New York: Rockefeller Foundation.

Campos, Nauro, and Jeffrey Nugent (1996), 'Institutions and Economic Growth: Can There Be a Link?', mimeo, Department of Economics, University of Southern California, Los Angeles.

Card, David (1998), 'The Causal Effect of Education on Earnings', Working Paper No. 2, Center for Labor Economics, University of California, Berkeley; forthcoming in Orley Ashenfelter and David Card (eds.), *Handbook of Labor Economics, Vol. 3* New York and Amsterdam: North Holland Publishing Co.

Carnoy, Martin (1997), 'Recent Research on Market Returns to Education', *International Journal of Education Research*, 27: 53–73.

Chenery, Hollis, Montek Ahluwalia, Cline Bell, John Duloy, and Richard Jolly (1974), *Redistribution with Growth*, Oxford: Oxford University Press.

—— Sherwin Robinson, and Moske Syrquin (1986), *Industrialization and Growth: A Comparative Study*, Oxford and New York: pub. for the World Bank by Oxford University Press.

Clague, Christopher, Suzanne Gleason, and Stephen Knack (1996), 'Determinants of Lasting Democracy in Poor Countries', unpub. MS, Department of Economics, University of California at San Diego.

Coase, R. (1993), 'Coase on Posner on Coase', *Journal of Institutional and Theoretical Economics*, 149: 96–8. (The earlier article by Coase is 'The Problem of Social Cost', *Journal of Law and Economics*, 3: 1–44.)

Cochrane, S. H. (1979), 'Fertility and Education: What Do We Really Know?', World Bank Staff Occasional Paper No. 26, Washington, DC: World Bank.

—— (1983), 'Effects of Education and Urbanization on Fertility', in R. Bulatao and R. Lee (eds.), *Determinants of Fertility in Developing Countries*, vol. 2, New York: Academic Press.

—— J. Leslie, and D. J. O'Hara (1982), 'Parental Education and Child Health: Intracountry Evidence', *Health Policy and Education*, 2, 213–50.

—— D. J. O'Hara, and J. Leslie (1980), 'The Effects of Education on Health', World Bank Staff Working Paper No. 405, Washington, DC: World Bank.

Colclough, Christopher (1994), 'Lessons from Cost Reduction in Education Systems of Developing Countries, and their Application to South Africa', mimeo, Institute of Development Studies, University of Sussex, Brighton.

—— (with Keith Levin) (1993), *Educating All the Children: Strategies for Primary Education in the South*, Oxford: Clarendon Press.

Coplin, William D., M. K. O'Leary, and Tom Sealy (various years), 'International Country Risk Guide', in *A Business Guide to Political Risk for International Decisions*, Syracuse, NY: Political Risk Services.

Cropper, M. L., and W. E. Oates (1992), 'Environmental Economics', *Journal of Economic Literature*, 30: 675–740.

Crouch, Luis (1991), 'A Note on an Inertia-Sensitive Shortcut to Cohort Component Projections', unpub. MS, Chapel Hill, NC: Research Triangle Institute.

—— Jennifer Spratt, and Luis Cubeddu (1992), *Examining Social and Economic Impacts of Educational Investment and Participation in Developing Countries: The Educational Impacts*

Model (EIM) Approach, Bridges Research Report Series No. 12, Research Triangle Park, NC: Research Triangle Institute.

Dasgupta, Partha, and Karl-Goran Mäler (1994), *Poverty, Institutions, and the Environmental Resource Base*, World Bank Environment Policy Paper No. 9, Washington, DC: World Bank.

De Haan, Jakob, and Clemens L. J. Siermann (1995), 'New Evidence on the Relationship between Democracy and Economic Growth', *Public Choice*, 86: 175–98.

Denison, Edward F. (1974), *Accounting for United States Economic Growth, 1929–1969*, Washington, DC: Brookings Institution.

Diamond, Larry (1992), 'Economic Development and Democracy', *American Behavioral Scientist*, 35: 450–99.

Diamond, P. A., and J. A. Mirrlees (1971), 'Optimal Taxation and Public Production', *American Economic Review*, 61: 8–27 and 61: 261–78.

Downs, Anthony (1957), *An Economic Theory of Democracy*, New York: Harper and Bros.

D'Souza, S., and A. Bhuiya (1982), 'Socioeconomic Mortality Differentials in Rural Bangladesh', *Population and Development Review*, 8: 753–68.

Eckstein, Otto (1961), 'A Survey of the Theory of Public Expenditure Criteria', in National Bureau of Economic Research, *Public Finances: Needs, Sources, and Utilization*, Princeton: Princeton University Press, 439–504.

Economist, The (1991), 'The Path to Growth', 13 July, 77.

——— (1994), 'Inequality: For Richer, for Poorer', 5 Nov., 19–21.

——— (1997*a*), 'Education and the Wealth of Nations: Who's on Top?', 29 Mar., 21–3.

——— (1997*b*), 'Emerging Africa', 14 June, 13–14.

——— (1997*c*), 'India and Pakistan at 50', 16 Aug., 17–20.

Ehrlich, I. (1975), 'Participation in Illegitimate Activities: A Theoretical and Empirical Investigation', *Journal of Political Economy*, 81: 521–65.

——— (1996), 'Crime, Punishment, and the Market for Offenses', *Journal of Economic Perspectives*, 10: 43–68.

Eisemon, T. O. (1988), 'The Consequences of Schooling: A Review of Research on the Outcomes of Primary Schooling in Developing Countries', BRIDGES Educational Development Discussion Papers No. 3, Cambridge, Mass.: Harvard Institute for International Development.

Eisener, Robert (1989), *The Total Incomes System of Accounts*, Chicago: University of Chicago Press.

——— (1997), 'Education in a System of National Accounts', in McMahon (1997*b*), 135–44.

Eliasson, Gunnar, S. Folster, T. Lindberg, T. Pousette, and E. Taymaz (1990), *The Knowledge-Based Information Economy*, Stockholm: Industrial Institute for Economic and Social Research/Almqvist and Wikell International.

Esim, Simel (1994), 'Contribution of Secondary Education to Economic Development in South Korea, Malaysia, and Thailand', 2nd draft of working paper for the World Bank, Education and Social Policy Department.

Fishlow, Albert (1996), 'Inequality, Poverty, and Growth: Where Do We Stand?', in Michael Bruno and Boris Pleskovic (eds.), *Annual Bank Conference on Development Economics*, Washington, DC: World Bank, 25–39.

Freedom House (various years), *Freedom in the World*, Lanham, Md.: University Press of America.

French, Howard F. (1998), 'In Africa Wealth Buys Only Trouble', *New York Times*, 25 Jan., sect. iv, p. 3.

Fuller, Bruce, and Prema Clarke (1994), 'Raising School Effects while Ignoring Culture? Local Conditions and the Influence of Classroom Tools, Rules, and Pedagogy', *Review of Educational Research*, 64: 119–57.

Gomes, M. (1984), 'Family Size and Educational Attainment in Kenya', *Population and Development Review*, 10.

Gottschalk, Peter, and Timothy Smeeding (1997), 'Cross-National Comparisons of Earnings and Income Inequality', *Journal of Economic Literature*, 35: 633–96.

Gradus, R., and S. Smulders (1993), 'The Trade-off between Environment Cure and Long-Term Growth: Pollution in Three Prototype Models', *Journal of Economics*, 00: 26–34.

Greenwood, Daphne (1997), 'New Developments in the Intergenerational Impacts of Education', *International Journal of Education Research*, 27: 95–112.

Griliches, Zvi (1977), 'Estimating the Returns to Schooling: Some Econometric Problems', *Econometrica*, 45: 1–22.

—— and W. M. Mason (1988), 'Education, Income, and Ability', in Zvi Griliches, *Technology, Education, and Productivity*, New York: Basil Blackwell, 182–212.

Grossman, Michael, and Robert Kaestner (1997), 'Effects of Education on Health', in Behrman and Stacey (1997), 69–123.

Ha, Han Jang (1992), *Educational Indicators of Korea*, Seoul: Korean Educational Development Institute.

Hanushek, Eric (1994), *Education and Quality in the U.S.*, Washington, DC: Brookings Books.

—— J. B. Gomes-Neto, and R. W. Harbison (1994), 'Self-Financing Educational Investments: The Quality Imperative in Developing Countries', mimeo, University of Rochester, Rochester, NY.

—— and Richard Sabot (1991), 'Notes on Changes in Educational Performances', paper prepared for the PEER meetings, Boston, Mass.

——, S. G. Riskin, and L. L. Taylor (1996), 'Aggregation and the Estimated Effects of School Resources', *Rewiew of Economics and Statistics*, 78(4): 611–27.

Harbison, Ralph W., and Eric Hanushek (1992), *Educational Performance of the Poor*, Oxford: Oxford University Press.

Hausman, J., and W. Taylor (1981), 'Panel Data and Unobservable Individual Efforts', *Econometrica*, 49: 1377–98.

Haveman, R., and B. Wolfe (1984), 'Schooling and Economic Well-Being: the Role of Non-Market Effects', *Journal of Human Resources*, 19: 377–407.

Hazledine, Tim, and R. S. Moreland (1977), 'Population and Growth: A World Cross-Section Study', *Review of Economics and Statistics*, 59: 253–63.

Heckman, James (1976), 'A Life Cycle Model of Earning, Learning, and Consumption', *Journal of Political Economy*, 84(4), pt. 2, pp. S11–S25.

—— (1998a), 'Explaining Rising Wage Inequality: Explorations with a Dynamic General Equilibrium Model of Labor Earnings with Heterogeneous Agents', faculty working paper, Department of Economics, University of Chicago.

—— (1998b), 'Rethinking Myths about Education and Training', David Kinley Lecture in Economics, University of Illinois at Urbana-Champaign, mimeo, Department of Economics, University of Chicago.

Hicks, John R. (1946), *Value and Capital*, 2nd edn., Oxford: Oxford University Press.

Hobcraft, J. N., J. W. McDonald, and S. O. Rutstein (1984), 'Socioeconomic Factors in Infant and Child Mortality: A Cross-Country Comparison', *Population Studies*, 38: 193–223.

Huber, Evelyne, D. Rueschemeyer, and J. D. Stephens (1993), 'The Impact of Economic Development on Democracy', *Journal of Economic Perspectives*, 7: 71–83.

Ibbsotson and Associates (1998), *Stocks, Bonds, Bills, and Inflation: 1998 Yearbook*, Chicago: Ibbsotson and Associates.

ILO [International Labour Organization] (various years), *Yearbook of Labour Statistics*, Geneva: O.

IMF [International Monetary Fund] (various years to 1996), *International Financial Statistics*, Washington, DC: MF.

—— (1998), 'Potential for Growth', *IMF Survey*, 27: 65–8.

Inter-American Development Bank (1993), *1993 Report: Human Resources*, Baltimore, Md.: distributed by Johns Hopkins University Press for the Inter-American Development Bank.

—— (1994), *Economic and Social Progress in Latin America: 1994 Report*, Baltimore, Md.: distributed by Johns Hopkins University Press for the Inter-American Development Bank.

Ito, Takatoshi, and Anne O. Krueger (eds.) (1995), *Growth Theories in Light of the East Asian Experience*, Chicago: University of Chicago Press, and London: NBER.

Jaffee, Adam (1997), 'Environmental Policy and Technical Change', NBER Working Paper, New York: Brandis/NBER.

Jang, Chang-Won (1994), 'Contributions of Secondary Education to Economic Development in Korea', background paper for the World Bank, Washington, DC: World Bank.

—— (1995), 'Endogenous Growth: Contributions of Education to Economic Development in Korea and Policy Implications', unpub. Ph.D. dissertation, University of Illinois at Urbana-Champaign.

Jayatunge, Jayantha (1993), 'Human Capital Development and Economic Growth', mimeo, Department of Economics, University of Illinois at Urbana-Champaign.

Kasarda, J. D., J. O. Billy, and K. West (1986), *Status Enhancement and Fertility: Reproductive Responses to Social Mobility and Educational Opportunity*, New York: Academic Press.

KEDI [Korean Educational Development Institute] (1992), 'Educational Indicators in Korea', Seoul: KEDI.

Kim, Jong-II, and Lawrence J. Lau (1996), 'The Sources of Economic Growth of East Asian Newly Industrialized Countries: Some Further Evidence', faculty working paper, Department of Economics, Stanford University, summarized in *AEA Papers and Proceedings*, May 1996.

Kiso, Isao (1993), *Secondary Education and Economic Development in Japan: A Case Study of Key Policy Decisions Affecting the Development of Secondary Education in Japan*, Tokyo: Ministry of Education, Japan.

Kmenta, J. (1986), *Elements of Econometrics*, 2nd edn. New York: Macmillan.

Knight, John, and Richard Sabot (1990), *Education, Productivity, and Inequality: The East African Natural Experiment*, Oxford: Oxford University Press (for the World Bank).

Kockerlakota, Narazana, and Kei-Mu Yi (1995), 'Is There Endogenous Long Run Growth? Evidence from the U. S. and the UK', paper presented at the AEA Meetings, Washington, DC.

Koopmans, T. C. (1966), 'On the Concept of Optimal Economic Growth', in *The Econometric Approach to Development Planning*, Amsterdam: North Holland Publishing Co.

—— (1967), 'Objectives, Constraints, and Outcomes in Optimal Growth Models', *Econometrica*, 35.

Krugman, Paul (1996), 'The Myth of Asia's Miracle', *Foreign Affairs*, 73(6): 62–78.

Kuznets, Simon (1955), 'Economic Growth and Income Inequality', *American Economic Review*, 65: 1–28.

—— (1971), *Economic Growth of Nations*, Cambridge, Mass.: Belknap Press.

Levine, R. A. (1987), 'Women's Schooling, Patterns of Fertility, and Child Survival', *Educational Researcher*, 16: 21–7.

—— and D. R. Renelt (1992), 'A Sensitivity Analysis of Cross-Country Regressions', *American Economic Review*, 82: 942–63.

Levy, Frank, and Richard Murnane (1992), 'U.S. Earnings Level and Earnings Inequality: A Review of Recent Trends and Proposed Explanations', *Journal of Economic Literature*, 30: 1333–81.

Lofgren, Karl-Gustaf, T. Aronsson, and P. Johansson (1995), 'Investment Decisions, Future Consumption, and Sustainability under Optimal Growth', University of Umea Department of Economics, Umea, Sweden.

Lucas, Robert E. (1988), 'On the Mechanics of Economic Development', *Journal of Monetary Economics*, 22: 3–42.

Mankiw, N. Gregory, David Romer, and David N. Weil (1992), 'A Contribution to the Empirics of Economic Growth', *Quarterly Journal of Economics*, 107: 407–38.

Mansfield, Edwin (1995), 'Economic Returns from Investment in Research and Training', background for World Bank Working Paper, Department of Economics, University of Pennsylvania.

Massun, E. (1990), 'Preventive Education to Cope with the Drug Problems of Latin America', *United Nations Bulletin on Narcotics*, 42: 49–55.

McMahon, Walter W. (1970), 'An Economic Analysis of the Major Determinants of Expenditures on Public Primary and Secondary Education', *Review of Economics and Statistics*, 52: 242–52.

—— (1971), 'Cyclical Growth of Public Expenditure', *Public Finance*, 26: 75–105.

—— (1974), *Investment in Higher Education*, Lexington, Mass.: D. C. Heath and Co.

—— (1975), 'Economic and Demographic Effects on Investment in Higher Education', *Southern Economic Journal*, 41: 506–14.

—— (1981), 'The Slowdown in Productivity Growth: A Macroeconomic Model of Investment in Human and Physical Capital with Energy Shocks', Faculty Working Paper No. 752, Bureau of Economic and Business Research (BEBR), University of Illinois, Urbana-Champaign.

—— (1984a), 'The Relation of Education and R&D to Productivity Growth', *Economics of Education Review*, 3: 299–314.

—— (1984b), 'Sources of the Slowdown in Productivity Growth: A Structural Interpretation', in John W. Kendrick (ed), *International Comparisons of Productivity Growth and Causes of the Slowdown*, Cambridge, Mass.: American Enterprise Institute/Ballinger, 93–108.

—— (1984c), 'Why Families Invest in Education', in Seymour Sudman and M. A. Spaeth (eds.), *The Collection and Analysis of Economic and Consumer Behavior Data: In Memory of Robert Ferber*, Champaign, Ill.: Bureau of Economic and Business Research, University of Illinois, 75–91.

—— (1987), 'The Relation of Education and R&D to Productivity Growth in the Developing Countries of Africa', *Economics of Education Review*, 6: 183–94.

—— (1990), 'A Macrodynamic Model of the U. S. with Investment in Human and Physical Capital', Faculty Working Paper No. 752, Bureau of Economic and Business Research (BEBR), University of Illinois, Urbana.

—— (1991a), 'Inefficiencies and Inequalities: Some Options for Improving Education in Latin America', for the World Bank, faculty working paper, Department of Economics, University of Illinois, Urbana.

McMahon, Walter W. (1991*b*), 'Inefficiency and Inequity Associated with Economic Decline; with Options for Improving Education in Latin America', background paper for the World Bank, LAC Division; copies available from the author, Urbana, Ill.

—— (1991*c*), 'The Relative Returns to Human and Physical Capital in the U.S. and Effective Investment Strategies', *Economics of Education Review*, 10: 283–96.

—— (1992*a*), 'The Contribution of Higher Education to R&D and Productivity Growth', in W. E. Becker and Darrell Lewis (eds.), *Higher Education and Economic Growth*, Norwell, Mass.: Kluwer Academic Publishers, 135–51.

—— (1992*b*), 'The Economics of School Expansion and Decline', in Bruce Fuller and R. Rubinson (eds.), *The Political Construction of Education*, New York: Praeger, 135–51.

—— (1994*a*), 'The Contributions of Secondary Education to Economic Development in Indonesia', working paper, University of Illinois.

—— (1994*b*), 'The Contribution of Secondary Education to Growth and Development in Japan, South Korea, Malaysia, Thailand, and Indonesia', working paper for the World Bank.

—— (1994*c*), 'Market Signals and Labor Market Analysis', paper for ILO Workshop on New Trends in Education and Training Policies, Geneva.

—— (1997*a*), 'Conceptual Framework for Measuring the Social and Individual Benefits of Education', in McMahon (1997*b*), 9–53.

—— (ed.) (1997*b*), *Recent Advances in Measuring the Social and Individual Benefits of Education*, special issue of the *International Journal of Education Research*, 27(7). 27.

—— (1998*a*), 'Education and Growth in East Asia', *Economics of Education Review*, 17: 159–72.

—— (1998*b*), 'Conceptual Framework for the Analysis of the Social Benefits of Lifelong Learning', *Education Economics*, 6: 309–46.

—— (1998*c*), *Knowledge for the Future: The Returns to Investment in Education and Research at the University of Illinois at Urbana-Champaign*, Urbana-Champaign: Office of Vice-President for Academic Affairs, University of Illinois, Urbana-Champaign.

—— (1999), 'Externalities, Non-Market Effects, and Trends in Returns to Investments in Education', *Evaluation of Educational Investments*, OECD-EIB, Luxembourg: European Investment Bank.

—— (forthcoming), 'Simulating Investment in Education and US Productivity Growth: The Growing Economy', in Buraton *et al.*

—— and Wendy Cunningham (1998), *Education for Great Cities: Measuring the Contribution of Investment in Higher Education at the University of Illinois in Chicago*, Urbana, Ill.: Office of the Vice-President for Academic Affairs, University of Illinois, Urbana.

—— and Terry Geske (1982), *Financing Education: Overcoming Inefficiency and Inequity*, Urbana, Ill.: University of Illinois Press.

Michael, Robert T. (1974), 'Education and the Derived Demand for Children', in T. W. Schultz (ed.), *Economics of the Family: Marriage, Children, and Human Capital*, Chicago: University of Chicago Press.

—— (1982), 'Measuring Non-monetary Benefits of Education: A Survey', in McMahon and Geske (1982), 119–49.

Milanovic, Branko (1994), 'Determinants of Cross-Country Income Inequality: An Augmented Kuznets Hypothesis', Policy Research Working Paper 1246, Policy Research Department, Transition Economies Division, World Bank, Washington, DC: World Bank.

Mirrlees, J. A. (1974), 'Notes on Welfare Economics, Information, and Uncertainty', in M. Balch *et al.* (eds.), *Essays on Economic Behavior under Uncertainty*, Amsterdam: North Holland, 243–57.

Moreland, R. S. (1982), 'Population, Internal Migration, and Economic Growth: An Empirical Analysis', *Research in Population Economics*, 4: 173–216.

Mortinson, Thomas (1997), *Post-secondary Educational Opportunity*, no. 48, Mar., Oskaloosa, Ia.: Mortinson Research Service on Public Policy Analysis for Post-secondary Education.

Musgrave, Richard (1959), *The Theory of Public Finance*, New York: McGraw-Hill.

National Institute of Justice (1980), *Searching for Answers: Research and Evaluation on Drugs and Crime*, Washington, DC: National Institute of Justice.

——(1990), *National Narcotics Intelligence Consumers Committee Report*, Washington, DC: National Institute of Justice.

NCES [National Center of Education Statistics] (1996), *Projections of Education Statistics to 2006*, U. S. Department of Education, NCES 96–661, Washington, DC: US Government Printing Office.

Nehru, Vickram (1993), 'New Measures of the Human Capital Stock', special study, Statistics Department, World Bank, Washington, DC.

New York Times (1998), 'Half Measures to Protect the Amazon', 2 Feb. A22, with follow-up articles on outcomes on 11 Feb., A9, and 13 Feb., A5.

OECD (Organisation for Economic Cooperation and Development) (1997), *Third International Maths and Science Study*, Paris: OECD.

O'Hara, D. J. (1980), 'Toward a Model of the Effects of Education and Health', in Cochrane, O'Hara, and Leslie (1980), 34–55.

Payne, Douglas W. (1993), 'Latin America: Democracy and the Politics of Corruption', in Freedom House (1993), 11–15.

Petrakis, P. E., and D. Stamatakis (1999), 'Growth and Education Levels: A Comparative Analysis', *Economics of Education Review*, Columbia, Sc.

Pernia, Ernesto M. (1989), 'Education and Labor Markets in Indonesia', Asian Development Bank Economic Staff Paper No. 45, Manila: Asian Development Bank.

Pigou, A. C. (1920), *The Economics of Welfare*, London: Macmillan.

Political Risk Services (various years), *International Country Risk Guide*, Syracuse, NY: Political Risk Services.

Population Crisis Committee (1987), 'Access to Birth Control: A World Assessment', Briefing Paper No. 19, Population Crisis Committee, Washington, DC.

Prescott, Nicholas, *et al.* (1993), *Public Prices and the Poor*, Indonesia Report No. 11293-IND, World Bank, Indonesia Country Dept., Washington, DC.

Psacharopoulos, George (1977), 'Unequal Access to Education and Income Distribution', *De Economist*, 125, NR 3, 383–92.

——(1994), 'Returns to Investment in Education: a Global Update', *World Development*, 22(9) 1325–43.

——and Ana Arriagada (1992), 'The Educational Composition of the Labor Force', Document No. PHREE/92/49, Education and Employment Division, Population and Human Resources Department, World Bank, Washington, DC.

——S. Morley, A. Fishbein, H. Lee, and B. Wood (1993), *Poverty and Income Distribution in Latin America*, Report No. 27, Human Resources Division, Latin America and the Caribbean Technical Department, World Bank, Washington, DC.

Ramsey, F. (1928), 'A Mathematical Theory of Saving', *Economic Journal*, 38: 543–59.

Rashid, Zainol Abadin (1994), *A Case Study of Secondary Education in Malaysia*, Economic Planning Unit, Kuala Lumpur, Malaysia.

Rawls, John (1977), *A Theory of Justice*, Cambridge, Mass.: Harvard University Press.

Romer, Paul (1986), 'Increasing Returns and Long-Run Growth', *Journal of Political Economy,* 94: 1002–37.

—— (1990), 'Endogenous Technical Change', *Journal of Political Economy,* 98: 571–93.

—— (1993), 'Two Strategies for Economic Development: Using Ideas and Producing Ideas', Proceedings of the World Bank Annual Conference on Development Economics, 1992, suppl. to the *World Bank Economic Review* and the *World Bank Research Observer,* 63–91.

—— (1994), 'The Origins of Endogenous Growth', *Journal of Economic Perspectives,* 8: 1–23.

Rosen, Sherwin (1987), 'Self-Selection and Education', in G. Psacharopoulos, (ed), *Economics of Education Research and Studies,* Oxford: Pergamon Press, 298–300.

Rueschemeyer, Dietrich, Evelyn Huber Stephens, and John H. Stephens (1992), *Capitalist Development and Democracy,* Cambridge: Polity Press and Chicago: Chicago University Press.

Rutter, M. (1985), 'Resilience in the Face of Adversity: Protective Factors and Resistance to Psychiatric Disorder', *British Journal of Psychiatry,* 147: 598–611.

Sachs, Jeffrey (1998), 'The Limits of Convergence', *The Economist,* Feb.

Samuelson, Paul (1955), 'Diagrammatic Exposition of a Theory of Public Expenditures', *Review of Economics and Statistics,* 32: 350–6, repr. in Joseph E. Stiglitz (ed.), *Collected Scientific Papers of Paul Samuelson,* vol. 2, Cambridge, Mass.: and London: MIT Press, 1966, pp. 1226–33.

Schultz, T. Paul (1993), 'Investments in the Schooling and Health of Women and Men— Quantities and Returns', *Journal of Human Resources,* 28: 694–734.

Schultz, T. W. (1973), *Economics of the Family: Marriage, Children, and Human Capital,* Chicago: University of Chicago Press.

Schumpeter, Joseph A. (1947), 'Theoretical Problems of Economic Growth', repr. in Richard Clemence (ed.), *Essays of J. A. Schumpeter,* Cambridge, Mass.: Addison-Wesley Press, 1951.

—— (1950), *Capitalism, Socialism, and Democracy,* 3rd edn., New York: Harper & Bro.

Segerstrom, Paul S. (1995), 'Endogenous Growth without Scale Effects', Faculty Working Paper, Michigan State University East Lansing, Mich.

Sen, Binayak (1995), 'Poverty', in Jayarajah *et al., The Social Impact of Adjustment,* Washington, DC: World Bank.

Shapiro, Carl (ed.) (1995), 'Symposium: Economics of Voting' (articles by Levin and Nalebuff, Tideman, Weber, Young, Rae, Myerson, and Sen), *Journal of Economic Perspectives,* 9 (1): 3–98.

Shaw, C., and H. McKay (1969), *Juvenile Delinquency and Urban Areas,* Chicago: University of Chicago Press.

Smith, V. Kerry (1997), 'Social Benefits of Education: Feedback Effects and Environmental Resources', in Behrman and Stacey (1997), 175–218.

Solow, Robert (1956), 'A Contribution to the Theory of Economic Growth', *Quarterly Journal of Economics,* 70: 65–94.

Stiglitz, J. E. (1974), 'The Demand for Education in Public and Private School Systems', *Journal of Public Economics.*

—— (1997), 'The Role of Government in Economic Development', in *Annual World Bank Conference on Development Economics, 1996,* Washington, DC: World Bank.

—— (1998), 'The Economics of Intervention: A Theorist's Persistent Questions', *New York Times,* 31 May, sect. 3, p. 12.

Sullivan, Dennis, and Timothy Smeeding (1997), 'Educational Attainment and Earnings Inequality in Eight Nations', in McMahon (1997b), 113–34.

Tallman, Ellis W., and P. Wang (1993), 'Educational Achievement and Economic Growth: Evidence from Taiwan', Working Paper 93–11, Federal Reserve Bank of Atlanta.

Tan, J. P., and M. Haines (1984), 'Schooling and Demand for Children: Historical Perspectives', World Bank Staff Working Papers No. 697, Washington, DC: World Bank.

Tunsiri, Viccai (1994), *Secondary Education in Thailand*, Bangkok: Office of the National Education Commission.

Ulph, David (1977), 'On the Optimal Distribution of Income and Educational Expenditure', *Journal of Public Economics*, 8: 341–56.

UNDP [United Nations Development Programme] (1994), *Human Development Report, 1994*, Oxford: Oxford University Press.

UNESCO [United Nations Educational, Scientific and Cultural Organisation] (various years), *Statistical Yearbook*, Paris: UNESCO.

United Nations (1966), *Covenant on Economic, Social, and Cultural Rights*, New York: Economic and Social Council, United Nations.

—— (1998), *Compendium of Social Statistics*, New York: United Nations.

USAID [US Agency for International Development] (1998), *USAID's Strategic Framework for Basic Education in Africa*, Africa Bureau Technical Paper No. 84, Washington, DC: US Department of State.

US Bureau of the Census (1997), *Current Population Survey, Series P-60*, Washington, DC: US Bureau of the Census.

—— (various years), *Statistical Abstract*, Washington, DC: US Department of Commerce, Bureau of the Census.

Uzawa, Hirofumi (1965), 'Optimal Technical Change in an Aggregative Model of Economic Growth', *International Economic Review*, 6: 18–31.

Wheeler, D. (1984a), 'Female Education, Family Planning, Income, and Population: A Long-Run Econometric Simulation Model', unpub. background paper for the World Bank Development Report.

—— (1984b), *Human Resources Policies, Economic Growth, and Demographic Change in Developing Countries*, Oxford: Clarendon Press.

Wintemute, Garen (1998), *Predicting Criminal Behavior among Authorized Purchasers of Handguns*, Washington, DC: US Department of Justice, Office of Justice Programs, National Institute of Justice.

Wise, David (1975), 'Academic Achievement and Job Performance', *American Economic Review*, 65: 350–66.

Witte, Ann Dryden (1997), 'Social Benefits of Education: Crime', in Behrman and Stacey (1997), 219–46.

Wolfe, Barbara, and Samuel Zuvekas (1997), 'Nonmarket Outcomes of Schooling', in McMahon (1997b), 74–94.

Wood, Adrian (1994a), *North–South Trade, Employment, and Inequality: Changing Fortunes in a Skill-Driven World*, Oxford: Clarendon Press.

—— (1994b), 'Skill, Land, and Trade: A Simple Analytical Framework', Working Paper No. 1, Institute of Development Studies, University of Sussex, Brighton.

World Bank (1989), *Sub-Saharan Africa: From Crisis to Sustainable Growth, A Long-Term Perspective Study*, Washington, DC: World Bank.

—— (1993a), *The East Asian Miracle: Economic Growth and Public Policy*, Policy Research Report, Policy Research Department, Washington, DC: World Bank.

—— (1993b), *Higher Education: The Lessons of Experience*, Education and Social Policy Department, Washington, DC: World Bank.

—— (1993c), *Indonesia Public Expenditures, Prices, and the Poor*, Indonesia Resident Mission, County Department III, Report No. 11293–IND, Washington, DC: World Bank.

World Bank (1995), *Priorities and Strategies for Education*, Education Sector Policy Paper, Education and Social Policy Department, Washington, DC: World Bank.

——(1996a). *African Development Indicators, 1996*, Washington, DC: World Bank.

——(1996b), *World Development Indicators* Washington, DC: World Bank (also available on CD-ROM and on the Network).

——(1998), *World Development Report 1998/99: Knowledge for Development*, Washington, DC: World Bank and Oxford University Press: Oxford.

——, *World Development Report* (various years), *World Development Report*, Washington, DC: World Bank and Oxford University Press: Oxford.

——, *World Tables* (various years), *The World Tables*, Washington, DC: World Bank.

Index